Music, Memory, Resistance:

MUSIC, MEMORY, RESISTANCE:

Calypso and the Caribbean Literary Imagination

Edited by

Sandra Pouchet Paquet

Patricia J. Saunders

Stephen Stuempfle

Ian Randle Publishers
Kingston • Miami

First published in Jamaica, 2007 by
Ian Randle Publishers
11 Cunningham Avenue
Box 686
Kingston 6
www.ianrandlepublishers.com

Selection and editorial material
© 2007, Sandra Pouchet Pacquet, Patricia J. Saunders and Stephen Stuempfle
All rights reserved. Published 2007

National Library of Jamaica Cataloguing in Publication Data

Music, memory, resistance : calypso and the Caribbean literary imagination / edited by Sandra Pouchet Paquet, Patricia J. Saunders, Stephen Stuempfle.

p. ;   cm.

Bibliography : p.   . – Includes index
ISBN 978-976-637-290-3 (pbk)

1. Calypso (Music) – Trinidad and Tobago – History and criticism. 2. Calypso (Music) Caribbean Area – History and criticism. 3. Music – Caribbean Area – History and criticism. 4. Music and literature. 5. Music – Social aspects. 6. Popular culture – Caribbean Area. 7. Literature – History and criticism.   8. Caribbean Area – Politics and government.

I. Paquet, Sandra Pouchet   II. Saunders, Patricia J.   III. Stuempfle, Stephen

781.64   dc 22

While copyright in the selection and editorial material is vested in the copyright holders, copyright in individual chapters belongs to their respective authors and no chapter may be reproduced wholly or in part without the express permission in writing of both author and publisher.

Cover and book design by Ian Randle Publishers
Cover photograph: Sparrow performing in a calypso tent. Trinidad, 1967. Courtesy of *Trinidad Guardian*; digital mastering by Kevin Burke.
Printed in the United States of America

CONTENTS

Preface / vi
Sandra Pouchet Paquet and Stephen Stuempfle

Introduction: Mapping the Roots /Routes of Calypso in Caribbean Literary and Cultural Traditions / xv
Patricia J. Saunders

MUSIC AS MEMORY, RESISTANCE AND POLITICAL CONTEXT

1. Eric Williams's Vision for the Development of Carnival
   Hollis 'Chalkdust' Liverpool / 1

2. Calypso as Political Con/Text: Reflections on the Legend of Eric Williams / 15
   Louis Regis

3. In the Battle for Emergent Independence: Calypsos of Decolonization / 59
   Ray Funk

4. Fugues, Fragments and Fissures: A Work in Progress /77
   M. NourbeSe Philip

SANS HUMANITÉ: THE SONG, THE SINGER AND THE STORY

5. Carnival Cannibalized or Cannibal Carnivalized: Contextualizing the 'Cannibal Joke' in Calypso and Literature / 99
   Gordon Rohlehr

6. Calypso and the Bacchanal Connection /141
   Earl Lovelace

7. Unmasking the Chantwell Narrator in Earl Lovelace's Fiction / 153
   Funso Aiyejina

TEN TO ONE IS MURDER: GENDER, SEXUALITY AND THE BODY POLITIC

8. Jamette Carnival and Afro-Caribbean Influences in the Work of Jean Rhys / 167
   Cynthia Davis

9. 'Big Fat Fish': The Hypersexualization of the Fat Female Body in Calypso and Dancehall / 189
   Andrea Shaw

10. Men in the Yard and On the Street: Cricket and Calypso in Caribbean Literature / 205
    Claire Westall

WHEN ALL THE WORLD'S A STAGE: PERFORMING CULTURAL IDENTITY AT HOME AND ABROAD

11. With a Tassa Blending: Calypso and Cultural Identity in Indo-Caribbean Fiction / 223
    Paula Morgan

12. Bop Girl Goes Calypso: Containing Race and Youth Culture in Cold War America / 255
    Michael S. Eldridge

13. (Not) Knowing the Difference: Calypso Overseas and the Sound of Belonging in Narratives of Migration
    Jennifer Rahim /285

14. 'Everybody do the Dance': The Politics of Uniformity in Dancehall and Calypso
    Kezia Page / 309

BIBLIOGRAPHY / 325

CONTRIBUTORS / 351

INDEX

PREFACE

Sandra Pouchet Paquet
Stephen Stuempfle

For over a century, calypso has flourished in the Caribbean at the intersection of diverse verbal traditions, both oral and written. It emerged as a modern art form around 1900, principally in Port of Spain, where it was shaped by a variety of African-Trinidadian oral traditions of stickfight and drum dance songs and orations of masqueraders in the pre-Lenten Carnival. Since then it has thrived during the Carnival season in the oral/aural dynamic of performances in streets, 'tents' and other venues in which calypsonians engage each other and their audiences in verbal exchanges. These performances have been augmented since the 1910s by audio recordings, which have greatly expanded the aural dissemination and experience of the song form. Yet calypso is also part of a written tradition. Some calypsonians have been keen readers who, in their compositions, draw material from sources ranging from current newspapers to literary classics. Moreover, calypsonians generally *write* their songs. Over the decades, countless calypsos have been published through broadsheets, pamphlets, newspapers and books. Any examination of the composition and reception of calypso must consider this interplay of literacy and oral tradition.

Since the 1920s and 1930s, calypsonians typically have composed songs that chronicle their observations and opinions on current events. Some calypsos focus on specific occurrences, from local scandals to world affairs, while others examine broader trends, such as changing gender relations or new types of popular culture. This topical commentary is expressed in a rich language of word play, dense irony and sharp humour. While many societies have topical song traditions, calypsonians developed a unique verbal style that combines vernacular expression and grandiloquence, realistic description and fantastic imagination, moral seriousness and irreverent laughter. In short, the language of calypso is resourceful and flexible enough to capture the many nuances, complexities and contradictions of life in the Caribbean and beyond.

Calypsonians' clarity of observation, trenchant social analysis and linguistic dexterity have long fascinated Caribbean writers of short stories, novels, poetry and drama. Given their often flamboyant personalities, as well as their ability to navigate various sectors of society, calypsonians have been compelling characters in the works of Samuel Selvon, Errol John, Derek Walcott, Earl Lovelace and numerous other writers. In addition, writers have frequently quoted calypsos and, in their own literary styles, experimented with the language and perspectives of the song form. The affinity of writers toward calypsonians perhaps stems, in part, from the similar position from which they have observed the Caribbean scene. Both have often operated at the margins of society, where their detachment has facilitated their critique. Both also gained greater international recognition during the era of the decolonization of the West Indies from Britain. In the years after World War II, calypso and Caribbean fiction offered key frames through which North Americans and Europeans, as well as local audiences, envisioned Caribbean life. In more recent times, calypsonians and other writers have continued to experiment with diverse verbal traditions and have remained vital figures in the representation of Caribbean experience at home and abroad.

The articles included in this book explore a variety of topics related to calypso and the Caribbean literary imagination. They derive from a conference organized in March 2005 by Caribbean Literary Studies at the University of Miami and the Historical Museum of Southern Florida. Located in Miami, a crossroads of the Americas, the University of Miami and the Historical Museum both have strong programmes of Caribbean research. The collaboration between the two institutions resulted in a dual-site conference that featured current scholarship on calypso and other literary forms, presentations in various media, and an audience that joined academics and the general public.

The Historical Museum of Southern Florida is one of the few museums in the United States that designates the study of the Caribbean as a central part of its mission. In addition to holding a substantial collection of rare maps, prints and photographs of the region, the museum has organized numerous exhibitions on the history of Caribbean societies and on the large communities of Caribbean peoples in South Florida. In 2001 the museum began work on a multi-format project, titled 'Calypso: A World Music', with the objective of exploring calypso's international history, particularly the increasing dissemination of the music throughout the Atlantic world from the 1930s to the 1960s. The project's catalyst was an extensive collection of calypso materials assembled by Ray Funk, a popular music researcher (and judge) in Fairbanks, Alaska. In the course of research carried out between 2001 and

2004, the museum supplemented Funk's collection with copies of items obtained from numerous public and private archives in New York, Washington, London and other locales.

These calypso collections provided the foundation for the development of two exhibitions. 'Calypso: A World Music' launched online at www.calypsoworld.org in 2004 and will remain accessible until 2009. This virtual exhibition features over 350 images, including photographs, sheet music, songbooks, record album covers, movie posters, advertisements and other graphics. Together, this material illustrates the spread of calypso, during the mid-twentieth century, from Trinidad to many countries in the Americas, Europe and Africa. Phonograph records, radio programmes, music publications, movies and television shows rapidly transmitted calypso to new audiences, while Caribbean migration, tours of artistes, Caribbean and US military service, and North American tourism constantly moved calypsonians and audiences to new locations for performances. Among the many calypso singers represented in the exhibition are such Atlantic travellers as Sam Manning, Frederick Wilmoth Hendricks (Houdini), Hubert Raphael Charles (Roaring Lion), Rupert Grant (Lord Invader) and Aldwyn Roberts (Lord Kitchener).

The Historical Museum also organized a travelling exhibition, 'Calypso Music in Postwar America', which focuses on the growing presence of calypso in the popular culture of the US from the end of World War II to the late 1950s. At various times during this period, numerous Caribbean and North American artistes released calypso records. Calypso was featured in shows on Broadway, nightclubs across the US adopted all-calypso formats, publishers churned out calypso sheet music and Hollywood produced calypso-themed movies. Featured in this exhibition are a wide range of artistes, such as Lancelot Pinard (Sir Lancelot), Cecil Anderson (Duke of Iron), Josephine Premice, Harry Belafonte and Maya Angelou (a dancer and singer before turning to literature). To date, the exhibition has been presented in Miami, New York, Port of Spain Kansas City, and Bloomington, Indiana.

In order to expand perspectives on calypso's international history, the Historical Museum worked with several other institutions to present public conferences. Among these was a collaboration with Dr Ray Allen and the Institute for Studies in American Music at Brooklyn College in October 2004. Brooklyn

College, in the heart of America's largest Anglophone Caribbean community, was a perfect venue to examine calypso's pan-Atlantic development and the significance of New York as a centre for the performance and media dissemination of the music. In addition to presentations of papers, Dr Hollis Liverpool (Mighty Chalkdust) performed a set of calypsos that illustrated the adaptations of the song form to diverse cultural contexts. In November 2005, musician and educator Geraldine Connor organized a calypso conference with the Centre for Cultural Analysis, Theory and History at the University of Leeds. This event, which brought together numerous scholars and artistes, focused on calypso and other Carnival arts in England, with particular attention to issues of memory, migration and displacement. In February 2006, librarian Joan Osborne and curator Sonja Dumas convened a final calypso conference at the National Library of Trinidad and Tobago in Port of Spain. Calypsonians Slinger Francisco (Mighty Sparrow), Chalkdust, David Rudder and Lutalo Masimbo (Brother Resistance) joined calypso writer Christophe Grant and several calypso researchers to discuss such issues as the language of calypso, the music's international appeal, the impact of electronic media and the importance of copyright.

The 2005 Miami conference Calypso and the Caribbean Literary Imagination included a number of students and alumnae of the University of Miami's Caribbean Literary Studies programme in English, past participants in the university's Caribbean Writers Summer Institute, and other researchers from the Caribbean, the US, Canada, England and Japan. Over the course of three days at the Historical Museum and the university, a vigorous dialogue developed on the aesthetics of calypso and the art form's multiplicity of connections with other types of Caribbean popular culture and literature. In addition to discussion of calypso as a verbal and musical form, conference participants examined visual representations of the tradition. The 'Calypso in Postwar America' exhibition was on display, and Ray Funk screened a series of film clips from his collection, such as Sir Lancelot performing Lion's 'Ugly Woman' in the Hollywood movie *Happy Go Lucky* (1943), Jeri Sullivan singing Invader's 'Rum and Coca Cola' in a 1945 'soundie' (a type of short film), Cy Grant rendering Kitchener's 'My Landlady' in the BBC television movie *A Man From the Sun*

(1956) and Maya Angelou performing 'Run Joe' in the Hollywood movie *Calypso Heatwave* (1957).

The scope and theme of the Miami calypso conference reflect the scholarship, creative writing and teaching in Caribbean literature that have thrived at the University of Miami since the 1990s. Caribbean Literary Studies at the university was envisioned initially as the Caribbean Writers Summer Institute, an initiative in partnership with writers from the nation states and territories of the Caribbean, that would bring Caribbean writers in dialogue with one another and with the US, in a rigorous, enriching, critical and creative space for studying Caribbean literary culture and producing new work. It was a prelude to the development of a programme for the study of Caribbean literature and culture at the university that would attract scholars, faculty, and establish the university as a premier site for such studies in the US in partnership with Caribbean institutions of higher learning and Florida institutions like the Historical Museum of Southern Florida.

The Otto G. Richter Library at the university, like the Historical Museum, has extensive holdings relating to the history of Florida and the Caribbean Basin. The Caribbean Collection includes dozens of books published in or about Jamaica between its conquest by the English in 1655 and the end of plantation slavery in the British Empire in 1834; travel narratives and other first-hand accounts that describe the societies and histories of the larger Caribbean islands as well as the smaller islands like Barbados, Antigua, Trinidad and Saint Lucia; and a number of rare titles on Guyana and Suriname. This is an addition to the Caribbean Writers' Summer Institute Video Archive the Cuban/Latino Theater Archive, and the generously endowed Cuban Heritage Collection.

The 2005 Calypso and the Caribbean Literary Imagination conference was the most recent of several international conferences organized first by the Caribbean Writers' Summer Institute and subsequently by Caribbean Literary Studies at the University of Miami. The success of these conferences prompted the establishment of a free access refereed online journal, *Anthurium: A Caribbean Studies Journal*, in collaboration with the Digital Lab at the Otto G. Richter Library. The articles featured in this collection were first published in *Anthurium* 3, no.1 in

December 2005. The conveners of the joint conference, Sandra Pouchet Paquet and Stephen Stuempfle, edited selected conference papers for that special issue with the assistance of Sheri-Marie Harrison, managing editor of *Anthurium*. The present volume was reassembled, designed, and edited with an introduction by Patricia Joan Saunders of the University of Miami. It was her initiative that secured a contract from Ian Randle Publishers to publish and market the collection of essays as a book that would enjoy a different kind of circulation among students, scholars, and calypso enthusiasts.

The articles featured in this book offer new perspectives on a wide variety of Caribbean artistes. Contributors explore the work of numerous calypsonians and other singers, including Sparrow, Kitchener, Chalkdust, Winston Bailey (Shadow), Denise Belfon, and Jamaicans Elephant Man and Carlene. Among the many writers discussed are Samuel Selvon, V.S. Naipaul, Jean Rhys, Errol John, Paule Marshall, Earl Lovelace and Lashkmi Persaud. As the articles suggest, Calypso encompasses and expresses a vast realm of social observation and philosophical thought in the Caribbean and the Caribbean diaspora. Over the past century, calypsonians and other writers have constantly reworked the form in efforts to fathom and interpret the Caribbean and its location in world history. We hope that this book will spark new interest in the possibilities of calypso research and encourage new readings of calypsos and other works of Caribbean literature.

The production of this book, the Miami calypso conference and the 'Calypso: A World Music' project would not have been possible without the multi-year assistance of the project advisory committee: Ray Allen, Kenneth Bilby, Geraldine Connor, John Cowley, Ray Funk, Donald Hill, the late Errol Hill, Gordon Rohlehr and Keith Warner. 'Calypso: A World Music' was funded in part by grants from the National Endowment for the Humanities. Many thanks are also due to the entire staff of the Historical Museum of Southern Florida for its work on the Miami conference and the online and travelling exhibitions. At the University of Miami, thanks are due to contributing faculty and graduate students in Caribbean Literary Studies in English, especially Patricia Saunders, Sheri-Marie Harrison, Anna-Bo Chung and Jessica Damian. Many thanks are also due to the Digital Media Lab at Richter Library, especially Bryanna Herzog, manager of the Digital Media Lab, and Peter Dooling, Digital Media Lab Specialist.

INTRODUCTION

MAPPING THE ROOTS/ROUTES OF CALYPSO IN CARIBBEAN LITERARY AND CULTURAL TRADITIONS

Patricia J. Saunders

This edited collection represents an array of convergences across critical perspectives, political and social agendas, generations and national boundaries. In its earliest manifestations, calypso music emerged in response to a cultural climate that demanded creative modes of expression that could both resist and record the historical and political changes taking place in Trinidad. Under the protective watch of another flourishing tradition of negotiation and resistance in Trinidad and Tobago (Carnival), the art form prospered by constantly remaking itself as the context and contours of the social landscapes in the country demanded. Some of the most significant demands came from other cultural institutions within the country. Since the 1900s, the development and continuous prominence of the steel pan in Trinidad and Tobago with contributions from East Indian culture, such as the tassa drums and chutney music, continue to transform the musical genre, making it one of the lasting pillars of Caribbean culture in the region and in diaspora.

The growing body of Caribbean literary texts which engage the relationships between Carnival, calypso, nationalism, gender and development, politics, youth culture and a host of other issues that affect the region, suggests that popular culture continues to emerge in more and more complex forms as a tool of cultural critique and education beyond the national boundaries of the Caribbean region.[1] There has always been an integral link between popular culture and politics in the Caribbean. C.L.R. James best captures this relationship in one of his seminal works, *Beyond the Boundary*, while the young Creole Trinidadian Ralph de Boissière, writing and living in Australia, published his novel entitled *Rum and Coca-Cola* (1956) which chronicled the growing voice of the discontented masses of workers toward American colonialism, a voice and sentiment in the novel rendered in song by the calypsonian. The growing interdependence (between politics and popular culture) was part of the practice of play and performance, so common in sports and dance, that was now being transformed in new arenas which included the political platform and the calypso tent in pre-independence Trinidad. The spirit of rebellion, which was an integral part of the stickfighting tradition was being heavily legislated against and blacks in the increasingly urbanized venues of Port of Spain had to find new resources to express their Selves and to record their experiences. John Cowley chronicles these changes in *Carnival, Canboulay and Calypso: Traditions in the Making*, noting that by 1896,

> It is possible that the Cedros "riot" was sparked by what was remembered by Joseph Clarke and Anthony, as a concerted effort to stamp out drumming (and, therefore, drum dances and stickfighting bouts). They recalled this happened in about 1895.... Legislation and its enforcement by the police had reduced the *diametre* element to a rump of its 1881 pre-eminence. Canboulay had been stopped, bands of more than ten persons carrying sticks were prohibited, pierrots were obliged to obtain police licenses, *pisse-en-lit* and transvestism were banned, as were obscene words and actions.[2]

The increasingly hostile sentiment towards Afro-Caribbean culture in the colonies hastened the emergence of new modes of cultural and political expression and the 'gamesmanship' of these two formidable spaces grew. Displaced from Calinda rituals, the chantwell honed his oratorical skill, making it a tool for verbal warfare, but these words also became the primary tool for recording an 'unofficial' account of the events taking place in the day to day lives of common people.

It has been well established by scholars such as Daniel Cowley, J.D. Elder, Errol Hill, Gordon Rohlehr and many others who study the various modes of cultural expression, that oral cultures in the Caribbean region have worked effectively as vehicles for ensuring the continuity of musical traditions in the Caribbean. Only folk tales and folk sayings, often used to educate people in the ways of life, have the same functionality as music within Caribbean cultures. However, the unique nature of calypso music and the historical context out of which it grew, allowed the art form to borrow from an already well established history of oral literature. This tradition was able to teach in ways the written text could not, primarily because of its capacity to reach a much larger audience, regardless of the degree of literacy. But this musical form also created a space for the musician to expose the limitations and playfulness of 'formal' language (the Queen's English) and the ways in which speakers and singers could make their own meaning beyond the formal boundaries of what colonial education provided its well educated masses. Some would argue that it is precisely these limitations within the *formal* educational institutions that prompted several teachers to cross over from the classroom, to the calypso tents, and swell the ranks of this cultural institution.

Music, Memory, Resistance: Calypso and the Caribbean Literary Imagination is divided into four sections — Section One: Music as Memory, Resistance and Political Context; Section Two: Sans Humanité: The Song, the Singer and the Story; Section Three: Ten to One is Murder: Gender, Sexuality and the Body Politic; and Section Four: When All the World's a Stage: Performing Cultural Identity at Home and Abroad. Each section reflects key critical concerns addressed both in calypso and literature, sometimes in relationship to its literary counterpart, other times in relation to other 'cultural texts' such as Jamaican music, cricket and dance. The critical premise of highlighting the formal, thematic, political and cultural links between calypso and a wide range of textual representations of Caribbean culture constitutes the framework for this collection. However, the section titles do not necessarily reflect a shared perspective on the themes represented in each essay in a given section. Rather, they act as companion texts based on the varied methodological approaches to the artistes as well as the art, its form and content. The collection considers the relationship between literature and calypso as similarly engaged in the project of subject formation (the making of Selves) within the Caribbean region and globally.

Historians have commented extensively that the roots/routes of calypso lie in its rebellious past as a form of ridiculing colonial masters, policies, values and traditions through verbal attack in song (also called picong), as well as a complex mode of negotiating the complex cultural terrain of the Caribbean. However, calypso music fulfils another social function, as a form of collective memory that is intimately linked to traditional constructions of cultural identity through history, legend, myth narration and performance. Long after the enthusiasm and awe of historical events die away, the narrative accounts rendered to melodic compositions immortalize these events in memories and imaginations across generations. From the early twentieth century, West Indians came to know the world more intimately; from events and battles in Britain to the battles of World War II and the struggles to end Apartheid in South Africa to the deaths of Martin Luther King Jr and John F. Kennedy and the continued struggles in Haiti for political and economic stability, through the lyrics and musical compositions of calypsonians. As an integral part of the institutional memory of the Caribbean region, music is an invaluable medium for maintaining a critical perspective on society by keeping contributions and controversies alive for future generations to learn from, borrow and ultimately, even revise. Finally, when the memory becomes susceptible to time, distance and the imagination, music is one of the 'sign-posts' that allows us to reconstruct our past out of the splintered recollections in the recesses of our minds and bodies. Because, like the mind, the body also remembers through movement and dance.

Not only has calypso served as an unofficial record of historical figures and events, it emerged as a cultural weapon that yielded tremendous sway within the general audiences of the region. Political leaders, from the colonial period through post-independence and the newly globalized Caribbean nation states, fear and respect the power of popular culture for conveying and transforming the sentiment of Caribbean politics at an (inter)national level. Calypsonians have long been the 'voice of the people', delivering the complaints, criticisms and even solutions to political leaders. Calypsonians created a tradition of textual narratives that contextualize the diverse political shifts in regional and global politics by situating them in relation to the everyday experiences of the nation's citizens. This popular art form has influenced how politics is practised and critiqued by state actors and citizens alike. The relationship between art and politics in Caribbean popular culture is a delicately maintained balance, with both institutions equally aware of the precarious nature of the relationship. Both are conscious of the need for each other, and yet they are unable to exist (comfortably) in the same political and cultural space without the occasional struggle to redefine the privileges, limitations and changes that characterize all meaningful relationships.

This collection includes contributions from calypsonians, critics, novelists and poets alike, all engaged in representing Caribbean culture in its myriad formations. The first two essays represent similar perspectives — from very different vantage points — on the historical stature, political contributions, and public image of Trinidad and Tobago's first Prime Minister, Dr Eric Williams. In his essay, 'Dr Eric Williams's Vision for the Development of Carnival', Hollis 'Chalkdust' Liverpool, the most famous teacher turned calypsonian, attributes his rise to prominence to Dr Eric Williams's vision of development in Trinidad. During his tenure as Prime Minister of Trinidad and Tobago, Williams drew endless criticism from calypsonians, including Chalkdust, in songs like 'Let the Jackass Sing' (1974), Maestro's 'To Sir with Love' (1974), and Scrunter's 'Crapuad Revolution' (1981). Yet he continuously encouraged citizens to participate in developing the art form because he saw it as crucial to developing a newly independent nation state. The consummate state manager, Williams understood calypso was essential to his vision of development for the nation, and encouraged businessmen, teachers and students alike to participate in developing the art form. Williams, and other scholars of this generation, including C.L.R. James, understood that development was not simply dependent upon economic success, but that cultural institutions were also an invaluable part of bringing Caribbean countries into their own sense of self, a selfhood that would no longer have to stand in the shadow of Britain.

This last factor led Williams to put systems — such as the Carnival Development Committee — in place to institutionalize and professionalize the art form by ensuring access to the channels of education because, as Chalkdust notes, formal training in the use of metre, rhyme and sequence of melody and other technical aspects of performance and production were crucial to advancing the art form, the nation and its citizens. Chalkdust's essay provides critical perspectives on Williams and his political interest in calypso and culture from his vantage point as a musician coming into his own voice at the same time the country was coming into its own identity. Louis Regis's essay, 'Calypso as Political Context: Reflections on the Legend of Eric Williams', offers a different vantage point on Williams, his contributions and his relationship to the nation's citizens — as he was praised as harshly as he was criticized. Eric Williams's gift as an orator raised him to a particularly revered status in the region, but his political position and insistence on focusing on the working class, concretized his place in the region's history. However, both essays reflect on the double-edged sword of Williams's popularity represented in songs such as Sparrow's 'William the Conqueror' and 'No Doctor No', the former which chronicles his rise as a political leader when challenged, and the latter, the rallying cry for protests against price increases implemented after the 1957 budget. Regis's essay traces the political cartography of Williams's ascension to power, and his slow demise as a political leader by comparing the calypsos of 1957–1970 and those of 1970–1981 which provide a rich cultural and political context for historians in the region.

In the broader regional context, calypso music has functioned as a critical tool for gauging the political atmosphere among Caribbean nation states, especially during the contentious periods of colonization, decolonization, federation and independence. Ray Funk's essay, 'In the Battle for Emergent Independence: Calypsos of Decolonization', examines this aspect of the art form, tracing the divergent terrain of songs in over 70 years, beginning in 1935. Calypsos effectively mapped the changing political sentiment between Britain and its colonies from proud British citizens celebrating the coronation of the Queen Elizabeth (Atilla the Hun); or King Edward VIII's abdication of the throne to marry the American divorcee Wallis Simpson (Lord Caresser, 'King Edward VIII', 1937); to allegiance with Africa, not Britain (Lord Kitchener, 'Africa My Home', 1951 and 'Birth of Ghana', 1956). With increased travel abroad the popularity of calypso grew in Britain and the United States. However, the growing popularity allowed calypsonians to travel and experience first hand, what they had only read about and heard over the radio. Lord Kitchener's songs about Africa were heavily influenced by his interactions with African immigrants in Britain during his time as a resident there, and out of these interactions emerged one of the first calypsos about an African nation gaining independence from Great Britain.

But there were two significant events that preceded World War II that provided the accelerant to an already low burning flame of pan-African anti-colonialist sentiment in the region. On October 3, 1935 Italy invaded Abyssinia (Ethiopia), aided by Britain and France, and forced the reigning Emperor, Haile Selassie, to flee the country less than a year later. The growing possibility of war in Europe meant that there was greater coverage in the colonies, particularly in newspapers like the *Trinidad Guardian* and *Port of Spain Gazette*. When news of the invasion reached Port of Spain, Trinidadians responded immediately and decisively against what many understood as an act of colonialist aggression. In addition to public marches and flag days that saw Trinidadians proudly flying the Ethiopian flag, calypsonians raised their voices in protest, demanding that Britain rise to intervene. Houdini's 'Ethiopian War Drums' and Roaring Lion's 'Advantage Mussolini' revived pan-Africanist political thought and sentiment which had been driven underground by the anti-sedition laws of the 1920s.[3]

Songs of African solidarity quickly became another impetus for encouraging independence — from Britain and the United States — within the Caribbean region. Most famously, Lord Invader's 'Rum and Coca-Cola' (1943) and Sparrow's 'Jean and Dinah' (1956) (originally recorded and released under the title *Yankees Gone*); but the push for Federation exposed the contentious nature of Caribbean nationalisms captured in songs such as the Mighty Bomber's 'Federated Islands' and Sparrow's 'Jump to the Tune' (1957). The nationalist sentiment that emerged as a result of the failure of West Indian Federation set the stage for independence movements throughout the region, all of which are chronicled in Funk's essay, right up to the 2005 calypso competition. Seventy years later, two women in the calypso arena — Singing Sandra and Marvelous Marva — reflect on the tradition of anti-colonial resistance and question whether the region has really progressed towards liberation in their song, '42 Years Gone', which chronicles an incident in which school officials deny education to young children because they have dreadlocks.

The rebellion and the memory evoked through calypso music are intimately connected to notions, imaginings and performances of self. Through the power of suggestion, metaphor and innuendo, the calypsonian modelled different modes of being-in-the-world. But, as Marlene Nourbese Philip suggests in her essay, 'Fugues, Fragments and Fissures: A Work in Progress', the increased popularity of Carnival has radically transformed calypso music as artistes are more concerned with getting radio air time than with the social significance of their songs. In both form and content, 'Fugues, Fragments and Fissures', details the concept of Caribbean identity as an amalgamation of these three physical and psychological states of experience. The various experiences of the 'fugue' or 'dissociative states' that occur between the lived experiences of the nation's citizens and the government's responses to them are the thematic focus of numerous calypsos. But more importantly, the calypso is a call to re-member, to bring back together the fragments by bridging the histories, spaces, languages, to form something anew. She reminds us that,

> It is sometimes the language of the calypso — not simply the words but the deeper language — the meta-language.... This for me is the mask coming to life through performance — the mask of history, a false history, being removed and through calypso our memory is animated. Calypso has the potential of bringing us out of that fugue state where we flee the reality of what has been and is still around us (91).

A primary tool for (re)membering the collective experience, calypso can effectively work to highlight, foster, and challenge the fragmented nature of Caribbean identity both in its form and content through its action on the imagination.

The poet's journal entries which span several years represent the fragments, or parts of the (w)hole — conversations with medical professionals about the spread of HIV/AIDS in Tobago, the poet's collecting seashells, pebbles, smoothed glass, music in the pan-yards, reading C.L.R. James on cricket and then Lamming, Mittleholtzer and BBC reports on an earthquake in Iran; the cultural texts that represent the 'clefts' created through the various fragmentations, or fissures — Sparrow's 'Jean and Dinah', *MACO*'s feature on Body Pond Estate in Antigua, the intellectual genius of Sylvia Wynter, Basil Davidson's 'African Genius', David Rudder's 'Madness', 'St Ann's', or 'Just Another Day in Paradise', reading issues of the *Trinidad and Tobago Review* that include no mention of women; these fissures and fragments of the (w)hole provide the poet with a context for interpreting the fugue state as a psychological and political mode of existence in the Caribbean, one that informs the shape and structure of memories and how we construct and perform our Selves daily. Ultimately, the questions posed through both the form and content of this piece ask us to speculate about the challenges faced by calypso and literature — and by extension the singer and the writer — of explaining 'who we are to ourselves and what we are doing here'.

Section Two, Sans Humanité: The Song, the Singer and the Story, traces the complex landscapes and strategies used by writers in their stories and songs. However, the title of this section also reflects on the contested terrains of engagement between the artistes and their subject matter which seem, at times, to compete for the hearts and minds of their audiences. The literal translation of the popularized refrain, *sans humanité*, is 'without human pity', a phrase said to have originated from stickfighting and which reflected the merciless nature of the battle in the gayelle.[4] The same phrase assumed a different meaning in the calypso arena, but one which still reflected the same boasting and skill associated with the calinda bands. The phrase was an invitation to participate in acknowledging the 'superior might and word-power of the calypsonian, while mercilessly deriding his opponent's lack of the same'.

The literal and figurative interpretation of sans humanité can best be understood in relation to the 'humour' which stems from the perversities of reality, so common in many calypso songs. Gordon Rohlehr analyses the 'cannibal joke' in Sparrow's calypso, 'The Congo Man' and in the narratives of the actual historical events from which the song emerged. 'Contextualizing the "Cannibal Joke" in Calypso and Literature' constructs a complex cartography of the cannibal in Africa, while linking it to cultural interpretations of other macabre developments throughout the African Diaspora. Reading Sparrow's plot in the 'Congo Man' as a metaphorical representation of the fissure between the terror of political violence and the artistic representation and responses to the song, Rohlehr suggests that the humorous elements of the song, when read against the history unfolding in the Congo during the departure of Belgium in 1960, is 'inseparable from the reductive spirit of Carnival masquerade, which, unmasked, reveal a horror, the skull beneath the skin-teeth'. In other words, the lack of human pity (sans humanité) speaks to the underlying masquerade which allows for humour in the face of such dire circumstances.

We are certainly encouraged to consider the interstitial dialogue between NourbeSe Philip's and Rohlehr's essays, where his is an equally elaborate deconstruction of the fugue or dissociative states that inform Caribbean cultural and political spaces. Rohlehr's analyses how cannibalism, the wry humour and irony implicit in these myths, and the underlying sexual innuendos of narratives, became part of the colonizing mythologies of Conrad's *Heart of Darkness* and James Joyce's *Ulysses*. His analysis traces the shift from colonizing mythologies to the sardonic humour later deployed in Carnival and literature as a means of diffusing the horror of political violence between African ethnic groups like the Baluba and the Lulula, two ethnic groups mentioned in Sparrow's song. The laughter and humour in the song is not simply aimed at cannibalism, it is specific to eating white women (white meat), who are travelling through Africa. The double entendre of consuming whites through violence, sex, and ironically religion highlights the allegorical relationship of these cultural texts and the social anxieties of the cultures they represent. However, as Rohlehr argues, the proverbial overbite of the 'skin teeth' has come full circle in contemporary calypsos, like 'Heaven' (or 'Tribal War', which NourbeSe Philip mentions) which call upon audiences in the regions to recognize the 'skull behind the skin teeth', as their complicit participation in political violence unfolding in Rawanda, Zaire and Haiti.

Regardless of cultural context, the story — tale, myth, lore, history — is capable of reaching across cultural and national boundaries, to address audiences around the world. The re-emergence of the African griot in the form of the 'chantwell' in Caribbean culture suggests that the art of storytelling certainly survived the Middle Passage. Much of what people in the Caribbean know of Africa and African culture emerges through performative aspects of Caribbean culture; from stickfighting to religious ceremonies, the art of *picong* and storytelling.[5] In African traditions the *griot* is charged with the responsibility for telling (his)stories of the community. Out of this oral tradition emerged New World narrators, unique to Caribbean cultures in different countries. In Trinidad's Carnival culture, the tradition is an integral link between the 'chantwell' and the tradition of stickfighting which is often described as one of the few remaining signs of African warriorhood in Carnival. The *chantwell*, 'possessor of the word, and a spokesman for the group, occupied a position of supreme importance' in the stickfighting arena (154). 'Unmasking the Chantwell Narrator in Earl Lovelace's Fiction', traces this tradition in calypso and its interpellation into Caribbean literary traditions. Like the chantwell, the calypsonian provided a voice which was a call to battle, to expression and recognition of the Self. Aiyejina's interpretation of *The Dragon Can't Dance, The Wine of Astonishment* and 'Jobell in America' asserts that Lovelace experiments with the chantwell as a narrative trope, a voice that documents the sensibilities of those in the text as they relate to the individual telling the story.

But even after independence stories of the working poor were not necessarily deemed 'worthy' of being told and preserved in some circles. Class and colour division in Trinidad and Tobago provided a clear demarcation between the spaces of 'high brow' and 'low brow culture'. No two spaces were more reviled by the middle and working classes alike than the pan yard and the stickfighting circles, for precisely the same reasons. For all those concerned with keeping their 'good' children out of such bacchanal and 'comess', the pan yard and stickfighting circle was a space and place where rum flowed as liberally as the stories, songs and fights, more often than not with the same sharp sting of wit and wood. In post-independence Trinidad, the street scene had been cleaned up significantly in order to encourage the middle classes to participate more extensively in Carnival. With the slow demise of stickfighting and the introduction of sponsorship in the steel bands middle classed participation in pan grew during the post-independence era. In 'Calypso and the Bacchanal Connection', Earl Lovelace speculates on the 'bacchanal space' in Creole culture in Trinidad and Tobago to suggest that the cultural production in this space is necessarily resistant because it emerged from a context in which African culture was constantly under threat of disappearance.[6] He argues that,

> [T]here were two basic spaces we entered when we came to this country: one I call the Ethnic Space, in which members of a group carried on the religion and cultural practices they brought with them, and the other the Creole Space, the general meeting place of cultures. Cultural and religious forms that were African were all banned at one point or another, and so that in order for Africans to express self they had either to abandon their gods or find ways to bring religion and culture into what was legitimate. So nearly everything they had brought had to be poured into the secular space, often not as a whole but as fragments. (146)

The bridge, therefore, between the literary trope of the chantwell and its relation to the political economy of culture in a country like Trinidad and Tobago, is outlined in the passage above. If there is any doubt about the relationship between the geographies of location in *The Wine of Astonishment* (that is, the rum shop, gayelle, the roadside, all of which are physical spaces generally deemed bacchanal arenas and Creole spaces) and the texts produced and distributed, we need only look closely at the conventions involved; the communal narration, multiple narrative filters, the extemporaneous elements of the stories and the shared thematic focus of the stories and songs sung by calypsonians of the day.

The communal nature of the discourses that circulate throughout these public, narrative spaces makes the exchange between the singer and the audience equally as vital to the story being told by the chantwell narrator in *The Wine of Astonishment*. The chantwell, who conveys (in this case) her narrative through a plural voice; 'Some say' (*Wine* 46), 'They tell this story' (*Wine* 83), 'They tell of another time' (83), and 'As he, Buntin, tell it later' (87), plays the role of emcee who facilitates the events for a given period until the 'main actors/actresses' are ready to continue the performance. This role is mediated through a call and response similar to that of the calypsonian, inviting the audience (through the chorus, sans humanité) to witness and participate simultaneously. The stickfighter also depended on the chantwell for inspiration and to set and modify the tone of the battle through music, song and his/her interaction with the crowd. The exchange does not exist in a unidirectional context, the audience has the power to influence the direction of the exchange, to rally the fighters and storytellers, to laud the skill of one performer while condemning the lack thereof in another; and in so doing shift the tenor of the exchange.

Section Three, Ten to One is Murder: Gender, Sexuality and the Body Politic, focuses more explicitly on the gender dynamics of Caribbean popular culture with particular attention to calypso, dancehall, soca and cricket — which constitute a significant portion of the cultural exports in the Caribbean region. The ideologies of national culture and national identity, so often espoused in conversations about popular culture implies that work and art produced in the region represents the sentiment or desires of a larger whole or the 'body politic' at large. However, as has been argued and clearly supported in political movements globally, there is a seemingly inevitable compression of historical and cultural specificities in the interest of promoting the idea of 'the nation' in culture and politics. The continued disparity of gender equity in the Caribbean region, despite the increasing visibility of women in cultural venues such as Carnival, where women now outnumber men (10 to 1), suggests that women's access to the technologies of citizenship and belonging remain limited, and are arguably, being rigorously repressed.

From its inital adaptation by enslaved Africans, Carnival was a site of subversion; a space of possibility for the poor to test the parameters of their strength and force against systems of oppression through stickfighting and the steel band movement, which was a later addition to Carnival. But this space was also an occasion to embrace African cultural forms which, though modified, presented black West Indians with a cultural bridge between the New World and their African ancestors. Oral narratives, storytelling and the folkloric figures that emerged out of this tradition symbolized not only the richness of the tradition, they also provided guides for surviving and prospering under systems that were less than favourable for women. Cynthia Davis traces the development of the 'jamette' in Carnival traditions and the appropriation of this figure in the works of the Dominican writer, Jean Rhys. 'Jamette Carnival and Afro-Caribbean Influences in the Works of Jean Rhys' situates Rhys's narrative style, as well as her thematic focus, within the context of a Carnival tradition. By contextualizing the social and economic conditions of urban women in the nineteenth century Davis examines Rhys's appropriation of the technical and political power of calypso and Carnival to empower her female protagonists in works such as *Voyage in the Dark*, 'Let Them Call it Jazz' and *Quartet*.

The notoriously scandalous behaviour of women in the marketplace and on the street earned them the title 'jamette', and this behaviour is embraced by Rhys in her own lifestyle as well of those of her protagonists. Drawing on the verbal cunning and other-worldly powers implicit in tales of Anancy spiders, la jablesse, and the Soucouyant, Rhys empowers her female protagonists with similar capacities in order to manoeuvre their way through social structures designed to oppress them. Although, as Davis notes, the term *jamette* would not have been used in the context of

Dominica's cultural landscape, what is more important in her reading of Rhys is the extent to which these traditions provided a literary and culturally relevant framework for her to imagine modes of resistance for her female protagonists, modes that were part of the African ancestry she insisted was integral to Caribbean identity. For Rhys's protagonists, their marginalization within colonial institutional structures meant that they had to assert themselves and their right to exist in public spaces like the 'street', where 'respectable women' were not seen unless accompanied by men. In other words, if they could not always be seen, they would certainly use their tongues and their wit to be heard, and turn less advantageous situations in their favour.

Like the street, the stage is another significant location for performance of cultural and sexual identity. While both calypso and dancehall have been traditionally masculine art forms, the lyrics of both musical traditions are overwhelmingly concerned with women's bodies — their size, shape, behaviour, sexual habits, domestic practices, et cetera. 'Big Fat Fish: The Hypersexualization of the Fat Black Female Body in Calypso and Dancehall', extends the discussion about the ways in which women's bodies are read and interpreted in public spheres. Shaw pays particular attention to how black women's bodies have 'come to play an instrumental role in the creation of "spectacle" in both the calypso and dancehall arenas' (193). Suggesting that in Jamaican popular culture, colour and 'size' matters, she critiques the ascendance of Carlene, one of the most prominent dancehall queens in Jamaica, arguing that her light skin worked effectively to offset — or lighten the affects of — her sexually suggestive dance moves. Interestingly, she asserts that Carlene's 'brownness' has helped to mediate her 'corporate and social mobility by rendering her crude public displays more palatable' (194).

The emergence and popularity of dancehall, commonly considered a form of 'low brow' culture (because of its lewd lyrics and 'vulgar' dances), has crossed class lines, through the enthusiastic embrace of middle classed, or at least middle coloured (brown) women seeking escape from middle-class propriety.[7] However, as Shaw asserts, colour is not the only modality for producing spectacle in performance. Women's size and sexual aura play equally important roles in both dancehall and calypso. Female calypsonians like Calypso Rose, Singing Sandra and soca star Denise Belfon are among several big bodied artistes whose bodies signify difference and resistance through their disruptions of white, upper- and middle-classed norms of beauty, prosperity and desire so often characterized by runway models in fashion magazines. More importantly however, the sexual suggestiveness of women who attend these fetes and performances, and their 'fleshy' displays — through clothing, or lack thereof — work to reclaim female sexual agency — if only momentarily through their performance in this public arena. However, raging debates continue among feminist scholars about the possibility of this 'sexual agency' as a mode of resistance, particularly since these performances are, more often than not, framed by masculinist discourses — in calypso and dancehall lyrics as well as through government policies — that define, police and appropriate women's sexuality.

Moving from the cultural arena of the stage, to another significant site for producing cultural identity in the Caribbean region — the cricket field — we are offered a different occasion to consider the nexus of gender/nation/sexuality. Our discussion up to this point has focused on cultural institutions that have heavily influenced the intimate links between calypso and the literary imagination. However, in the same way that Carnival and calypso have been integral to Trinidadian identity, no other cultural institution has defined the identity of the Caribbean region as cricket. C.L.R. James, George Lamming, V.S. Naipaul deployed the game of cricket as an analogy for the region's complex and, at times, antagonistic relationship to its British colonial history and inheritance. More than simply a game, cricket has become one of the most important conduits for social and political expressions of a uniquely Caribbean identity as embodied in the various modifications of the game brought about by the style of play in the region.

'Men in the Yard and On the Street: Cricket and Calypso in Caribbean Literature' examines the public domain of the yard and the street as sites for negotiating Caribbean identity especially across race, gender and class boundaries. Westall asserts that the colonial inheritance of cricket, once revised to meet the needs of the players in the Caribbean, provided a means for men to 'beat the master' at his own game. However, as her critique of *Miguel Street* suggests, the 'gentleman's game' remained limited to working-class men who were locked out by colonial prejudices which excluded them from some clubs and teams. Efforts to exercise their masculinity occur through their domination of women in their communities and other spaces where the cricket bat becomes the tool of abuse and the phallic symbol of imposed order. The local hero of the Caribbean cricket pitch, immortalized through calypso songs, is emasculated when he is denied the opportunity to compete on the international stage. His inability to at least be measured against the standard of white masculinity locks him into the position of a 'small boy' playing a grown man's game.

The yard, in Errol John's play, *Moon on a Rainbow Shawl*, emerges as another sphere in which men and women jostle for recognition. Although the biting verbal wit of the women in the yard controls the discursive terrain, there is a maternal element to this space that allows men to imagine a different kind of relationship with the women in their lives. But even in these more intimate spaces, there is limited growth for the men in the yard, who must still look to their colonial masters for approval and for upward mobility. The novel and the play speak to the larger issue of social stratification in the Caribbean and the social injustices suffered by the working classes throughout the region. Through a socio-historical analysis of cricket and representations of the sport in Caribbean literature, Westall highlights the intimate relationship between sports, culture and Caribbean masculinity. The question that remains, however, is where are the socially acceptable outlets for women who are also struggling for their recognition as subjects and citizens?

The final section, When All the World's a Stage: Performing Cultural Identity at Home and Abroad, considers the impact of migration and immigration on how cultural identity is performed, imagined and contested globally and regionally. The myriad roots and routes of Caribbean culture and its various manifestations in the diaspora are difficult to imagine, far less to piece together in a continuous narrative. And yet, the ongoing effort on the part of artistes to create out of this tapestry, a garment capable of representing and celebrating all of these histories encourages the production of newly emergent art forms and identities. Convergent patterns of migration, forced and voluntary, and divergent cultural traditions forged a region that is still struggling to come to terms with its complex colonial past. For many, travel to the imperial metropoles provided the route to self discovery, while for others the key to creating a Self lay firmly in forging a unique Caribbean identity from the social and cultural remnants of what various groups brought to the New World.

East Indians, who were brought to the Caribbean region as indentured labourers during the colonial period, have certainly made their mark socially and culturally in countries like Trinidad and Tobago, and Guyana. They arrived in the Caribbean with their own religious, linguistic, and cultural traditions, many of which continued to grow and transform into new practices and rituals as they settled into the newly formed societies of the region. Discourses on national identity depend largely on cultural hybridity, which borrows symbols and icons from an array of ethnic groups in the respective countries. This is most definitely the case in Trinidad and Tobago where recent debates about whether the steel pan should be the national symbol of artistic expression and culture and, most recently, the national debate about whether the country's highest award for achievement in the service of the nation, should remain the Trinity Cross. In May 2006, the High Court of Justice ruled that Trinity Cross amounted to discrimination against those who were not of the Christian faith. However, the court stopped short of demanding the government to change the symbol. Instead, they urged the ruling People's National Movement (PNM) government to engage in public discussions about how best to accommodate the ethnic diversity of the country in the symbol of its highest honour. Prime Minister Patrick Manning agreed that such a venture should be undertaken because 'the Government of Trinidad and Tobago has one responsibility and one responsibility only and that is to remove the unnecessary impediment to the smooth conduct of our national life.'[8] Subsequently, the Prime Minister appointed a committee — headed by University of the West Indies Professor of History, Bridget Brereton — to review the country's highest award, and others like it, to assure that no discriminatory symbols were present that might exclude the citizens of Trinidad and Tobago. The committee was also charged with making recommendations to the government about how best to resolve the current issue of the Trinity Cross.[9]

'With a Tassa Blending: Calypso and Cultural Identity in Caribbean Fiction' contemplates a similar set of questions about representations of ethnic identity in national culture in Trinidad. Calypsos have historically satirized and ridiculed Indo-Caribbean identity and cultural traditions. But recently, it was a female soca singer, Denise 'Saucy Wow' Belfon, who donned a sari and declared, in her song, Indo-Trinidadian men as sexually desirable. Many segments of the Hindu community felt her performance in a sari constituted a disregard for the sacred nature of the sari, while others wondered about the necessity of the sari in making this proclamation. Would the song have been read or interpreted as somehow less offensive or, for that matter, less artistically creative if it were performed by an Afro-Trinidadian woman, in African clothing? What is clear is that songs that openly express sexual desire across ethnic lines always receive critical attention from religious and community leaders within both communities. This suggests in the end that culture, more than any other arena, is the battleground on which contestation for national and even political recognition is fought.

Seepersad Naipaul's *Gurudeva and Other Indian Tales* (1943) and V.S. Naipaul's *Miguel Street* (1959) are two of the earliest Indo-Caribbean fictional texts to include references to calypso. According to Morgan, for both writers, calypso provides a philosophical framework by analysing and magnifying the domestic dramas. In later short stories like Sam Selvon's 'Calypso in London', the art form is 'deployed as a contradictory marker of Trinidadian distinctiveness and the translocation of Anansi-style coping strategies within the metropolitan scenarios' of London and other Caribbean diaspora spaces (238). For Indo-Trinidadian male authors, their deployment of calypso music represents shared experiences, rather than ethnic disassociation. Their representations were very limited in how they dealt with the experiences of East Indian women in their shared social environments. For Indo-Trinidadian women writers, the post-independence period made more educational and job opportunities available and out of these opportunities emerged a new body of writing which represented their experiences within their communities and within the larger Trinidadian landscape. Lashkmi Persad's *Butterfly in the Wind* (1990) and *For the Love of My Name* (2000) explore the binaries that exist between Brahminical

Hinduism and Afro-Creole nationalism to suggest that both of these spaces limit the possibility for transformation for East Indian women.

Other women writers experiment with what Morgan describes as 'intentional hybridity', which highlights the more transgressive elements of ethnic, sexual and political identities. Ramabai Espinet's 'Indian Robber Talk' and Rajandaye Ramkissoon-Chen's 'When the Hindu Woman Sings Calypso' both borrow and revise Indo-Trinidadian and Afro-Trinidadian art forms from soca chutney to 'robber talk', bringing East Indian women's voices into debates about national culture. Ramkissoon-Chen's poem is based on the emergence and success of the Indo-Trinidadian female calypsonian, Drupatee Ramgoonai, and traces the complex boundaries she traverses to enter this predominantly male, Afro-Trinidadian cultural space — from rural village to the urban centres, from the secluded, female space of the matikor prenuptial ritual, to the calypso tents and stages. The response to Drupatee's 'transgression' from within the East Indian fraternity was comprised of condemnation, shame and censure, but Ramkissoon-Chen's poem provides another voice into the usually male-dominated discourse. This intervention shifted the terrain by highlighting the privileges enjoyed by men in the cultural arena and the double standards implicit in the patriarchal structures of Hinduism and how these structures transform — as is evident in the growing popularity of tassa drums in soca and calypso music — and are transformed when they travel and encounter new cultural and social 'contact zones'.[10]

The intercultural exchanges that characterize the meeting of cultures in 'contact zones' are very often negotiated on unlevel playing fields. The terms of negotiation are set out from positions of power and left for those with limited access to manoeuvre for their right to access and existence socially, culturally and politically. Michael Eldridge's 'Bop Girl Goes Calypso: Containing Race and Youth Culture in Cold War America' gives an account of an important moment in American popular culture when calypso music was heralded as a bona fide contender to displace rock and roll music, or so the film *Bop Girl Goes Calypso* imagines. In an effort to capitalize on the growing passion for the exotic new genre and to hedge its bets against other films of the same genre which included, *Calypso Joe* (with Ellington alumnus Herb Jeffries in the title role, opposite a then unknown Angie Dickinson) and Columbia's *Calypso Heat Wave* (featuring aspiring song-and-dance man Joel Grey and lounge singer Maya Angelou), United Artists decided to throw their hats into the entertainment ring before the craze died down. Though it seemed clear from the beginning that this competition was not going to be long lived, the energy around the new art form certainly served to bolster the life and durability of rock and roll music while also assuring white Americans that their daughters, though susceptible to music crazes, were safe from the assumed 'vagaries' of this new cultural art form.

Eldridge traces the cultural and political logic that framed the codification of West Indian identity in the North American landscapes during the 1950s. Explaining the context in which calypso music emerged as a viable alternative to other more 'militant' music forms in America, Eldridge poses an interesting question, and an even more surprising response that would redefine the cultural connections between the US and the Caribbean:

> How, then, could suburban parents in a panic over rock and roll's threat to their children's moral hygiene (and, by implication, its menace of contagion of the social order with the germs of restiveness increasingly associated with black people) possibly see calypso as a preferable alternative to the demon rock and roll? They could do so, above all, by personifying it in Harry Belafonte (261)

As the climate of the Cold War grew even colder, Belafonte's own political persuasions came into conflict with the (stereotypical) images of West Indians that the American public wanted to consume. With the emergence of more 'authentic' calypsonians from the Caribbean region — who were recording and performing in the US and Britain — and the growing fear of the proximity of all things black in the 'intimate spaces' (the ears, minds and hips) of white youth, the possibilities for calypso music were increasingly limited to acting as a taming force for rock and roll music.

Where 'Bop Girl' explores the appropriation and interpolation of Caribbean music into the American racial landscape, 'Not Knowing the Difference: Calypso Overseas and the Sound of

Belonging in Narratives of Migration', continues the discussion about how culture is translated as it travels in Caribbean narratives of migration. Examining Sam Selvon's *The Lonely Londoners* (1959) and *Ways of Sunlight* (1957), Paule Marshall's *Brown Girl, Brownstones* (1959) and Lawrence Scott's *Aelred's Sin* (1998), Rahim argues that Caribbean societies recognize and comprehend 'the logic of travelling cultures given the dual forces of rootedness and itinerancy which shape its diasporic ethos' (286). This contradiction reflects the dialectical relationship between culture and identity, showing it to be the source of inclusion and exclusion simultaneously. By its very definition, culture is a process of signification that is inherently contradictory and often alienating through its discourses of 'sameness' while simultaneously consolidating systems of meaning out of which notions of community and collectivity emerge. In these narratives, music is the conduit through which we see protagonists struggle to maintain the delicate balance between culture as a means to alleviate the hegemony and racism of their 'host country' and culture as a means of excluding Others whose differentiation violates the sameness so often demanded for inclusion.

One particular aspect of cultural and national identity most rigorously contested and policed through Caribbean popular culture is sexuality. Rahim asserts that calypso and dancehall music 'work to reinforce, rather than challenge the exclusionary politics of the status quo on the issue of sexual citizenship' (297). While not as rigorously concerned with homosexuality as its first cousin (dancehall), calypso music certainly consolidates notions of West Indianess through heterosexual relationships which are positioned as 'normative' and necessary for inclusion. Caribbean migration narratives, through their focus on issues of authenticity, belonging and citizenship, speak to the necessity for continued renegotiation of cultural identity through cultural forms of expression. The opportunity for what Rahim describes as the 'homotextuality' of novels such as Trinidadian Lawrence Scott's *Aelred's Sin*, to emerge and disrupt the fixed boundaries of Caribbean identity depends largely on the willingness of readers to engage the ethical and moral questions that these texts pose. The questions raised in the nearly unrecognizable terrains of these texts are troubling ones about the costs of negating same sex relationships in the literary and cultural landscapes of the region. The conclusion of Scott's novel suggests that the 'sacred' territory of homosexuality is one of the necessary sites of discursive and political engagement about questions of citizenship and equal rights and protection by the state and indeed, the church. Equally as important to this critique, however, is the need to recognize the multiple transitions between national, cultural and sexual boundaries which create a 'third' or interstitial space where traditional insider/outsider binaries no longer define the realms of possibility.

The last essay in this collection signals a new area of critical focus in Caribbean cultural studies, a change that might well represent a return to an area of 'popular' culture that has been overlooked in contemporary criticism; dance. In Earl Lovelace's novel, *The Dragon Can't Dance*, we are summoned to remember the restorative and rebellious nature of dance.

> There is dancing in the calypso. Dance! If the words mourn the death of a neighbor, the music insists that you dance; if it tells the troubles of a brother, the music says dance. Dance to the hurt! Dance! If you catching hell, dance and the government don't care, dance! Your woman take your money and run away with another man, dance. Dance! Dance! Dance! (310).

Tracing the origins of dance, from its roots/routes in the work of resistance, to the contemporary phenomenon in soca and calypso described by some cultural critics as 'overly instructive' and organized and banal dances, 'Everybody do the Dance: The Politics of Uniformity in Dancehall and Calypso' contextualizes the dance craze that has migrated from the Caribbean to the 'global massive'. Some of these dances (and songs) include 'Signal de Plane', 'Get Something and Wave', and more recently, 'Chakka, Chakka'.

Far from simply representing growing fads in pan-Caribbean culture, Page suggests that the songs which accompany these 'instructive dances', and the movements themselves, can be read as moments in popular cultural history that 'capture an ethos that is at once concerned with making space for the outsider and marginalizing that same outsider' (312). What is most significant about these acts of inclusion and exclusion, however, is the processes through which they are performed. Considering Super Blue's 1991 road march winning song, 'Get Something and Wave', Page argues that there are multiple registers of meaning and movement that rely primarily on the 'choreographic maps' or registers of the participants. When Super Blue's song is read through Trinidadian political history — the failed Muslimeen coup led by Abu Bakr in 1990 and Blue's repeated evocation of Mother Muriel, the Spiritual Baptist icon — we are asked to consider a more complex nexus of negotiations taking place. These negotiations are couched between the contemporary realities of a 'tradition of subversion that inspired the very roots of Carnival' symbolized by Mother Muriel's chanting 'no curfew' during Super Blue's performance and her 'presence in Carnival as a Spiritual Baptist [which] unsettles (European based) notions that the spirit and the flesh are separate' (317).

Similarly, Page examines dance crazes launched by Elephant Man and his dance troupe — John, Bogle, Keeva, Stacy — and asks reading audiences to consider dance movements (like signal the plane) which mimic 'working bodies' in the travel industry, as symbolic resistance against immigration laws which function at complex levels to arrest or limit the mobility and motion of poor bodies. This critique posits that dancers in the audience may well participate in *both* spaces as insiders and outsiders which includes white and black Americans who can travel to Jamaica without obtaining visas or owning passports for that matter; middle-classed Jamaicans who see dancehall culture as antithetical to their puritanical ethics, and working-class Jamaicans who are 'outside' (in a foreign country) struggling to make ends meet. In short, the spaces of inside and outside are not as hermetically sealed as we would like to imagine. While the dance moves may appear on the surface to encourage uniformity and even 'sameness' we might also consider how this sameness, more often than not, is 'organized around resistance' whether against governments, industries or technologies of globalization, all of which impact how, when and why bodies move and are moved.

The sounds and songs of Caribbean popular culture are the impetus which guides the direction of movement in the region. Just as slaves and indentured labourers working in the fields depended on rhythms and songs to steady their souls, as their sweat and tears melded in building the New World; so too do their ancestors, now struggling to reap the fruits of their labour whether in the Caribbean or in its broader diasporas. The technologies of producing sound and song have been transformed, but what is all the more important is reexamining the locations and spaces out of which these cultural productions emerged and are represented. The relationship between music and literature, and their shared discursive structures, modalities for producing meaning and performances of the imagined self, offers us an array of epistemological paradigms through which to read, deconstruct, and reconstruct Caribbean subjectivities.

This collection of essays contributes critical perspectives on Caribbean popular cultural movements that have long been a part of the landscape of the region. In this respect, the music and culture under consideration here is by no means 'new'. The innovation of this collection rests in how these writers, artists and critics interpret the new demands made of cultural traditions in the regions in the face of renewed globalization and empire building. The dialogues represented in the convening of the Calypso and the Literary Imagination Conference are part of an increasingly relevant debate about the way we interpret and engage music, literature, and dance; all of which are bound up in our readings of culture, contemporary society and politics. Where other works have maintained somewhat rigid boundaries between popular culture and more institutionalized modes and forms of cultural production, the truly unique nature of this collection is its close attention to the 'back' (or hidden) routes and roots out of which Caribbean music and literature emerge. The works gathered here would have us believe that both calypso and literature were born of the same parents (the imagination), grew out of resistance against colonial legacies of oppression, and continue to revise and re-invision the continued changes taking place in Caribbean culture.

These essays provide some reflections on what David Scott describes as our 'refashioned futures'. Apart from simply providing interpretive lenses for reading Caribbean popular culture, the essays represent a more deliberate, strategic practice of cultural criticism that rereads the impact of colonial power through the various transformations in artistic production and the arts of the imagination.

Notes

1. For more detailed discussions of the significance of Caribbean popular culture in the construction of national identity, politics, religious identity, gender and society see Gordon Rohlehr's *Calypso and Society in Pre-Independence Trinidad* (Trinidad: self published, 1990); Stefano Harney's *Nationalism and Identity: Culture and the Imagination in a Caribbean Diaspora* (London and Kingston: Zed Books and the University of the West Indies Press, 1996); and Louis Regis's *The Political Calypso: True Opposition in Trinidad and Tobago* (Florida: University Press of Florida, 1999). These relationships are explored in early novels by Caribbean writers; Ralph de Bossière's *Rum and Coca-Cola* (Melbourne: Australasian Book Society, 1956); Earl Lovelace's *The Dragon Can't Dance* (UK: Longman Group UK, 1981); and *The Wine of Astonishment* (London: Heinemann, 1983): Willi Chen's *King of the Carnival* (London: Hansib Publications, 1988); and Michael Anthony's *The Chieftain's Carnival and Other Stories* (UK: Longman, 1993; reprint, Kingtson: Ian Randle Publishers, 2007).
2. John Cowley, *Carnival, Canboulay and Calypso: Traditions in the Making* (Cambridge: Cambridge University Press, 1996), 132–33.
3. Michael Anthony's *Port-of-Spain in a World at War 1939–1945* traces this development with particular attention to the shifting political sentiment among Afro-Trinidadians in relation to the British Crown. This shifting sentiment was most visible in Port of Spain, and most immediately in the popular cultural productions of the period. Gordon Rohlehr focuses more specifically on how the popular music of this period reflected and influenced the shape of the discursive terrain about Trinidad's place in the war as it developed. His chapter, 'World War II and its Aftermath', in *Calypso and Society in Pre-Independence Trinidad*, offers an analysis of the songs written and performed throughout Trinidad as well as how the Abyssinian War reached further into Caribbean culture as the Rastafarian movement proclaimed Haile Selassie as their religious leader.
4. Richard Allsopp's *Dictionary of Caribbean English Usage* (Kingston: the University of the West Indies Press, 2003), 487, gives a more detailed description of the historical and cultural evolution of this phrase.
5. The term *picong* refers to the practice (and art) of verbally ridiculing or satirizing another person (usually an opponent in calypso) while in their presence. The etymology of the term is connected to the cultural performance and adaptation of the term by Africans in the New World. A creolized form of the French word, 'piquant', meaning cutting or stinging, picong is part of the verbal warfare and rivalry that takes place between calypsonians in which they highlight one another's shortcomings and boast of their own strengths, all toward the end of embarrassing opponents into submission. In the context of contemporary calypso, the art of picong has been increasingly reserved for the extemporaneous singing.
6. Interview with Patricia Saunders entitled, 'The Meeting Place of Creole Cultures', *Calabash: A Journal of Caribbean Arts and Letters* 2, no. 1: 10–22.
7. For an extensive historiography and discussion on discourses of desire, the complexity of colour and class, and the nexus of race, femininity and skin colour in Jamaican society see Patricia Mohammed's '"But Most of All Mi Love Me Browning": The Emergence in Eighteen and Nineteenth-Century Jamaica of the Mulatto Woman as the Desired', *Feminist Review* no. 65 (Summer 2000): 22–48. Mohammed traces shifting attitudes and policies on miscegenation between black and white populations in Jamaica from

the diaries of Thomas Thistlewood and Lady Nugent through contemporary shared notions of female desirability expressed by artists like Buju Banton, from whose song the title of the essay is taken.

8. Roxanne Stapleton, 'No regrets in changing Trinity Cross, says PM', *Trinidad and Tobago Express*, Monday, June 5, 2006.

9. Richard Lord, 'New National Award: PM appoints committee to change Trinity Cross', *Trinidad and Tobago Express*, June 3, 2006. The other members of the committee include: Gillian Bishop (designer), Prof. Selwyn Ryan (political analyst), Devanand Ramlal (lawyer and businessman), Gregory Aboud (business leader), Dr Ralph Balgobin (Head, Arthur Lok Jack Institute of Business), Anslem Richards (Tobago House of Assembly) and Sandra Marchack (Permanent Secretary to the prime minister). While it appears that the prime minister sought to comprise the committee from an ethnically and professionally diverse group of individuals, Opposition leader, Kamala Persad-Bissessar, was reportedly heard complaining during the announcement of the members that there were no Muslim members appointed to the committee.

10. I borrow this phrase from Mary Louise Pratt's book, *Imperial Eyes: Travel Writing and Transculturation* (New York and London: Routledge, 1992). She defines 'contact zones' as the 'social spaces where disparate cultures meet, clash, and grapple with each other, often in highly asymmetrical relations of domination and subordination like colonialism, slavery, or their aftermaths as they are lived out across the globe today' (4). In this case, the cultural hybridization represented in art forms in Trinidad and Tobago emerge in precisely the social and political context described by Pratt. After emancipation, the culture of the Caribbean region is still engaged in the processes of redefining and representing the notion of cultural identity in the aftermath of centuries of imperialism.

MUSIC AS MEMORY, RESISTANCE AND POLITICAL CONTEXT

1

ERIC WILLIAMS'S VISION FOR THE DEVELOPMENT OF CARNIVAL

Hollis 'Chalkdust' Liverpool[1]

A few years ago, I wrote an article for a newspaper, the *Bomb* actually was the name of it, and the editor of the newspaper called me in and told me I couldn't write that article.² So, I asked him why, and he told me that I was a calypsonian and calypsonians can't write.

Of course, he was insinuating that calypsonians were simple singers and not academics. So, let me begin by saying that Eric Williams saw the calypsonian in a different light. Williams saw the calypsonian as an academic and indeed more than an academic.

For Williams, the calypsonian was a political scientist in his own right. And I want to begin by singing the calypso, 'Let the Jackass Sing.' It is a very true calypso because Williams used to talk to me about calypso and what calypsonians do and I learned a lot from him. And I also learned from his cook, the woman who used to look after him. And when I asked her how he liked the calypso and what Williams said, she told me, 'Let the Jackass sing!' So I got that actually from the woman in the house, who told me: 'Let the Jackass sing!' And I want to begin my talk by singing the first and third verses of the calypso, to show you how he thought of the calypsonian and, hopefully, you will have a better idea of Williams in terms of his imagery about the calypso and the calypsonian. And if you follow me …

'Let the Jackass Sing'

1

PNM women against me
They report me to Deafy
Last year after Dimanche Gras
Deafy Chalkie gone too far
How come someone in Trinidad
Tell this young man
That someone in White Hall mad
It's an insult to your office
Let us take him to court for this.

Chorus   *Leave him alone women*
Eric Williams tell them
Is caiso men like he
Contribute to me
When dem caisonians sing

Is de tourists dey bring
And it is cash come in
For de treasury
and de party
and some for me
He goin to tie a noose
Around his own throat
Give him plenty rope
Is I go win
All yuh let the jackass sing

3

Eric, Chalkie is a damn scamp
It is time we out his lamp
Tings we don't want people know
He does tell dem in calypso
Although the man criticizin we
You still send him university
Let's dismiss him for some stupid breach
Or send him in Toco to teach

Chorus   *Leave him alone women*
Eric Williams tell dem
Is time you ladies know
More bout calypso
Without calypso lawwe
Who go jump and sway
What will steelbands play
The calypsonian makes me
Understand public opinion
Though he neigh and bray
Though his tongue does wag
Let him fly his flag
Eric is still de king
Phyllis Mitchell let de jackass sing[3]

    I think that the calypso captures the man, but my talk this morning is not on calypso. I am talking generally on Carnival, Eric Williams, and his vision for Carnival. Let me begin by saying that, in 1957, when the Carnival Bands Union demanded that their prizes be raised from $8,000 to $16,000, and the calypsonians decided to boycott the national Carnival competition, the newly formed government of Eric Williams had already instituted the Carnival Development Committee (CDC), concertedly, to develop the Carnival.[4] His Carnival Committee at the time promised to provide better prizes, et cetera.

Contrary to what many people believe, Williams did not dismiss the *Guardian* Committee. The *Guardian* Committee, as if by consent and attrition, dismissed themselves. Since then, until now, the CDC has run every Carnival celebration in Trinidad and Tobago, and right through all the Caribbean islands they have appointed Carnival development committees.[5] And they have all utilized the Trinidad and Tobago model, but they have not however instituted the full Eric Williams model.

In 1968 I was at a calypso audition for selecting individuals for the Calypso Theatre, then managed by the CDC. Note that Williams found the audition important enough to go and I was there. In an aside and private conversation with me, he told me, 'I have instituted the Carnival Development Committee to bring all the calypsonians into the fold. The word is development now, don't forget, development.'

I will never forget that. This is 1968. Dr Williams way back in 1956 had this profound vision. He was only one year in office at the time but already he had seen the need for development of the art form. Hence, he did not dismiss the *Guardian* Committee, and when George Goddard of the Steelband Association (George Goddard introduced me to the prime minister) asked him, 'Well, what about the *Guardian* Committee?' He told George that the *Guardian* Committee was to see about the operational aspects of the Carnival in terms of competition and prizes and the CDC was to see about development.

There was a time ten years ago when development was only seen as economic growth. In terms of Carnival, it meant chairs and prizes, et cetera, et cetera, in other words, the awarding of prizes and large sums of money, et cetera. Williams knew all of that but what then is development. What was Eric Williams's vision for development? As early as 1965, and I was there at [the Government] Training College in 1965, when Williams gave the address to students graduating in 1965 at Teachers' College [Government Training College], they played pan for him, and they sang calypsos. I sang. And he informed us of the need not only to take part in cultural events but also to make culture become part of educational practices. In other words, if any human development was to take place, Williams was saying that there could be no development without an appropriation of one's culture. When he instituted the CDC, and he stressed the word *development* at the 1968 audition, I was reminded of his consistency. You see people look at the words Carnival Development and they do not know what it means.

The World Commission on Culture and Development put it very nicely.[6] A fellow called Boutros Boutros-Ghali, the old Secretary General of the United Nations, said: 'Development divorced from its human or cultural contexts is growth without a soul.' In other words, the commission was saying two things. They were saying that first of all, development must be seen as a full, satisfying, valuable way of life. It is the flourishing of human existence in all its unified forms. And secondly, the commission was saying that a human being could not be developed if one was divorced from one's culture.

If this point of reference is generally acceptable, and Carnival and its concomitant behaviours link the West Indian to his culture, then in the Caribbean especially, where historically Carnival means so much to so many as a genre of art, of movement in song, and song in play, and transposes itself into functional art, then it must be welded into the elements that are basic to our development. May I remind you that for us in the Caribbean, Carnival is a concatenation of things — it is movement, it is colour, it is food, it is drink, it is fete, it is feast, it is ritual, it is celebration, it is what keeps BWIA flying, it is foreign exchange, it is a harbinger of blessings and woes. So, for us in the Caribbean, there can only be an arid education, no centre of development, no holistic schooling or training without directional focus on the annual Carnival Bands. A few years ago, I attended a conference — when I was Director of Culture — in Nicaragua, and they came to the conclusion, the cogent conclusion that Carnival must be seen as the rhythm of our development.

Yesterday there was talk of sustainable development. Today, in keeping with that Williams vision, sustainable development must embrace more than just the physical environment, and it must bring in maintenance and placement and capital assets, et cetera.

It means therefore, first of all, that if we are to develop Carnival in the Caribbean there must be a great deal of concentration placed on the education of our people with a view to alerting talent, developing skills, training administrators, practitioners, maintaining the human resource, documenting our past, ensuring the retention of our traditions, and recognizing the artistic creations and cultural expressions of our population. And secondly, it means that governments and state agencies that are entrusted with the development of Carnival must also develop cultural policies that are profoundly sensitive to and inspired by Carnival itself. And such policies must not be seen as a handout but as a correction of a market failure.

You will agree, I am sure, that to produce a Carnival Band, or to play a pan, to sing a calypso, or to manage a calypso site, be it a pan yard or a tent, calls for skills. You know, Kitchener [Aldwyn Roberts] was telling me that when he came back, one of the reasons he started to sing with the pan was because he saw the skill in the pan yard. When the guy hit that *palang, palang, palang*, everybody kept quiet.[7] Kitchener said that was what made him start singing on pan.

It is said by social scientists that in the field of management, human beings are the most difficult of the elements to manage. Well, if they had studied Carnival, they would have found out that panmen and calypsonians are among the hardest people to manage. Carlyle 'Jazzy' Pantin told me, the Carlyle 'Jazzy' Pantin who managed Kitchener's Revue [Kaiso tent] from 1965 to his death in 2004. When I asked him the reason for his success, he told me you have to be a friend, a referee, an adviser, a marriage counsellor and a father, a tactician and above all a moneylender who must forget who he owes. And these characteristics surprisingly, these characteristics developed in the Calypso tent by the manager, represent fundamentals of modern management.

Hugh Borde, the longest reigning captain of a steel band, had been a captain since 1948. He told me that he learned to steal his father's money — his father used to have a pharmacy — and his mother's too, to give to panmen, or else pan [the steel band] would have mashed up in the first year. He learned too to avoid steel band clashes with other steel bands he said, by not taking any sides whatsoever when disputes arose. Clearly the management requirements, empathy, and objectivity had developed naturally in Hugh Borde without the university lessons of the practising psychologist. And last, in 2003, there was a satirical calypso song on Mr Afong who was the chairman of the NCBA, the National Carnival Bands Association, and the guy sang a calypso called, 'Ahfong [I found] the thief'.

Besides skills of administration and management, producing the Carnival band calls for skills in painting, in welding, in wire bending, designing, decorating, sewing, and above all the use of metals and other materials for the construction of mas'. Today, the correct materials must be used to provide that masquerade with balance, and resilience, and movement, et cetera.

In the area of pan playing and tuning, everyone knows that it takes a special skill to play the pan, and more skill to tune it. And would you believe that Trinidad only has six pan tuners. When I talk about pan tuners, I am talking about tuning pan to a professional level.[8] In the discipline of the calypso, the art of composing, singing, playing a musical instrument, reading music and discerning different rhythms and tunes are skills that all calypsonians need to have.

A few years ago I met a guy in London. He came off the stage and he asked me, 'Chalkie, what you think about the calypso?' And I said, 'You need training.' He watched me in my face with pain, 'I need training.' He watched me with a startled look on his face. For calypso, you need training. He couldn't understand that calypsonians need to be trained in the use of metre and rhyme and sequence of melody and even in the proper use of the microphone. Over the years we have been trained by apprenticeship training. In the recording industry everyone knows that to compete in the international market, calypso CDs must be at a high standard in terms of sound and musical arrangement and musical chords and musicianship. One simply has to go to a recording studio today to see the very changes in recording. You can put on your voice in Miami, put on the synthesizer in Toronto, et cetera.

In the area of education, in keeping with Dr Williams's vision that a person cannot be termed as educated if he or she is not grounded in their culture, let me give you an example of what I mean. I went to a secondary school once in Couva, and I heard, Rudy Piggott, the history teacher teaching the history of the Amerindians, and what was he using? He was using Carnival, 'Tears of the Indies', George Bailey's [masquerade] band. I went once to listen to a teacher teaching a lesson in a primary school. She was talking about slavery and she was using [Sparrow's calypso], 'The Slave'. I went to the University of Lund in Sweden and the guy was teaching physics using the steel band — steel band is physics.

And today what happens? Today, we see, in the streets today [during the Carnival parade of bands], we see thousands of Romans and Vikings and Egyptians and marines and sailors and tribal warriors and Chinese philosophers and Apache Indians, to name a few. They are all roaming the streets in all their glory — giving us lessons in history and sociology and anthropology and math and music and science, and very little of this rich and informative data reaches the classroom. It has not reached the halls of our universities, far less the primary and secondary schools of the Caribbean. We cannot call ourselves developed and have no understanding of the psychical elements driving the Carnival on the streets. We cannot be developed and still not be moved by the masses of human beings drawn into cohesion through natural bonding.

And our governments and universities in the Caribbean, they know that Carnival [is] culture, they know the part that it plays in the life, et cetera. The mere fact that the University of the West Indies bestows honorary degrees on our carnival practitioners is an apology and proof that they recognize their own failure to regard culture as a necessary ingredient for development. Sparrow was just granted an honorary degree, but it came years after C.L.R. James compared Sparrow's calypso on Federation . . . as being the best paper on the Federation. If I had the time, I would sing you a verse . . .

> People want to know
> Why Jamaica run from de Federation
> If you want to know
> Why Jamaica run from de Federation
> Jamaica have a right to speak she mind
> That is my opinion
> And if you believe in democracy
> You agree with me

> If they know they didn't want Federation
> And they know they don't want to unite as one
> Tell de doctor you not in favor
> Don't behave like a blasted traitor
> Dis ain't no time to say
> You ain't federating no more.
> The Mighty Sparrow, "Federation"[9]

C.L.R. James said it was the best paper on Federation. I like the word paper because as I told a university professor, when I applied for a job and he told me that I did not produce, I said, 'Which university professor has produced more than I?' I said, 'I produced 300 papers!'

On the matter of training, I went to the University of Portland and I saw this guy putting up all these beautiful things at an exhibition of African masks in the museum in Portland, and I asked him:

'Where you learned that?'

And he said, 'Carnival.' And he said, 'But Chalkie you can't get a certificate for me?'

I said, 'A certificate for what?'

'A certificate to show I am a carnivalist or something,' he said. 'If I had a paper I'd a get so much money, eh. But I eh have no paper.'

In other words, thousands of our Carnival artistes make their living out of Carnival, but they have no paper or certificate to show that they are committed people, or they are educated people, so they roam our shores only recognized by other practitioners like themselves. That is one of the faults we have and Eric Williams's vision now becomes perceptible in manifold applications. The wide world recognized the wizardry of Boogsie Sharp, but our universities do not. The Carnival world, the world of Miss Universe, and the world of the Olympics, hired the skills of Peter Minshall. The English-derived education system does not. The Japanese ambassador in Trinidad praised band leader Jason Griffith who has been playing fancy sailor for over 50 years.... And I remember in 1984, J. O'Neill Lewis telling Penguin (Seadley Joseph) and me that we had turned out more people over all the years in Washington even though he was ambassador.

It was in keeping, therefore, with Williams's vision of the art form that I sang the calypso, 'Let the Jackass Sing.' And I am saying that most people only see Eric Williams calling me a jackass but they neglect to see in the song the role of the calypsonian, and on that role he had lectured to me many times. As prime minister, he visited the tents, and I was secretary of the Calypso Association and talking to him all the time, and he pointed out to me as the song showed, that calypsonians by their creative abilities not only increase the general revenues of the treasury, but the political party. He pointed out to the women who had complained about me that businessmen too are exploiting the calypso, mercilessly. They make calypso paint, calypso dish, and calypso sandwich. Above all, in 1965, with his vision for development, he had told the graduates [of Teachers' Training College] that as educated sons and daughters they should be involved in calypso. He told them that even though I was criticizing him, he still sent me to university. Thus I was a bona fide part of his vision for a developed populace, for Williams saw the need to develop the artistes by giving them the educational tools to reach their highest potential. And when I was at university and the university people turned down — we were part time people — our getting in full time, we went to Williams and Williams okayed it. And when, in 1968 I was charged by the Teaching Service Commission for receiving 'emoluments while in the employ of the Crown', it was Williams who came to my assistance with the famous words, 'I don't know why they humbugging the young man for.' Those words caused the Commission to drop the charges and reinstate me into the teaching profession from which I'd been temporarily shelved. So, I want to close by singing the last two verses of that calypso, the second and the fourth.

'Let the Jackass Sing'

> 2
> PNM women don't like me
> They tell Deafy that Chalkie
> Castigatin him daily
> An bad talking de Party
> Doc if you could say that Shorty was rude
> Well then we believe Chalkie rude

             Though there's some truth in the things he tell
             Doc we could charge him for libel

Chorus   Leave him alone women
             Eric Williams tell dem
             Is caiso men like he
             Help build dis Party
             Many men before he
             Took a pride you see in attackin me
             Melo and Christo bad talk me for so
             They dead out you know
             They a pounce on him
             Causing him such strife
             Crapaud smoke his pipe
             No don't stop him
             Ruby Felix let the jackass sing.

                         4
             You ladies Eric said
             Caiso brings us plenty bread
             Singers get wages from it
             Records bring others profit
             [Is] so Calypso means to Carnival day
             And from Carnival many get their pay
             People sell from pudding to water
             Alcohol sales make the firms richer

Chorus   *Leave him alone women*
             Eric Williams tell dem
             People learn of our country from records by he
             Business men take slangs from he
             Put dem on jersey and make big money
             Dey make calypso paint calypso dish
             And calypso sandwich
             His song call "Ah 'Fraid Karl"[10]
             Almost make Karl king
             So let Chalkie flap his wing
             Is fame I getting
             [Rita Guy] let the jackass sing.

Years after, I met Karl and he had a nice button on his shoulder marked: 'Karl ain't 'fraid.' God bless.

Notes

1. On Friday, March 18, 2005, Dr Liverpool presented a paper entitled 'Dr Eric Williams's Vision for the Development of Carnival', at the conference on Calypso and the Caribbean Literary Imagination, March 17–19, 2005. His presentation was part of a panel of three on Policy, Politics, and Promise in Calypso: The Eric Williams Era, that was chaired by Dr William Aho, Professor Emeritus, Department of Sociology, Rhode Island College. In his presentation, Dr Liverpool focused on Carnival development in at least two ways: the value of Carnival to personal and national development and the need to further develop Carnival arts through (formal and informal) education and through stronger government support. His presentation slipped in and out of the vernacular and included the singing of his calypso 'Let the Jackass Sing' and a few lines from The Mighty Sparrow's 'Federation.' This script was transcribed and edited for publication by Sandra Pouchet Paquet from an original video recording of Dr Liverpool's presentation, and is reproduced here in its present form with Dr Liverpool's permission.
2. The *Bomb* is a long-running political weekly in Trinidad and Tobago.
3. Chalkdust (Hollis Liverpool), 'Let the Jackass Sing', *Stay Up* LP Strakers GS 7789, 1974.
4. An article in the *Trinidad Guardian*, February 23, 1957, pp.1–2 suggests that the Government of Trinidad and Tobago organized the Carnival Development Committee in late 1956. Originally, the committee did not intend to implement its plans in time for the 1957 Carnival, but a crisis occurred that forced it into action. That crisis, as Dr Liverpool indicates, was the threatened boycott. See also, Gordon Rohlehr, *Calypso and Society in Pre-Independence Trinidad* (Trinidad: Gordon Rohlehr, 1990), 448–56.
5. In the period following a change of government in 1986, the CDC was renamed the National Carnival Commission (NCC).
6. The independent World Commission on Culture and Development (WCCD) was established jointly by UNESCO and the United Nations (1992–1995).
7. The *palang, palang, palang* refers to the knocking on the side of a pan by a steel band arranger, when he wants everyone in a pan yard to stop playing during a rehearsal.
8. There are actually many more than six, but Dr Liverpool is making the point that he feels only six are of the highest quality.
9. The Mighty Sparrow (Slinger Francisco), 'Federation', *Sparrow Come Back*, Matrix N804 1114/5, 1962.
10. Chalkdust (Hollis Liverpool), released a calypso called 'Ah 'Fraid Karl', on *Ah 'Fraid Karl / We is We* A/B 7 Strakers S-0052, 1972.

2

CALYPSO AS POLITICAL CON/TEXT: REFLECTIONS ON THE LEGEND OF ERIC WILLIAMS[1]

Louis Regis

David Rudder's 'Calypso Music' (1987)² describes the Calypso as 'a living vibration rooted deep within my Caribbean belly'. This 'Caribbean belly', preserving the patterns of behaviour of the African folk, contains memories of ancestral practices among which is the role of the poet in the community and society. Poetic traditions that survived the practices of New World plantation society have been perpetuated in the calypso that articulates personal and group experiences, attitudes and emotions. Eric Williams, the nation's Father and Founder, has been the subject of constant calypso celebration and censure, commentary and interrogation from his first election success in September 1956 to his death in March 1981. No other individual occupying the prime ministerial chair has been examined and evaluated as much and in as many ways, and this scrutiny has followed him in death where he is generally remembered favourably as the standard against which his successors, to their disadvantage, are compared.

Three major interconnected facts can be adduced in support of this. Firstly, Williams served the nation in the highest capacity for an unbroken 25 years during which time the country experienced constitutional independence as well as rigorous challenges, to what Rudder calls in 'Hoosay' (1991)[3] the 'lovely lie' of island paradise. Secondly, during his 25 years as the highest elected official, Williams dominated national public life and was often the focus of the national collective gaze. Thirdly, although mulatto, he was regarded by Afro-Trinidadians as being African. Afro-Trinidadian perceptions of Williams, reflected and refracted in and through the calypso, derive from ancestral African notions of the hero/villain, notions carried subliminally in the memory of the group.

This paper examines dualistic calypso constructions of the Williams legend. Calypsonians celebrated Williams as hero, but for the most part were never so blinded by his aura as to lose their own rooted sense of reality. Generally, Williams is perceived in song as a man, a very special man but a man nevertheless. However, even while they evaluated him as a man and subjected his name to an irreverent — sometimes reductive — *picong*,[4] their rites of passage into shared communal experience, they seemed wary of the man who was known to have exclaimed publicly: 'Don't get me damned blasted vex!' Calypsonians have represented Williams variously as *obeahman*, as *ananse*, as *badjohn*, or *ananse*-turned-*badjohn*, all concepts deriving from the folk/urban experience that also gave birth to the calypso.[5] These representations allowed calypsonians to access Williams imaginatively and to a large extent it was the only way they could make contact with him. Employing the lenses provided by folklore and folk practice, calypsonians negotiated several layers of the Williams mystique to arrive at notions or explanations that are understandable both to calypsonians and their public from whom these populist notions ultimately derive.

The Hero Talks to the Crowd

Williams's first signifying acts in the movement towards claiming political power in Trinidad and Tobago were his public addresses at what was called the University of Woodford Square, Port of Spain, and at the neighbouring Public Library. His intellectual duel with Dom Basil Mathews, the coal-black Trinidadian scholar who represented the Roman Catholic Church, and by extension the socio-politico-economic order represented by that church, generated much attention in the local community. Thanks to this debate, Williams established himself as the champion of those Trinidadians — and especially those Afro-Trinidadians — who resented the marginalized condition imposed on them by the forces personified by the French Creole Roman Catholic elites.

One suspects, however, that while the content of the formal academic discourse of the Williams–Mathews debates may have been beyond the understanding of the man and woman in the street, what would have registered with them was Williams's mastery of erudition and language. The latter achievement would have made a profound impression on a traditional African-based community where 'the eloquent speaker is capable of garnering a great deal of power, respect and in many cases admiration through his artful speaking'.[6] Abrahams highlights the importance of the man-of-words in traditional performances and differentiates between the 'good talkers' and 'good arguers'.[7] The former are characterized by 'the use of long speeches suffused with overly decorative elevated diction and elaborate grammar and syntax',[8] while the latter are characterized by 'strongly colloquial diction and the rapid thrust of invective'.[9] Abrahams notes further that although one man could be both, his skills were rarely called for on the same occasion:

> The man-of-words not only provides the tone and subject for traditional performances, but also serves as principal organizer of the activity ... he has an equivalent in the man-of-action, the physically adept one who focuses the proceedings by his leadership and performance abilities.[10]

Eric Williams was the hero for whom Afro-Trinidadians had long been waiting. He was at one and the same time the 'good talker', 'good arguer' and man-of-action.

Considering Williams as a personification of continuity in West African traditions of power, expressive and instrumental, prompts this examination of the correspondence between politics and calypso. Politicians and calypsonians depend upon mastery of the word. They pay attention to one another in performance, they rely upon one another for inspiration, and they quote one another appropriately and conveniently. The logical calypso extension of this relationship is The Mighty Chalkdust's 'Eric Loves Me' (1979)[11] which avers that Williams's otherwise inexplicable actions were designed merely to give Chalkdust topics for calypso. This peculiarly 'calypsoesque' perception of the politician–calypsonian relationship is confirmed in Manchild's 'Politicians Love Calypsonians' (1999).[12]

Selwyn Cudjoe appreciated Williams's verbal magic as a function of a calypso-type appeal to a calypso-appreciative audience. He understood that Williams communicated with the general audience which included semi-literates and illiterates by presenting them with the necessary information seasoned with humour, folkloric wisdom, aspects of popular culture and 'robber talk' — all the verbal weapons in the calypsonian's arsenal. Cudjoe concluded:

> Thus to attend an Eric Williams public meeting was like going to a calypso show at the Queen's Park Savannah or a Port of Spain calypso tent. It always possessed a dramatic air of the unexpected, an

element of the festive, and a shared sense of participation in a common experience.[13]

Cudjoe observes that instead of 'Kaiso' or 'Dat is Kaiso', the audience chorused, 'Dat is man! He could *really* talk.'[14] Implied in this is the reality that the audiences who crowded the calypso tent to hear calypsonians sing were the voters who congregated to hear Williams talk. Further, the major attraction of both experiences was the practice of the word functioning simultaneously as message and as entertainment.

Cypher's prize-winning 'Last Elections' (1967)[15] translates Cudjoe's thoughts into the economical verse of calypso. After ridiculing all of Williams's electoral opponents, the narrator of 'Last Elections' ends triumphantly:

> Up came a short little fellow
>
> And he turn the whole program yellow
>
> He said to support my party
>
> And don't vote for no rum and roti
>
> In Princes Town I support Maharaj
>
> He give me a drink, people say I bad
>
> That little man was the public choice
>
> And they for his tone of voice
>
> He say
>
> "The other party they call the *macafouchette*[16]
>
> Only running like loved him that can't find a hole
>
> [This line is hopelessly garbled]
>
> On the 7th of November the leader and
>
> his followers shall go to hell"

Lloyd Best offers another shorthand version of the Williams mystique as represented by his utterances and actions: 'The nation at heart still loves and reveres him, because he is still the best guntalker, *picong*-slinger, opposition crusher of all.'[17] What commentators and calypsonians agree upon is that Williams was the master of the word, the word as agency of power, the word as key to the hearts and minds of Trinidadians and Tobagonians. It was this mastery as much as his political achievements and actions that endeared him to the calypsonians.

The Twin Portraits of Williams

Sparrow's 'William the Conqueror' (1958)[18] and 'No Doctor No' (1957)[19] establish the dualism of calypso representations of Williams by delineating the parameters for calypso address to and engagement with Williams. 'William the Conqueror' celebrated Williams's 1956 success in this way:

1

I am sure you've heard the story
About Big Brains and Big Belly
Well, Sparrow ain't fraid to talk
Who don't like it take a walk
Fight finish, no bruise no cuts
But a man fall down on he guts

Chorus
Praise little Eric
Rejoice and be glad
For we have a champion leader here in Trinidad
PNM
It have nothing like them
For we have a champion leader
William the conqueror

2

I am no politician
But I could understand
If wasn't for Brother Willie
And his ability
Trinidad wouldn't go nor come
We used to vote for food and rum
But nowadays we eating all the Indians and them
And in the ending, we voting for PNM

> 3
> Many lives were in danger
> They murdered a stranger
> Then they went and threaten the doctor
> Concerning his daughter
> It's there I prove he was the man for us
> Because he didn't make any fuss
> He addressed the crowd with a smile
> And when he finished Big Belly was with child

William the Conqueror, the Norman adventurer who captured England in 1066, is transformed in calypso into Eric Williams, the native intellectual who had first scaled the walls of English academia and then conquered the neocolonial political 'kingdom' of Trinidad and Tobago. At the risk of personal injury and threats to his beloved daughter, this folk hero rescued Trinidad and Tobago from the old-style politics and electioneering represented by Albert Gomes and his associates. Williams's victory over the old-style politics promised a bright future for Trinidadians. The last image of Big Belly being impregnated by Big Brains is a calypso euphemism for a sexual yoking which constructs Williams as potent masculinizing actor and feminizes Albert Gomes as the dominated partner.[20]

But while 'William the Conqueror' sets the calypso standard for panegyric, its partner song 'No Doctor No' establishes the bar for protest. In this second song Sparrow articulates the discontent of the masses, who felt the burden of price increases imposed after the 1957 budget:

> Listen, listen carefully
> I am a man who does never be sorry
> But Ah went and Ah vote some for council men
> They have me now in a pen
> After promising to give so much tender care
> They forget me as they walk out of Woodford Square
>
> Chorus   Because they raise up on the taxi fare
> No Doctor No
> And they have the blasted milk so dear
> No Doctor No

> But Ah want you to remember
> We support you in September
> You better come good
> Because I have a big piece of mango wood

Although the second stanza begins by suggesting a softening of this position, this seeming softening is countered immediately however, by protest against the lifestyle changes imposed by the PNM's drive to support local industry. The charge of neglect, which became popular in the 1970s, was levelled against Williams as early as 1957. To the untutored man-in-the-street, the business of government remains a mystery if he interests himself only in his immediate short-term interest and is indifferent to the grand strategies of long-term policy planning, its mystifying rationales and forbidding language. Sparrow wonders at the opacity of transactions whose ultimate result is distress for the man-in-the-street. He further chastises the educated elite for what he perceives as the unforgivable sin of abandoning the collective good. To his mind, education and political position are merely the vehicles by which the man-in-street is empowered and Williams's failure to deliver on promises reeks of irresponsibility.

The final stanza establishes a gulf between the supporting calypsonian and the political directorate and also provides an early instance of that self-abasement adopted by some calypsonians when challenging or confronted with Williams the colossus:

> Ah only hope they understand
> I am just a calypsonian
> What I say may be very small
> But I know poor people ain't please at all

At the end of the final chorus however, the mango wood threat is downgraded as Sparrow reverts to the pose of a sullen grumbling citizen who promises to hold on to his 'mango wood'. Despite this robust affirmation, the mango wood threat remained just that: the rhetorical aggression of the powerless. Williams who was sufficiently 'Trini-to-the-bone' to appreciate Sparrow's mango wood *gran' charge*[21] for what it was, may have been more concerned about alienating the one calypsonian who had the ability to rally Trinidad's disaffected, discontented and disillusioned. Although

Sparrow declared himself 'just a calypsonian,' Williams may have perceived him as the second political force to have emerged in 1956, the year when both men independently declared a majestic presence on the relevant public stages.[22] As a consequence Sparrow was called in for what he referred to laconically as 'consultations'.[23] Sparrow did not elaborate upon this cryptic phrase but I imagine that the Calypso King of the World would have heeded only the summons of Williams himself. I cannot imagine the *sagaboy/badjohn* Sparrow responding to a summons from any of Williams's ministers or associates whose names he never mentions in his songs. The exceptions to this are Patrick Solomon ('Solomon Out' in 1964 and 'Get to Hell Out' in 1965),[24] and John O'Halloran whose fondness for the illegal sport of cock fighting is satirized in 'Cock Fight' (1969).[25] The consultations of 1957 may have been responsible for the PNM-friendly propagandizing in Sparrow's 'PAYE' (1958),[26] 'You Can't Get Away From The Tax' (1959),[27] 'Leave the Dam Doctor' (1960)[28], 'Present Government' (1961),[29] 'Balisier' ['Wear Your Balisier'] (1961)[30] and 'Federation' (1961).[31] Although these songs promote a more favourable image of Williams, they nevertheless treat Williams as man.

Many other singers of the Sparrow and the Independence generations address or engage Williams as man, shorn of the mystique credited to him by his adoring constituents. It is significant that even faithful calypsonian supporters of Williams perceive him as human. Striker's 'Don't Blame the PNM' (1958)[32] satirizes those supporters who rush to Williams for solution to their every situation even their most intimate problems:

> Annabella stocking want patching
> She want the doctor help she with that
> Johnson trousers falling
> He want the doctor help he with that
> Some want a Zephyr motorcar
> Others want a piece of land
> Dorothy loss she man
> She want to complain to Dr Williams

While this testifies to a public perception that Williams was the source of power, it implies that Williams is merely a mortal man and should be spared the strain of every man's burden. Williams himself cited this fragment in his career autobiography *Inward Hunger* when he recounted how he drafted for the PNM a code of responsibilities designed to relieve 'the strain on the Political Leader'.[33]

Bomber's 'Political Wonder' (1970)[34] affords another example of the calypsonian supporter testifying to Williams as a man. Bomber situates Williams among the pantheon of international twentieth-century giants, but his major concern in 'Political Wonder' is the quality of the legacy Williams would leave. Bomber thus engages Williams's mortality, a major feature of the human condition, but he carefully ignores Williams's fallibility which is another major feature of the human condition.

The generation of calypsonians who perceived themselves as being in opposition to Williams inclined to the sternness of 'No Doctor No' and eschewed the celebration of 'William the Conqueror'. Valentino's 'No Revolution' (1971)[35] submits a respectful memorandum refuting Williams's theory of revolution and explaining what he saw as the true purpose of the 1970 demonstrations. He acknowledges Williams as a source of power — 'Them talking bout power, doctor / But is you who have power' — and concedes Williams's restraint — 'Yuh give them a inch they take a whole yard' — but this concession does not deter him from threatening Williams with the judgement of history:

> A citizen should withstand the wrong things in his country
> Regardless of what happen, that is my ideology
> All we meeting with is oppression and a set of strain
> Trials and tribulations, sorrows and pain
> When we try to shake up the government
> The result was police ill treatment
> But justice must be done otherwise History
> Is going to punish you worse than you punish we

Invested with the mantle of People's Calypsonian and encouraged by the restless post-1956 Black Power generation, Valentino was emboldened to a more stinging reproach. His 'Barking Dogs' (1973)[36] addresses Williams as a man with seeing and hearing impairments that impede communication with the society of which he was the leader. Williams himself had carefully cultivated the public mystique by persisting with his trademark dark glasses and hearing aid.[37] In 'The Spoiler's Return', Derek Walcott has the Spoiler persona confess to what may well have been Walcott's own fascination with Williams:

> and those with hearing aids turn off the truth
> and their dark glasses let you criticize
> your own presumptuous image in their eyes[38]

Valentino, undazzled by the Williams mystique and the Walcott reflection, addresses Williams sternly in 'Barking Dogs', a song which answers the *badjohn* rhetoric, 'When I talk/ No dam dog bark' of 'Get to Hell Out.' Alluding to the chorus of dissent that had resulted in the unrest of the early 1970s, Valentino declares:

> Now this word is me
> And I am this word
> So let my voice be heard
> Fix your hearing aid and hear what I say
> Wipe your glasses and see things my way
> The song that you hear is an angry one
> And I'm sure if you see things clear
> you'll see that all happiness is gone
> But the dogs, the dogs are barking too long
> It is a sign that something is wrong

Maestro's 'To Sir with Love' (1974)[39] accuses Williams of betraying the national constituency of African voters with whom he had established a teacher–student relationship in the University of Woodford Square where he had founded programmes on political education:

> Mister, mister, is me yuh Black brother
> Pressure, pressure, indeed inward hunger
> The people who oppose you endlessly
> They get plenty but you ent care 'bout we
> With the twenty eight percent I vote
> Now yuh turn 'round and stroke a yoke on mih throat

Chorus
> Ninety percent of all who buying is of African origin
> But they ent hiring blackhen chicken
> although is my money they banking
> The only time they want the knottyhead fella
> Is when I come over they counter to spend my dollar
> No Bossman, I ent talking race
> Ah only tracing what taking place in this place

'Dread Man' (1977)[40] is starker in its condemnation of the effects of Williams's stewardship on said poor black community:

> Dreaming of a dread man
> Dread man on an island
> Where bigger brother squander
> While smaller brother suffer
> Dread man mash the small man down
> They used to love the ground he walk on
> They voting but now they groaning

Williams's actions and policies in the oil-boom period and especially the events of Bloody Tuesday 1975 are highlighted:[41]

> Plenty money making
> Plenty belly aching
> Them buy self-loading rifle
> To hassle who give trouble
> Workman say
> They want more pay
> They send away for the CIA

In Maestro's mind Williams has graduated from being the Black leader/teacher who abandoned his brother constituents/students to being 'Big Brother', George Orwell's futuristic controller of the minds of the people in *1984*.

In reproaching Williams for his 'gifts' of oil money to Caribbean governments, and demanding the share due him by virtue of citizenship, Black Stalin's 'Piece of the Action' (1976) invokes the equality enshrined in the incurable democracy taken for granted by the calypsonian in performance and adopted unconsciously by many citizens:[42]

> Oil drilling, money making
> Mr. Divider here is a warning
> Mih blood in this country
> Mih sweat in this country
> So when yuh sharing yuh oil bread
> Ah say remember me
> This ent no Black power talk
> This ent no talk 'bout revolution
> Ah say Mr. Divider listen to me
> This is man talking to man

We can profitably examine the difference between 'Piece of the Action' and 'No Doctor No'. Sparrow's threat to beat Williams into compliance was premised on a personal relationship to Williams, a relationship based on a 1955 association in Gayap.[43] Stalin, however, would have suspected that to Williams he was merely another of the anonymous Black Power boys or the revolutionaries of the early 1970s. By representing himself as a citizen entitled to voice his dissent and have it heard, he attempts to distance himself from those agents who had disturbed the peace of Williams's kingdom. Despite this, he still delivers the rhetorical threat 'Stalin old and begging/ Is one thing he ain't seeing/ Is six feet first I going.' Williams, who had outlived the Sparrow *gran' charge* of 1957, the Black Power unrest, the guerrilla movement of the early 1970s, and the challenge to his leadership of the party in 1973 ignored this rhetoric.

Relator, listening to a report from one Dr Aziz that indicated that panmen were gradually growing deaf, and noting that Williams had remained deaf to all appeals, satirized the panmen, and the prime minister in the skillfully constructed 'Deaf Panman' (1974):

> Ring ting ting ting, ping pong, ping pong
> Steelbands going to wail in town
> They sounding sweet, they sounding sweet
> Masquerade on Frederick Street
> Some playing in C, some lost the key
> Some are very near to WC
> But they going to jam
> And the name of the mas' is Dr Williams
> Ah hope you understand the masquerade
> Pan men in dark shade wearing hearing aid. [44]

Relator follows up this abrasive satire with the plainspeak of 'Take a Rest' (1980),[45] which concedes the futility of complaint, censure and satire — 'It is useless that we continue to blame/ A horse that is tired and almost lame.' Because the traditional calypso weapons have been rendered ineffectual by Williams's silence and disregard, Relator offers direct advice to the nation:

> I would like to suggest a good rest for the doc
> Before the poor man fall down on the work.

This statement, the equivalent of Delamo's grim vision of 'Apocalypse' (1979)[46] that which likened the corruption-laden racing complex to the Laperouse Cemetery, was remembered in April of 1981 when Williams died in office.

When we compare the calypsoes of 1957–1970 and those of 1970–1981, we observe that the praise singers of the earlier period concede Williams's mortality but acknowledge his specialness; the disapproving voices of the later period, however, consistently withhold that celebration of specialness. But celebration and censure have operated as alternating voices in the calypso on Williams; while one is dominant the other is quieter. In the 1957–

1970 period when celebration was the dominant mode, some calypsonians challenged Williams, while some praised him in the years 1971–1981 when censure was the dominant mode. What is common to both periods and both sets of voices is the perception that Williams, either as political personality or as representative of institutionalized power was not a man not to be trifled with. The familiar addresses Deafy, Eric and so on, as well as the calypso *picong* of Prince's 'Come as You Are Party' (1974);[47] Kitchener's 'Twenty to One' (1974);[48] Squibby's 'Streaker' (1975);[49] Scrunter's 'Crapaud Revolution' (1981),[50] and so on do not disguise the fact that calypsonians trod warily around Williams. The heavy-handed PNM riposte to Tiger's irreverent 'The Doc's Secret Wedding' (1959), which criticized Williams for his one-day marriage, signalled the end of the performing career of an icon of modern Calypso.[51] After 1959 those who protested generally did so with a sense of deference or adopted the mask of satire.

Despite its heterogeneity, however, the corpus of songs on Williams testifies to a fundamental respect for him in his public capacity, which is the dimension in which he has been apprehended. The open disrespect of the calypsos for his successors may be a function of the degradation of society as much as it is a perception that Williams and Williams alone was worthy of respect.

'Let the Jackass Sing'

Chalkdust falls between the two extremes of perception of Williams defined by 'William the Conqueror' and 'No Doctor No'. His Calypso on Williams is marked by an ambivalence which develops out of his own internal conflict where Williams is concerned. Chalkdust, the tireless Williams-watcher, first came to public attention when his 'Brain Drain' (1968)[52] critiqued Williams's own use of the term against those professionals who were fleeing the country in the wake of the first devaluation in the independence period. The fall-out from that song was that the Teaching Service Commission and the Ministry of Education and Culture sought to restrain Chalkdust, then a primary school teacher.[53] Off the record Chalkdust has claimed that only Williams's personal intervention rescued him from the clutches of officialdom. This admission, one of several contradictory Chalkdust statements about the issue, is all the more remarkable because one would have thought that the institutions were acting to save Williams possible embarrassment at the hands of a junior functionary.

After Williams's censorship of Shorty's 'The Art of Making Love'[54] at the 1973 national Calypso Crown competition, members of the Trinidad and Tobago League of Women's Voters wrote to Williams requesting that Chalkdust be disciplined for his performance of the irreverent 'Somebody Mad.'[55] Chalkdust, who had heard from an informant within the Williams household that Williams had privately dismissed him as a jackass, then created a scenario which harmonized the PNM women's public complaint and Williams's private dismissal in 'Let the Jackass Sing' in 1974:

>
> PNM women against me
> They report me to Deafy
> Last year after Dimanche Gras
> "Deafy, Chalkie gone too far
> How come this young man tell Trinidad
> That somebody in Whitehall mad
> It's an insult to your office
> Let us take him to court for this

Chorus
> *Leave him alone, women*
> Eric Williams tell them
> It's kaiso men like he contribute to me
> When them kaisonians sing
> They tourists they bring and is cash coming
> For the treasury and the party and some for me
> He going to tie a noose around his own throat
> Give him plenty rope
> Is I who go win
> Allyuh, let the jackass sing[56]

'Let the Jackass Sing' is among many other things a traditional calypsonian endorsement of the economic viability of the Carnival, of the supreme importance of the Calypso to the Carnival, and of its value in commercial advertising and in political propagandizing. Chalkdust's self-promotion in this regard, however, may not be as significant as projected in the calypso.[57] There is no mistaking, however, vital features of Chalkdust's thinking in respect to Williams.

Several important things emerge from other stanzas. First, Chalkdust seems to think that his enrolment at the St. Augustine campus of the University of the West Indies (UWI) is a personal favour granted by Williams. The generation of 1956 gratefully accepted the benefits of secondary and tertiary education that only became possible under Williams. The corollary of this is that some of the beneficiaries of this privilege — and their parents, in my case — felt that UWI students would be ingrates if they were to criticize the person who had made possible their advancement in society. Chalkdust would have been aware that he would have been so accused and the calypso suggests that he may have felt so. He may have felt especially favoured given the state response to his 'Brain Drain'.

Secondly, Chalkdust believes that the reclusive Williams appreciates that calypsonians are the voice of the people — 'The calypsonian makes me understand public opinion' — but his employ of the derogatory 'Deafy' indicates that he thinks that Williams is deaf to the appeals transmitted through calypso. The employment of reductive *picong* signalled by 'Deafy' does not disguise the fact that Chalkdust is aware that Williams controlled institutionalized power of office. According to the calypso, too, the PNM women request that Williams invoke this power to dismiss the junior teacher 'for some stupid breach', or banish him to remote Toco, or just as easily 'out his lamp'. But the Williams persona arrogates the option of spontaneous, terrifying action — 'The day Ah pounce on him for singing such tripe /Crapaud smoke his pipe.' This persona has too much political and business acumen to be provoked to public anger by the lese-majesty of Chalkdust or any other calypsonian. He has faith in his own staying power and the record of having outlasted 'Many men before he', among whom he identifies Melody and Cristo — 'They dead out you know.' He is perfectly convinced that singing protest is suicidal — 'He going to tie a noose around his own throat' — because the colossus is guaranteed ultimate victory — 'Is I who go win.' Given all of this, Williams can dismiss Chalkdust's songs with the contemptuous, 'Let the jackass sing'.

Chalkdust's self-designation as jackass, a pre-emptive self-conscious self-abasement in face of the colossus, is an interesting phenomenon.[58] Sparrow had defined himself as 'just a calypsonian' reducing himself to subaltern in the face of Williams's 'knowledgism'.[59] Valentino, Maestro, Stalin and Relator do not consider donning the mask of the subaltern. Chalkdust, however, seems actuated by the conflict within himself where Williams is concerned. As said before, he may have been impressed and humbled by the gift of free tertiary education which Williams had granted him — and thousands of other citizens. He has claimed that he and Williams had met and talked as equals, but he also claims off the record that Williams refused to publicly acknowledge any link between them or to publicly acknowledge his worth as calypsonian. Chalkdust's relentless targeting of Williams can be explained in part by a need for public acknowledgement and recognition even if this were to take the form of an angry contemptuous outburst.

'Clear Your Name' (1974),[60] another clear response to the Williams comment on 'Somebody Mad', is a clear instance of attempted provocation. In requesting that Williams declare himself to the nation and to posterity, Chalkdust shifts the burden of jackass from himself onto Williams:

> In the near future our young children will study you in class
> They would want to know if you were a giant or simply a jackass

To this and to several intrusive questions posed about his public stewardship and private life posed in the calypso, Williams characteristically made no public answer. I do not know if this refusal by Williams to be provoked may have inspired or contributed to 'Eric Williams Loves Me' ['Eric Loves Me'] (1979),[61] which is Chalkdust's confession that Williams remained to him an absolute mystery. Listening to Chalkdust's calypso odyssey and reading his prose outside of calypso, I have concluded that Chalkdust is fascinated with Williams. I suspect that he perceived him as a giant, a giant who in decline could be helped by a Lilliputian calypsonian. And yet this attraction on the part of Chalkdust was compounded with the need to maintain safe distance from the man who controlled the power that could so easily 'out his lamp'.

The jackass metaphor survived the Williams–Chalkdust interface. In 1998 Luta's 'Pack Yuh Bags' reminds then prime minister Panday, who had put himself on a war course against dissenting calypsonians, that

> The culture of the people is what you must understand
> You have to learn to handle *mamaguy* and *mauvais langé*[62]
> Take a tip from Eric Williams and let the jackass bray
> But listen attentively to what the jackass say[63]

Luta advises Panday that his perceptions and definition of the calypsonian are irrelevant; what matters is that he listens to the calypsonian as attentively as Williams did. This favourable post-facto imaging of Williams against the witness of the many contemporary calypsos, which reproached him for inattention to his supporters and to the national good as a whole, is evidence of the hold he still exerts on the minds of calypsonians.

Badjohn Willie

The image of Williams as leader in the mode of steel band captains of the 1950s and 1960s is established in Blakie's 'Doctah Ent Dey' ['De Doctor Eh Dey'] (1965).[64] In this song Blakie creates the scenario of a concerned citizen who had earlier discussed the problem of resurgent youth violence with Williams. Prominent among the warring youths, were those steelbandsmen who had formed Williams's unofficial janissaries,[65] and who had been rewarded in the Special Works programmes. Blakie, who was an associate of San Juan All Stars, and a major player in this steel band unrest, laments in song that Williams was not present to implement the schemes they had concocted together, according to the fiction of the calypso, and to this end he reproaches the prime minister:

> Doctor, Ah find yuh getting on funny
> Ah talking mih mind, believe the Lord Blakie
> Ah believe is 'fraid you 'fraid
> Of San Juan All Stars and Renegades

> But remember you is the leader
> All you got to do is to pass an order

The irreverent Blakie looks for his prime minister in unexpected places like the madhouse and the prison, echoing a popular *oletalk*[66] that Williams was mad or corrupt.[67] Faulting Williams with failure to arrest a deteriorating situation has been a common calypsonian reproach against him. Penguin's eulogy 'Betty Goaty' (1982)[68] goes as far as to have him gloating over those corrupt subordinates whom he was powerless to control and who would be exposed to their just deserts when he is not there to protect them.

While Blakie was faulting Williams with failure to live up to the authoritarian image of steel band leader in the pioneering age of the 1940s and 1950s, Sparrow's classic 'Get to Hell Out' (1965)[69] which purports to be Williams's defiance of those who challenged his handling of the Solomon Affair, reinforces the notion of Williams as politician appropriating the language and posture of *badjohn*:

> I am going to bring back Solomon
> Who doh like it complain to the Commission
> None of them going to tell me how to run my country
> I defy any one of you to dictate to me
> I am no dictator
> But when I pass an order
> Mr. Speaker, this matter must go no further
> I have nothing more to say
> And it must be done my way
> Come on, come on, meeting done for the day
>
> Chorus   This land is mine
>   I am the boss
>   What I say goes
>   And who vex lorse
>
>   2
>   Who the hell is you to jump and quarrel
>   PNM is mine lock stock and barrel

>
> Who give you the privilege to object
> Pay yuh taxes, shut up and have respect
> I am a tower of strength yes
> I'm powerful but modest
> Unless
> I'm forced to be blunt and ruthless
> So shut up and don't squawk
> This ent no skylark
> When I talk no damn dog bark

Chorus
> My word is law
> So watch yuh case
> If yuh slip yuh slide
> This is my place

> 3
> I am going to do what I feel to do
> And I couldn't care less who get vex or who blue
> And if you want to test how ah strong in a election
> Let we bet some money, Ah giving odds ten to one
> I control all the money
> That pass through this country
> And they envy me for my African safari
> I am politically strong
> I am the weight of town
> Doh argue with me
> You can't beat me in John John

Chorus
> Who's not with me is my enemy
> And dust will be their destiny
> And if I say that Solomon will be minister of External Affairs
> And if you doh like it
> Get to hell outa here

It proved impossible for Williams to live down this *badjohn* image that had been inscribed during his heyday. Chalkdust's 'Two Sides of a Shilling' (1971)[70] has the Williams persona threatening a defecting Robinson with the words, 'Yuh waiting on election but

Ah go pound yuh behind like a nail.' In a calypso drama preview of the 1976 election, Chalkdust has Williams proclaiming himself a master of electoral warfare and of street rhetoric:[71]

> I accustom fighting wars
> That is why they call me "Jaws"
> I eating from kingfish to salmon
> In this general election

The Williams of Crusoe's 'I Eric Eustace Williams' (1982)[72] boasts of his invincibility in national elections and of his uncontested pre-eminence within his party:

> Opposition know they never stood a chance
> Five elections I whip them on the conscience
> In my Party I am absolutely boss
> Who defied me I simply told them get lost
> With brains, intellect and charisma
> My visions were always superior
> Anyone who attempted to move me from the head
> I just raise my hand and they politically dead

Chalkdust's 'Bad John Willie' (1980)[73] ascribes to Williams a *badjohn* attitude, which informs all of his political actions either domestic or regional:

> A *badjohn* named Saga went to fete
> He got drunk and stabbed a man to death
> The police was sent
> To get a statement
> So this big *badjohn*
> Start to say what went on
> Same time Mr. Guerra the lawyer was listening
> And very abrupt he jump in and stop
> this *badjohn* man from talking

Chorus   Guerra say, Learn to shut yuh mouth
            Shut yuh mouth
            You must always stay calm like Eric William
            Man yuh doh see Eric doesn't talk to Manley
            Burnham he cut off completely
            He blank his permanent secretary
            So now we telephones ent working
            Is Selby Wilson we blaming
            And the real culprit sit down quiet and saying nothing
            Shut yuh mouth, shut yuh mouth
            You could kill and get way free
            Once yuh live like badjohn Willie

The events surrounding Williams's resignation and return (September to December 1973) excited the suspicion among some calypsonians that he was playing high stakes political poker. Composer's 'Different Strokes' (1974), for example, presents Williams as a combination of *ananse* and *badjohn*.[74]

> They playing with me
> Yuh think it easy
> Like a *mapepire*[75]
> Ah come back indefinitely
> Ah pretend to resign they had to beg and coax
> But now Ah ready to give them rope
> Is different strokes for different folks

When asked his reasons for employing 'such a creole tact', the 'Williams' of Superior's 'Why I Left, Why I Returned' (1974), excuses himself on the grounds of being human and politically pragmatic:[76]

> I have many problems within my party
> Don't talk about problems in the whole country
> I have to settle this bacchanal
> Party groups don't want Kamal
> And as you know, the country 'fraid Karl

The issue of Williams's motivations has divided political analysts. Composer and Superior, however, operating out of a cynical street context, are convinced that Williams was playing a cynical game with the Creole cunning of an *ananse* and the viciousness of a *badjohn*. They were projecting onto Williams the motivations typical of the folk characters with which they were familiar.

Stalin's 'Breakdown Party' (1980) reverses the image of Williams as *badjohn*. In 1979, Stalin's 'Caribbean Unity'[77] had advanced a controversial thesis for Caribbean unity declaring that Rastafarianism was the only cohesive to unite the millions divided by insularity. Williams refuted this thesis in a long address at the twenty-first annual PNM convention. Stalin replied with 'Breakdown Party' which blames Williams for the breakdown in services and national purpose — 'Mr. Divider start the habit/ Brother, Trinidadians copy it/ Now he trying he utmost best to stop it.' Having opened Pandora's box of evils, Mr Divider is now powerless to reverse his actions. Stalin then offered his streetwise solution to the national debacle:

> But if this was my party
> Ah woulda stop the dam thing already
> When Ah say "Stop!"
> Stop the jam
> Else Ah break a DJ hand

Even if we discount the practicability of this in a society whose 'pronounced materialism and disastrous individualism' were recognized by Williams himself,[78] the point is that Williams seems no longer able to even summon up the rhetoric of violence to stabilize a society which he kept somewhat in check by his mere presence and his ability to invoke the appropriate rhetoric.

Williams the *Obeahman*

It is impossible to consider West Indian society without considering the presence and influence of the supernatural. Vestiges of the magico-religious power of the West African king/ leader/hero are still present in Caribbean society. The fortuitous appearance of Williams in 1955 was seen by many of his followers as nothing less than providential. Ivar Oxaal writes that, 'For many lower class Negroes particularly Creole women, Dr. Williams was nothing less than a messiah come to lead the black children into the Promised Land.'[79] According to Oxaal, placards carried at PNM public meetings boasted the messages, 'The Master couldn't come so he sent Williams' and 'Moses II'.[80] This perception has been immortalized in at least two calypsos that celebrated independence. In his offering at the inaugural Calypso King competition of 1962, Dougla alluded to this when he sang 'Independence' (1962):[81]

> Dr Williams come like Moses in biblical history
> And he led us like the children of Israel to independency

Twenty five years later Shadow echoed that sentiment in his 'From Then to Now' (1987) when he affirmed that Williams:

> Led us like Moses
> Led the children to the Promised Land
> He built the stages
> Then left us to perform[82]

After Williams's death, Calypso Rose, a member of the Spiritual 'Shouter' Baptist faith whose members venerated Williams, offered the unique eulogy of 'Balance Wheel' (1982).[83] Rose, who in 'I Thank Thee' (1978), thanked Williams for encouraging her to become a calypsonian, begins her eulogy by establishing:

> Williams as the balance wheel:
> Hold on to the balance wheel
> Eric was the balance wheel
> Who can't hear they got to feel
> So get to the balance wheel
> Now that Eric Williams gone
> I know that you'll miss this son
> Do not think his days are done
> He gone[84]

In Spiritual Baptist iconography, the balance wheel which graces all Spiritual Baptist churches, is a wheel which is suspended horizontally from the ceiling and which contains holders for lighted candles. This wheel symbolizes the equilibrium that Spiritual Baptists are encouraged to aspire to in their daily lives; the candles represent spirituality. After her semi-mystical introduction, Rose invests Chambers, Williams's successor, with the mantle first worn by the master:

> Hold on to the balance wheel
> Chambers is the balance wheel
> Watch out Trinidadians
> For them crooked politicians
> But I know my lips are sealed
> Is so much I can't reveal
> Eric tell me, "Peace, be still"
> He gone

Rose delivers her message with the air of an initiate reluctant to betray too much of the sacred mysteries. I do notknow if that cryptic reference to crooked politicians implicates those PNM politicians condemned in Sparrow's 'Honesty' (1966)[85] and 'Sam P' (1984);[86] Commentor's 'The Opera of the Midnight Opera' (1981);[87] Rudder's 'Panama' (1988),[88] and exposed relentlessly in so much of Chalkdust. Chambers seems to be differentiated from those around him, singled out because of the role that fate had called him to play.

Stanza three of the calypso moves us into the traditional eulogy:

> Eric Williams say, "Hold on!"
> Eric Williams was the boss
> Oh what a great man we loss
> His spirit still have a boss
> Show remorse
> Eric Williams was the balance wheel
> Trinidadians make him screel
> He still standing behind a wheel
> He gone.

Then Rose enters that domain of dream/vision that transcends conventional religious denominational boundaries and carries weight with a large inter-religious congregation of Trinidadians:

> I saw Eric in mih dream
> Still holding the balance wheel
> He say "Rosie tell Chamber
> Call election November
> And tell Chambers I say
> Give the Baptists a holiday
> And tell the nation don't mourn
> Ah gone"

But popular belief also situates and anchors Williams in *obeah*, that elusive dimension of popular religion.[89] Some calypsonians chose to accept that Williams's return after resignation was miraculous. Scraper described Williams as 'the greatest *obeahman*' ('The More You Look the Less You See' 1974)[90] while in the same year and adverting to the same situation, Crusoe also arrives at the same conclusion 'like he working *obeah*' to explain Williams's successful 'escape'. I am not quite certain how seriously calypsonians and some of their audiences took this matter of working *obeah*. I have heard much speculation about Williams's religious beliefs and practices. It is believed by some that he was either a Spiritual Baptist,[91] or had sought out *obeah*.[92] I do not now know to what extent calypsonians like Scraper and Crusoe believed this, if they were playing to their audiences or merely exploiting a popular metaphor.

Chalkdust, nominally a Roman Catholic, makes literary capital of the folk perceptions of a nexus between politics and *obeah*. In 'Goat Mouth Doc' ['Goat Mouth'] (1972)[93] he employs internationally renowned seer (psychic) Harribance Lalsingh as the voice for his own comments on the lunacy which overtook some of those who had opposed Williams:

> Quite in a place called Tableland
> *Obeahman* Harribance called me

> And said to me, "Look here, young man
> Watch yuh tail with that man Deafy
> Because yuh tickling him and yuh lying too
> Getting way with murder
> But if that man put his mouth on you
> Well, boy, dog eat yuh supper"

Chorus
> Shut up yuh big mout'
> Beyond any doubt
> The doc have a light Chalkie
> He does put on his enemy
> The man pass he mout' on Gene Miles and George Goddard
> Is mad both of them gone mad
> And some like Spence can't get no wuk for life
> Keep out, Chalkie, keep out
> Eric Williams have goat mout'

In another stanza Chalkdust calls Williams Papa Doc thus equating him to the feared Haitian dictator Francois Duvalier whose mystique was built upon a cultivation of an image as *obeahman*, backed by arbitrary and generous employ of violence. In parting, Harribance warns Chalkdust that if he persists in his rhetorical attacks he could become the victim of 'Eric spirit lash/And end up like Skerritt under a lettuce patch'. This reference to a notorious murder of the early 1970s removes Chalkdust's fears about his own safety from the nebulous realm of the spiritual to the domain of political assassination.

I do not know how seriously Chalkdust feared for his life. Certainly the 'goat mout'' notion was a literary device, one in the range of masks employed by Chalkdust in his relentless political *picong*. Chalkdust's fearlessness certainly qualified him for martyrdom or some form of severe censorship as he intimates in 'Who Next' (1972),[94] which was composed in the wake of the conviction of a fearless popular journalist. In the climate of fear created by the passage of repressive legislation and the arbitrary house searches and detentions that characterized the early 1970s, it was natural for Chalkdust to anticipate some retaliation, but I am not sure that Chalkdust thought that Williams would have him assassinated. I have not heard or read accusations that Williams himself was complicit in assassination; the nearest I have come across in calypso is Stalin's 'Nothing Ent Strange' (1974)[95] which, apropos of the system's elimination of the National Union of Freedom Fighters, declares: 'The system have a vicious way of operating.' But not even Williams's enemies have alleged assassination against him personally.

Williams as Sexual Man

Caribbean masculinity is centered on virility. Our calypsonians, cricketers and other popular public personalities seem expected to master the bedroom as they do the stage, the field of play, or the parliamentary chambers. Melody's 'Doctor Make Your Love',[96] a song response to those who criticized Williams for his 24-hour marriage, presents and praises Williams as a sexual being. After a snide remark at the maintenance of secrecy and elitism, the calypso engages Williams as man and encourages him in his amorous activities:

> I know the wedding confuse they brain
> Socialism must be maintained
> Mama the wedding confuse they brain
> Socialism must be maintained
> Doctor yuh right
> Man can't be always lonely at night
> Doh mind they washing they mouth on you
> You have a right to make romance too

Chorus
> Hold on to yuh turtle dove
> Doctor make yuh love
> They jealous you from heaven above
> Doctor make yuh love

> 2
> Enjoy yuh life as a man
> They want to put you in confusion
> They confusing yuh life
> Concentrate on yuh lovely wife

> Doctor ah telling yuh plain
> Is yuh brain that driving the dogs insane

To Melody's way of thinking, Dr Williams was essentially man and so needed the romance and sexual release that men enjoy and take for granted. But Williams, like politicians and public personalities everywhere, suffered the occupational hazard of having his private domestic situation sensationalized in the public domain. In his defence, Melody first chastises those Afro-Trinidadians who 'washed their mouths' on Williams:

> The rumour was the Doctor too old
> Some people really brass-faced and bold
> That is the fault of the Negro race
> Putting they mouth in the wrong place
> If I was you, Brother, this is what I will surely do
> I will build a family

Melody's final lines here, that would be recorded in the pages of history, suggest that he, then in his early thirties, may also have felt that Williams was creating history by attempting to start a second family at age 48. Despite what seems as a private doubt or misgiving, he endorsed the effort as a means of silencing censorious and gossiping Afro-Trinidadians.

This done, he denies Indo-Trinidadian detractors the right to pass judgement on the Afro-Trinidadian messiah whose role had made possible a better life for all Trinidadians:

> It is Dr Williams apparently brought us all out of slavery
> I don't understand this constant provocation
> What is wrong with this Indian man
> He should be in Calcutta, believe me
> Not in this land of milk and honey
> He too fas' and outa place

In this way, Melody removes the affair from the purely personal and private domain to the public: Williams the politician supersedes Williams the private individual and the focus shifts from the sexual to the political.

The image of Williams as sexual being is rudely shattered in Shorty's 'PM's Sex Probe' (1974).[97] For reasons that are still unclear, Williams had initiated the moves that led to Shorty being arrested for indecency for his performance of 'The Art of Love Making' at the 1973 Dimanche Gras competition. The first stanza of 'PM's Sex Probe' sketches the affair:

> Newspapers around the globe
> Wrote about the PM's sex probe
> Never before in our history
> Has one calypso caused such a controversy
> I did my best to try and educate my people
> But my good intentions were made to seem so terrible
> How it all began, believe me, I cannot comprehend
> All I know is my calypso somehow offend the PM

Unable to read Williams's mind or to penetrate the circle of his confidantes, Shorty then contrives a situation in which Williams confronts Ivan Williams, then chairman of the CDC:

> Cause I hear him say
> "Ivan Williams, I want to know
> Why this love-making calypso
> Was put on the Dimanche Gras show
> Come on, come on. Come on. Come on, Ivan
> Tell me if this is not disrespecting me
> I am sitting with company
> My legs are crossed quite socially
> When this long streak o' misery
> Embarrass me with some dam tomfoolery about scooggie-woogie
> The audacity
> Bernard right to charge his backside with indecency"

Although Shorty's 'Williams' credits then commissioner of Police, F. Eustace Bernard with the arrest, everyone else saw the hand of Williams in the entire matter, which began with the spectacular blanking of television screens when Shorty stepped up to perform 'The Art'. Some of the individuals commenting on the matter, and these include Shorty himself, felt that the Shorty affair was a rehearsal for a public censoring of Chalkdust, who it was believed had annoyed Williams by the boldness and recklessness of his exposés of PNM corruption and inefficiency.

The second stanza of 'PM's Sex Probe' purports to present the reaction, in Shorty's private circle, to the news of the charge:

> When mih wife heard about the scandal
> The shock was so great she end up in hospital
> From all throughout the country letters came to me
> People offering their support and sympathy
> A woman say, "Shorty, I go pay all yuh lawyer fee
> If you would only teach me the art of love making please
> How the PM could object when things like this are happening
> Ah have a feeling yuh singing touch him
> Where he most lacking"

Whether a literary creation or an actual person impressed into the calypso commentary, Shorty's unidentified female fan simply echoes the arrogant assumption of the 31-year-old Shorty that Williams's 62 years were *ipso facto* evidence of sexual incapacity. 'Williams' confesses same in the third chorus:

> Ivan Williams, I want to know
> Why this love-making calypso
> Was put on the Dimanche Gras show
> Come on, come on, come on, come on, Ivan
> Tell me if this is not disrespecting me
> A man such as I way past sixty
> Dammit, Ivan, I am no baby
> Now who the hell is Lord Shorty
> To advise me what to do in case of emergency

Tell him for me 1970 emergency
This finger was no use to me"

In 'The Art of Making Love' Shorty had advised his male students to keep the little finger handy 'in case of emergency'. This means that lovers must be prepared to be creative when intimate situations warrant deviation from the script. In 'PM's Sex Probe' Shorty supposes that during the national emergency of 1970, the seemingly womanless Williams had found no use for the exercise of the little finger as Shorty had taught.

Shorty's derogation of Williams implies that Williams did not understand the subtlety of sexual innuendo in calypso. In 'The Art of Making Love' Shorty advises old impotent calypsonians to take their dates to cricket and soccer. Apropos of this advice, 'Williams' complains in 'PM's Sex Probe', 'Most irregular, he make me look small/ How a man could make love and still play football.' The mere thought that Williams could misread the sexual connotations of a calypso suggests that he was out of touch with his people for whom such connotations and their normative practice form the basis of life. Time, according to Shorty, which sidelined Williams from the game of lovemaking, also rendered incomprehensible to him the informed commentary on the finer points and subtle nuances of that game.

Shorty followed up this derision of Williams with 'Oh Trinidad' (1976),[98] which demolishes the image of Williams as paterfamilias. Representing Trinidad as a neglected woman whose children are frustrated, crazy, in exile, or imprisoned, he advises Trinidad to take positive lifesaving action:

If the breadwinner of your family
Making mistakes continually
Put him out
He ent care 'bout you
Is the thing to do
And again:
If yuh man old and falling on he face
Get a younger fella to take he place
Put him out

Shorty's final stanza crystallizes the reasoning of the post-1970 generation, which is either unaware of or indifferent to Williams's achievements and aspirations of the 1960s:

> You are grateful, yes I know
> For things he did long ago
> But how long can gratitude last
> Oh Trinidad forget the past
> With someone new
> It might be rough
> But I'm telling you now
> We'll make out somehow
> Change is inevitable
> Don't sit on yuh bottom and wait for trouble

Chorus
> Too much of one thing good for nothing
> Dig it dig it
> If you have a hernia that can't get better
> Cut it cut it
> For twenty years now he holding on
> Poor fella he get old and worn
> *Put him out*
> It's the thing to do

Images of unhealthy growth, of extreme tiredness and of futility attend Williams in decline. Within 20 years, Sparrow's triumphant William the Conqueror has been sadly reduced to Shorty's doddering old man.

'Oh Trinidad', like several other songs mentioned in the essay, echoes those magico-religious practices of some West African communities in which the sexuality of the king is connected organically to the fertility of the land — and thence the well-being of the people. This is yet another of those vestiges of West African kingship which have survived the Middle Passage and remain part of the collective memory of New World Africans. Reflection on all the ways that Williams has been represented in calypso conjures the thought that calypsonians may have been viewing him through the prism/prison of their own expectations. They expected him to be a Caribbean king invested with all the attributes of a dimly-remembered kingship. When he appeared as conquering hero and as paterfamilias to the nation they felt satisfied. When, on the other hand, he did not live up to their expectations they were scathing in their condemnation.

Conclusion

Poet Eric Roach, reviewing the experience of Williams's early years in politics, writes in 'Hard Drought' (1973):

> Williams called us
> and we thought we'd won;
> we set him on the golden stool,
> gave him Kingdom upon Kingdom
> of the heart; our pride and love
> ringed him with janizaries[99]

Roach creates the impression of West African potentates specifically the asantahenes of what is now modern Ghana. If one recognizes Roach's 'janizaries' as the *badjohns* and steelbandmen who formed an unofficial bodyguard around Williams, then one must add to Roach's list the griots like Sparrow, Striker and Superior who championed Williams in song, defended him against the attacks of his enemies, and translated his policies for the people who might have problems understanding his realpolitik. Sparrow et al. undertook this agreeable task with energy and enthusiasm, transforming themselves temporarily into the court poets of West African kingdoms. When Williams did not deliver as the African underclass had expected, a generation of calypsonians undertook to censure him. The end result of all this calypso attention, which has followed him posthumously, is a corpus of songs that propagate the Williams legend.

Given the transience of our collective conscious memory and the relative paucity of printed material, the calypso record is the most viable and accessible history of popular attitudes towards Williams. Over 200 calypsos have documented his existence and achievement in the public sphere. Unfortunately, the exigencies of the recording industry have marginalized the political commentary and threaten to reduce the calypso record of Williams to the memory of a few scholars and the libraries of a few collectors.[100] The post-1981 generation barely knows who Williams was and the post-1970 generation can hardly boast of greater knowledge. If they and those coming after them are not introduced at least to the calypsos on him, Eric Williams will remain that unexplained person after whom the medical sciences complex at Mount Hope has been named.

In parting salute to Williams, Trinidad's great enigma, I wish to cite deFosto's 'Reflections of Our Late Prime Minister' (1982):

> He lived and died for his country
> A death so suddenly
> He was the godfather for the Caribbean
> A chosen leader, a blessed son universally
> It was a dull-looking Sunday night, '81 the 29th of March
> Only to hear at 8 o' clock next day our leader passed away

Chorus
> The time had come for him to go
> Shed no tears, don't prop sorrow
> The nation's future lies in your hands
> Let honesty prevail as man
> It was written and so well done
> God did appoint Eric Eustace Williams
> Raise your flag red white and black
> Supreme colours a living fact

2
> Every light carries a reflection
> Just like the shadows of yourself
> But as for one man who had so much vision
> With his three watchwords discipline, tolerance and production
> Who is his reflection where could he be if he's not yet born
> I hope that chosen one do all his best for our nation

Chorus
> The time had come for him to go
> Shed no tears, don't prop sorrow

> He did his part, his voice was heard
> For twenty five years through this third world
> It was written and so well done
> A king must go for one to come
> He used to say "Bring ballot box, cardboard box or onion box for this throne
> Still PNM will go marching home"
>
> 3
> His vibration was one in a million
> Just like the power of the rising sun
> He was the Right and truly Honourable
> A philosopher, author, premier, teacher, the Nation's Father
> He put aside luxury which was of no importance to him
> He was the people's majority, a simple man, a simple king
>
> Chorus The time had come for him to go
> Shed no tears, don't prop sorrow
> An illustrious master that's who he was
> A true born saviour send from above
> It was written and so well done
> His number was called his time had come
> Together we aspire, together we achieve
> Parts of his thoughts and his belief [101]

Everything considered this seems the best calypso tribute to Williams.

Notes

1. 'Reflections of a Legend' was originally presented as part of a panel at the March 2005 conference on Calypso and the Caribbean Literary Imagination hosted by the University of Miami and the Historical Museum of Southern Florida. That panel, Policy, Politics, and Promise in Calypso: The Eric Williams Era, was chaired by Dr William Aho, and organized by Erica Williams Connell, Eric Williams Memorial Collection.
2. David Rudder, 'Calypso Music', *Calypso Music 10th Anniversary Album*, LP with bonus 7", Lypsoland CR06/CR07, 1987.

3. David Rudder, 'Hoosay', *Rough and Ready*, LP Lypsoland CR06/CR07, 1991.
4. *Picong* includes a range of repartee that is satirical in nature.
5. The *obeahman* is a shaman and folk healer. *Ananse* is the cunning rascal and hero of many Caribbean and African folk tales; he is always amusing in his greed and selfishness, hence a manipulative, self-centred person. The *badjohn* is a street fighter, or a person who is prone to violence.
6. Roger D. Abrahams, 'Traditions of Eloquence in Afro-American Communities', *Journal of Inter-American Studies and World Affairs* 3, no.4 (October 1970): 505.
7. Roger D. Abrahams, 'The Shaping of Folklore Traditions in the British West Indies', *Journal of Inter-American Studies and World Affairs* 9 (1967): 470.
8. Abrahams, 'Traditions of Eloquence', 506.
9. Abrahams, 'The Shaping of Folklore Traditions', 470.
10. Ibid., 471.
11. The Mighty Chalkdust, 'Eric Loves Me', *Origins*, LP Strakers GS 2220, 1979.
12. Manchild, 'Politicians Love Calypsonians', No album information available, n.d.
13. Selwyn Cudjoe, 'Eric E Williams and the Politics of Language', in *Eric Williams Speaks: Essays on Colonialism and Independence*, ed. Selwyn Cudjoe, 100 (Wellesley, MA: Calaloux, 1993).
14. Ibid., 101.
15. The Mighty Cypher, 'Last Election', *Top 10 Calypsoes from the Original Young Brigade 1967* (aka *Calypso 1967 Top Ten*), Various Artists, LP National NLP 8099, Hilary SP 3004, 1967.
16. *Macafouchette* are leftovers or stale food.
17. 'God help our gracious king', *Tapia* 23 (May 1971): 8.
18. The Mighty Sparrow, 'William The Conqueror', William The Conqueror/Sailor Man/Yankees Back Again/Third Eye on the Finger. 7" EP Balisier EXJA 101, 1958.
19. The Mighty Sparrow, 'No Doctor No', *No Doctor No*. 78 Pirates Records V 100, 1957.
20. Albert Gomes, a Portuguese Creole, was also a master of the word. His opposition to Williams to whom he had been something of a patron led to his derogation and near erasure from the annals of social history. This is lamentable because Gomes had been the proprietor and editor of the *Beacon* in the 1930s, and had spearheaded the anti-colonial movement in the 1940s and 1950s, championing the steel band as well as the calypso. During his tenure as chief minister in the early 1950s the ban on the Shouter Baptists was lifted.
21. *Gran' charge* is bravado or rhetorical flourish.
22. C.L.R. James accepts Sparrow as a political force when he examines two political personalities: Williams and Sparrow. See C.L.R. James, *Party Politics in the West Indies,* ed. R. Walters (1962; reprint, San Juan, Trinidad: 1984), 151–72.
23. Sparrow [Slinger Francisco], personal interview, January 24, 1991.
24. See Louis Regis, *The Political Calypso: True Opposition in Trinidad and Tobago* (Barbados: The University of the West Indies Press; Gainesville: University of Florida, 1999), 29–33.
25. John O'Halloran, an intimate of Williams, was a promoter of the illegal sport of cockfighting. His public participation in cockfighting in West Indian islands where the O'halloran was also widely reputed to be a ladies man or cocksman, as is said in some islands. Years later when he exonerated himself from charges of corruption he declared that his only sins were to fight

game cocks and love women. Sparrow's 'Cock Fight' (1969) is a satirical double entendre which thanks O'Halloran for leading the charge for the legalizing of cockfighting in Trinidad but even more it advertises his (Sparrow's) championship of his own (most likely fictitious) fighting cock Duncan.

26. The Mighty Sparrow, 'PAYE', *Calypso Carnival 1958*. LP Balisier HDF 1005, Cook 920, 1958.
27. Sparrow, 'You Can't Get Away From the Tax [You Must Pay Tax]', *This is Sparrow*. LP Balisier HDF 1008, 1959.
28. Sparrow, 'Leave the Damn Doctor', *Lulu/Leave the Damn Doctor*. 7" RCA 7-9030, 1960.
29. Sparrow, 'Present Government', *Sparrow the Conqueror*. RCA LPB-2035, 1961.
30. Sparrow, 'Wear Your Balisier', *Wear Your Balisier/Panama Woman*. 7" RCA 7-2067, 1961.
31. Sparrow, 'Federation', *This is Sparrow Again*, 7" EP Kalypso XXEP4, 1961.
32. King Striker, 'Don't Blame the PNM', *Don't Blame the PNM/No Jobs Suit Striker*, 7" Cook CC5807, 1958.
33. Eric E. Williams, *Inward Hunger: The Education of a Prime Minister* (London: Deutsch, 1969), 269.
34. Bomber, 'Political Wonder', No album information available, n.d.
35. Valentino, 'No Revolution', *No Revolution/Birth Control*. 7" Antillana 968, 1971.
36. Valentino, 'Barking Dogs', *Barking Dogs/Be Aware*. 7" Strakers S-107, 1973.
37. Williams admits in *Inward Hunger*, 28–29 that his hearing problems may have originated in the knock he had taken at soccer as a young man. Errol Mahabir, his crony who had accompanied him to China in 1974, revealed in 1996 that after they had observed Chinese medicine in practice, he had approached Williams about having his hearing restored. To this Williams replied: 'Are you mad?' See Errol Mahabir, 'Errol Mahabir', Special Issue: *Capitalism and Slavery* Fifty Years Later: Eric Williams and the Post-Colonial Caribbean hosted by the Department of History, University of the West Indies, St. Augustine, 1996. *Caribbean Issues* 8, no.1:159–62.
38. Derek Walcott, 'The Spoiler's Return', in *The Fortunate Traveller* (London: Faber, 1980), 55.
39. Maestro, 'To Sir With Love', *Mr. Trinidadian/To Sir With Love/Poor Man*. 12" Hildrina H 1007, 1974.
40. Maestro, 'Dread Man', *Savage/Dread Man*. 12" Charlies PKL 150, Kalinda PKL-15, 1977.
41. See Regis, *The Political Calypso*, 69–120.
42. Black Stalin, 'Piece of the Action', No album information available, n.d.
43. This was one of the many organizations that prepared the way for Williams in 1955. Before formal entry into politics, Williams had built up a network of associations that worked independently of each other.
44. Relator, 'Deaf Panman', *Deaf Panman/The Bomb*. 7" Pan Records P 3150, 1974.
45. Relator, 'Take a Rest', *The Real Master*. EP Makosssa MD 9060, 1980.
46. Delamo, 'Apocalypse', *Apocalypse/Musical Rasta/Doreen Party*. 12" Semp SDI 24, 1981.
47. Prince, 'Come as You are Party', No album information available, n.d.
48. Lord Kitchener, 'Twenty to One', *Tourist in Trinidad*. LP Trinidad TRCS – 0004, 1974.
49. Squibbly, 'Streaker', *The Chook/Streaker*. 7" Strakers GS 188, 1975.

50. Scrunter, 'Crapaud Revolution', *Crapaud Revolution/Sheila Run Away.* 12" KN-003, 1981. In the age of streaking, Prince portrays Williams as a participant in a nudist fete while Squibby represents him as a masquerader in a band of streakers. Kitchener wants Williams to jump into a Carnival band with all of the police force to offset the imbalance in numbers between males and females. Scrunter represents Williams as being afraid of a revolution started by an orchestra of toads.
51. The Growling Tiger's 'The Doc's Secret Wedding' (1959) satirized Williams's secret wedding and one day marriage. Tiger's satirical tone which challenged Williams's integrity annoyed PNM faithful to whom the affairs of their chosen Caesar were above suspicion and these indignant faithful boycotted the Senior Brigade at which Tiger was appearing. This resulted in a loss of revenue and Tiger was forced to retire from the tent. For further details see Rawle Gibbons, *No Surrender: A Biography of the Growling Tiger* (Tunpauna, Trinidad and Tobago: Canboulay, 1994) 83–89.
52. Chalkdust, 'Brain Drain', *Brain Drain/Devaluation.* 7" RA NSP 193, 1968.
53. See Regis, *The Political Calypso*, 47–52.
54. Shorty, 'The Art of Making Love', *The Art of Making Love.* Shorty S-003, Caravan CX-160, Sakanda SAK-737, 1973.
55. '"Chalkie was disrespectful" say women,' *Sunday Guardian*, March 11, 1973, p.1.
56. Chalkdust, 'Let the Jackass Sing', *Stay Up.* LP Strakers GS 7789, 1974.
57. See Regis, *The Political Calypso*, 99–108.
58. As part of his contribution to the conference, *Capitalism and Slavery: Fifty Years After*, held at St. Augustine in 1996, Chalkdust revealed that on the request of some of the residents of Diego Martin, he had written a letter to Williams about some or other grievance. According to what he heard from the delegation tendering the letter, Williams had been impressed by the quality of the writing and complimented Chalkdust as a writer. When reminded that he had dismissed Chalkdust as jackass, Williams allegedly retorted: 'In letter-writing he is good, but in Calypso he is a jackass.'
59. Epigraph to *Eric Williams Speaks*, edited by Selwyn R. Cudjoe.
60. Chalkdust, 'Clear Your Name', *Stay Up.* LP Strakers GS 7789, 1974.
61. Chalkdust, 'Eric Loves Me', 1979.
62. *Mamaguy* is flattery and deception. *Mauvais lange* is malicious gossip or injurious half truths.
63. Luta, 'Pack Yuh Bags', *Double Silver.* Double CD Dimensions DPR003C, 1999.
64. Blakie, 'De Doctor Eh Dey', *Sparrow Lost/De Doctor Eh Dey.* 7" Telco TW – 3240, 1964.
65. It is popularly believed that these steelbandsmen declared themselves Williams's bodyguards in the wake of the threats on his life and on that of his daughter.
66. *Ole talk* is rhetoric or idle talk.
67. Gordon Rohlehr, 'Calypso and Political Criticism after 1965', Port of Spain, Government Broadcasting Unit, Sunday, June 10, 1973: *From Atilla to the Seventies* #20.
68. Penguin 'Betty Goaty' (1982) co-opts the children's game 'Betty Goaty' to represent the recently deceased Williams as a child. According to the logic of the calypso, Williams now safely in a location described only as 'down here' can jeer at those subordinates whom he was powerless in life to control. See Louis Regis, *The Political Calypso: True Opposition in Trinidad and*

Tobago 1962-1987 (Barbados: The University of the West Indies Press; Gainesville: University Press of Florida, 1999) 155–56.
69. Sparrow, 'Get to Hell Out', *Congo Man,* LP National NLP 5050, Melodisc NLP 17 155, Hilary SP 3006, 1965.
70. Chalkdust, 'Two Sides of the Shilling', *Answer to Black Power/Two Sides of the Shilling.* 7" Tropico T7-1109, 1970.
71. The calypso drama in which Chalkie sang the piece on Williams was a drama in which singers represented all of the many leaders contesting the 1976 elections. Chalkdust scripted the entire calypso drama for the 1976 season at the Regal Calypso Tent in which he had a proprietary stake. Naturally he assumed the role of Williams performing the stanza in which there is mention of Jaws. At the time the movie *Jaws* had been playing to full houses in Trinidad and Tobago as elsewhere. After the elections he also scripted the sequel, which was presented at the Regal in 1978.
72. Crusoe, 'I Eric Eustace Williams', No album information available, n.d.
73. Chalkdust's 'Badjohn Willie' (1981) represents Williams as one of those colourful but dangerous street hooligans who made life unsafe in Port of Spain in the late 1950s up to the early 1970s.
74. Composer, 'Different Strokes', No album information available, n.d.
75. *Mapepire* is a venomous snake found in the West Indies.
76. Superior, 'Why I Left, Why I Returned', No album information available, n.d.
77. Black Stalin, 'Break Down Party', *Just for Openers/This is it.* Double LP Makossa MD9054/55, 1980; Stalin, 'Caribbean Unity', *Play One/Caribbean Unity.* 7" Wizards MCR-147, 1979.
78. Eric Williams, *History of the People of Trinidad and Tobago* (New York: Praeger, 1984), 278.
79. Ivar Oxaal, *Black Intellectuals Come to Power: The Rise of Creole Nationalism in Trinidad and Tobago* (Cambridge, MA: Schenkman, 1968), 100.
80. Ibid.
81. Dougla, 'Independence', No album information available.
82. Shadow, 'From Then to Now', *National 25th Anniversary of Independence Calypso Competition.* Various Artists. LP Stag H18701, 1987.
83. Calypso Rose, 'Balance Wheel', *Mass in California.* LP Strakers GS 2234, 1982.
84. Calypso Rose, 'I thank Thee', *Her Majesty.* LP Charlies CR 444, 1978.
85. Sparrow, 'Honesty', *Going Home Tonight/Honesty.* 7" National NSP 078, 1966.
86. Sparrow, 'Sam P', *King of the World.* LP Bs BSR-SP-002, 1984.
87. Commentor's 'The Opera of the Midnight Opera', No album information available.
88. Rudder, 'Panama', *Haiti.* LP Lypsoland CR 008,1988.
89. Obeah is normally taken to mean the complex of magico-religious practices inherited from West Africa. Earl Lovelace's 'Working Obeah', in *Growing in the Dark: Selected Essays,* ed. Funso Aiyejina (San Juan, Trinidad: Lexicon, 2003), 216–26 offers a philosophical disquisition of the phenomenon of *obeah* (217–28).
90. Scraper, 'The More You Look the Less You See', No album information available.
91. Stephen Glazier comments on Williams's membership in the Baptist faith in 'Funerals and Mourning in the Spiritual Baptist and Shango Traditions': I have been unable to determine his true status within the faith.

> But then again, William's "true" religious preferences are of minor importance to this discussion. For me the most

> important thing is that many Baptists believed that he was a member. Also I think it is significant that Williams made no attempt to deny it (6).

I suspect that this silence meant that Williams could not be bothered to answer one way or the other, or felt that leaving credulous people in doubt was useful to the cultivation of his mystique.

92. Lovelace places the celebrated Papa Neezer [Ebeenezer Elliot] at the call of Williams ('Working Obeah', 219). Lovelace also writes:
   > Suddenly a difference emerges between C.L.R. James and Williams that explains Williams. James didn't live here after a while; Williams returned to seek power and power brought him to Obeah.

   'Working Obeah', (219).
93. Chalkdust, 'Goat Mouth', *Goat Mouth/Immigration Problems*. 7" Strakers S-0061, 1972.
94. Chalkdust, 'Who Next', *Who Next/We're Ten Years Old*. 7" Strakers S0067, 1972.
95. Black Stalin, 'Nothing Ent Strange', No album information available, n.d.
96. Lord Melody, 'Doctor Make Your Love', *Again!! Lord Melody Sings Calypso*. LP Cook 914, 1959.
97. Shorty, 'P.M. Sex Probe', *The Love Man, Carnival '74 Hits*. LP Shorty SLP 1000, 1974.
98. Shorty, 'Oh Trinidad', *Sweet Music*. LP Shorty SLP-1003, 1976.
99. Eric Roach, 'Hard Drought', *The Flowering Rock: Collected Poems 1938-1974* (Leeds: Peepal Tree, 1992), 165–66.
100. When Sparrow released his 40-CD suite, he compressed 'William the Conqueror', 'P.A.Y.E.', 'No Doctor No', 'Get to Hell Outta Here', 'You Can't Away from the Tax', 'Leave the Dam Doctor' and 'Drink Your Balisier' into an Eric Williams Medley on the CD entitled *A Living Legend*. In fairness he does present 'Get to Hell Outta Here', 'Honesty', 'Solomon Affair', 'Present Government' and 'Popularity Contest' as singles on the CD.
101. The Original DeFosto Himself, *Reflections of Our Late Prime Minister*, Cucumba TODH 005, 1981.

3

IN THE BATTLE FOR EMERGENT INDEPENDENCE: CALYPSOS OF DECOLONIZATION

Ray Funk

Introduction

Earl Lovelace, in one of his essays notes, 'Decolonisation ... to be the process by which the previously colonized wrestled to achieve some sense of self, some independence as they disengage from colonialism.'[1] In another of these essays Lovelace observes, 'What characterized the calypsonian throughout his long fight for social acceptance has been his acute sense of his own freedom.'[2] This essay focuses on certain calypsos in the decades leading up to Trinidad's independence in 1962 in which the calypsonian's sense of his own freedom is manifested in calypsos that focus on the larger struggle for freedom and autonomy for his society. In these calypsos, there is a subversion of the status quo, a move from a respectful deference to colonial rule to a new postcolonial consciousness. These calypsos focus on changing attitudes toward the British Royal Family, a growing allegiance to a homeland other than Mother England and the major events during the 1950s as plans for a West Indian Federation develop and collapse.

Griot to the British Crown

In tracing the African roots of calypso and Carnival, commentators like Dr Liverpool, Trinidad's seven-time calypso monarch, have seen strong connections between the West African griot and the calypsonian. Griots were hired by African royalty to sing their praises, celebrate their lives and document their achievements. Applying such a loose definition, there are a goodly number of calypsos that seem to fit in this category in reference to the British government and its tangible symbol of the government, the Royal Family, for example: Roaring Lion's 'Coronation of Queen Elizabeth', George Browne's 'I Was There At the Coronation', Kitchener's 'Festival of London', and the many calypsos supporting the war effort during World War II. Visits to the British colonies by members of the Royal Family or visiting dignitaries like President Roosevelt resulted in calypsos and calypso contests to sing songs of praise.

Panther's international career was launched by winning a contest for the visit of Princess Margaret to Trinidad in 1955. In general these calypsos were reverential. For example, the first recorded calypso of this type, Attilla the Hun's 1935 recording of 'Duke and Duchess of Kent', is typical of these commemorating the visit of the British Royal Family to Trinidad:

> Trinidadians regard with pride
> The visit of the Prince and his bride.
> With banners flying happy and gay
> The whole island was on holiday
> And it seems everyone was bent
> On welcoming the Duke and Duchess of Kent.[3]

The message that they are to take back to King George is explicitly referenced in the song which hopes the Duke and Duchess 'will speak of our loyalty' to the king.

In 1955, Princess Margaret visited Trinidad, the first such visit by a member of the Royal Family in 20 years. This led to the calypso competition won by the Mighty Panther, which led in turn to his travelling to the United States and also created some excitement in England. The *London Daily Express* published the text of Panther's tribute to Princess Margaret and the *Express* offered a cash prize to the best British calypso on the same subject.[4] The newspaper reported that 'thousands (mostly women)' entered the competition. The winning entry was far from memorable and its chorus went:

> There is plenty to see and plenty to do.
> Everyone is happy and waiting for you,
> Our singing can be heard for miles around
> Because our lovely Princess Margaret is West Indian bound.[5]

But there was, almost from the beginning, a less reverent tone in certain calypsos. The most famous calypso on the Royal Family in the first half of the twentieth century was subversive rather than subservient. Lord Caresser's 1937 calypso 'King Edward VIII' is generally known by the hook line of its chorus, 'Love Love Alone'. The subject was King Edward VIII's abdication of the throne to marry the American divorcee Wallis Simpson. It became immensely popular and was sung throughout the Caribbean and beyond for decades to come. Harry Belafonte recorded it in 1957 during the Calypso Craze when his album called *Calypso* sold a million copies and launched a major hysteria when the American entertainment industry for six months thought it would kill rock 'n roll. Most recently, the American blues artist Taj Mahal recorded it.[6]

'Love Love Alone' is not a celebration of the king as the leader of the British Empire, no mightier-than-thou ruler of his subjects whose exploits in battle are being celebrated. This calypso was on his human nature rather than his kingliness. His abdication was itself a bold act of independence and this is what was celebrated in Caresser's song. The hook in its chorus made it memorable: 'It's love, love alone, / That caused King Edward to leave the throne.' The song celebrates the well worn theme of 'love conquers all', but what is unique was the king's voluntary surrender of power and his decision to flaunt the power structure, 'Oh, what a sad disappointment / Was endured by the British government', and risk all, 'And if I can't get a boat to set me free / Well, I'll walk to Miss Simpson across the sea.' By his abdication the king was set free, free of his kingly duties and indeed free of England for he immediately left Great Britain to live in exile. Edward attained a freedom the colonists would long for in the decades to come.

Lord Kitchener, From Mother England to Mother Africa

If one looks at the calypsos of Lord Kitchener while he lived in England during the period from 1948 to 1962, this subversion, this striving for identity and freedom is clear. As Kitchener got off the *Windrush* in 1948 after making the journey from Jamaica to England, he was confronted by a newsreel crew and sang a new calypso that he wrote in anticipation of his arrival, 'London is the Place for Me.'[7] Kitch proclaimed his intentions in the chorus and in the second verse:

                Well, believe me, I am speaking broadmindedly
                I am glad to know my mother country

Chorus   To live in London you really comfortable

> Because the English people are very much sociable
> They take you here and they take you there
> And they make you feel like a millionaire
> London that's the place for me (2nd verse)

But this rosy view was not what he sang in the years to come, after he had actually lived in England not just fantasized about it. British subject or not, being a Caribbean person of colour in cold, damp England was tough in the 1950s as Lord Kitchener was to learn and was to sing about extensively. As Donald Hinds who immigrated to England from Jamaica in 1955 wrote:

> Despite the fact that in a few years thousands of West Indians had settled in Britain, the migrants' world was a lonely one. The crowded boat train is the only reminder that a large number of his countrymen are over here. Once the station is behind him, if he looks through the window of the taxi at the pedestrians hurrying quietly along, then he must realize that he is a long, long way from home. The streets are not lit with the vulgar brilliance of West Indian cities and towns; the vehicles do not hurtle along at breakneck speed with their headlamps blazing and horns blaring angrily at the mistakes of others. No one shouts at a friend on the street. It seems that the city is walking in its sleep.[8]

The experience of exile and separation was vividly portrayed at the time in the comic novels of Trinidadian Sam Selvon, especially his aptly titled *The Lonely Londoners*.[9] The conditions were equally vivid in Lord Kitchener's calypsos. In 'Sweet Jamaica' (1953),[10] he didn't mince words:

> Thousands of people are asking me
> How I spend the time in London City
> Well, that is a question I cannot answer
> I regret the day I left sweet Jamaica
> I mean you would pity my position
> Because I nearly die here from starvation

Kitchener went on to sing about the weather — 'I can't stand the cold in winter / I want to buy an incubator' — problems of getting transportation, difficulties of finding good housing — 'My landlady's too rude / In my affairs she likes to intrude' — and his dislike of British food in his 'Food from the West Indies':

> No, no, no, this wouldn't do
> Give meh rice I'm begging you
> Dorreen, Darling, if you please
> Give the Lord some rice from the West Indies

His famous song 'Nora' which reflected a longing to go home to Trinidad was a classic of expatriate feeling.

But besides documenting the harsh reality of life in the Mother Country, Kitchener was shifting his focus and his allegiance from England to what was for him the real mother country. Kitchener proclaimed his allegiance in his 1951 calypso, 'Africa My Home': 'I want to come back home, Africa / Girl, I tired, roam, Africa.' Around this time, the BBC was broadcasting calypsos on the Overseas Service not just to the Caribbean but also to West Africa where they were proving immensely popular. Meanwhile, Kitchener was coming into contact with the expatriate population of Africans arriving in England. From Kitchener's pen, his 1956 'Birth of Ghana' then became the first calypso to directly address the subject of a country receiving independence from Great Britain. This song proved very popular. Indeed, a recording firm manager is quoted in the *Jamaica Gleaner* in October 1957 as stating that it had sold an amazing 300,000 copies.[11] This would make this record a best-selling real calypso of its time. It is unlikely that these sales were largely in Britain but instead from export sales to Africa and the Caribbean.

Kitch's description of Nkruma is somewhat prophetic of Eric Williams and revealed that independence came only with struggle and a forceful leader:

> Dr. Nkrumah went out his way
> To make the Gold Coast what it is today
> He endeavored continually
> To bring us freedom and liberty

> The doctor began as agitator
> He became popular leader
> He continued to go further
> And now he is Ghana's prime minister

Kitchener's lyric points to the wider goal of getting out from under the yoke of colonial rule as Markus Coester wrote in a recent article that looked at both Kitchener's 'Birth of Ghana' and Laurel Aitken's mento about Ghana's independence, 'They Got It.'[12] Kitchener leaves no doubt that Nkrumah's struggle was for the benefit of all 'Africans' under colonial rule, be it in Africa or elsewhere, or be it only as a means of creating pan-African solidarity. He does not hesitate to emphasize his identification with those who benefit from Nkrumah's achievement — independence. Indeed, all subsequent calypsos in direct celebration of independence from British colonial rule owe a debt to Kitchener's song. Lord Kitchener himself returned to Trinidad not long after independence. If one reviews the broad sweep of his calypsos over the prior decade and a half, one of the themes they reflect is a gradual disenchantment with life in England, a growing allegiance to his African roots, and a support for the decolonization of the British Empire.

Yankee Gone

During the 1950s, while there was a move toward formal independence from Great Britain, there was also one of independence from the United States. The military base at Chaguaramas that had been established during World War II had a profound effect on the life of most Trinidadians. For some Trinidadians the base offered job opportunities and increased wages not there previously, but there was also the sense that the country had been invaded by a second foreign power and the results were not all beneficial. Indeed, two of the best-known calypsos of all time are about the effects of the American occupation, specifically on prostitution in Trinidad. When Lord Invader in 'Rum and Coca Cola' in 1943 proclaimed 'Mother and daughter working for the Yankee Dollar', he did not mean handicrafts. The American base caused an enormous increase in

Trinidadian women who were making their living as prostitutes with American soldiers as their clientele.

By 1956 things were starting to change, with what would now be called downsizing at Chaguaramus, and Sparrow won the Calypso monarchy that year with 'Jean and Dinah' proclaiming an end to the American domination of this sector of the local economy. The song was originally called, in print and on its first record release, 'Yankees Gone':

> All the girls in town feeling bad
> No more Yankees in Trinidad
> They going to close down the base for good
> Them girls have to make out how they could

The women 'round the corner posing' are told, 'Don't make no row / Yankee gone / Sparrow take over now,' and 'It's the Glamour Boys Again / We are going to rule Port of Spain.' Sparrow's proclamation was putting the colony on notice of a new force in calypso, a new pride in throwing off the yolk of foreign control. Sparrow soon became the voice of the People's National Movement (PNM) and Eric Williams as he advocated support for the Doctor in an entire series of calypsos in the next few years.

American departure was not as swift as Sparrow reported in 1956, and during the next few years, the calypsonians sang about the continued American ownership of the base in Chaguaramus. There were a number of calypsos about it, and all were supportive of Eric Williams's efforts to get the Americans to depart. Cypher in his 'The Chaguaramas Issue' (1959) sang:

> We want Chaguaramas
> Say what thou like
> The Doctor is right
> We want Chaguaramas[13]

These calypsos seem to be all part of the wrestle to be free and independent of foreign occupation.

While there was this tension with American occupation, a master calypsonian reached into American history for the subject of his calypso. Though it remains little known, there is a calypso written by Growling Tiger in the period leading up to independence that reflects a yearning for freedom. In 1960, in the collection of the latest calypso lyrics, Tiger included his 'Abraham Lincoln Speech at Gettysburg'. He had already given up appearing in the tents and the song was not commercially recorded but he did sing it at the Newport Folk Festival in 1964.

> Lincoln's historic speech given at Gettysburg
> Was an incentive the living and the dead had heard
> Eulogizing those who fought the civil war
> To defend the liberty of both rich and poor
> Some were wounded some were living many dead
> As Lincoln again in his oration said
> We are highly resolved again
> The men who have died
> Should not have died in vain
> Lincoln told them then
> That his word would never fall
> In this nation all men are created equal

Just as things were heating up for independence in Trinidad, Growling Tiger went back to the famous American presidential address from a century before to draw inspiration. Was it the freeing of slaves or the concept of a civil war that attracted him? Certainly, Pretender's 'God Made Us All' had in the 1940s eloquently voiced the right to racial equality. For Tiger, when you consider this calypso, it is liberty, equality, and democracy — principles that men were dying to defend during the American Civil War — that he emphasized and found in Lincoln's speech to be the cause for the great celebration.

Federation

The first plan for liberation of colonial rule in the Caribbean was a plan for federation of the Caribbean colonies and there were a number of calypsos on different aspects of federation in the 1950s.[14] I wish to point to but a few lines from a couple of the many written on this topic. One of the issues that were central to the eventual dissolution of the federation was the placement of the capital in Trinidad which Jamaicans were especially unhappy with. In 1957, Sparrow was singing in the tent:

> Bajans sorry but Sparrow glad
> We have the capital in Trinidad
> They try all kind of botheration
> To wreck West Indian Federation.[15]

Sparrow was hoping for the best but Federation was not to survive. Lord Melody asserted Trinidad's success and Jamaica's failure quite proudly in his calypso, 'Capital Site', and is clearly chortling at Trinidad's success.[16]

> All they got in Jamaica is plenty banana
> And poor people hungry
> They ain't got a penny
> 5 shillings for ordinary chow
> Their life but I still wondering how
> They could say that they want supremacy
> And all they got is banana industry

The partisanship between Trinidad and Jamaica was a central failure in federation planning.

Other countries were not on board either. King Fighter from British Guiana in the same tent in 1957 was extolling:

> I really can't understand
> Why BG afraid of federation
> BG you're fooling yourself
> Why hide like a mouse upon the shelf
> You losing a progressive chance
> You'd better jump in the brew and dance.[17]

Even as these calypsos reflected tensions in the process of trying to establish a West Indian Federation, they reflect a heightened implicit excitement in freedom from colonial rule. Mighty

Bomber's 'Federated Islands' spoke of the need for cooperation, 'May the islands co-operate independently', and in the third verse, of the next step:

> There's a task before us
> We must fight dominion status
> Free trade and free movement
> And have a sound devoted government
> So to speak we want to accomplish
> We must forget everything about racial business
> Giving our leaders their every need
> Regardless of colour, their class or creed

Striker's 'Ah Glad for Federation' focused on the hope that with Federation discrimination as to people from member countries would end. As federation collapsed, renewed dreams of sovereign nations emerged and the process of decolonization continued.

1962 Independence Calypso Competition

Success was finally at hand in 1962, and with the pending celebration of independence, a calypso competition was put together by the Celebration Committee. Thirty-six calypsonians were chosen to audition at Radio Trinidad on August 9 and featured were all the leading calypsonians of the time. Twelve were chosen for the final to be held at the new Town Hall on August 15, and the event was broadcast on Radio Trinidad.[18] The first prize was $1,000, which was substantial in light of other competitions at the time. The competition proved a very popular event as the *Guardian* noted: 'Hundreds packed the auditorium of the Port-of-Spain Town Hall where the competition was being staged. Nearby Woodford Square was filled to capacity as loudspeakers relayed the proceedings from the Town Hall.'[19]

A young singer, a relative outsider, won the competition. Kade Simon, Lord Brynner, took his sobriquet from the fact that he was bald and was a reference to the famous American actor Yul Brynner. All the songs from that radio broadcast survive in only the poorest quality of tape recording with a terrible hum and have largely slipped into oblivion. That is, except for two which were commercially recorded. They are, the contest winner Brynner's piece and Sparrow's entry. Brynner's song was issued as a single on RCA and not long after was featured on his first album called *Mr. Calypso* and the song is re-titled as 'Our nation's calypso' (1962).[20] Lord Brynner sang:

> Because this is your land, just as well as my land
> This is your place and also it is my place
> So let we put our heads together
> And live like one happy family
> Democratically, educationally,
> We'll be independently.
> ....
> Conscientiously, Independence
> And constitutionally, Independence
> Forget all this lousy rumour about racial equality
> If you are an East Indian and you want to be an African
> Just shave your head like me
> Then they can't prove your nationality

The most interesting and bizarre conceit in the song is the foreshadowing of racial tension that continues to plague Trinidad and Tobago, that the East Indian population should conclude that racial unity is only a 'lousy rumour' and that Indians should all pretend to be of African decent by shaving their heads. A simplistic solution but one that is the kind of exaggerated idea that sparks controversy and some thought, like Cro Cro's solution to kids not learning that their arms be cut off in the calypso that brought him to the Big Yard that year, or Singing Sandra's 'Equaliser' from several years ago that advocated castration for all sex offenders.

Brynner beat the Mighty Sparrow who had been the 1962 Calypso Monarch and came in second. The *Trinidad Guardian* noted:

> Sparrow, with his wine-coloured coat, white shirt and black trousers, was "Mr. Showman" himself. He was as a schoolmaster lecturing his audience, with a word of advice for foreigners: "You people who

are foreigners, Spread the word where you pass, There is a Model Nation at last."[21]

Sparrow's song 'Our Model Nation' was featured on both a single and his latest album and ultimately has had a more lasting history as a well-known calypso in part because Sparrow himself has gone on to be recognized as the country's greatest living calypsonian, while Brynner like so many other calypsonians died in poverty with little recognition:

> Trinidad and Tobago will always live on
> Colonialism gone Our Nation is formed
> We go follow our leaders they always do their best
> We want to achieve so we're going to aspire
> And we bound to be a success.
> It is a miracle all these different people
> Can dwell so well
> You see we are educated to love
> And forget hatred
> You see tis so
> You people who are foreign
> I've got a message to give you when you're going
> Spread the word anywhere you pass
> Tell the world there's a Model Nation at last

Sparrow's calypso like Brynner's looks to past leaders and is a celebration, a griot's homage to a remarkable achievement, but these calypsos celebrate the achievement of becoming free and independent of the kingly rule by a foreign power that had preceeded.

Jamaica

Kitchener sang of independence in Africa and many calypsonians sang of Trinidad's independence. But there were others who sang calypsos as Britain granted independence to other former colonies in the Caribbean. Jamaica was made independent in August 1962 as well. As in Trinidad, the joyful event was celebrated by a number of songs in local pre-reggae styles that reflected American R&B, for example, Al T. Joe's 'Rise Jamaica', or more ska and mento sounds, such as, Derrick Morgan's 'Forward March'. But while these songs might have had some popularity, it was a song by a recent immigrant from Trinidad, Kenrick Patrick, that was the hit song in Jamaica. Under his sobriquet Lord Creator he recorded a classic calypso called 'Independent Jamaica' (1977)[22]. Indeed, it was the first hit for record producer Vincent 'Randy' Chin who would go on to produce hundreds of records after this success. It was reportedly the first single issued by British record producer Chris Blackwell on his Island label which later had many worldwide hits with Bob Marley.

Known for his calypso 'Evening News', he had spent a few years in the tents in Trinidad and went on a tour in 1961 through the islands. He ended up in early 1962 at the Club Havana in Kingston and sought out Chin, owner of Randy's Record Store to record. In a *Jamaica Gleaner* interview a few years ago he described how this song came about: 'It was January, but Chin asked me to make an Independence song for him in tribute to the independence referendum that was approved by the people. I did the song, then I left Jamaica to complete my tour, he explained.'[23] It was while on the next leg of his tour that an excited Chin called him and informed him that the song 'Independent Jamaica' was selling like 'hot bread'.

> Jamaica getting their independence
> And everyone is happy
> So I will now to tell the story
> So please listen carefully
> Manley called up a referendum
> For you to make up your own decision
> So the people voted wisely
> Now everyone is happy
> There's no more federation
> These two men came from England
> They came the very same day
> On two different planes that stopped Montego Bay
> They separated down to Kingston

> But still we are very pleased
> But they got independence
> The first in the West Indies
> Lord Creator, "Independent Jamaica"

Although Creator did record a 'Jamaican Anniversary Calypso' for the next year, he abandoned calypso and instead made his name singing ska and ballads. Lord Creator seems to have abandoned any loyalty he might have had to Trinidad in the song. In his embrace of the collapse of Federation, which was more favourably viewed in Trinidad that had been picked as the capital, and was something that stuck in the craw of many Jamaicans at the time, Creator emphasized that this was one of the issues that led to the collapse. In addition, the song emphasizes that Jamaica was made independent August 6, 1962, a couple weeks before Trinidad. It is not likely that line would have made him any fans in Trinidad.[24]

Coda: Patriotism and Postcolonialism

But to get back to Trinidad, with independence there would be many other patriotic calypsos that would catch the fancy of the new nation. Best known of these are Sniper's 'Portrait of Trinidad' from 1965 and Lord Baker's 'God Bless Our Nation' in 1967. With independence, the Brain Drain of great calypsonians who had gone to England was reversed. Lord Kitchener, Lord Beginner, Roaring Lion and the Mighty Terror came home. Several independence calypso competitions have been held since the first, most notably for the tenth and twenty-fifth anniversary in 1972 and 1987 and another just recently in 2005.

If there is any song that represents a different attitude toward the 'Mother Country' and more specifically the Royal Family as a symbol of the former British Empire, it is Sparrow's perennially popular calypso, 'Philip My Dear', about the break-in at Buckingham Palace by a 32-year-old labourer Michael Fagan on July 9, 1982. Queen Elizabeth woke to find Fagan sitting on her bed. Sparrow, who had in 1956 proudly declared the 'Yankee Gone', and who in 1962 proclaimed Trinidad the 'Model Nation', was now comfortably referring to what was the Mother Country as just 'good old England' with no reverence or really even any respect at all, and to the Queen as being a not unreceptive subject to a bedroom intrusion by someone who was younger, stronger, harder than the Prince of Wales. The calypsonian's consciousness is clearly postcolonial and his independence from the Mother Country seems by such a calypso to be complete.

Meanwhile, independence is never far from the calypso consciousness in Trinidad. Remaining issues of freedom from England such as the use of Britain's Privy Council for the final court of legal appeals has continued to be the subject of calypsos railing at this last vestige of colonialism. Independence is also a frequent touchstone for calypsos that seek to gauge the progress of the country. This year in the calypso tents Marvellous Marva and Singing Sandra both sang calypsos of outrage at an incident last fall involving a nun who was principal of a Catholic school and who refused to let a young student attend school because of her dreadlocks.[25] Marva's calypso, '42 Years Gone', which I got to hear at Kaiso House only a few months ago during the height of the 2005 calypso season, harkens back to independence as part of her outrage, finding such lack of tolerance unacceptable in a country that has come so far since 1962:

> 42 Years Gone
> We are independent now
> It's we who are running our own affairs
> While we still have issues with Rasta hair

The calypsonian is not finished with wrestling to achieve a sense of self, personal independence and nation building as the disengagement from colonialism continues.

Notes

1. Earl Lovelace, 'Dignity Without Apology', *Growing in the Dark*, ed. Funso Aiyejina (Trinidad: Lexicon, 2003), 47.
2. Earl Lovelace, 'Watch, Your Freedom is in Jeopardy', *Growing in the Dark*, 65.
3. Reissued on the CD, *Roosevelt in Trinidad: Calypsos of Events, Places and Personalities, 1933–1939*, Rounder Select 1142, 1999.
4. 'Offer to U.K. Calypsonians', *Trinidad Guardian*, February 6, 1955, p. 1.

5. 'Prizewinning Calypso – London Style', *Trinidad Guardian*, February 10, 1955, 3.
6. You can hear the live recording that Duke of Iron, Lord Invader and Macbeth the Great sang at Town Hall in 1946 on the Calypso: A World Music website, <www.calypsoworld.org/noflash/audio.htm>
7. Lord Kitchener later recorded 'London is the Place for Me', Melodisc 1163, 1950, and it was reissued on anthology *London Is the Place for Me, Trinidadian Calypso in London, 1950–1956*, Honest Jon's Records HJRCD2, 2002.
8. Donald Hinds. *Journey to an Illusion: The West Indian in Britain* (London: Heinemann, 1966; reprint, London: Bogle L'ouverture, 2001), 48.
9. Sam Selvon, *The Lonely Londoners* (London: Longman, 1989).
10. Lord Kitchener, 'Sweet Jamaica', Lyragon J700, 1952.
11. Londoner (sic), 'West Indian Table Talk', *Jamaica Daily Gleaner*, October 15, 1957, 16.
12. Markus Coester '"Ghana is the Name We Wish to Proclaim" –Two Popular Caribbean Voices and the Independence of Ghana', *Ntama Journal of African Music and Popular Culture*, <http://ntama.uni-mainz.de/content/view/92/29/>
13. Calypso Souveniur edited by Small Island Pride [Theophilus Woods] (Trinidad, 1959).
14. See Gordon Rohlehr, *A Scattering of Islands: Essays on Calypso* (Trinidad: Lexicon, 2004), 25–42 for an extended discussion on a wider range of calypsos related to Federation.
15. 'Jump to the Tune', *Trinidad Guardian*, February 12, 1957, p.1.
16. *Calypso Carnival 1958*, Balisier HDF 1003, 1958.
17. 'Jump to the Tune', *Trinidad Guardian*, February 12, 1957, p.1.
18. 'Calypso Finals Tonight', *Trinidad Guardian*, August 15, 1962, p.1.
19. 'Lord Brynner – Boy Who Wanted to Be Somebody', *Trinidad Guardian*, August 26, 1962, p.8.
20. Lord Brynner, 'Our Nation's Calypso' recorded as 'Trinidad and Tobago Independence', RCA (Trinidad) 7-2116, 1962.
21. 'Independence Crown to Brynner', *Trinidad Guardian*, August 16, 1962, 1.
22. Kenrick 'Lord Creator' Patrick, 'Independent Jamaica'. *Don't Stay Out Late, Lord Creator's Greatest Hits*, VP Records, 1997 and *Island 40th Anniversary Vol. 1: Ska's the Limit*, Island Records, 1997.
23. Claude Mills, 'Lord Creator has a Passion for Ballads', *The Sunday Gleaner*, April 12, 1998, p.3E.
24. Albert Ribero, aka Lord Hummingbird and another Trinidadian expatriate, recorded a calypso that celebrated the independence of The Bahamas a few years later, and my guess is that calypsos were sung as Guyana, Bermuda and Barbados among others became independent, but so far my search has not located these.
25. <http://www.africaspeaks.com/articles/2004/23092.html>

4

FUGUES, FRAGMENTS AND FISSURES: A WORK IN PROGRESS

M. NourbeSe Philip

In fact, Americans of African descent might be *the* alienated people in this century. For if America represents for others an emancipation from the past, it means for black Americans an abduction from the past, into first the apocalypse of chattel slavery and then the more subtle horrors of racism, segregation, and "invisibility," creating the especially acute psychic tensions that we see in Ellison's novel.

Robert W. Rudnicki, *Percyscapes*

	Two white women travelling through Africa
Chorus:	*Africa*
	Find themselves in the hands of a cannibal witch doctor
Chorus:	*Witch doctor*
	He cook up one and he eat one raw
	She taste so good he wanted more
Chorus:	More more more
	He wanted more

The Mighty Sparrow, 'Congo Man'[1]

I am about 12 years old, legs lengthening into puberty and I know this calypso is rude — sexually suggestive — but I don't know how, although the laughter of the adults tell me all I need to know. Is big people business Sparrow singing about — about eating white meat and travelling through Africa. Of course, I know all about Africa: every Saturday we make our way to the local cinema, there to feast on cowboys and Indians and me-Tarzan-you-Jane. But this is my first introduction to Africa through the up-from-the-ground-behind-the-bridge art form of calypso. My first conscious memory, or so I believe for a long time, is of Africa.

Some of the most powerful and enduring tropes of Africa are present: travel, cannibals, witch doctors and sorcery. Through the white woman's body, gender will be the weapon of choice with which to challenge colonialism and racism. The black man will have his own back through consuming the white woman — literally and sexually. This was payback time in the nation's and people's history — the white man's trophy would be sexually used and bred into extinction through these metaphors of the raw and the cooked which, unknowingly, signalled Levi Strauss' organizing methodology of the raw and the cooked.

As many calypsos have done, 'Congo Man' was functioning as an aide mémoire about Africa. A fragment. Of a whole. A sliver or shard of memory in the psyche which if left would fester and suppurate. 'Congo Man' was also functioning, however, as an aid to amnesia, a way of erasing the past and allowing us to forget that which we didn't know as colonial subject — that Africa was and is more than cannibalism, witch doctors and sorcery. And in the between of these two states — remembering and forgetting — memory and amnesia lies the fissure.

I am always (re)turning. To the Caribbean. To Trinidad and to Tobago. The latter being my birth as well as spirit home in this part of the world.[2] On this particular visit I am staying in Bacolet, Tobago, on the Atlantic coast. The closest beach, a mere stone's throw away, Minster's Bay is washed by the Atlantic Ocean. If you stand on the beach facing the sea you are (re)turned towards Africa. The beach is seldom used because of the presence of rip tides; this means I often have it to myself. However, being a woman on a beach alone, even in Tobago, conjures up anxieties — how safe is this place? My s/p(l)ace?[3]

I had always believed 'Congo Man' to be my first introduction to Africa. It was not. Some years earlier, when I lived in Tobago, my family was visited by Coptic priests who had come to bless the then and still only Coptic Church in Tobago. These priests were from Ethiopia and they stayed with us. Tall slim, brown men in long black clothes and long hair that hung down their backs in curls. One of them wished to marry my older sister who would then have been about eight. The proposal was that she would continue to live with us until she came of age, at which time my mother would send her to him. In Ethiopia. In Africa. Unlike the case of 'Congo Man' where Africa becomes the over-determined trope, I cannot recall the word Africa being mentioned around the visit of the Coptic priests, although I imagine it must have been. Several times.

Had I fulfilled my dream and become a back-up singer, coolly riding the rhythms of the calypso, my role would have been to echo the word 'Africa', highlighting it, emphasizing its mystery, its apparent fathomlessness. As witness, recorder, griot, poet and teller of tales my role is similar to the back-up singer, echoing the word, but perhaps glossing it in another way.

If there were an earlier memory than this one it would have been Tarzan of Africa. The same Africa, complete with cannibal witch doctor that Sparrow sings about. Like the woman's body in 'Congo Man' which becomes the means through which he will challenge racism and colonialism, my sister's body was intended to be the means through which the broken circle would be completed. She would be the bartered bride — one body for a memory. Lost. And found.

Each and every Sunday we ate the white-host body of Christ, so that we could be saved; although not cannibal we drank his blood. In 'Congo Man' we would all participate in an entirely different eating — of the white woman's body. In both cases, however, we sought salvation as history pulled and pushed us along the trajectory of freedom. And Sparrow's laugh, 'Cyah cyah cyah,' riding over the sweet crooning voices of the back-up singers, explained without words what no adult would explain about the eating of humans. And gods.

Fragment

Journal, January 2004

I walk the beach almost every day — as is my custom I collect shells — if I manage not to pick up one then I can walk without picking up any — having picked up that first shell, or pebble, or piece of smoothed glass, I am then condemned to keep picking them up. This time I am keen to know their species and names — I have left my book on shells in Toronto so I buy another in a store in Black Rock and begin my quest. For fragments.

I find the fragments of shell more beautiful than the whole ones and today, reading a book on shells of the Caribbean, and again on the beach, am aware of preferring the broken ones and liking the challenge of trying to figure out the identity of the shell from the fragment. Have been able to identify Common Spirula, Decussate Bittersweet, Measle Cowrie and Magnum Cockle to name a few. Not to mention Atlantic Hairy Triton and West Indian Top Shell.

- am aware of how this idea of the fragment mirrors issues here in the Caribbean — we are fragments of a whole but can still be identified as such. Or can we?
- the islands themselves are volcanic and coral fragments.
- the w/holeness exists in the fragment — as the w/hole exists in the fragment of the text.
- found a cowrie shell — lovely the whole back missing but from the front it appears w/hole
- can fragments be an organizing principle for the Caribbean?
- how much of a shell can be lost before it is no longer a shell?
- *when does the fragment cease being a part of the w/hole? To become its own w/hole?*

Elvira: I had been lying on my bed at the hotel one afternoon and I came awake very suddenly. The radio was playing Eddy Grant. Do you know his song "Neighbour, Neighbour."[4] (*She hums the refrain and he shakes his head.*) There was something in the timbre of his voice –

Rohan: So, I've got Eddy Grant to thank for this?

Elvira: It was the first time I'd ever felt like that.

Rohan: Like what? Are you having an affair with Eddy Grant?

In *Coups and Calypsos*,[5] Elvira, an African–Trinidadian woman married to and separated from Rohan, an Indian Trinidadian, hears a fragment of a calypso which reverberates within her, stoking a desire to be with an African man. Something in Grant's voice, not to mention the melody, dislodges a memory of a former wholeness long forgotten. By the play's end she has embarked on a journey to find herself and ground that discovery in a discarded history and culture.

Fragment

Journal, 2002

There are three bands. In a pan yard. In Woodbrook. One of them is small — some youngsters or youth men and a few older men; some dreadlocked and some not; a couple of women. The pans — tenor, guitar and bass licking up the music; congo drums calling, shak shak shekere and scraper keeping the rhythm — thok thok thok thoc — two cylindrical sticks knock knocking together and keeping the beat and just so we right inside the music. There is a fire, an urgency, a calling out, a longing, an acknowledgement of a history — the savagery, the beauty, the absolute will to survive and the unquenchable impulse moving to the rhythm of the music and I seeing me myself and I and I in the young boy beating his heart out on a tenor pan as he laughing to dead into a riff that is the call that the other pans answering and the old man laughing too and shaking the tambourine with a joy on his old, gap-toothed face and I knowing in an instant that this too passing and we surviving, that we not dying, that we here — with sun shining bright bright, sea, sand, and poverty; with anger and with joy — that we be and be here — always moving, never standing still, never static.

A truly subversive thought that, given the AIDS pandemic that is ravaging the Caribbean and, in particular, Trinidad and Tobago, not to mention Africa. But there is a fragment. Of a w/hole that that pan side captured that evening — and through the fragment I could recognize the w/hole. Of something long forgotten.

My father demonstrates the jazz of memory by remembering everything he did not do and so filling the gaps, the black holes, the lacunae left by his failing, faltering and essentially fragile memory that crumbles at the touch of reality, so that everything you mention, each landmark, each place you pass, he has dreamt of or thought of — just — and so he riffs on absences and gaps, filling them with his own fictions, metamorphosing into a Lord, knighted by the Queen. Why not? Why the hell not? Like the calypsonian weaving from a fragment a whole, as s/he improvises on the fragments of his/her memory. Our collective fragments of memory. And isn't this what we do — improvise, filling the gaps in our memory with our fictions masquerading as truth dress up as lies playing ole marse with we minds,

Meantime is what I doing in dis here dream dat is not my own — is somebody else dream dis who dreaming me and we because I have memory and memory don't dream, memory is forever, is a melody you don't have to make up, not dream and pretend; and if you have memory how you forgetting because dreaming is only forgetting and what I doing in dis here dream — who dreaming dis dream, who dreaming dis dream ... calypso does remember and pan does remember and rapso and caiso but I does forget and dream and forget to dream or ... as Rudder saying, 'Is shake down time' and 'just another day in paradise'.[6]

Jean, Dinah, Rosita and Clementina were four prostitutes. They all lived in a calypso by Sparrow, the world's greatest calypso man. Jean, Dinah, Rosita and Clementina, their space a corner, a street corner, where they posing and selling what all men wanting — a piece of their space, the space between their legs. Jean, Dinah, Rosita and Clementina:

> Bet your life is something they selling
> And of you catch them broken
> You can get it all for nothing
> The Yankees gone and Sparrow take over now.
> Sparrow, "Jean and Dinah"[7]

Once again Sparrow going up in the white man face — the face of Empire but dis time is de yankee dem he taking on and once again is woman body and woman space he usin to score he points — calypso working in the service of memory — challenging us to remember those who meant us no good as slaves, peasants, negroes, coloured, black men and black women, yet working to erase woman and the reasons why Jean, Dinah, Rosita and Clementina might be forced to sell the space between their legs; forgetting that Sparrow might be taking over but all a we losing in the forgetting. Of woman.

Risking the sin of generalization I suggest that if we re/turn to the idea of how African cultures perform ritual we observe the mask or the costume (the artefact?) that has been created that is then extended into and by performance, the better to call down the ancestors or the spirit through prayer, spoken and unspoken, through utterance, spoken or sung, and once the spirit is called down and caught and the devotee mounted, all things are possible which is where what in the West is called improvisation begins. It is the catching of the spirit through performance that generates 'Caiso! Caiso!' Or the applause at the end of a jazz riff. There is memory and recognition. Of something once lost and regained. If only temporarily.

The mask is the given, the static, as is our history, and in the history of raw deals ours is one that brooks little competition. It is the calypsonian, like the reggae artist, the rapso performer, the jazz musician who takes the given into our modern day rituals of performance and through the performance of memory calls down the spirit on us. Often the mask is in fact the amnesia or the forgetting that the calypsonian or reggae artist transforms into memory. Calypso is our call to the ancestors through performing memory and with an incisive economy is also simultaneously newspaper, therapist, priest, confessor, is lament, exhortation, exultation and ululation — a call to arms with 'lyrics to make a politician cringe'.[8] But that memory is a two-edged sword on the one side of which is amnesia and on the other forgetting. In other words memory carries within it forgetting.[9] Just like 'Congo Man' carried both memory and forgetting.

Fragment

Journal, 2004

A blue sea — the horizon, white clouds, a blue sky, a butterfly and bird song — so much beauty, so much cruelty, so much, so very very much savagery:
de dream dead long live the dream of be — longinging, trying to weave a network of relationships dead in the blood.
here a cousin, there a cousin, every where a cousin but absent family.
Where you from?
Here.
Where.
Anywhere.
De one on monkey mountain or de one dat say massa day done, or de one massa say done. We is we own boss now. Is dat dream you talkin bout? Or remember how we use to sing how Africans never never never shall be slaves. Except is not Africans we used to be singin bout but Britons — cause we still slaving — dat dream never dead and dat is not we dream.
Lord Yeats (my father) once had dreams, as a boy — dreaming as he cutting grass for cow, horse an goat in a little village name Moriah in Tobago, dreaming as he dancing the cocoa dreaming

the dream dreaming him of bigger and better days — a piece a lan a piece a pork, dreaming the dream of an island independent an free who massa day done, not an island where der sprechen deutche and black still serving ... white, where dey resurrecting de plantation and calling it hotel and everybody still free. To dream:

> In words — in a "language of the people. Language for the people. Language by the people, honed and fashioned through a particular history of empire and savagery. A language also nurtured and cherished ... in the mouths of the calypsonians, Jean and Dinah, Rosita and Clementina, Mama look a boo boo, the cuss buds, the limers, the hos (whores), the jackabats, and the market women."[10]

The fragment is both/and: containing the w/hole while being at the same time a part of the w/hole — it compels us to see both the w/hole and the hole: impulse to memory and impulse to amnesia. The fragment is not static; it contains its opposite and it is that opposite — the impulse to forgetting and erasure that I call the fugue.

In *Percyscapes* Robert Rudnicki explores the dissociative disorder known as the fugue state:[11] 'A fugue state has no pre-determined length, the condition may last hours or months. Thus fugue represents a flight in two senses: an escape from one mode of consciousness to another, and a literal escape from home to a new or unfamiliar place'.[12] In fleeing from the usual, the individual forgets his or her earlier life and adopts a different identity. Trauma is often the precipitating factor and the new personality is not recognizable as having any link with the earlier one. The fugue state can, therefore, be seen as a way of protecting the mind and the psyche from overwhelming trauma and allows the individual to live 'normally'; it is a state of amnesia, often associated with wandering, and 'can be literal or figurative'.[13]

Chantwell Rudder's 'Madness', 'St. Ann's', or 'Just Another Day in Paradise' represent the fugue state in two senses: in one sense the fugue state is descriptive of the behaviour of an individual; in fact that is its most common usage.[14] I am suggesting that not only is it descriptive of our society but also of the state itself — our nation state can be described as a fugue state. Indeed, much of what I find incomprehensible in Trinbagonian society becomes comprehensible when I apply the concept of the fugue state to it — a state that allows groups and individuals to function as if 'normal' but whose behaviour is dissociative. Beginning with the political shenanigans which manifest as general corruption and contempt for the populace, whatever the party in power, the apparently utter contempt for life in Trinidad and Tobago and the loosening of the bounds that once held families and society: 'Whey we goin?' Rudder asks. 'St. Ann's' (the home for the mentally disturbed) the chorus replies. Many of these behaviours are a direct result of the poisonous legacy of colonialism — but it is a legacy we must confront in order to enter a more integrative state. And one of the ways to confront it is through memory — the memory fragment.

Calypso does remember, but calypso does forget too: calypso as memory or amnesia or both. Many calypsos and calypsonians serve to wake us from our dissociative states — Calypso Rose, David Rudder, Black Stalin, Ella Andal, Singing Sandra, Sparrow to name but a few. One overdetermined example would be Cro Cro and his 2004 calypso on kidnapping in which he advocated kidnapping the politicians ('Face Reality').[15] They had him to hang, as the saying goes, but the calypso was a wake up call, forcing the audience to engage with the issues of kidnapping. And to ask questions about how the state was dealing with the issue. Nor, am I only talking of the political calypso, or the calypso of social commentary — Melody's 'Mama Look a Booboo',[16] for instance, was funny but was also riffing on ideas of our 'ugliness' left by our erstwhile masters and still rampant in our collective psyche.

Increasingly, however, calypsos, particularly those that receive the most air play work to heighten and continue the dissociative, fugal state. They work to keep the people hived off from what it is they will not — cannot — face; from the 'normal' which is in fact a disturbed state, particularly if it is a fleeing from what cannot be faced. Many of these calypsos are nothing but a set of instructions, which the audience is expected to follow. Often they are primarily sexual in content but no longer indulging in the clever word play and double entendre of earlier calypsos. Carnival culture, which is the primary context of the calypso, has been evacuated of much of its substance. As the carnival bands have become little more than bikinis and beads, so too have the calypsos that are given prominence become little more than empty refrains exhorting the crowds to move left or right, or take something and wave. To fugue.

In this age of the brand and the logo, Trinidad and Tobago's brand is Carnival. Unfortunately this results in the carnivalization and accompanying sexualization of society. While it is important that carnival arts like calypso have become a part of the school curriculum, what we also have now is teachers taking time off before carnival to prepare and to fete and after carnival to recover.[17] Students, unsurprisingly, follow suit. The fall-out from the increased sexualization is often fatal. Particularly as it relates to the increase in HIV/AIDS in Trinidad and Tobago. Sexual tourism is now very much a part of the tourist industry in Tobago and it is commonplace to read news reports of doctors expressing concern about the increase in HIV/AIDS testing after Carnival, which speaks to the increase in risky sexual behaviour during the season.

Newspapers are in the business to sell newspapers not necessarily news, and anything that smacks of the extreme, particularly in matters sexual will make the news. But surely, photographs of Machel Montano a hair's breath away from performing cunnilingus on one of his Powder Puff girls, while being described as a role model for youth passes all understanding. Unless, as I am suggesting, we understand Trinidad and Tobago society to be in a dissociative state. A fugue state. Fleeing from a trauma — an unacknowledged trauma — it simply cannot face.

Neither Trinidad and Tobago nor Caribbean societies in general are unique in having to grapple with the psychic, societal, and material disintegration that are an integral part of the modern capitalist society: the atomization of society, the breakdown of communities, the dissipation of family ties, the hiving off of generations, the emphasis on youth culture at the expense of the wisdom of the elders. The list is infinite. To which we must add, within the context of a society like Trinidad and Tobago, the legacy of empire, colonialism and its attendant scourges like racism. And to which again we must add the fact that it is a 'developing' society, a 'Third World' country that leads the pack in terms of modern day plagues like HIV/AIDS. The matrix of all this is the 400 year history of slavery which destroyed so much in African life.

Fragment

Journal, January 2004

I met a doctor yesterday at Bacolet Bay — we talk of life in Tobago. He is a gynaecologist. He talks about the rampant sexuality indulged in by young people in Tobago. Older professional women now are entirely celibate, he says, compared to ten years ago when there was an assumption that having a sexual relationship was an expected part of life. Women in low-end jobs, at hotels for instance, 'have to have one man to pay the light bill, another for the phone bill'. Older men prey on young girls. There is a lack of leadership, he says. He is Indian from Guyana where he was a member of the Ratoon group in Guyana in which Indians and Africans worked together to understand each other's cultures. Where he grew up, he tells me, all the teachers were black. If you needed a letter you went to the teacher who was black. There was a very low literacy rate among Indians, he says, now it's reversed among his black brothers and sisters. Now they're the ones with low literacy. And, I think to myself, in Port of Spain, Toronto London and LA they are shooting each other. All the little black boys that Baron sang about. He works on an individual basis, he tells me, trying to encourage young women he meets to get into nursing. In 50 years, he says, the demographics in Tobago will be entirely different as a result of HIV/AIDS. He seems a fair man and much of what he says I agree with. He shares with me that he has married outside his group — to a Black woman — which gives him a certain perspective on both sides of the racial divide so to speak.

The waves push us this way and that. I am nervous — wary of the sea and mindful that this is the Atlantic side of the island where you're cautioned to take your passport if you go swimming.

The question in my journal: why has their spirituality appeared so much more resistant than ours? Even on the continent. Why aren't we convinced of the beauty of what we have and who we are?

In *African Genius*, Basil Davidson, in describing how different groups came to terms with their often harsh environments, writes of the 'deep wisdom' of Africa that understood that: 'religious needs (lay) at heart of social evolution. Social needs, that is, were conceived in religious terms'.[18] Religious not in terms of how we think of religion today, but a deep, spiritual understanding of the relationships between ancestors and the land and community that bind us. These connections have been severed, ruptured by our peculiar history into fragments and fugues or fuguing fragments.

Memory/amnesia. A memory triggered when Rudder sings the Our Father exhorts us to give thanks and we, the chorus, answer him and do (give thanks, that is, albert through the veil of Christianity), thereby overriding the amnesia generated by slavery and colonialism.

Fragment

Journal, January 2004

Here there are stairs — either of buildings that once existed but now no longer, or buildings once in the process of being built but now abandoned. In either case they lead nowhere.

Yesterday driving along the Bacolet Road that borders the cemetery — cars line the way — people are dressed in white, lavender, purple or black–but they are drinking and dancing in the street. At a funeral.

The whole society appears to have lost any moral bearing despite the plethora of churches of all denominations. We have aped our erstwhile master — the European — who had nothing to teach us in morals or spirituality.

Fragment

Journal, February 2004

In the morning I read C.L.R. James — I laugh a lot. He has quite a way of skewering the English. Then I read Lamming this morning. Ten years ago when I moved back to Tobago I was reading Lamming. Also Mittleholzer — re-reading a *Morning at the Office* — as pertinent today as when it was first written. Then I read Mario Varga Llosa and I come upon a longing for a woman's voice in all this — James is surprising at times in the nonsense he writes about women but oh for a woman's sensibility and what do I do as a woman when I look back and all I see is this unending line of men stretching back — James, Lamming, Mittleholzer, Dessalines, Toussaint. The only woman who comes to mind is Sylvia Wynter. And Claudia Jones. These men are the planks over the swampy bogs of history — mangrove swamps perhaps?

I envy the women their cool calm collected acceptance of the largesse of their flesh, their sang-froid, their slowness. Yet I am at times irritated by it.

Read the Review *yesterday and my god! Not a single woman was mentioned in the entire edition — all the photographs are of men!*

Fragment

(Excerpt from letter) February 2004

I think it interesting that at one time the West Indies was known the world over for its cricket teams, which kicked butt, albeit in an entirely male-focused activity, and today we're known for carnival — not kicking butt but showing butt. And there's no coincidence that we are witnessing the currently disastrous performance of the West Indian cricket team.

Having said that, however, as I read and re-read *Beyond the Boundary*, I am overwhelmed by the fact that this activity that defined the Caribbean and shaped how the region was seen is so male. This is a game that we didn't even play as girls or women– how then do I position myself in this activity? As spectator? Beyond the boundary? I want to resist that impulse to find the female equivalent — Sylvia Wynter is one of the most brilliant thinkers, with a formidable intellect and I believe that her failure to garner more attention in the region is because she is female. So too with Claudia Jones. But finding the female equivalent is not the answer; although I must say the other day I was thinking that the Admiral of the Oceans, Columbus, was actually sent by a woman, not a man. It was Queen Isabella, wasn't it, who charged him with the task of finding a way to the east. That's a bit too close to the behind every great man is a woman. No, I see the men of the African Caribbean as continuing the project of patriarchy, much as I value their insights and scholarship. They have answered the master in the language of the master — it's like cricket, isn't it, beating the master at his own game. (And I am reminded of

Audre Lorde and the impossibility of using the master's tools to dismantle the master's house.) But that particular game is over and maybe the language doesn't exist yet in which what has yet to be done must be done. Is it the language of Sycorax? After all, Caliban acknowledged that he held the island through and by her. And what is her language?

It is sometimes the language of the calypso — not simply the words but the deeper language — the meta-language. The German scholar Leo Frobenius was of the opinion that in African cultures language did not, as in the West, serve only to communicate ideas, but also brought the imagination to life and enlivened the object world. This for me is the mask coming to life through performance — the mask of history, a false history, being removed and through calypso our memory is animated. Calypso has the potential of bringing us out of that fugue state where we flee the reality of what has been and is still around us. Using the Caribbean demotic, vernacular or nation language, calypsonians have sung our hopes and our dreams, have sent up the stupidities of the colonial masters, and present day politicians; have poked fun at ourselves and bigged us up; reminding us to remember.

In contrast:

> Whole cadres of educated elites in the Caribbean are selected for eminence by schooling on the confident premise that they know little or nothing about the societies for which they are responsible. The great merit for which our validating elites are celebrated is their half education. There is so much that they know about the rest of the world. It is of course the root cause of the signal incapacity of Afro Saxon culture to abandon its obsession with formulas and clichés ... an elite unable to describe its own reality by using concepts and designations that spring out of its own experience.
>
> Lloyd Best[19]

The inability of Afro Saxon culture to 'describe its own reality' is, I'm suggesting expressive of a dissociative state — a fugue state. A state of amnesia.

Fragment

Journal, February 2004

Estate and plantation houses are always seen as romantic places, showpieces with nothing of the history of terror that attaches to them.

There is a BBC report of an earthquake in Iran: the presenter speaks of the people losing their bearings because of loss of family, loss of home — he says they are suffering from post-traumatic shock syndrome. And I realize that, indeed, that is what we — this society, our society — suffers from, post-traumatic shock syndrome. That is also perhaps what Africa suffers from.

Body Pond Estate, Antigua

The article appears in the lushly produced *Maco*, a magazine about luxury living in the Caribbean. The article describes a renovation to an old plantation house. As always, a romantic old plantation house. But its name, Body Pond, disturbs me and I fear what further reading confirms, that the estate got its name from a pond where Africans, in an attempt to escape, drowned. Now, the estate, house, garden and pond, owned by a Syrian woman is displayed as a showpiece, with but a brief reference to 'the island's only river *legend*' (emphasis added) which takes 'its name from the fact that in a desperate bid to flee servitude, plantation slaves had been known to hurl themselves into the water where they met with a tragic death'. Body Pond. Antigua. Body Pond. The Atlantic. Memory/Amnesia. Fragment/fugue.

Fragment

Journal, March 2004

When I am here I live in History — it is all around.
– That time of the day when everything darkens becomes silhouetted, black cut outs — the fringed coconut palm — an image so associated with the tropics — the Caribbean — it comes as a surprise that they are not indigenous but they have made

these islands home and metamorphosed into a visual signifier of sorts for the area. Their manner of arrival — nuts borne or carried on the seas to wash up here, there, or anywhere is a metaphor for how we came here as well — to make this place our home unhome.

– *Stumps of the coconut trees like so many dismembered arms lacking hands having clawed their way out of the sand, reach out, yearning, reaching reaching ... towards sea, the ocean, the Atlantic — to Africa. Over there. Past the horizon ...*

– And the sea, her hunger sated, spits us up — so much flotsam and jetsam on these hard rocks of indifference passing as island paradises of sun, sea and sex. Where revolutions and dreams in equal measure are born only to die.

– *The architecture, if you can call it that, approximates the fort — big square and obzoky, no concession made to the environment that invites openness; houses modelling themselves instead on the closed-in northern type of house — by passing for the most part the gracious, graceful elements of the colonial period, to imitate villas of the Mediterranean with red clay roofs, or approximations of the pared down postmodern style, or simply, the big white fortress towering above the landscape — a dinosaur on concrete legs. Ugly is the word that comes to mind often in a land so overwhelmingly beautiful.*

It is an absolutely beautiful day — on the plantation — clear blue skies, bird song, the huge leaves like sculptures — am struck by how certain plants occupy space.

Am on the plantation and in the great house — literally and it is pleasant being in the great house, but I can never forget myself. We can never forget ourselves.

A bird is on the table, a brown dove walks across the tiled floor head moving in that funny propulsive way that birds do.

An alternate but original meaning of the fugue is a musical composition with polyphonic elements in which 'themes are developed contrapuntally'.[20] Usually there is a melody or melodic phrase that is repeated in different keys and at different intervals. In this sense of the word, too, Trinidad and Tobago and the Caribbean can also be described as fugal societies — polyphonic societies, culturally and racially and ethnically. Societies in which the harsh melodies of loss and exile and be/longing for a re/turn are repeated over and over again in different keys and at different intervals. Societies in which these melodies come from different societies and cultures, some of which, like the African and the Asian carry with them polyphonic and polyrhythmic musical traditions. Fugal societies in two senses of the word — both dissociative and polyphonic. And it is the calypsonian that has the potential to heal the former and allow the polyphonies to grow.

What, if anything, does this have to do with the literary imagination? Calypso and literature both attempt to explain who we are to ourselves and what we are doing here. Wherever here may be. But the literary imagination is directed to the written and calypso to the oral and performative traditions. They both serve important functions in these postcolonial societies and remain in productive tension with each other as complementary ways to integrate and move a fractured society toward w/holeness.

... And just like the names Totoben and Maisie giving themselves when they singing calypso-Exploiter, Roaring Lion, Tiger, Lord Kitchener, Lord Melody. The Mighty Sparrow, Calypso Rose — the names talking about how Totoben and Maisie moving from slave shack to the street, about how Totoben and Maisie through Black Stalin ready to fight for their moving:

> I spend so much money to buy this costume
> now I ready to jump
> you better give me room
> I make so much a plan just to play dis marse
> now is time to play
> give me room to pass
> I want to jam down
> roll down
> shake down
> all around town
> dis marse is for you and you and you
> so move move you blocking up the place
> so move
> I want to shake my waist
> the people want to jam
> so get out of the band
> I say move
>   Black Stalin, "Move"[21]

Notes

1. The Mighty Sparrow, (Slinger Francisco), 'Congo Man'. *Congo Man/Patsy* 7" National NSP 052, 1965.
2. According to the Haitian Quebecois writer, Max Dorsinville, in his work *Le Pays Natal: Essais sur les littératures du Tiers-Monde et du Québec* (Dakar: Nouvelles Editions Africaines, 1983), the archetype of return marks the work of writers of the Afrospora — whether it be a metaphorical return in literature or a real return as in writers like Aimé Cesaire returning to their homes after an extended sojourn in the metropolis. Return to Africa is also a significant aspect of this archetype.
3. In 'Dis Place—the Space Between', *Genealogy of Resistance and Other Essays* (Toronto: Mercury Press, 1997), 74–112, I argue that for women the outer space is inflected by the perception of how safe the space between the legs is.
4. Eddie Grant, 'Neighbour Neighbour'. 12" Ensign, 1981.
5. Marlene NourbeSe Philip, *Coups and Calypsos: A Play* (Ontario: The Mercury Press, 1996).
6. David Rudder, 'Another Day in Paradise', *No Restriction*. Triple CD Lypsoland CR 027, 1997.
7. Sparrow, 'Jean and Dinah', *Sparrow in London*. LP RA RA 2127, 1970.
8. David Rudder, 'Calypso Music', *Calypso Music 10th Anniversary*. LP Lypsoland CR06/CR/07, 1987.
9. Bernice Reagon a folklorist and founder of the musical group, Sweet Honey in the Rock, in talking of African culture in the new world, has said that because our societies were so materially impoverished, we had to make our cultures work for us; it had to carry everything. Barnard College, 109th Commencement, New York, May 15, 2001.
10. Marlene NourbeSe Philip, *'The Absence of Writing or How I Almost Became a Spy.' She Tries Her Tongue: Her Silence Softly Breaks* (Charlottetown, PEE: Ragweed Press, 1988), 84.
11. Fugue is from the Latin word meaning flight. The term is also used to describe musical composition that is polyphonic and contrapuntal in style.
12. Robert W. Rudnicki, *Percyscapes: The Fugue State in Twentieth-Century Southern Fiction* (Baton Rouge: Louisiana State University Press, 1999), 9, especially the chapter on 'Fugue and the Modern Literary Mind', 1–35.
13. Rudnicki, *Percyscapes*.
14. As Philip explains subsequently, 'St. Ann's' is a refrain in the chorus of David Rudder's 'Madness', *Calypso Music 10th Anniversary*. LP Lypsoland CR06/CR/07, 1987.
15. Cro Cro, (Weston Rawlins), 'Face Reality', *Face Reality 2004*. CD Abstracts Entertainment, 2004.
16. Lord Melody, (Ftizroy Alexander), 'Mamma Look a Booboo', *Mamma Look a Booboo /Missin' Chicken*. 78; 7" Monogram M950, 1955.
17. Coversation with a teacher at a high school in Tobago.
18. Basil Davidson, *The African Genius* (Oxford: James Curry, 1969), 9, 50.
19. Lloyd Best, *The Express*. December 13, 2002.
20. Rudnicki, *Percyscapes*, 7.
21. Black Stalin, (Leroy Calliste), 'Move', *The Bright Side*. LP Strakers GS 2337, 1991.

SANS HUMANITÉ: THE SONG, THE SINGER AND THE STORY

5

CARNIVAL CANNIBALIZED OR CANNIBAL CARNIVALIZED: CONTEXTUALIZING THE 'CANNIBAL JOKE' IN CALYPSO AND LITERATURE

Gordon Rohlehr

Congo Man

The Mighty Sparrow first performed 'Congo Man' at Queen's Hall, Port of Spain, Trinidad, early in October 1964.[1] Over four decades since then, he has performed it regularly and recorded it six times.[2] Treating it as a sort of signature tune, Sparrow delights in creating a new version of strange sounds every time he performs it. 'Congo Man' has been cited by journalist Debbie Jacob as 'Sparrow's own all-time favourite'.[3] An intriguing calypso that only Sparrow can convincingly perform, 'Congo Man' has raised questions about the centuries-old encounter between Africa and Europe in arenas of ethnicity, culture, gender and politics; the racial stereotyping that has been an almost timeless aspect of this encounter; the erasure of any clear image of Africa from the minds of diasporan African-ancestored citizens of the New World, and the carnivalesque performance of 'Africa' in the transfigurative masquerades of Trinidad and New Orleans.

The plot of 'Congo Man' is very simple: two white women travelling through Africa — for what reason the calypso does not say — find themselves in hostile Congolese terrain, deep in the hinterland of the fierce and hungry Baluba, one of whose warriors captures them, cooks one in a big pot and devours the other one raw. The Congo Man, unnamed in the first version of the calypso, but identified by the narrator in subsequent versions as 'my big brother Umba' is almost delirious with delight and laughs, giggles, growls, screams, dances round and round his marinating prey, joyfully chanting the refrain: 'Ah never eat a white meat yet.' The narrator, a typical 'macco' frequently found in barrack-yard type calypsos, claims to have witnessed the Congo Man's performance from his vantage point among the bushes, and proclaims his envy for the Congo Man whom he feels an urge to congratulate because, like him, the narrator 'never eat a white meat yet'.

The narrator offers no explanation for his presence in Africa, which seems to be as gratuitous as that of the two white female travellers or adventurers. This paper will seek to locate 'Congo Man' within the context of the post-independence 'Congo crisis' and to determine as far as possible where Sparrow stood as a person of African descent observing this ever unfolding catastrophe. Using the metaphor suggested by 'Congo Man', this paper will try to determine from what bushes, from what vantage point in the jungle of his heart does Sparrow gaze on his Congolese brother and double. This paper will be particularly concerned with both 'big brother Umba's' strange ecstatic laughter and the seemingly inexhaustible delight with which Sparrow as narrator/protagonist has over four decades performed Umba's laughter. Our enquiry points to the conclusion that the grotesquerie of both Umba's laughter and Sparrow's enactment of it is inseparable from the reductive spirit of Carnival masquerade, which, unmasked, reveal a horror, the skull beneath the skin-teeth.

Historical Background to the Making of 'Congo Man'

In 1966 Sparrow, in an interview with journalist Wayne Brown, explained how 'Congo Man' came to be composed:

> "The Congo Man" came to me on a subway in New York — just the melody. And the lyrics came from the many activities in Africa at the time. So many nuns and priests were being ambushed and beaten, you know.... And I got the idea that this was probably happening there: white people were just traveling through and found themselves in the hands of head hunters, you know, who put them in a pot, had a fire at the bottom, and had a chant. (That's where the "haw, haw, haw" comes in). Jump up and down and see how the food is cooking, and forbid anybody to fraternize with the meat.[4]

According to Sparrow 'Congo Man' was purely humorous and completely unsuggestive. If even one were to take the calypso on a purely literal plane, one would still be faced with the problem of explaining how such grim circumstances as the killings and cannibalism that were being reported about the Congo, could engender such pure and unsuggestive humour and laughter.

What Sparrow calls 'the activities in Africa at the time' was really the tragic disintegration of the Congo in the years after Belgium on June 30, 1960, suddenly thrust independence on the over 200 ethnic nationalities whose land Belgium had invaded, exploited with barbaric ferocity and left completely unprepared for the challenge of independence and nation building. Two weeks after he was elected prime minister of an independent Congo, Patrice Lumumba was faced with the secession of mineral-rich Katanga and army mutiny. He spent a desperate few months trying to regain the power he had never been allowed to exercise with what remained of his army, but was captured by Mobutu's troops, handed over to his rival, Tshombe, and executed on January 17, 1961.

Martyred, Lumumba became a greater inspiration to resistance than when he was alive. The Simbas, a ragged guerilla army of youth led by Pierre Mulele, Lumumba's Minister of Education, developed a reputation for fierce merciless modes of fighting. Reinterpreting the idea of the primitive for the purpose of inspiring terror, they wore war paint, armed themselves with bows and arrows, spears, machetes and sharpened bicycle chains nailed to pieces of wood. They regarded themselves as the true and pure flame of Lumumba's revolution and viewed the monument that had been set up in his honour in Stanleyville as a shrine. Advancing United Nations (UN) peacekeeping troops destroyed the Lumumba monument in 1964.

Disintegration had set in even before independence with the departing Belgians, who actively encouraged tribal rivalries that had traditionally existed between such large ethnicities as the Baluba and the Lulula (Lulua). The Belgian strategy was the simple time-honoured one of divide and rule. Their interest lay in Katanga, whose mineral wealth in copper, uranium, cobalt, diamonds and gold had replaced the original commodities, ivory and rubber, as the main pillars upon which the economy of modern Belgium had been erected. Inter-tribal warfare would, it was believed, drain the new nation of the energy and unified focus necessary for controlling its own resources. They were correct, but they did not anticipate that the warring tribes, together with the young lions, the Simbas, would not only destroy each other, but would also direct their energies against the most defenceless among their common enemy, the Belgians. So the Baluba–Lulula holocaust of burnt villages, hacked corpses and raped and cannibalized cadavers spread from being an almost self-contained 'sacrificial crisis'— to appropriate René Girard's term in *Violence and the Sacred*[5] — to becoming a free-for-all of killing in which isolated lumber camps or Christian missionary outposts were as much prey as the thatched rural villages of the Baluba or Lulula.

It was at that point that the Congo catastrophe became for Europeans a crisis, and the killings a massacre.

D'Lynn Waldron, foreign correspondent and war photographer for the *New York Herald Tribune*, describes the growing anarchy that ensued even in the months before Independence. At one mission, Baluba villagers 'butchered Lulua (sic) women and children for meat'.[6] Both groups continued the tradition of King Leopold II's pacification troops when they chopped off the hands of captured enemies; but they also improved on Leopold's style by 'slaughtering and eating their victims'.[7]

Some commentators were puzzled at the upsurge of cannibalism that accompanied the dreadful, inter-tribal war. One missionary surmised: 'They are fighting a war, so they must have protein. The bodies of their enemies are the only source of protein available'. Waldron, however, disagreed.

> But, as I have seen, the cannibalism in the Congo was also used as a form of terrorism. Very soon there were so many bodies that only the rump roasts were removed and the rest left to rot. Entrepreneurs saw the commercial value of what the warriors left behind and the government had to pass a law that no meat could be sold without some sort of hide attached.[8]

Waldron complained that the newspapers in America to which she wired her articles tended to omit her political and economic commentaries and ask for more cannibal stories. But who could blame them when she produced such delicious tit-bits as the last quotation? It was, perhaps, such stories about cannibalism that might have inspired Sparrow's 'Congo Man.' *Time* magazine carried a weekly column on the Congo in which occasionally, as on January 18, 1963, stories of cannibalism occurred. There, however, it was two white men, not women, who were eaten. *Time* reported:

> The point was underlined in blood last week in Kasai province, where feuding tribesmen were at one another's throats over a border dispute. Natives kidnapped and reportedly ate two Belgian lumbermen, then began slaughtering one another in the town of Kakenge. Such gruesome incidents no longer surprised anyone.

A Leopoldville newspaper reported that event as matter-of-factly as it were a baseball-box score. Its headline: KILLED AT KAKENGE – 370 LULULAS, TWO BELGIANS, ONE MUSONGE, ONE KANYOKA.[9]

Sparrow, no doubt influenced by Spoiler's bed bug, would not for the world be inveigled into eating any hard-arsed male. The particular incident that may have prompted Sparrow to compose 'Congo Man' was the January 1964 uprising in Kwilu province, 250 miles east of Leopoldville, where 'roving gangs of youths hacked to death three Belgian Roman Catholic priests — one of them bedridden'.[10] Also attacked in this raid were two white American women, Ruth Hege and Irene Ferrel, both of whom were Baptist missionaries. Ferrel was killed by an arrow, while Hege survived only because her assailants thought that she too had been killed when they saw her lying prostrate, covered with blood but feigning death. Here, then, was a graphic report of two white women who were not just travelling through Africa, but committedly sharing their lives in the perilous and ambiguous adventure of bringing the Christian word and Western civilization to Sparrow's 'big brother Umba' of the Baluba. These Kwilu killings, taking place as they did in the middle of the Carnival and calypso season of 1964 and involving priests and missionaries, provided Sparrow with the connection he was to make later in the year, between the horrible events that were taking place in real life and their grotesquely twisted, carnivalesque misrepresentation in the calypso 'Congo Man.'

Congo Man 'Cannibalizes' Carnival 1965

One person in Trinidad who had good reason to connect 'Congo Man' to lurid news reports on the Congo crisis, was schoolteacher Valda Sampson who in mid-February 1965 invited Sparrow to Mount Lambert Roman Catholic primary school to perform 'Congo Man' to an audience of school children and old age pensioners, many of whom entered into the festive spirit of the calypso and sang along with Sparrow. Ms Sampson, founder and patron of an arm of the Red Cross, the Verbena Junior Red Cross Link, thought she was performing an act of charity by hosting the event. She was, however, bitterly condemned in the press by the Roman Catholic Archbishop, Count Finbar Ryan, for bringing Sparrow to school 'to teach children filthy songs'.[11] The Catholic Teachers Association 'probed' the Mount Lambert incident.[12] Several schools decided to boycott a Junior Calypso King competition that Sparrow was sponsoring, and to stage, instead, their own in-house competitions.[13] On top of all this, the Director of the Junior Red Cross wrote Sampson a letter condemning her and her effort.[14]

Recalling the incident nearly 20 years later, Sampson simultaneously exonerated herself and unmasked what she thought to be the real source of 'Congo Man' and the unstated reason for the rancorous Roman Catholic reaction to the song. She wrote:

> A few days later, on a visit to the Red House, I spied a copy of *Time Magazine* and chose to read an article titled "Massacre in the Congo." According to the article, cannibals had eaten two nuns and two priests in the Congo in Africa. I could only come to the conclusion that Sparrow, apparently better read than many people, was relating in his own inimitable style, a true story. There was nothing filthy about the calypso ... unless, as in the words of another ditty, it was "de vice in dey own head".[15]

Sampson was both right and wrong. Sparrow's calypso had indeed been a reaction to several news reports since 1960 about cannibalism in the Congo, including those in early 1964 about attacks on nuns and priests, such as the *Time* report on the January 1964 uprising in Kwilu province. But the *Time* magazine that Sampson had discovered in the Red House with the front-page headline, 'The Congo Massacre' (not 'Massacre in the Congo') was dated December 4, 1964,[16] while Sparrow's first performance of 'Congo Man' had happened two months earlier in October 1964. By the second week of January 1965, the calypso had been played so many times on the radio that a tough San Fernando audience, claiming to have grown tired of both 'Congo Man' and 'Get to Hell Outa Here', booed Sparrow when he performed in January 1965.[17]

Such negative responses as the Roman Catholic and San Fernando ones were, ironically, testimony of the degree to which 'Congo Man' had captured the imagination of the Trinidad public, with its simple graphic lyrics, its easy sing-along chorus, and the opportunity it offered for mime and role playing. 'Congo Man' was a performance piece that had grown out of two contexts that were widely familiar to mas-playing Trinidadians. First there was the context of the whole wide/white world of cannibal jokes, jungle movies set in Africa or Haiti and cartoons such as the well-known one of the cannibal who was looking forward to his second taste of the clergy. Secondly, there was the specific performance context of the Trinidad Carnival, which was replete with portrayals of wild, savage men, warriors, Warrahoons, headhunters, devils of all hues and varieties, monsters of the folkloric and cinematic imagination and Ju Ju warriors. Besides this, Sparrow had erupted on the calypso scene at precisely the same time that the great mas' designer George Bailey had generated an interest in rendering picturesque carnivalesque representations of 'Africa' and other 'exotic' places. Bailey produced *Back to Africa* in 1957, the same year as King Fighter's calypso of the same name. Bailey continued with *The Relics of Egypt* (1959), reflecting the then current trend in pan-Africanist discourse to explore linkages between Egyptian civilization and those of sub-Saharan Africans both in the eastern and western regions of the continent. Dennis Williams's novel *Other Leopards*[18] is a neglected but important illumination of the anguish and complexity of relocating the hybridized diasporan in either ancestral or contemporary postcolonial African spaces.

Masqueraders in San Fernando Carnival 1964 presented *The Glamour and Horror of Africa* as if to summarize the ambivalence that current events in the Congo and many other parts of Africa had reopened in schizophrenic diasporan consciousnesses. Walcott's celebrated 'A Far Cry from Africa'[19] was, in the early 1960s, the most powerfully articulated poetic expression of this ambivalence. The *Glamour and the Horror of Africa* featured among the characters, a gigantic gorilla, first cousin, no doubt, to Mighty Joe Young or King Kong. George Bailey crowned his late 1950's achievements with *Somewhere in New Guinea* (1962) in which he included individual masqueraders such as the witchdoctor and the magician. Bailey's last great production would be *Brightest*

Africa (1969). This however was long after the 'Congo Man' and, like the Stanleyville Massacre of December 1964, could not have influenced its making.

Interest in Africa was certainly awakened by Dr Eric Williams's 1964 tour of 11 African states which virtually coincided with some of the grim events described above (for example, the Kwilu uprising that had occurred only a fortnight before Williams and his touring party set out for Africa). The objective of Williams's tour was, according to him, to form 'a political bridge between the West and Africa, mindful too ... of how dangerous a bridge can be if it is not soundly constructed and properly maintained'.[20] President Tubman of Liberia generously showered his nation's highest honours and titles on both Williams and his 12-member entourage. Williams was awarded 'The Grand Band of the Star of Africa', Liberia's oldest title, while tour members Lee, Halsely McShine, Kamaluddin Mohammed, Isabel Teshea, Ellis Clarke and others, all became Grand Commanders of the Order of African Redemption.[21]

Sparrow in 'Get to Hell Outta Here' (1965)[22] did not seem to be particularly inspired by Williams's attempt to build a bridge across the Middle Passage. Sharing a scepticism that was in fact, quite widespread in Trinidad, he referred to the tour as Williams's 'African Safari'. One, indeed, speculates that it was his irreverent portrait of Williams in 'Get to Hell Outta Here,' much more than the crowd's tiredness with 'Congo Man', that earned Sparrow the boos he received in San Fernando when he presented both songs there in January 1965. Lord Blakie in 'The Doctor Ent Deh' (1965)[23] ungenerously viewed the tour of Africa as Williams's attempt to escape from the growing social chaos in Trinidad, particularly in Williams's own South-East Port of Spain ghetto constituency. The safari was, according to Blakie, a dereliction of the responsibility to govern that as a leader Williams had undertaken.

While Williams was touring Africa, his then young Minister of Finance A.N.R. Robinson was publishing every week in the *Trinidad Guardian* a series of articles on Africa entitled 'The New Frontier and the New Africa'.[24] Published on Fridays between January and February 1964, Robinson's articles endeavoured to present Africa in a new light to readers who had only been offered glimpses of the horror of African peoples, politics and society.

Like George Bailey's carnival productions then, Robinson's articles sought to counter traditionally negative stereotypes about Africa and Africans by suggesting the possibilities that were realizable if the rest of the world were to approach Africa with an unbiased gaze. When Robinson mentioned the Congo it was in relation to what the Cubists had been able to derive from the sculpture of the Basonge, Balege and Ababua, as well as the 'round sculpture' in the Western and Southern Congo.[25]

'Congo Man' was inspired neither by Williams's historical voyage of reconnection nor Robinson's effort to relocate African civilizations within the congress and discourse of all 'otherworld' civilizations. Its relationship to pan-Africanist consciousness, to what Naipaul, quoting John Hearne, termed in *The Middle Passage* 'the sentimental camaraderie of skin',[26] was at best ambivalent, oblique and skeptical. Sparrow in 1964, despite the moving sentimentality of 'Slave' (1963)[27] and 'Martin Luther King for President' (1964)[28] seemed to feel no real commitment to African causes, Africans or Africanity. In his 1966 interview with Wayne Brown, Sparrow denied any notion that he as a diaspora African ought to demonstrate some sort of loyalty to African roots: 'I'm not aware of any roots in Africa. I know where my ancestors came from, but I don't see why I should go BACK to Africa when I've never BEEN there. 'Back to Africa' should be for those who WERE in Africa.'[29] This was standard diasporan ideology at the time. One might compare Louise Bennett's poem, 'Back to Africa', with its scathing lines: 'Yuh haffe come from somewhere first / Before yuh go back deh!'[30]

This sentiment was irrefutable in its straightforward, honest literalness, and even such masters of double-meanings and indirectness as calypsonians could be plain and literal when it suited them. Yet this near total denial of linkages to Africa also reflected the colonizer's success in erasing both memory and consciousness of Africa from African-ancestored diasporans. It was this obliteration of the past along with Caucasian control, dissemination and manipulation of stereotypical images of Africa and Africans at home and abroad that had made Sparrow indifferent to African sensitivity in his appropriation of the cannibal–monster stereotype for the purpose of subversive laughter.

Carole Boyce Davies observed in 1985, when the issue of the meaning of 'Congo Man' was clearly still not settled, that critics had taken two basic positions on the calypso:

> Discussion of this calypso is best summarized in the positions taken by Gordon Rohlehr and Lloyd Brown. Gordon Rohlehr sees it as 'the most disturbing example of the "phallic calypso" which Sparrow has projected throughout his career, especially since it was the recreation of an actual rape of some Belgian nuns in 1964. He adds that it is an excellent indicator of the West Indian's cultural limbo for Sparrow has used the white man's stereotype of the African, which reveals his divorce from the African, to make a deep and serious joke against the whites, which reveals his alienation from the whites. But in so doing, he reveals a deep psychic need within the West Indian to prove his manhood through a fulfilled phallic vengeance for ancestral rape; which proves his alienation from himself.

Lloyd Brown provides another excellent analysis, seeing 'Congo Man' as an important reversal of the stereotypes of Africans created by whites, an expropriation of the 'grinning Beast mask' for ironic ends.

> The Congo Man is an object of ridicule, not as an African reality, but as an image which White Westerners have about Africans and other blacks: Africans are savages, and all Black men have an insatiable bestial appetite for White women. Hence the song's laughter becomes an important satiric weapon that is typical of the calypsonian's irony. The animal sounds of expectation reproduce White myths about Black sexuality ... the Black man's desire–hate for the White woman, as an object of sexual craving and racial 'revenge' is dramatized by the sadistic fulfilment implied by the cannibal motif.[31]

This essay, by tracing 'Congo Man' to its several possible sources, reinforced Rohlehr's 1970 observation about Sparrow's alienation from the African. Sparrow himself had in 1966 proclaimed his disconnection from, or more precisely, his sense of never having been tangibly connected to Africa. Sparrow's entry into and laughter through and at the Cannibal stereotype was, as I hope to show, even more complex and certainly more ambiguous and ambivalent than Brown allows.

Derek Walcott, in reviewing the first night of Sparrow's 1965 Original Young Brigade, commented on 'some odd cannibal jokes' that had been given or that had appeared in some of the calypsos. 'Congo Man' apparently was not the only calypso in 1965 on the cannibal theme. One surmises that its relatively early release in the first week of October 1964 might have triggered a few other calypsos on the same theme: a normal tendency in the Calypso where sudden song cycles can spring up on any current popular theme. 'Congo Man' had effectively 'cannibalized' the 1965 Carnival. Walcott recorded that:

> Dougla's [calypso] had a terrible one [joke] about child-eating and Sparrow, following Killer, delivered the virtuoso piece of the evening, one which I feared for, but which had just the right tent flavour of dubious taste, "Congo Man." Doing superb imitations of orchestra instruments, drumbeats and jungle noises, miming, growling, leaping and howling like a Congo cannibal, Sparrow demonstrated again that as a performer he is unsurpassable. In fact, he is now better than the songs he sings. It's a problem the finest artists face. There are moments in their career when they are superior to the material they have to hand.[33]

The performance, the play, was the thing whether — the role demanded the tear-jerking lamentation of the 'Slave' (1963) or the grotesque laughter and demoniac shrieks of 'Congo Man.' Beyond the moment and occasion of the performance itself, Sparrow, as we have seen, claimed to have no concept of or responsibility to Africa, that 'land so far'. Thus the Congo crisis with its relay of coups d'état and massacres, was relevant only as a source for the performance of grotesque humour, in a way that resembled how the phenomenal history of the Zulu nation became in early twentieth-century New Orleans, reduced to the Mardi Gras blackface minstrel krewe, Zulu.

The carnivalesque representation of history cannot be read outside of the context of carnival performance; and carnival performance generally has its own purposes and clusters of coded meanings. In the case of Zulu, this purpose was the satirical reduction of the white supremacist krewe, Rex. In the case of 'Congo Man', it was the pouring of scornful laughter on everyone and everything: universal Caucasian supremacism, the white man's 'god complex': local Trinidadian black and white racial prejudice, a so far unexplored dimension of 'Congo Man'.

It was also the self-vindication and self-celebration of Sparrow as 'king', and this kingship must be located in the context of Carnival and the conventions that determined the bestowal of kingship and the acclamation of the king. Such acclamation was visible in the number of headhunter masquerades played in 1965 and the popularity of 'Congo Man' at parties and on the radio. Sparrow himself was fully aware of the power of 'Congo Man' as a performance piece and the affinity of this calypso to masquerade. Michael Anthony records that in 1965: 'The Mighty Sparrow, whose popular calypso *Congo Man*, must have inspired the band *Chiefs of Africa*, was appearing in the band as Congo Man, a fierce head-hunter in that colourful band led by Big Sarge of Tunapuna.[34] Sparrow, who had lost both the Calypso Monarch and the Road March competitions in 1964 (to Bomber and Kitchener respectively) was illustrating with 'Congo Man' where his immense powers lay; and though he would win neither the monarchy nor the Road March in 1965, 'Congo Man' was undoubtedly the most startlingly, original and memorable calypso of that and many a year.

The *Sunday Guardian* of February 21, 1965 published a photograph of two Ol Mas characters that had won a prize in their division at the Ol Mas Competition of Tranquillity Tennis Club, Port of Spain, held on February 19, 1965. The masqueraders were both light complexioned and the caption of the photograph read: 'The Congo Man is about to achieve his ambition — eating a piece of white meat. He is seen dropping his captured white meat into the pot during 'Ole Mas' competition at Tranquillity Tennis Club, Port of Spain'.[35] Ten days earlier, a similar, most likely the same mas had won the first prize in the couples' section at the Ol Mas Competition of the Arima Tennis Club. This apparently white Trinidadian couple, the man painted with streaks of black grease jab jab style, the woman masked, was described as depicting 'the popular theme, "Ah never eat a white meat yet"'.[36] Caucasian laughter here was probably of the same order as that of the French Creole planter-class males, who in pre-emancipation times played Jab Molassie, a masquerade that simultaneously caricatured, demonized, empowered and reduced to manageable proportions the figure of the rebellious field slave. Played blackface by white players, Congo Man was neutralized and robbed of the menace he still represented — masquerade notwithstanding — to Caucasian Trinidad.

Two commentators were not at all amused at the popularity of 'Congo Man' and the cannibal-headhunter theme it had stimulated in the 1965 Carnival season. One wrote sarcastically 'commending' the local TV station for broadcasting a Sparrow performance of the song and 'congratulating' the radio stations for playing it, and RCA recording company for the recording and proposed worldwide dissemination of 'Congo Man'. The writer who termed himself or herself a 'Free Thinker' noted that time had been when such a calypso would have elicited a flood of condemnatory letters to the press from citizens who believed: 'That the country was on the threshold of hell. Nowadays, I notice that nothing happens. Hooray! And congrats to TTT for breaking new ground'.[37] L. Milne from Maracas Valley commended 'Freethinker' and added his or her drop of sarcasm to the discourse:

> Something tells me that if Sparrow entered politics he would be elected to the highest office in the land. Anyone who can command so much adulation for singing "Congo Man" can surely get away with anything, especially since his type of "Art" is aided and abetted by our radio and television stations. I reel with shame.[38]

There was in this discussion a delicate silence as to the source of such intense shame and rage as 'Congo Man' had inspired in these two commentators. The only commentator who in 1965 came close to unmasking the calypso's real theme was Clifford Sealey a true freethinker and proprietor of The Book Shop. In a letter answering 'Free Thinker' he came out against that critic's implied recommendation that censorship be directed against calypsos (as had and would no doubt have happened three decades earlier). Sealey wrote:

> With the third implication that "Congo Man" is objectionable, I cannot agree; and I would invite him to reconsider his opinion. For, without stating its object, this song brings into the open an often alleged longing of the black man, objectifies it, enacts it, ridicules it, depriving it thereby of its warping potential. This calls for an amazing degree of self-distancing on the part of both the artist and the responding audience, which in Trinidad includes both races. Finally, the fact that 'Congo Man' produces this cathartic effect, as can be witnessed at any jump-up this year, places it in my opinion far above the indisputably brilliant essays of James Baldwin as a contributor to the relaxation of racial tension.[39]

Sealey's letter to the editor identifies 'Congo Man' as enactment and the demolition through ridicule of a traditional and damaging stereotype; the nightmare that white colonizers since Prospero had engendered of the African male as oversexed monster hungering for a taste of 'admired Miranda,' trying every trick in order to 'tup' the white ewe, Desdemona. Sealey locates the calypso squarely within the then current dialectic of black–white race relations, involving African-American authors such as James Baldwin, Ralph Ellison, Richard Wright, Eldridge Cleaver, and radical humorists such as Dick Gregory. By challenging and deconstructing traditional stereotypes and attitudes, this dialectic had by the mid-1960s already transformed the ways in which black and white inter-racial desire was to be discussed in the future.

Sealey had unmasked the implied and unnamable theme of 'Congo Man' and its subversive intent and method. Sparrow, according to Sealey, was really exploding the cannibal/monster stereotype by entering and wearing it as his mask. Beyond this, he was exploring the metaphorical possibilities of the cannibal fable through which the act of 'eating' becomes either the sexual act itself or the act of oral stimulation. For, despite Sparrow's statement that 'Congo Man' was simply a humourous song, one that should be taken on a purely literal plane, he knew very well that a society nurtured on *double entendre* and the coded visual vocabulary of Carnival masquerade, would read the calypso as metaphor and explore the range of its possible meanings and social implications.

Sparrow had, through performance, 'carnivalized' the cannibal. Anyone attending a performance of 'Congo Man' in 1965 would automatically have recognized its affinity to masquerade and the question it posed about the relationship between Sparrow (who, via performance, transformed himself into or entered and was possessed by the persona of the cannibal) — and the Congo Man — (whose joyous 'eating' of white meat the calypsonian claims he has never experienced himself, despite all his travels and travails, his trips and traps).

> I envy the Congo man
> Ah wish ah coulda go and shake 'e han
> All you know how much trap I set
> Until ah sweat
> But ah never eat a white meat yet

'Congo Man' is narrated and performed in the tradition of the African folktale, in which the narrator/calypsonian plays all the characters, changes gesture and tone of voice as the tale demands, interrupts narrative flow with songs and choruses. In some performances of Afro-Caribbean folk tales, the narrator might repeat the 'crick crack' formula in the middle of the tale. Sparrow as narrator becomes, yet is not the Congo Man. The narrator becomes, yet is not the Congo Man. The narrator identifies himself as a voyeur, 'peeping through the bushes to see what's taking place.' In short, he behaves as generations of calypso narrators have behaved: as a 'macco', a watcher, a person always on the scene to witness someone else's private affairs.

Yet, as folk narrator, he must 'become' the Congo Man and be able to reproduce his war-whoops, yodels, primal screams, gurgles, giggles, belches, anticipatory lip-smackings, joyfully orgasmic feeding frenzy. In the process of 'becoming' the Congo Man, the narrator claims to envy him his good fortune and superior skill as a hunter. This confession of envy is contradicted by his statement in the 1967 and 1988 remakes of 'Congo Man', that he would never have eaten the women, had they strayed into his domain, but rather he would have 'sent them home to their husbands' — a statement that he expects no one to believe, no more than he expects them to believe that he too 'never eat a white meat yet'.

In the 1965 recording, the original, a chorus of voices proclaims the narrator a liar, when he declares his innocence of having eaten white meat; but he defends his honour and integrity to the very end with: 'Who lie? Who lie? Is who all you calling a liar?' A denial that is meant to enhance his image as a sort of globetrotting Casanova, a global village ram willing, ready and able to serve a world of women as in his early calypso 'Sailing Boat Experience.'[40]

'Congo Man' cannot be adequately read outside of its initial and, afterwards, its constantly changing contexts of performance. The original 1965 version had already established enormous distance between the actual events taking place in the Congo and Sparrow's reduction of them to a bizarre celebration of his own elaborately denied conquest and consumption of the much desired, white meat. Subsequent recorded versions seem to be more formulaic performance pieces with the introductory, 'Ooday, ooday oo', repeated in chorus by a sing-along audience within the body of the song. The naming of the Congo Man, Big Brother Umba of the Baluba, is new. It is not meant to signal any knowledge of Baluba distress, but to provide a frame for the comic enactment of what in its origin was tragedy. The insertion of the chant, 'yabba dabba, doo', that is, the Stone Age caveman jabber of Fred Flintstone, jokey Caucasian cartoon version of the African headhunter, allows the listener not only to measure African primitivity against its European counterpart, but to observe the mergence of both primitivities into one globalized and hybridized chorus of screams, giggles, belches and ecstatic laughter. Later versions of the song were popular as party songs, and though totally dislocated from the original sociopolitical context, evoked bitter and trenchant commentary from black nationalists angry at what they saw as Sparrow's shallowness and disrespect for Africa and Africans.

The Skull Beneath the Skin-teeth

The type of humour that so startles the listener to 'Congo Man' has had a long history in literature. It is a variant of modes such as 'black' — no pun intended — comedy or grotesque comedy, of laughter that grows out of usually other people's pain. What is it about the cannibal or the idea of cannibalism that inspires such strange mirth?

One thinks of the famous 'A Modest Proposal' of Swift, who suggested that the best way to convert the homelessness, destitution and wanton fertility of overpopulated Ireland into a profit, was to breed and father babies for butchery and human consumption. Literal cannibalism, Swift declared, was reasonable and, properly managed, could become a profitable substitute for the metaphorical cannibalism of an aristocracy of imperial landlords who were, so to speak, devouring the human and material resources of the country.

The Stanleyville massacre of November 1964 with its reports of Belgians chopped to death and Congolese cannibalism evoked two distinctly different types of response from the British Press: the pathetic and factual and the grotesquely satirical. One example of the factual was this news report of November 25, 1964:

> The survivors of the Stanleyville massacre, their ordeal made plain in their haggard faces, flew into Brussels today. The welfare workers waiting to care for them wept at the sight of orphaned children and husbandless wives, and Princess Paola wept with them.

Princess Paola, in a mink coat with fur-lined knee-length boots, wiped tears from her eyes as a priest, who was wrapped in a blanket against the cold, told her husband, Prince Albert of his experiences. Later she mixed with women evacuees at a Red Cross coffee stall and kissed some of them on the cheek. She was in tears again when she left them.[41]

> No hint of satire here, though anyone who had read *Heart of Darkness*, *King Leopold's Soliloquy*, or Roger Casement's reports on the atrocities perpetrated in the Congo towards the end of the nineteenth century by Belgian King Leopold II's genocidal administrators, might have felt that the Stanleyville massacre was no more than the inevitable end of a horrible beginning, many atrocities before; history's grim judgment passed on Leopold's hypocritical *mission civilatrice*.

One example of the grotesquely satirical response was a cartoon that appeared in England a few days after Stanleyville — November 24, 1964; the author recalls that he was in England at the time working on Joseph Conrad's *Heart of Darkness*,[42] and while he has a copy of the cartoon, he does not have the name of the publication. This cartoon took the form of a diptych on the left half of which an English boy was soliciting donations from passers-by for his Guy Fawkes effigy with the traditional entreaty: 'A copper for the Guy.' The drawing on the right depicted a black cannibal headhunter alongside a huge bubbling pot, entreating passers-by for 'A guy for the copper.'

It was hugely funny, but coming when it did, raised in my mind many questions as to its meaning beyond its magnificent play on words. Guy Fawkes Day, is celebrated on November 5 each year by the burning of an effigy of Guy Fawkes, mastermind of the November 1605 Gunpowder Plot to blow up the British House of Parliament. Reduced now to a straw-filled bobolee, Guy Fawkes was a warning that civilized society did and does not tolerate subversive anarchy. It was the opposite with the Congolese cannibal who, as a still untamed and unappropriated Neanderthal, was a living menace to civilization, not a distant or symbolic threat.

This hilarious representation of the cannibal caused me to revisit *Heart of Darkness*, which is one of the places that cannibals appear in Conrad's work. The 30 able-bodied sailors and woodcutters, who accompany Marlow and four other white men up the dark serpentine river, are eaters of human flesh. Recruited at the Company's Outer Station close to the river's mouth, they are 800 miles from home and as unfamiliar with the deep hinterland as the Europeans. Having, according to Marlow's surmise, no sense of time, they have entered into contracts to work for six months. No one assumes responsibility for feeding them, and the dead hippopotamus they brought with them has gone rotten and has had to be thrown overboard. They seem to eat nothing except 'some stuff like half-cooked dough, of a dirty lavender colour, they kept wrapped in leaves',[43] and would, if they could, capture, kill and eat any of their black brethren howling in the bushes on the banks of the fog-bound river. They are very angry and perhaps on the verge of mutiny when Marlow dumps overboard the body of his dead African steersman, killed by a spear hurled from the bank of the Congo.

What I am calling Marlow's 'cannibal joke' concerns his two reactions to being on the same boat with men he believes to be cannibals. The first is unstated, but constantly hinted in his several references to his crew. He talks about their well-muscled physiques slowly degenerating because of starvation; he mentions their gleaming eyes, and he is clearly a worried man. The second reaction is openly stated: Why don't these desperately hungry cannibals attack, kill and eat the most easily available prey, the white men? With a wry, self-directed jest he surmises that the white men must look too 'unwholesome' to serve as prey for 30 hungry cannibals. Marlow also hopes — attributing this feeling to his encroaching illness and sense of being involved in a dream sensation — that *he* does not appear to be so 'unappetizing', and that the cannibals have not placed him in the same category as his despicable Belgian fellow travellers. In other words, Marlow is worried that he might be eaten and even more worried that he has not been!

Giving more serious consideration to this bizarre circumstance, Marlow moves beyond the stereotype to surmise that these Congo men may have developed a moral code of honour and restraint far superior to that of their European employers and civilizers of the master race. The cannibals' allegiance to this code is more powerful than 'the devilry of lingering starvation, its exasperating torment, its black thoughts, its somber and brooding ferocity'.[44] If we locate these words — 'devilry', 'torment', 'black thoughts', 'somber and brooding ferocity' — within the patterned imagery and tonal rhetoric of the novel, we will recognize that Conrad has attributed to hunger and its absolute dimension starvation, the same qualities he accords the African (and Malaysian) forests, and that stereotypically menacing primitive man, the cannibal. Yet this crew of 30 cannibals has confounded the accepted stereotype and shamed the 'othering' eye of 'civilized' man, so that in the end both the constructs of 'cannibal', civilized man's ultimate Other and 'civilization' are interrogated. The cannibal joke here, then, has been employed unconventionally, to subvert the complacency and self-ignorance and to unmask the hypocrisy beneath King Leopold's *mission civilatrice*.

Lurking at the edges of Caribbean discourse, cannibalism has historically been attributed to native Caribbean peoples by Columbus and other conquistadores needing a moral excuse for the atrocities of conquest. The cannibal is an inalienable part of colonizing mythologies, perhaps since time began. He provided Roman imperialism with justification for the persecution of the early Christian communities. Seventeen centuries later, he provided Robinson Crusoe with the moral justification he needed for gunning down Friday's captors. That is, he provided British imperialism with the same excuse that Columbus's Caribs had bestowed centuries before on Spanish imperialism. As America declared her right to hegemony in the Western hemisphere, her writers of pulp fiction and her filmmakers recognized the need to reconstruct the cannibal in the image of whomsoever could lay claim to prior occupancy of invaded territory.

Leasa Farrar Fortune, commenting on *la mission civilatrice* American style, says of voodoo novels and movies:

> They contained all the necessary elements for box office success: cannibalism, hapless black people, zombies and witch doctors, death, spirit possession, and helpless white women to be saved by the virile white male.'[45]

Such stereotypes, implanted in the consciousness of cinema-loving West Indians, are joyously and scathingly dissolved in Sparrow's 'Congo Man', where the white hero does not appear in the nick of time, and the women are eaten by a cannibal who inverts the hierarchy of who laughs and who is laughed at.

In 1965, the year when 'Congo Man' cannibalized the Trinidad Carnival, Derek Walcott in 'Crusoe's Journal' sardonically contemplated the ambiguous effect of Crusoe's imposition of language and religion on Friday, the cannibal he has converted to Christianity after having saved him from being eaten by his own cannibal kind.

> like Cristofer he bears
> in speech mnemonic as a missionary's
> the Word to savages,
> its shape an earthen, water-bearing vessel's
> whose sprinkling alters us
> into good Fridays who recite his praise
> parroting our master's
> style and voice, we make his language ours
> converted cannibals
> we learn with him to eat the flesh of Christ[46]
>
> *The Castaway and Other Poems*

Walcott's cannibal quip has had a long history, though its immediate predecessor in modern literature may be found in James Joyce's *Ulysses*.[47] There, Leopold Bloom the Jewish protagonist wanders into a church at communion time and comically meditates on Christian liturgy and practice: 'Shut your eyes and open your mouth. What? Corpus. Body. Corpse. Good idea the Latin. Stupefies them first. Hospice for the dying. They don't seem to chew it, only swallow it down. Rum idea: eating bits of a corpse why the cannibals cotton to it.'[48] Bloom sardonically surmises that the success of Christian imperialism, *le mission civilatrice*, in converting cannibal nations must be due to the affinity that the cannibals recognize between the symbolic Christian practice of 'eating bits of a corpse' and their own literal and ritualistic consumption of human flesh to gain possession of, or be possessed by the power and spiritual energy of the slain foe. Joyce's sardonic, wry, jibing humour marks and mocks that uneasy border where cannibalism and divinized human sacrifice overlap. Walcott's musing laughter arises out of his ironic recognition that 'Friday's progeny' have mastered Crusoe's imposed language and religion to such an extent, that they are simultaneously more articulate and more pious than their former masters and teachers. The wryly comic result of *la mission civilatrice* is illustrated when Friday or Caliban/cannibal becomes more 'civilized' than Crusoe/Prospero and displays a sort of postcolonial subaltern triumphalism by flaunting his learning in his teacher's face.

The deeper and primary source of Walcott's cannibal joke, however, lies in the origins of Christianity itself: that era when Christians were regarded as the ultimate barbarians in a crisis-ridden and decadent Roman Empire. Psycho-historian Norman Cohn states in *Europe's Inner Demons* that it was widely believed that Christians in the first and second centuries AD were subversive and indulged in promiscuous and incestuous orgies, infanticide and cannibalism. Such notions were according to Cohn: 'widespread both in geographical and in the social sense. Christian apologists referred to them as flourishing in all the main areas where Christians were to be found — north Africa, Asia Minor, Rome itself; and not only amongst the unlettered populace, either.'[49]

Such accusations, fuelled both by the Christians' belief in the apocalyptic destruction of the kingdom of this world and the coming of a divine ruler, and by pagan confusion at the Eucharistic practice of eating the body (bread) and drinking the blood (wine) of Christ, provided Romans with moral and political justification for the persecution, torture and in some cases massacre of Christian communities.

Of particular interest is the connection that existed in the minds of highly civilized Europeans, between politically subversive intent, cannibalism and sexual promiscuity — a connection, according to historian Livy, which was clearly illustrated in the socially threatening behaviour of the Bacchanalia. Cohn concludes that:

> By Livy's time — that is to say, on the eve of the Christian era – erotic orgies of a more or less perverted kind belonged to the stereotype of a revolutionary conspiracy against the state. Directed against the Christians, the accusation of holding such orgies points precisely in the same direction as the accusation of cannibalism. By assimilating the Christian *Agape* to the Bacchanalia the pagan Romans were, once again, labeling Christians as ruthless conspirators, dedicated to overthrowing the state and seizing power for themselves.[50]

Warnings against cannibal and Carnival share a common source. Transport Crusoe backwards in time two millennia and he becomes Friday or Caliban or Congo man, stereotypically hungry, oversexed, bacchanalian, carnivorous, subversive: civilization's ultimate Other and sombre Shadow, and a useful excuse for justifying imperialist wars of pacification and humanization such as the Belgian intervention that had reduced the Congo to such sad dereliction.

Antecedent, Ancestor, Archetype

Curiously, one of the first songs remembered and recorded from old French Creole Trinidad mocked at the confusion that surrounded the Christian ritual of 'eating the body' and 'drinking the blood' of a sacrificed victim who is simultaneously human and divine. This song which was also connected with Carnival and which played harshly with the cannibal stereotype, was the archetype and ancestor of Sparrow's 'Congo Man'. I am not saying that Sparrow — or whoever else might have been responsible for the lyrics and concept of 'Congo Man' — was aware of the older song, but that certain texts, ideas and types of performance become archetypal, inscribe themselves in a society, and finally achieve permanence via the commemorative process of masquerade. Trinidad, it turns out, has been making mas and creating subversive picong out of the cannibal/savage stereotype and the Euro-Christian civilization/pacification mission from the island's foundation as a theatre for the interface or confrontation of European, Native Caribbean and African tribes.

The ancestral song in question went this way:

> Pain nous ka mangé
> C'est viande beké
> Di vin nous ka boué
> C'est sang beké
> Hé St. Domingo
> Songe St. Domingo

This translates:
> The bread we eat
> Is white man's flesh
> The wine we drink
> Is the white man's blood
> Hé St. Domingo
> Remember St. Domingo

This song, cited in 1805 as evidence of a slave plot to murder 'all the whites and free coloured inhabitants' of the island in a revolt that was being planned on the Shand estate, might have been little more than the battle cry of one of the Convois or Régiments, as the African dance societies used to be called at that time.[51]

The governor and planters, however, sitting in their Supreme Tribunal, interpreted the song as damning evidence that African (that is, Africans 'liberated' from non-British slave ships who, according to Dom Basil Mathews,[52] were reconstructing replicas of their lost communities) and French Negroes (that is, creolized black Trinidadians born in the Caribbean) had been contemplating 'the destruction of all the white men, and the dishonour of all the white women of the island'.[53] Four slaves were executed, others tortured and mutilated, in a manner that in the *Time* reports of the Congo massacres 160 years later, would be termed 'savage', 'barbaric', and 'uncivilized', but which had for countless centuries been standard practice in all the great civilizations of the world. The fortunate few of the alleged insurrectionists were merely flogged and banished from Trinidad.

Cannibal war-song or Caliban's aboriginal road march, 'Pain nous ka mangé' contains a number of familiar masquerade or carnivalesque features. It ritualizes the confrontation of two socially unequal antagonists. One protagonist is Caucasian, authoritarian, Christian, Catholic, established, endowed by the 1783 Cedula with property in proportion to the degrees of whiteness and wealth in cash or chattel slaves he had brought to Trinidad. This protagonist is empowered to impose his text and image, his religion, his vision of this world and the next, on a savage, subservient black Other. The Other(ed) protagonist is an alliance of African and black Creole Trinidadian. Implicit in the text of 'Pain nous ka mangé' is his felt resentment at and firm rejection of the image of the African as monster and cannibal. Such resentment, however, is conveyed via an apparent 'acceptance' by the black subaltern of the very image of the cannibal and blood-drinking savage that his Caucasian owner and tormentor constructed and imposed on the African. Indeed, this 'acceptance' of stereotype which is a denial of stereotype must also have informed the regression of modern Congolese groups like the Simbas to traditional weapons, war-paint and atavistic rituals such as cannibalism.

The song-text of 'Pain nous ka mangé' also harshly rejects and mocks *the white man's 'cannibalism'* — as suggested by the flesh-eating and blood-drinking metaphors of the Eucharist — and valorizes and acclaims the African-Caribbean equivalent of this metaphorical cannibalism: Haitian-style revolution. There is a bitter racial baiting here; a vicious picong, a mocking laughter at the familiar nightmares of slaves in revolt as in Haiti or Fedon's Grenada ten years earlier; the possibility of retaliatory rape, murder, 'gastronomical transgression'[54] and violence equal in every degree to what Caucasians had habitually visited on Africans in the Caribbean. One recognizes the vocabulary of threat and the technique of grotesque caricature that are common to all forms of male-versus-male rhetorical discourse that were later to become enshrined in the Trinidad Carnival. The style and aesthetic of inter-racial encounter were being established and inscribed in that Christmas/Carnival season of 1805–1806, 160 years before Sparrow became, with 'Congo Man', the medium for a commemoration and reincarnation through performance, of that founding aesthetic.

'Pain nous ka mangé' raises the same sort of questions as 'Congo Man.' Were the 1805 Convois or Régiments — societies, social clubs, social unions — boldly signalling their current intentions to demolish the master race and class, or commemorating and defiantly celebrating the one great example of successful African warriorhood in the New World: the Haitian Revolution? How much of the song was masquerade as E.L. Joseph seemed to believe and how much a serious declaration of an intent to exterminate the planter class? Are we dealing here with play, picong, jibe, threat, the self-glorifying rhetoric of the permanently disempowered, for whom verbal militancy must compensate for lost warriorhood? The white French and English Creoles, with the memory of Haiti and Grenada ever on their minds, were not going to take any chances. Many of them were first generation refugees from Haiti, Grenada and other parts of the crumbling French empire in the New World. The sadistic severity of their retaliation was meant to be — like the British slow-torturing, hanging, drawing and quartering of the gunpowder plotters two centuries earlier — both just punishment for current offence and pre-emptive warning against any future attempt at revolt.

The nightmare of 'another Haiti', together with the fear of extermination of all white men and dishonour (that is, rape) of all white women by vengeful and monstrous black males, remained a subliminal part of Caucasian consciousness long after emancipation and has become a sort of vestigial phobia of the newer Indo-Trinidadian bourgeoisie that is in the process of locating and defining itself within the complex of Trinidadian ethnicities.[55] In short, the history of European/African encounter in the New World created, fed on and subsequently required the validating nightmare of the monstrous black male lurking in the bushes just beyond one's fence. That nightmare needed to be policed and confined to its proper place. White xenophobia in Trinidad, the terror of 'another Haiti', remained alive and well into the twentieth century.

After the waterfront workers' strike of 1919, right into the 1930s the white urban elite sought and procured permission to bear arms, as their ancestors did, and to organize themselves into vigilante patrols against the impending doom of awakening pan-Africanist consciousness via the heavily-censored Garveyite movement.[56] The *Trinidad Guardian* reported a conspiracy that involved,

> the destruction of organized Government and the elimination of the white population. The propaganda framed by the leaders of the organization is saturated with racial animosity in its most extreme form. Every negro child was to be trained to hate the white man, every device was to be used to irritate the negro people against Europeans. Schemes were drawn up for the establishment of a boycott of white merchants, all these movements having as their essential and avowed object the driving out of the British Government and the creation of a negro republic in Trinidad.[57]

The *Guardian* never released the names of the 'conspirators,' men who were plotting nothing more than the establishment of trade links between Africa and the African Diaspora in the Caribbean and America. This Garveyite scheme never materialized; and would not have been allowed to take shape in the atmosphere of paranoia that had, apparently, never quite disappeared since Haiti.

Sparrow's 'Congo Man', then, located in the context of Trinidad history, was a revisitation of one of the archetypal themes of colonial encounter. It was a latter-day enactment of a masquerade older than, though reinforced by the Cedula. There is, however, little evidence of the paranoia of 1919 in the 1965 responses to 'Congo Man'. True, some felt that the uncensored broadcasting of the song signified that the country was on the verge of moral collapse, and predicted imminent hellfire for those involved in the song's promotion. But 'Congo Man', unlike '*Pain nous ka mangé*' could not be linked to any obviously subversive political or racial conspiracy to subvert the status quo. It was just a carnival song, and seemed to have registered with even white masqueraders as no more than a weirdly funny performance piece. There is no sense in the conversion of 'Congo Man' to Caucasian tennis-club ol' mas, that the players were aware of the extent to which the song's laughter may have been directed at them.

Yet, there can be little doubt that part of 'Congo Man's' laughter was focused on the racist absurdities of Trinidad society. Sparrow had in the late 1950s become both an example and a victim of such absurdities. In 1957 he married a white American woman, who, according to Melody in 'Corbeau Flying High',[58] he initially said was his manager. The marriage facilitated his acquisition of work permits to perform in the US Virgin Islands and mainland USA. Lord Melody, Sparrow's companion in song had, for much the same reason, married an African American.[59]

Whatever the motive for marriage, love or convenience, the 22-year-old Sparrow had placed himself in a different situation, given the state of inter-racial relationship in a still rigidly colonial Trinidad. Most black/white marriages at the time tended to be Othello/Desdemona affairs between black male professionals — doctors, lawyers, engineers, et cetera — and white women from the US, UK, Ireland, and later Canada. Marriages between local white Creole women and local black males were relatively few, regardless of the achievement or social position of the male. No particular excellence of achievement beyond the mere fact of whiteness was ever required of the female.

The marriage of a lower-class, grass-rooted black male to any kind of Caucasian woman, a phenomenon in the metropolis where a whole generation of West Indian and other colonial migrants had by the late 1950s lived for nearly two decades, was an even rarer occurrence in the islands, than that of the upper middle-class black professional and the local white woman. The Growling Tiger in 'Let the White People Fight' told the story of a black World War I veteran who returned to Trinidad crippled and with a blue-eyed wife. Unemployed, he resorted to selling bush-rum to earn a living, was caught — one cannot run from the police while confined to a wheelchair — and sent to jail where he subsequently died. The white community took care of his wife, one of their own who had, indeed, strayed, but was now redeemed of the social error of a transgressive marriage. Tiger bitterly commented to those British officials and local patriots who were again seeking to recruit a fresh batch of West Indian soldiers to fight in yet another World War.

> The boys went to the last war. What did they get?
> The way they treat them I'll never forget.

Cyril lose both legs beneath the knee
He got twenty dollars a month. How niggardly!
And after those people mash up his life
And even saddle him with a blue-eyed wife
He sell a pint of rum and they did not fail
To give the war veteran six months in jail

Tiger's resolution in this passionately delivered and passionately acclaimed calypso was: 'But I going plant provision and fix me affairs / And the white people could fight for a thousand years.'[60]

Even in the first decade after Independence such black/white marriages as Cyril's were beset by challenges. Sparrow, the Roaring Lion and Lord Kitchener would all marry Caucasians. All of these marriages failed. Sparrow, our primary concern here, did himself little good by flaunting his American wife in the faces of his colleagues. In 'Reply to Melody' (1958),[61] the third calypso in the famous Sparrow/Melody picong series, Sparrow sang taunting Melody: 'I marry a wife, you go and marry one too / But your wife ain't have eyes of blue.' Clearly indicating his belief that his Caucasian wife was in some way the social or ethnic superior to Melody's black one, even though both women were creatures of convenience. Neither white nor black Trinidad was amused. Sparrow's plaintive cry: 'Everybody washing they mouth on me' gives some indication of the real pressure he was receiving from the public at large ('*everybody*') and his colleagues ('dem calypsonians') along with 'some of my friends and family', in particular.

Accusing his critics of 'interfering in my private romance' and not giving him a chance to live happily ever after with whomsoever he chose to marry, Sparrow exploded: 'But ah love me wife and to hell with everybody.' Later in 'Reply to Melody', he confessed with unusual and unmasked frankness that all the hatred he had been receiving from his formerly enthusiastic and supportive audience, had left him feeling 'miserable':

What have I done to these people
They have me so miserable
My poor wife never trouble them
They hate me worse than the PNM[62]

Sparrow had opened himself to attack, first by crossing the historically inscribed racial taboo lines and secondly by boasting about it. Melody, at whom Sparrow's taunt had been directed, retaliated in calypso with the stinging 'Corbeau Flying High,' a song that pokes harsh ironic fun at the disintegration of Sparrow's marriage. In 'Corbeau Flying High' Melody depicted Sparrow as the despised corbeau, the black vulture, who flies high in the brief period of his improbable marriage to the white bird of passage, but has to descend disconsolately to earth when she flies away from him. Since vultures are by nature attracted to dead meat, Melody's calypso may contain a hidden and vicious derogation of his friend's wife as carrion.

In July 1960,[63] Sparrow explained the failure of that marriage as having been 'because people would not let us love.' Later, though, in January 1965, a few days after his first performance of 'Congo Man' in the Original Young Brigade Tent at the opening of the tent's 1965 Carnival season, Sparrow accepted all the blame, saying: 'In those days I didn't have the understanding I have now.'[64] Interestingly enough, Melody in 1965 sang 'Mas' in which he anticipated playing a splendid mas with George Bailey, in the climax of which would be the revelry he would make with his 'white woman'. The white woman had suddenly established a carnival identity as tourist and accessible Carnival trophy, or as naïve transgressor into native Trinidadian space, needing to be instructed in the ways of masquerading; or as intruder and rival to angry black women fearful of losing their men to these pale-faced antagonists (see 'Mas', 'Miss Tourist', 'Find a Fellar', or 'Sock It to Me' by respectively, Melody, Kitchener, Duke and again Kitchener).[65] The white woman as target for the black voyeur and as trophy, makes another appearance in Sparrow's 'Toronto Mas' whose chorus ends with, 'And all them white woman will be in the street.'[66]

Given Sparrow's sensitivity about the failure of his first marriage, it is not stretching our interpretation of 'Congo Man' to view it as a striking back through laughter at all those people who had placed obstacles in the path of, or viewed as unnatural his black and white love and marriage. 'Congo Man', read in the context of Sparrow's failed marriage and dearly bought 'understanding' invites his detractors to examine the absurdity of their own prejudices. Insofar as the calypso is a baiting of Trinidad Causcasians, 'Congo Man' brings them face to face with their own xenophobia, their nightmare that white ancestral promiscuity has irreversibly contaminated the Caucasian bloodstream. 'Congo Man' mischievously confronts this group with deeper and more horrifying levels of transgression as it baits the old archaic rump of ethnic supremacists.

But, it can be argued, the majority of those who would not let Sparrow and his first wife love, were as he indicated in 'Dey Washing Dey Mouth,' his family, friends and fellow calypsonians: and these were mostly black. What message, under its multifaceted mask, was 'Congo Man' sending to black nationalists who could be as against mixed marriages as any local Brabantio or Iago? Such nationalists, a growing body in that age of Martin Luther King, Malcolm X and neo-Garveyism, would have objected to Sparrow's adoption of the cannibal mask whatever the satirical intent behind that action. There really was no room for the Congo man in the constructions of 'Black dignity'; and 'Black dignity' rather than Black Power would in the late 1960s and early 1970s become the preferred slogan of the black middle class.

'Congo Man', however, was as subversive of this bourgeoisie whose watchwords were respectability and dignity, as it was of the white chauvinists. One feature of Sparrow's self-representation from the late 1950s into and beyond the mid-1960s, visible in calypsos such as 'Mr. Rake and Scrape' (1961)[67] and 'The Village Ram' (1964),[68] was as the anti-hero, a totally depraved sexual anarchist whose lusts were insatiable; an imp from the underground; a Casanova of gutter, garbage and la basse. The narrator of 'Mr. Rake and Scrape', a sexual scavenger, declares himself 'a busy man with no time to lose'. He is indiscriminate in his choice of women and will hunt down even the pregnant, the crippled women with 'one foot or one hand', the elderly and destitute in the almshouse. No one actually believes the protagonist's outrageous and gross claims. There is a large element of the impish, the mischievous in this persona, and 'mischievous', significantly, is the adjective that Sparrow once said to an interviewer best summarizes his character and stage personality.[69]

'The Village Ram' similarly presents the public with a sexual superhero, albeit reduced to the ramgoat of medieval lust. This persona too is anti-heroic with respect to how 'straight' society constructs the hero. But according to the scheme of values of the demi-monde, the village ram is hero. He is a taunter, a flaunter, a teaser; one whose aim is to irritate his opponents or rivals — that is, all other males — with a narrative of his exploits and a boast of his credentials and capabilities. He offers at one point, to help his rivals by doing for them the jobs they are inadequate to perform.

> In case of emergency
> If you ain't able with she
> And you find yourself in a jam
> Send for the village ram

The Village Ram is a butcher whose penis is his cleaver, who cuts down 'black is white' (that is, indiscriminately). He is a sex-machine who works 'day and night' without recess. Three years later, Sparrow's protagonist, unable to perform his sexual boast without medicinal stimulation, recommends to men like himself the use of bois banday (bois bandé), a bark that long before Viagra and all the other substances now available online, used to help aspiring village rams to maintain their ramajay.

Less grim than his successor eight months later, the Congo Man, the Village Ram is still imp; still a maker of mischief with his boast, his false modesty — 'I ain't boasting, but ah know ah have durability'— still a performer for the crowd of overawed listeners; a fertility king who somehow represents them all: Osiris resurrected after reassembly, and now perpetually aroused; 'a busy man with no time to lose' since he knows that his cycle of potency will not last forever; that the king, inevitably, must die. So the Village Ram has to make the most of each limited time-cycle before his charisma wanes and a new king takes his place, eating his vitals in order to subsume his power.

Sparrow has over the years expended much energy in making the public aware that he is and will always be the king. This has generally meant either defense or reaffirmation of kingship by means of confronting and defeating in competition all rivals to his throne. This has also meant the constant boasting and celebration of himself as cocksman, phallic warrior or fertility god. 'Congo Man', coming as it did after 'Mr. Rake and Scrape' and 'The Village Ram', and before 'Cockfight' (1969)[70] and 'SaSa Yea' (1969),[71] was part of Sparrow's effort at reconstructing his image of himself as king. Sparrow's king was caught between two worlds: the jamette demi-monde of fierce, subversive encounter and the bourgeois world of property and respectability, whose hypocrisy he had angrily condemned in 'The Outcast' (1964),[72] but towards whose consolidated materialism and celebrity he was steadily moving, by virtue of his very success as a grass-roots entertainer. The king of the demi-monde was, by definition, anti-hero in 'straight', 'decent', bourgeois society. So the Congo Man is society's ultimate Other, the anti-hero at his most offensive, mischievous and anarchic. Yet, paradoxically, the Congo Man represents society's suppressed shadow side, its secretly celebrated yet publicly denied sexuality. 'Congo Man', the calypso, probes and severely tests society's schizophrenia by presenting society with its other side, the cannibal, and by luring the respectable to participate in the Congo Man's infectious laughter, even as they shudder at the grim origins of that laughter: the horror at the heart of humour, the skull beneath the skin-teeth.

Aftermath and After-call

The 'after-call' is a low humming echo that a Guyanese buck-top makes after it has sung its high-pitched, half-crying, half-whistling melody at the beginning of its spinning, circling dance. The several versions of 'Congo Man' after 1965 produced an after-call of discourse in the 1970s and 1980s, in which Sparrow's representations of Africa and Africans came to be rigorously interrogated. One category of listeners, people who had been deeply affected by Black Power and pan-Africanist ideologies of the late 1960s and early 1970s, demanded of calypsonians serious reflection and 'conscious' well-researched opinion on all issues concerning Africa and Africans at home and abroad. These were usually impatient with the complex, playful, mischievous and anarchic laughter of such a song as 'Congo Man', and despite Sparrow's espousal of a typically neo-Garveyite creed such as 'black economics — that black people support black men in business',[73] doubted both his sincerity and authenticity as a spokesperson on black people's affairs.

It is worth noting that apart from the remakes of 'Congo Man' — the most significant of these being the 1967 *Spicy Sparrow* and 1988 *Party Classics* versions — virtually all but one of Sparrow's calypsos about Africa between the 1970s and the 1990s have been identified by Winsford 'Joker' Devine as his (Devine's) compositions. These calypsos are 'Du Du Yemi' (1978), 'Idi Amin' (1978), 'Gu Nu Gu' (1979), 'Love African Style' (1979), 'Isolate South Africa' (1981), 'The Witch Doctor' (1990), and 'I Owe No Apology' (1991).[74] The only calypso not mentioned by Devine in his 1994 listing of calypsos he had composed for Sparrow was 'Invade South Africa' (1985).[75] It is, therefore, problematic to talk about Sparrow's representation of Africa in the three decades after 'Congo Man' (1965),[76] and more correct to speak of the representation of Africa and Africans in calypsos performed by Sparrow during those three decades into the 1990s when he continually restored 'Congo Man' as a 'party classic' and his 'all-time favourite'.

In 1974, the year before 'Du Du Yemi' with its Yoruba chorus and 'Idi Amin' that hostile portrait of the Uganda dictator who in the calypso was condemned as a tyrant, terrorist, human rights abuser and venereally diseased sexual predator, was also the year that Sparrow visited Nigeria as part of the Trinidad and Tobago contingent to Festival of Arts and Culture (FESTAC). At FESTAC he was royally welcomed as Eric Williams and his African 'Safari' contingent had been welcomed in Liberia 13 years before, and invested with the title of 'Chief OmoWale of Ikoyi' by the Nigerian government. Major General Danjuma, well-known in Trinidad as the head of the court martial team that judged the Trinidad and Tobago army mutineers of 1970, sent Sparrow 'an honorary hat and letter', the certificates, as it were, of his chieftainship. Almost a decade later in December 1986, Sparrow returned to Nigeria as part of a contingent of calypsonians and Jamaican reggae singers, who together with popular Nigerian entertainers performed at several concerts, winning enthusiastic responses from the Nigerian public.[77]

Yet, such acclaim was sharply questioned by a handful of sceptics back home in Trinidad who criticized Sparrow for 'insulting Africans' with calypsos such as 'Du Du Yemi' and 'Idi Amin'. For instance, Modibo Kambon Karamoko of the African Advancement Association (AAA) stated that: 'Most calypsos sung by Sparrow pertaining to Africa and African people, those at home and abroad, have been very negative, degrading, baseless, cultureless, and very insulting.'[78] Karamoko argued that Sparrow propagated stereotypes learned from the Western media whose journalists were particularly hostile to 'progressive African leaders' among whom he numbered Idi Amin: 'one of our courageous brothers on the African soil'.

To illustrate his contention that Sparrow had always insulted Africans in his calypsos, Karamoko cited the still popular 'Congo Man' in which, he said, 'Sparrow was describing the Africans of the Congo as cannibals.' Karamoko questioned Sparrow's sincerity and depth of black consciousness, noting that although Sparrow had expressed pride in his African name, Omowale, and the title had been bestowed on him after FESTAC (1977), he had demonstrated no genuine African consciousness in his two 1978 calypsos. Nor had he a good track record of protest against the atrocities perpetrated by Vorster in Soweto or Ian Smith in Rhodesia. Sparrow, according to Karamoko, had not been truly sensitive either to the fates of black people in the diaspora.

Karamoko's case for the indictment of Sparrow received support from Reuben Cato and Learie Alleyne-Forte. Cato felt that Sparrow's focus on Idi Amin was sadly misplaced:

> Vorster and Smith have been murdering and dehumanizing our people for years, but you did not see fit to do a recording of them. In the past month, 4,000 women and children were slain by Ian Smith's forces, where they crossed the border from Southern Rhodesia into Mozambique.[79]

Like Karamoko, Cato viewed Sparrow as a sort of white man's black man and a mouthpiece for the white media. Alleyne-Forte, even more openly insultive, complained that Sparrow, whom he had always admired as one of the country's true geniuses along with Kitchener, Eric Williams and V.S. Naipaul, had begun to go 'off-key', 'basodie and stupid'. Sparrow, according to Alleyne-Forte, needed to admit and correct his ignorance of international affairs if he wanted to remain a spokesperson for black people in a more enlightened age.

> "If Sparrow say so, is so," then yuh have to do much better than yuh doing at present. Wha yuh have to appreciate, being a man in your position, is that if yuh decide to go out in dat arena of international politics "inna dis ya age" yuh have to start analyzing facts of a wider

and more varied source, because yuh catering to a more intelligent and educated black public now.[80]

Neither Devine, who penned Sparrow's 1978 calypsos, nor Sparrow who performed them, bothered to answer these black nationalist critics; though one 'Black Brother' of Five Rivers, Diego Martin did undertake the task of refuting 'the sentimental hyperbole of Modibo Kambon'.[81] Black Brother argued against any facile dismissal of the so-called white media, since it was the same white media that provided the evidence by which one condemned both Idi Amin and Vorster and Ian Smith. Karamoko was being inconsistent when he accepted and exploited their news reports where they revealed white atrocities, and rejected them where they uncovered black African human rights abuses. Karamoko's African Advancement Association, who was advising Sparrow of the need to protest against Vorster and Ian Smith, had not themselves been loud or sanguine in their praise of calypsos sung by Tobago Crusoe/Crusoe Kid and Cypher that had attacked racist and imperialist policies in South Africa and Rhodesia. Black Brother also noted that while Karamoko and his AAA had jumped to defend the dubious Amin from the scathing irreverence of Sparrow's calypso, they had not protested against the 'unjustified personal attacks made on our Prime Minister in calypso song'.[82] Amin deserved to be criticized for both his brutality and his buffoonery, and no pan-Africanist sentimentality should protect him from his just deserts.

This mini-controversy, an after-call of the earlier 1965 wrangle over 'Congo Man', signalled a number of things. First of all, the Black Power and Black Consciousness discourses had made the representation of Africa and Africans in Africa and in the African diaspora a deadly serious business. Indeed, leaders and rhetoricians of the 1970 Black Power marches in Trinidad had sought constantly to attack the stereotype of grinning, laughing, devil-may-care, unserious, don't give-a-damn black person, and would, if only they could, have abolished laughter from their movement. Thus, curiously, although Black Power advocates welcomed such political picong as calypsonians like Chalkdust and Relator had begun to direct against Eric Williams and his relay of governments, they could not countenance the anarchic and subversive freedom with which the same political picong could turn inwards and critically unmask such fragile and insecure constructions as black identity or the African image, or black dignity, or black solidarity. In such an age of seriousness, the reductive subtleties of humour tend to be replaced by a more straightforward literalness, that is impatient with the word-play, masking, mind-play and ambiguity that wit and humour require.

Secondly, the controversy over 'Idi Amin' and 'Du Du Yemi' seemed to illustrate the truth of Vidia Naipauls's observation in *The Middle Passage* that 'the insecure wish to be heroically portrayed'.[83] This meant that in the drive to negate the hostile stereotypes of the colonial era, the new liberated, post-independence Caribbean person had begun to construct more positive but equally questionable stereotypes that discouraged scrutiny of a phenomenon or mode of behaviour, however unacceptable, on the grounds that such scrutiny might violate a now sacrosanct pan-African solidarity. Thus the phenomenon of African postcolonial tyranny manifest in the monstrous behaviour of an Idi Amin, needed not only to be ignored, glossed over and explained away as typically imperialistic white media propaganda, but also to be transformed into the laughable notion of Amin as a progressive African leader and 'one of our courageous brothers on the African soil'.

Conversely, Learie Alleyne-Forte's contention that the black public had grown more intelligent and better educated, and required of its spokespersons a wider and more varied range of facts than Sparrow–Devine had revealed in 'Idi Amin', was probably true. How true, it would not have been easy to say. Sparrow's 'Congo Man' with its portrayal of what one of my English colleagues in 1966 termed 'the ignoble savage', remained in the 1970s and 1980s and well into the 1990s, far more popular than, say, the Mighty Duke's post-1970 images of the black diasporan as the much-abused, but still erect and militant warrior, the 'manchild of a slave'. If aspects of the society's black consciousness had changed, other aspects had remained substantially the same. The society moved into the 1990s bearing this paradox of change and unchange; of greater intelligence and a wider range of information available about Africa and everywhere else, and yet greater or equal indifference to how the Caribbean people located themselves both within the world of international affairs and with respect to notions of ancestors and identity.

Sparrow–Devine would, between 1981 and 1991, focus on the anti-apartheid campaign and the worthier — than Idi Amin to be sure — figure of Nelson Mandela. This could mean that the unanswered criticisms of Karamoko, Alleyne-Forte and Cato had made some impact on their representation of Africa and African affairs. Maybe. But 'Congo Man' continued to be Sparrow's 'all-time favourite', and the release of yet another updated version in the late 1980s could still evoke harsh criticism from an offended member of the public. This time the response took the form of the published lyrics of a 'counter-calypso' (my term) penned by Vernon Alexander of San Fernando, who in 'The Noble Congo Man' condemned Sparrow as 'a disgrace' to 'we race'; 'wicked to [his] people'; 'playing the game to get Uncle Sam fame' and 'selling his brother for Uncle Sam's dollar'.[84] Alexander asked Sparrow to burn all recordings of 'Congo Man.'

This urge to replace Sparrow's ignoble cannibal by a noble Congo Man has survived; but so has the reality of the Congo basin as a venue of postcolonial chaos, in which the cutlass — inscribed since the late nineteenth century as the tool and weapon with which King Leopold's African police amputated the right hands of men, women and children who rebelled, or did not work hard enough, or could not pay the required taxes — re-merged in the late twentieth century as the genocidal weapon in the inter-tribal wars in Kigali, Rwanda Burundi. In 100 days, Hutu militants butchered 800,000 Tutsis and liberal Hutus. The cutlass, and the thousands of corpses floating in the Congo in 1994, have become the living and nightmarish icons of the Congolese millennium. Since 1999 in the Democratic Republic of Congo, according to recent reports on what seems like a recycling of the post-independence Congolese situation, 'ethnic warfare, marked by atrocities including cannibalism, has killed 50,000 people'.[85]

It would be difficult, after all the killings that have taken place in Africa, Viet Nam, Cambodia, the Middle East and the Balkans since the mid 1960s, for one to approach the Congo situation today with the same macabre flippancy that Sparrow employed in 1964 over the then Congo crises. The shift in consciousness in the 1990s was best illustrated not in anything Sparrow sang, but in David Rudder's entire album about Apartheid (*Rudder 1990*) [86] and more particularly in his 1995 composition, 'Heaven.' 'Heaven' regards latter day genocide in the adjoining states of Rwanda and Zaire without the sort of Carnival mask that Sparrow had employed 30 years earlier to negate the horror of current events and convert the Congo crisis into a metaphor or backdrop for his own phallic fantasy. Rudder's 'Heaven' presents the Congo region of the 1990s as a landscape of the kind of genocide that he feels is possible in a multi-ethnic Trinidad, fractured into 'tribes,' competing ethnicities, vestigial castes and both rigid and fluid class formations. Rwanda and Kigali cease to be thousands of miles away in space and time and consciousness and become the living omen of what is in this era of highly racialized politics, an imminent inter-tribal imbroglio. 'Tribal war,' Rudder warns his turbulent nation, 'is only one dark emotion away,' and societies structured like that of Trinidad and Tobago's cannot afford to be complacent about such matters.

In Sparrow's 'Congo Man,' catastrophe in that land of the distant ancestors served as the backdrop for a grim yet hilarious cannibal joke. In Rudder's 'Heaven' catastrophe is presented unmasked, uncarnivalized, with the calypso-lament ending not with the narrator baiting his audience to either confirm or deny rumours of his phallic competence, but with the narrator quoting Kurtz's last words from Conrad's *Heart of Darkness,* 'the horror, the horror'. Humour is absent from Rudder's landscape of possibility, not because he is a disciple of the post-1970's Black nationalist commitment to seriousness, dignity, and focused, unsmiling warriorhood against the castrating imperialist system, but because he has through contemplation of postcolonial African catastrophe, recognized that genocidal ethnic nationalism usually begins or continues in the power vacuum left by the strategic withdrawal of predatory and authoritarian imperialism. So Rudder in 1995 assumes the mask and rhetoric of the prophet who warns the nation about the stress-cracks he has observed in the edifice of its human relations, where Sparrow in 1965 mocked subversively at its substantial residues of racism, its bourgeois pretence at respectability, and the schizophrenic ambivalence with which it simultaneously affirmed and denied his kingship.

Notes

1. *Trinidad Guardian* (hereafter *TG*), October 5, 1964.
2. Linda de Four, *Gimme Room to Sing: Calypsoes of the Mighty Sparrow 1958–1993: A Discography* (Port of Spain: Linda de Four, 1993).
3. Debbie Jacob, 'Sparrow's Own All-time Favourite', *Sunday Express* (hereafter *SE*), February 10, 1991.
4. Sparrow, interview by Wayne Brown, *TG*, October 2, 1966.
5. René Girard, *Violence and the Sacred*, trans. Patrick Gregory (Baltimore: Johns Hopkins University Press, 1977).
6. D'Lynne Waldron, 'Tribal War in Luluabourg, Belgian Congo', 1960, p.13 http://www.dlynnwaldron.com/Luluabourg.html
7. Waldron, 'Tribal War in Luluabourg, Belgian Congo', 16.
8. Waldron, 'Tribal War in Luluabourg, Belgian Congo', 34.
9. *Time*, January 18, 1963.
10. Ibid.
11. Valda Sampson, 'De Vice in Dey Own Head', Letter to the Editor, *Express*, December 20, 1984, 9.
12. *TG*, February 24, 1965.
13. Sampson, 'De Vice in Dey Own Head', 9.
14. *Express*, December 20, 1984, 9.
15. Sampson, 'De Vice in Dey Own Head', 9.
16. 'Massacre in the Congo', *Time* vol. 84, no.23 (December 4, 1964).
17. *TG*, January 4, 1965.
18. Dennis Williams, *Other Leopards* (London: New Authors Ltd., Hutchinson Group, 1963).
19. Derek Walcott, 'A Far Cry from Africa', in *Derek Walcott: Collected Poems 1948–1984* (New York: Farrar, Straus & Giroux, 1986), 17–18.
20. *TG*, February 16, 1964.
21. *TG*, February 25, 1964.
22. 'Get to Hell Outta Here', *Get Outa Here*. Matrix NLP 5050 ½ c. pre carnival, 1965.
23. Lord Blakie, 'The Doctor Ent Deh, *Sparrow Lost/De Doctor Eh Dey*. 7" Telco TW–3240, 1965.
24. Arthur Robinson, 'The New Frontier and the New Africa', *TG*, Friday, January 17, 1964 (one of a series of articles running weekly in the *Trinidad Guardian*, January/February 1964).
25. *TG*, January 17, 1964.
26. Vidia Naipaul, *The Middle Passage* (London: André Deutsch, 1962), 83.
27. Sparrow, 'The Slave', *Kruschev and Kennedy/The Slave*. 7" Jump Up JU-507, 1963.
28. The Mighty Sparrow, 'Martin Luther King for President' on *Sparrow Sings the Outcast*, Port of Spain, National NLP 4199, 1964 ($33^{1/3}$ rpm, Side 2, Track #1).
29. *TG*, October 2, 1966.
30. Louise Bennett, 'Back to Africa', *Jamaica Labrish* (Kingston: Sangsters Book Stores, 1996), 214.
31. Carole Boyce-Davies, 'The African Theme in Trinidad Calypso', *Caribbean Quarterly* 13, no.3 (June 1985): 67–86.
32. Carole Boyce-Davies, 'The Africa Theme in Trinidad Calypso', 73–74.
33. Derek Walcott, 'Efficient Birdie Minus the Feather-ruffling', Review of the Original Young Brigade. *TG*, January 6, 1965.
34. Michael Anthony, *Parade of the Carnivals of Trinidad 1839–1989* (Port of Spain, Trinidad: Circle Press, 1989).

35. *SG*, February 21, 1965.
36. *TG*, February 9, 1965.
37. Freethinker, Letter to the Editor, *TG*, February 18, 1965.
38. L. Milne, 'I Am Ashamed', Letter to the Editor, *TG*, February 18, 1965.
39. Clifford Sealey, 'Ah Mr. Censor', Letter to the Editor, *TG*, Thursday, February 23, 1965.
40. 'Sailing Boat Experience', No album information available [c. 1957].
41. The *Birmingham Post*, November 25, 1964.
42. Joseph Conrad, *Heart of Darkness*, ed. Robert Kimbrough (1899; reprint, New York: Norton, 1963).
43. Ibid., 42.
44. Ibid.
45. Leasa Farrar Fortune, 'Hollywood's Haiti: the Genesis of "Voodoo Movies" (abstract of paper presented at Conference of the Centre for Black Music Research, Port of Spain 2001), quoted in Bruce Paddington, 'Caribbean Cinema: Cultural Articulations, Historical Formation and Film Practices' (PhD thesis, University of the West Indies, St. Augustine, Trinidad and Tobago, 2004).
46. Derek Walcott, 'Crusoe's Journal', in *The Castaway and Other Poems* (London: Jonathan Cape, 1965), 51.
47. James Joyce, *Ulysses* (1922; London: The Bodley Head, 1960).
48. Ibid., 99.
49. Norman Cohn, *Europe's Inner Demons* (1975; St. Albans: Paladin, 1976), 3.
50. Ibid., 11.
51. John Cowley, *Carnival, Canboulay and Calypso: Traditions in the Making* (Cambridge: Cambridge University Press, 1996); E.L. Joseph, *History of Trinidad* (London: H.J. Mills, 1838; reprint, London: Frank Cass & Co. Ltd, 1970).
52. Dom Basil Mathews, *Crisis of the West Indian Family* (Port of Spain, Trinidad: the University of the West Indies, Extra-mural Department, 1952).
53. Cowley, *Carnival, Canboulay and Calypso*, 12.
54. Cynthia Davis, 'Calypso and Carnival Influences in the Works of Jean Rhys', Calypso and Caribbean Literature Panel, Calypso and the Caribbean Literary Imagination, University of Miami, Coral Gables, Florida, March 19, 2005.
55. Gordon Rohlehr, *A Scuffling of Islands: Essays on Calypso* (Port of Spain: Lexicon Trinidad, 2004), 281–334.
56. Gordon Rohlehr, *Calypso and Society in Pre-Independence Trinidad* (Port of Spain: Gordon Rohlehr, 1990), 103.
57. 'Seditious Publications Act Passed', *Weekly Guardian* March 27, 1920, 11.
58. Lord Melody, 'Corbeau Flying High', *The Devil/The Beast/Caroline/Corbeau Flying High*. 7" EP Cook CC 5811, 1958.
59. Lord Melody, interviewed by Gordon Rohlehr, November 24, 1987, Library, University of the West Indies, St. Augustine, Trinidad.
60. Raymond Quevedo, (Atilla the Hun), *Atilla's Kaiso: A Short History of Trinidad Calypso* (St. Augustine, Trinidad and Tobago: University of the West Indies Extra Mural Dept., 1983).
61. Sparrow, 'Reply to Melody', *Calypso Carnival 1958*. LP Balisier HDF 1005 Cook 920, 1958.
62. Sparrow, 'Dey Washin Dey Mouth', *120 Calypsoes to Remember*. Port of Spain, 1963.
63. *TG*, July 7, 1960.
64. *TG*, Janaury 10, 1965.

65. Lord Melody (Fitzroy Alexander), 'Mas', Port of Spain, RCA Victor, 7-2172 (B-7-900), 1965 (45 rpm).
66. Sparrow, 'Toronto Mass', *Hotter Than Ever*. Matrix RA 3112, 1972.
67. Sparrow, 'Mr. Rake and Scrape', *Veronica/Mr. Rake and Scrape*. 7" RCA 7-2041, 1961.
68. Sparrow, 'The Village Ram', *Bull Pistle Gang/The Village Ram*. 7" Jump Up JU-523, 1963.
69. Vaneisa Baksh, 'The King and I', *Sunday Express*. October 6, 1991.
70. Sparrow, 'Cockfight', *More Sparrow More*. RaRa 2020, Island Series CCS 2020, 1969.
71. Sparrow, 'Sa Sa Yea', *More Sparrow More*. RaRa 2020, Island Series CCS 2020, 1969.
72. Sparrow, 'The Outcast', *The Outcast*. LP National NLP 4199, 1964.
73. *TG*, June 8, 1970.
74. 'Du Du Yemi', *Sparrow N.Y.C. Blackout*. Matrix CR139, 1977; 'Idi Amin', *Idi Amin/Du Du Yemi (Black Beauty)*. Charlies 1906, 1978; 'Gu Nu Gu', *London Bridge*. Matrix JAF-001, 1979; 'Love African Style', *London Bridge*. Matrix JAF-001, 1979; 'Isolate South Africa', *Sweeter Than Ever*. Matrix JAF 1005, 1982; 'The Witch Doctor', *Sparrow V/S The Rest*. Matrix DSR SP, 1976; 'I Owe No Apology', *We Could Make It Easy If We Try*. Matrix BLS 1011, 1991.
75. *Sunday Punch*, November 6, 1994; 'Invade South Africa', *A Touch of Class*. Matrix BSR SP 041, 1985.
76. Sparrow, 'Congo Man', *Congo Man/Patsy*. 7" National NSP-052, 1965.
77. *The Sun*, December 12, 1986.
78. Modibo Karamoko, Letter to Editor, *Express*, Wednesday February 15, 1978.
79. Rueben Cato, 'Oh Sparrow, You Have Shocked Me', *Express*, January 16, 1978.
80. Learie Alleyne-Forte, 'Open letter to Sparrow on That Idi Amin Calypso', *TG*, January 21, 1978.
81. Black Brother, Letter to Editor, *Express*, Wednesday, February 22, 1978.
82. Karamoko, Letter to Editor, *Express*, Wednesday February 15, 1978.
83. Naipaul, *The Middle Passage*, 68.
84. Vernon Alexander, 'The Noble Congo Man', *Sunday Express*. February 5, 1989.
85. *TG*, March 4, 2005.
86. David Rudder, *David Rudder 1990*. Port of Spain, Lypsoland, 1990, 33S! rpm LP Record, CR013.

6

CALYPSO AND THE BACCHANAL CONNECTION[1]

Earl Lovelace

Calypsonians really ketch hell for a long time
To associate your self with them was a big crime.
If your sister talked to a steelband man
The family want to break she hand
Put she out, lick out every teeth in she mouth. Pass
You outcast!

The Mighty Sparrow, 'Outcast'

This calypso, 'Outcast' by The Mighty Sparrow tells the story of calypso and of calypso's men and women as undesirables, at that time relegated by society to what I call the bacchanal space, the jamette or underworld space in the Creole culture of Trinidad and Tobago.² It was sung sometime in the 1960s. So a conference on calypso 40 years later indicates to us the distance that we have travelled. We owe debts of gratitude to calypsonians like Sparrow, Kitchener, Chalkdust, Shadow, and Rudder, but are specially grateful to people like Gordon Rohlehr, Chalkdust, and Louis Regis, to name a few, who have brought home to us the wealth of calypso production, the variety of its concerns and its significance to us as achievement and history.

   I myself have had a long relationship with calypso and if I had been bold-faced enough I might have become a calypsonian. My calypso name was Lord Farmer. I was working in the late 1950s in the Agricultural Department at the government farm in Rio Claro, when it was given to me by Lord Blakie, who had come up to Rio Claro to visit Supey, Lord Superior, who is from Rio Claro. The highlight of my possible career was as a backup singer for Bas of Rio Claro. Bas is Lord Superior's brother, and a very good calypso singer, in fact Bas could sing anybody's calypso very well but he wasn't very much of a composer. He had great presence, great voice, and Supey agrees that if Bas had taken this calypso singing seriously he would have been very successful. I was backup for him in a competition in Rio Claro, I believe at Railway View Hall where fetes were held in those days. Bas himself was a favourite citizen of the town, a limer and a livewire, a footballer, sprinter and a great humorist and storyteller, I mean, Bas could really tell you stories. I am a joke compared to him. And Bas himself was the subject of his most humorous stories. Many of them were connected with his adventures as an events and fete promoter.

On one occasion, Bas had organized things well, had a good band — Joey Lewis or Clarence Curvan or Dutchy Brothers or Fitz-Vaughn Bryan — and had sent out invitations far and wide. Everything set. Fellars ready. Girls dressed. People on their way to the fete. And then rain. People right next door to the fete just a few yards away and rain falling so heavy that they can't move. The rain fall whole night, not letting up for anybody to move. Another time, the weather good, fete start; fight. The fete mash up. It was these among many disappointments, which led him to migrate.

So I was a backup singer for Bas in a competition in which he sang two songs. One was a composition of mine and the other one was his. My composition — and I remember these things from then — was kind of topical. Saliah had a parlour in Rio Claro that had just been broken into and there was much speculation as to who was responsible for the break in. This is what I remember of my song:

> When you have you news that you want to spread
> About who getting married or who is dead
> Don't tell me at all
> Leave me out of that
> Go and tell your story
> To Tom, Dick, or Harry
> Or tell your good friend Parrot
> I don't want to know who frenin with Miss Olga
> ... Something or other ...
> Or who break Saliah parlour
> I'm not inquisitive
> Of that I'm positive
> When you have your news
> Put it in your shoes

And Bas who was equally talented, had his song. This is what I remember of it:

> Don't look for help from me
> See the Salvation Army
> Don't look for help from me

> See the Salvation Army
> When you and your man was going okay
> You didn't have one damn thing to say
> Now he kick you and he buss your face
> Your coming home to my place
> Get out my place Miss Emily
> I don't want you here
> Get out my place Miss Emily
> This thing go cost you damn dear
> Stick to your man doo-doo la
> Stick to the end
> I am your enemy
> Run by your friend

That competition took place in Rio Claro. The other competitors included the late Zandolie, Michael Anthony's brother from Mayaro and McGruff from Dades Trace. I believe it is the same McGruff who came out with a song either this year or last year. Bas the hometown boy was placed third, McGruff was second, and Zandolie won the competition with two calypsos, which later became well known on the national stage. One was 'The Jockey' in which he said, 'I ride cow, goat, horse, sheep, jackass and all / and up to now I never fall,' or something like that.[3] And the other was called 'Man Family' in which the calypsonian found that his woman, Millicent, was always bringing to their house strange men whom she claimed to be relatives.[4] As far as he was concerned that was a bit unnatural, she had too many male relatives. He had never met a woman like that who all her family is man. So he said:

> Millicent, like you take me for Mickey Mouse
> Always bringing man in my house
> And they always with the government
> Either police or regiment
> I don't want to break your jaw
> I don't want to tangle with the law
> So I want you to write all your family name
>   on a piece of paper for me.

To check, I suppose, on whether they were all really bona fide relatives.

As I said Bas was an organizer and in a spirit of entrepreneurship he organized a roving calypso tent and asked me to be a member. Principal participants of this tent were fellars from the same team I played football for, Penetrators. Bas was the right-winger and really loved to play, he had speed and determination but he only kicked effectively with his right foot. Once he got injured and we wanted to drop him and he decided no, he was fit to play. I was the captain of the team at that time. So I say, you're injured, your foot not good. He said, no, no, no. I alright. Okay, I said, let us run a race, if I beat you, you can't play, if you win, you play. I was a pretty fast runner, but Bas was a real sprinter. So we lined up in the road in the night. I said Go, and we take off. I had beaten Bas. He say, no, no, no, false start, so we went again about three times until finally Bas kind of edged me on the tape, or told me that he kind of edged me on the tape, and so he played.

With us at that time also was Aji and Lord Shoes. Shoes is a character that appears in *A Brief Conversion and Other Stories*.[5] He was given the name Shoes because he was the first person in Rio Claro to wear a blue shoes among the fellows so they called him Blue Shoes at first and then they shortened it to Shoes. Shoes used to dance on broken bottle and eat fire. He was quite an intriguing guy and I wrote about him in 'The Fire Eater'.[6] He had come to Port of Spain with BoyBoy and Toy a half-Chinese acrobat, and BoyBoy also was an acrobat who later I was told settled in Britain as an obeah man. Shoes became a calypsonian, at least in Rio Claro. He never wrote anything, he just got on the stage and he started to sing a song about a Chinese fellow and all the words he had were: 'Chung, chickee, Chung, chickee, Chung.' He managed to have people collapsing with laughter, and became a star in Navet, Tabaquite and the places where the tent went.

At Rio Claro, I was also involved in stickfight. There was a lot of stickfighting on the Mayaro road in front of Khandan shop as well as on the road to Biche, with stickmen like Short Boy and Seven Days John. Seven Days John was so named because he was a Seven Days Adventist. I don't know how he became a stickfighter. He was a man with massive forearms and when he made a blow, it looked like the force would break the stick his opponent was parrying with. He was really powerful. Other stickfighters included Panther and Garbo, both from Mayaro. They played football for us too, for Penetrators. I remember going to stickfights, standing up behind the drummers and learning the lavways and singing. One of the songs, was: 'Crow, crow, jumbie bird crow / jumbie bird wouldn't crow.' It is about a jumbie bird that fancies himself a fighting cock, a song in which one fighter ridicules others as they hesitate to come into the gayelle. And you may know this chant, 'mooma, mooma, your son in de grave already'; and this, 'mooma, mooma pigeon flying, / O Lord, pigeon flying today'; and, 'Joe Pringay, lend me your bois to play.'

I saw stickfighters, saw the dances, heard the chants, and came to note that every stickman had not only his own chant, but his own special movements, and I recognized the influence of Shango on stickfight. Later I would conclude that much of what Africans brought by way of religion — this may seem like somewhat of a jump but later it will become clear — did not die but were taken into the secular domain. And it is my view that much of what we have now in what is called the Creole culture came out of African religious and cultural forms, principally because there was no other outlet in which they (Africans) could legitimately express self.

As we know, apart from the few Amerindians native to this country, everybody else came here or was brought here. I have taken the view that there were two basic spaces we entered when we came to this country: one I call the Ethnic Space, in which members of a group carried on the religion and cultural practices they brought with them, and the other the Creole Space, the general meeting place of cultures. Every group but the African was allowed an Ethnic space in which they could maintain the religion and culture they had come with. Cultural and religious forms that were African were all banned at one point or another, and so in order for Africans to express self they had either to abandon their gods or find ways to bring religion and culture into what was legitimate. So nearly everything they had brought had to be poured into the secular space, often not as a whole but as fragments. Carnival would become one such space because it was a legal and legitimate festival, and what might now seem to be independent activities — calypso, stickfight, the carnival characters, were, I suggest, linked to a larger cultural–religious whole. Recently someone told me that she had gone to an egungun festival — in Trinidad — where the masks were the carnival characters, baby doll and jab molassie and blue-devils, et cetera. I remember going to Carriacou (at that time I had no idea of the connectedness between Shango and stickfight), so I went to Carriacou to witness the Big Drum Dance or Nation Dance as it is called, and I went with great anticipation to see all these African survivals that had been kept alive in dance. And when they started to play the drums and to dance, I recognized all the dances from the stickfights that I had seen over the years in Rio Claro and Grande and Mayaro. I always knew that every stickman entered the ring with his own chant, moved with his peculiar movements just as you see with calypsonians, each had his own rhythm, his own movements. It was then it struck me that these movements, these dances of the stickfighters — there is a word for it that escapes me now — represented the different nation dances. So it seems that even while Africans transcended tribe here in Trinidad and Tobago and in the Caribbean, they retained — without necessarily recognizing it — particular tribal songs and dances and movements.

Not only did the forms move into the secular area, it seems that the spirit did as well. I am referring to spirit possession. Now, I used to think of possession as occurring in a Shango palais brought on by the influence of the drums, the beat to a particular Orisha, and I have witnessed in a Shango ceremony someone possessed exhibiting extraordinary strength and balance which he could not have had without being possessed. I have seen actually, a small man, carrying a big woman on his back while dancing and moving and stopping and darting. I believe that this extraordinary strength by means of possession is the same kind of strength a man displays when he is possessed, when he has a spirit on him. It is the same thing. The people know it. They say so and so has a spirit on him to fight. And so you will see a single man so strong that it will take seven men to hold him down. Shango — if it is Shango doing the possessing — has moved from the religious to the secular space.

And I also attended wakes, which were great social events in the countryside. In Valencia, I remember a fellow there, Sam Primus, who *could* sing. At wakes, Sam was a star, and he always had a little pleasant smile as if he was very conscious of his star status. And I remember him at a wake singing what was literally the test piece for wake singers:

> And thou, Bethlehem, in the land of Judah
> art not the least among the princes of Judah
> for out of thee shall come a governor
> and he shall rule thy people Israel.

And the chant that followed:

> Aunty Rachel oh,
> Aunty Rachel oh, she big and she able
> Bring de bottle and she put it on the table
> Whole night we going to sing,
> Aunty Rachel sing for joy ...

And of course, there was also fine play, which consisted of games and songs: 'I have a tree to cut, Zelina / Woy woy, wop, Zelina.' And of course, as well there was bongo at a wake. In Rio Claro I got to know Sylvan who was the champion bongo dancer, who had a voice like a bell and who was also a good singer, a good chantwell. And these are some of the chants that I remember very fondly,

> When de corporal dead and gone,
> the place was in a mourn
> nobody know
> where de corporal dead and go.

And there was another one in which the call and response motif is clear:

> When I sol
> far sol ,
> when I dead,
> bury me,
> in Marabella
> Junction,
> in Marabella
> Junction,

in Marabella
Junction

And there was parang for Christmas and we would go around singing if not the Spanish, which was sung by my neighbour, a county councillor I think his name was Fuentes, old calypsos, or sentimental songs that we liked. One was 'Lady in Red' with Tommy on the guitar and others of us with whatever instrument we could make from Christmas toys, bottle and spoon, tins, boxes. Later, I would see the Bel Air dances in Mayaro taken there by Aldwyn Boynes, himself a dancer, and so on. What I have been describing are my first hand experiences of cultural forms within the Creole culture.

Now from these experiences, I have come to see calypso not only as a song, but as a voice emerging from the Creole world, indeed the voice of the Creole world in which the ordinary people lived, in which they celebrated themselves, their heroes, recalled important events, and expressed attitudes to life and the world. There were of course the elements of double entendre as well as the singing of sexually suggestive wake songs, for example:

> the bull, the bull, the bull jump the woman in the open savannah,
> when he take out his pistle, he make the woman whistle
> the bull, the bull jump de woman ...

One can note that there is a whole body, if you want, a base of different types of songs that would influence calypso. But the calypso was not the only voice of that world. We had Sam Cooke, Elvis Presley, Bing Crosby, Nat King Cole, Ella Fitzgerald, Ray Charles. And I don't think we should forget that because that too is part of what influenced us in the Creole world.

How then did Calypso arrive at the outcast status alluded to by Sparrow? We have to remember that before the negative treatment of calypso and calypsonians, the same treatment — indeed worse — was meted out to the Shouters, the Shango and the stickfight — all of them were banned, drumming was banned. But calypso was a powerful force. It was linked to Carnival which was already in the bad books of the colonial authorities and which from the 1840s onwards the press made an all out drive to stop, describing it as *a relic of barbarism and the annual abomination* and so on. Calypso could not be banned, it could be limited, and the most effective way of limiting calypso was to demonize it, to link it to carnival and to bacchanal. This didn't require any fresh imagination. Shango and the Shouters had already been demonized; so in linking calypso to the bacchanal aspect of Carnival or to the idea of Carnival as bacchanal, both Carnival and calypso were consolidated in the Trinidadian's consciousness as bacchanal.

As we know, Carnival was one thing for the black masses and another thing for the whites and mulattoes, one growing out of the Camboulay (cannes brules) and the emancipation struggles, and the other out of the French masked balls and festivities, one on the street and the other in ballrooms. It was the African inspired Carnival that was blasted by the press with a characterization that was so off-putting that until very recently — indeed even now — black people associated with mas have been contemptuously referred to as having a carnival mentality, an attitude to the world that emphasizes wastefulness, revelry, lack of discipline and whatever else is unseemly and unwelcome. And I think that in promoting the idea of Carnival and calypso as bacchanal was one way of discouraging the assigning of too great an importance to them and maintaining them in a nether world of social acceptability. Having calypso identified with bacchanal meant that calypso was linked and limited to the bacchanal season of Carnival. Once Carnival was done, Lent came in and we went back to Nat King Cole and Bing Crosby and others. We were not allowed to sing calypsos in Lent, so imagine the frustration. You dying to tell someone about a calypso you had heard or a band you had seen in Carnival, and you couldn't speak. Now I wasn't a Catholic but somehow the law extended to me. Until Kitchener sang: 'Ah go dance in Lent I don't care who say / ... I can't wait until Glorious Saturday.' Because I remember that in those days you had to wait until Glorious Saturday which was sometime in the middle of the Lenten season which lasted for 40 days, which by the time it came to an end, Carnival would be a thing of the past.[7]

The development of soca and calypso that limits itself exclusively to Carnivals has helped to link calypso even more firmly to Carnival and to bacchanal, and to justify calypso's appearance on radio as a strictly seasonal thing. Soca of course does not provide the social challenges that calypso has always done and that is fine with those who see Carnival as bacchanal and calypso/soca as functioning in its service.

And today you have a new song, I don't know whether you call it raga soca or what exactly it is, but it presents a fast paced frenzied beat, guttural sound, an aggressive tone and a performed militancy — I don't know that these fellas stand up for anything that I know — and it occurred to me — we were talking about this, this morning — that this form of music might be mirroring the harshness in the society or be somehow connected to it. There is a lack of humour, lack of balance. I mean, when Gordon Rohlehr was talking about Sparrow's 'The Congo Man', there were aspects of it that were difficult to swallow, still, the calypso in the end with its humour, made it a little easier for us to relate to each other and understand each other and to come to grips with whatever problems we were having.

I was saying that we have come from disparate places to this country and have had to occupy two spaces: the Ethnic space and the Creole space, and that Africans have poured a lot of themselves into that Creole space because they were denied a legitimate ethnic space. I think that makes them therefore very responsible for seeing that this space is made into a real meeting place for all. We all have a lot to lose if that space becomes corrupted, bacchanalized, rendered impotent. The idea of having ethnic spaces as reference points has many merits in what is still very much a Eurocentric world, but the vision of ethnic spaces as a retreat from the bacchanal of the Creole world is a temptation we must resist. The space for adventure, for newness, for growth is the Creole space. It is this space that we have to get right. It is here we have to challenge definitions and pose questions and utilize what we have inherited to shape a real space of our own.

I am thinking that calypso represents the promise and confusion of the Creole culture. There is a lot more to be said and I am about to end now. I think we have some good signs on the horizon, actually not on the horizon but very present, for example, we have Three Canal and Brother Resistance and a whole brigade of young rapso people who have in a way taken the responsibility that this is their place and who understand what has gone on and that we have to go beyond the bacchanal space by continuing to define who we are, to reclaim the fullness of our experience and not to persist with an identity imposed on us by a colonial order whose objective was to keep us on the cultural defensive, the better to sustain its rule. We have to re-examine the history and present as well a vision of the past that impels to our future. We cannot have a past in which we are going to get stuck; it's like writing, you have to start from where you could go forward. We have to answer questions, at least: Who we are? What kind of society we want? How to treat the poor, if we want the poor at all? What rules do we want to live by? What it means to be human in this world? We are not living in a borrowed culture, but one that we are creating, against a background of a lot of struggles an important one of which is to disengage from the bacchanal characterization that began in colonialism and create a self confident culture of our own.

Notes

1. Keynote Address, Conference on Calypso and the Caribbean Literary Imagination, University of Miami, March 18, 2005.
2. The Mighty Sparrow (Slinger Francisco), 'Outcast' or 'The Outcast', *The Outcast* LP National NLP 4199, 1964.
3. Mighty Zandolie (Sylvester Anthony), 'The Jockey', not commercially recorded, n.d.
4. Mighty Zandolie (Sylvester Anthony), 'Man Family' or 'Too Much Man Family', *Too Much Man Family/Merchant of Venice*. 7" National NSP 167, 1968.
5. Earl Lovelace, *Brief Conversion and Other Stories* (London: Heinemann, 1988).
6. There are two such stories in *Brief Conversion and Other Stories*: 'The Fire Eater's Journey' and 'The Fire Eater's Return'.
7. Glorious Saturday (Holy Saturday) actually comes at the end of the Lenten period.

7

UNMASKING THE CHANTWELL NARRATOR IN EARL LOVELACE'S FICTION

Funso Aiyejina

With the publication in 1979 of *The Dragon Can't Dance*,[1] which is now widely regarded as the quintessential carnival novel, Earl Lovelace established himself as a sensitive, perceptive, and rigorous interrogator and manipulator of carnival and the carnivalesque for thematic and aesthetic purposes. However, his preoccupation with carnival and the carnivalesque dates back to his very first novel, *While Gods Are Falling* (1965)[2] in which calypsoes such as Spoiler's 'Himself Tell Himself' are deployed as meta-narrative threads. Of his five novels, one collection of short stories, and one collection of plays to date, only one, *The Schoolmaster*,[3] does not engage with carnival or the carnivalesque. This paper continues my exploration of Lovelace's narrative strategies initiated in 'Novelypso: Indigenous Narrative Strategies in Earl Lovelace's Fiction', where I identified and analysed a number of carnival and carnival-related paradigms deployed by Lovelace as narrative signifiers. In this sequel, I explore the possibility of reading many of Lovelace's narrators as chantwells or approximations of the chantwell. I suggest that although Lovelace experiments with first-, second-, and third-person (limited or omniscient) narrators, the narrative tradition that conditions his main narrators is, more often than not, the tradition of the chantwell/calypsonian.

Gordon Rohlehr dates the emergence of the chantwell figure in Trinidad to the early nineteenth century.[4] By the 1840s, there was a chaotic linguistic situation in Trinidad with Spanish, French, and English contesting for official supremacy, with French Creole emerging as the dominant language for verbal communication. A number of African languages were negotiating their status among the majority of Africans of the underclass in squatter settlements that sprung up around the urban centres to which many Africans had drifted in search of jobs.[5] One of the consequences of the competition for limited resources and jobs within such squatter settlements was the rise of calinda/stickfighting street gangs, formed to defend turfs. Each such band had a lead singer/chantwell whose duty it was to 'harangue the stickfighters into action, to sustain the courage of his champion, and to pour scorn on the rival group or champion'.[6] The chantwell functioned as a soloist and the other members of the gang as the chorus. The chantwell, as the 'possessor of the word and as a spokesman for the group, occupied a position of supreme importance',[7] and the performance of the chantwell would go on to form the foundation of the calypso art. In essence, 'calypso grew out of this milieu of confrontation and mastery, of violent self-assertiveness and rhetorical force; of a constant quest for a more splendid language, and excellence of tongue.'[8] The chantwell as a storyteller, critic, commentator, creator of delightful turns of phrase, and astute user of double entendre, often with humorous effect, is reminiscent of African griots who, among other things, 'recount genealogies, narrate epics, compose songs to mark important events, sing praises of others ... teach people of all ages about the past ... interpret speeches, announce news, maintain the legal, family, and historical records of a people, and give advice to their patrons'.[9] The chantwell as a storyteller is central to the survival of every civilization because, in the words of the Old Man in Achebe's *Anthills of the Savannah*, 'it is the story ... that saves our progeny from blundering like blind beggars into the spikes of the cactus fence. The story is our escort; without it, we are blind.'[10]

The Dragon Can't Dance, a novel that owes its inspiration to carnival, closes with the voice and vision of the calypsonian; not with Aldrick, the questing native intellectual and central hero of the narrative; not with Fisheye, the warrior and defender of tradition; not with Pariag and Dolly, the male–female idealization of the latest cultural addition to an emerging multicultural/cross-cultural mosaic; and not with Sylvia, the new generation of the Black woman whose ultimate self-discovery, along with that of Aldrick, represents the most overt articulation of a positive vision for the society, one that includes the female perspective in an otherwise patriarchal society. The inevitable question is: Why has Lovelace, who has consistently demonstrated that he is a deliberate artist, opted to close with Philo, a man who is viewed by the Hill as a traitor, following his material success, his relocation to middle-class Diego Martin, and his in-your-face flaunting of the miracle of his escape from the poverty of the Hill?

One way of looking at Lovelace's narrative choice here is to consider the fact that the voice of the calypsonian is actually the unidentified voice presiding over the novel in the same way that the voice of the calypsonian presides over carnival — his calypsos are listened to, jumped up and danced to, and played by steelbands. The novel, therefore, is presented from the perspective of the calypsonian as he engages in the documentation of the trials and tribulations of the Hill. That these are possible interpretations is hinted at in the introspective, ritualistic, and retrospective nature of the novel's closing coda, in which the details of Philo's development as man and calypsonian are presented as an intrinsically intertwined ethos of personal and communal developments. Philo is presented at once as a hero and a villain, a victim and a victimizer; he is both the narrator and the subject of the narrative, hence, his double-vision consciousness. Philo's double vision, articulated in part in the radical difference between his views about the Hill before and after his material success, is an intrinsic consequence of the circumstances of the history of the region; it is an expression of

> the psychological flexibility of the Trinidadian, and even perhaps the Caribbean person. So the sense of joy, when it surfaces, must not be seen as trivial, nor totally descriptive of the whole person; similarly, the very serious concerns when they are expressed should not be seen as an aberration to be dismissed
>
> *Growing in the Dark* [11]

When Philo reviews his life without attempting to sanitize it, he is merely affirming the critical tradition of the chantwell/griot who is capable of simultaneously praising and deflating his subject, including himself.

Against the background of these comments about Philo, it is possible to re-examine the prologue of the novel and to recognize the embedded call-and-response pattern of the chantwell/chorus paradigm in the novel's single-voiced, single-versioned, and unidentified but involved third-person narration. At the beginning of the Prologue,[12] the narrator's 'This is the hill tall above the city where Taffy', introduces the observing voice of the chantwell/teller-of-tales, and at the end of the Prologue 'dance' establishes the choral refrain, such that the Prologue can be re-formatted as follows to convey the underlying call-and-response tradition at work:

Solo: There is dancing in the calypso.
Chorus: Dance!

Solo: If the words mourn the death of a neighbour, the music insists that you

Chorus: dance;

Solo: if it tells the troubles of a brother, the music says

Chorus: dance.

Solo: Dance to the hurt!

Chorus: Dance!

Solo: If you catching hell,

Chorus: dance,

Solo: and the government don't care,

Chorus: dance!

Solo: Your woman take your money and run away with another man,

Chorus: dance.

Solo: Dance!

Chorus: Dance!

Solo: Dance! It is in dancing that you ward off evil. Dancing is a chant that cuts off the power of the devil.

Chorus: Dance! Dance! Dance!

Once analysed in this way, it becomes possible to see the novel as the narrative of an observing calypsonian operating as a master of ceremonies who is presenting a parade of carnival bands with chapters like 'Queen of the Band', 'The Princess', and 'The Dragon' as individuals/kings/queens in a carnival band that could easily be named the 'Calvary Hill Band'. In fact, although the narration is not undertaken in the first-person/direct voice of the calypsonian, it is executed in a style that acknowledges the calypsonian as the master of ceremony, as a documenter and articulator of events and sensibilities as they relate to him as an individual participant in the human dramas around him, and as they affect the community as a whole. 'If I consider my novel, *The Dragon Can't Dance*,' Lovelace confesses, 'I think of the whole book as the movement of a calypso,'[13] thus affirming the need to approach this and his other novels with an awareness of the nuances of the calypso art form.

In *The Wine of Astonishment*,[14] Lovelace continues to explore the figure of the chantwell as a narrative trope. Of course, *The Wine of*

Astonishment is narrated in the first-person voice of Eva who is not a chantwell by normal definition although she affirms the notion of women as the active carriers and, by extension, vocalizers of tradition. Eva is the Mother in the Spiritual Baptist Church over which her husband Bee presides. The strategies she adopts for structuring and narrating the story of her family and community echo those of the chantwell. She is an aggregate of the multiple voices in her community, and, by the end of the narrative, she evolves into a chantwell/griot figure entrusted with the task of identifying the heroes and anti-heroes of the community, and chanting their stories.

When Eva narrates traditional female spaces and consciousness, such as her household, she narrates with the confidence and authority of a participant or witness. When, however, she narrates traditional male spaces, such as the rumshop and the stickfighting gayelle, she is quick to establish that she is a secondary or tertiary filter inspired to re-tell her inherited stories, and re-shape them into collectively beneficial visions. The primary and secondary filters are more often than not the chantwell and her husband respectively:

> Most evening he [Bee] would go down to Buntin shop where the men congregate to play draughts, and he would drink a rum with Clem and listen to the men talk about Hitler, the war and Churchill.
>
> Clem is a chantwell, a singer leading stickfight chants and bongo songs and he will sing a nice sentimental, like Bing Crosby. Clem always had a guitar with him. And he would sit down there picking his guitar above the talking, watching with Bolo what all of us seeing: the Yankees zooming about the place, the village girls parading ... their eyes full with the sickness for money that was the disease taking over everybody...
>
> Clem could make up a song on anything ... and sometimes Clem wouldn't sing at all, just sit with his head lean to one side, the way I see him sometimes when I passing, his fingers pulling soft hard notes out of the guitar strings to match the things that was happening; for it wasn't only the girls, it was the men.[15]

This passage invites a number of observations: (1) Bee participates in the 'story sessions' at Buntin's shop and relays them to Eva; (2) Clem is the village's resident storyteller and social critic; (3) Eva occasionally observes Clem operating as an extemporaneous artist; (4) Clem is a fictive approximation of the calypsonian, especially since the content and design of his songs echo The Mighty Sparrow's comments about war-time Trinidad in 'Jean and Dinah'.

Eva is conscious of her role as a secondary filter. Through narrative-hook lines like, 'As they tell it', she constantly reminds her audience that she is merely re-telling stories she inherited from others. In spite of her confession of her lack of direct access to her stories, however, like the calypsonian, she narrates and recreates with the confidence of a witness. For example, when she reports Bolo saying to Clem: 'We playing the arse here,'[16] we wonder how she managed to know the content of a dialogue that would have, according to her own admission, taken place in the exclusive male domain of the stickfighting gayelle.

The centrality of the chantwell as the repository of the stories of the community becomes manifest after Clem's departure from Bonasse. Before his departure, he functions as the primary source of stories and comments about the sociopolitical landscape of the community, but with his departure, Eva is forced to shift the focus of the narrative away from male/public spaces to private/family/church spaces. She also becomes the primary synthesizer of all the tales rather than the inheritor of Clem's synthesized versions. Ultimately, she offers generalized versions of stories which are so public that everyone in the village is privy to their basic details, or narrates other people's conversations with Bee to which she would have been privy. Ironically, Eva's post-Clem–chantwell sources of stories become more democratized to include Buntin, the store keeper and local ideologue who would become the primary source of the accounts of events at the gayelle in front of his shop, and out-of-Bonasse events like Bolo's visit to a government office to enquire about land: 'Brother Ambrose nephew work there. So between what Ambrose nephew say and what Bolo tell Buntin, it ain't hard to put together what happen there that day,'[17] and that of Komono, 'a half-Carib fellar who always drunk ... and who have on his head more bumps than an alligator have on its body ...'[18] who would narrate the story of Bolo's destruction of Mitchell's bar to a group that includes Eva. They include Cap, who would narrate Bolo's ban from the gambling club to Sister Elaine who would re-narrate it to Eva: 'And I telling the story just as Cap tell Sister Elaine and Sister Elaine tell me,'[19] and Trotman, who would narrate the fight between Bolo and the ten policemen.[20] This section of the novel is replete with narrative source-identifiers like 'Some say',[21] 'They tell this story',[22] 'They tell of another time',[23] and 'As he, Buntin, tell it later',[24] which reinforce the notion of multiple contributory perspectives and a structure of narrative relays that would be refined into central narrative and thematic devices in *Salt*.[25]

Throughout *The Wine of Astonishment*, Lovelace presents Eva as a narrative pool or channel, with some editorial latitude, into which the stories collect and through whom they are organized and disseminated. By the time most of the public stories get to her, they have been mediated by the consciousness of the primary or secondary witnesses. Eva's major task is that of collating, shaping, and giving a unifying and coherent voice to all the stories that are entrusted to her. She is at once inside and outside the stories she tells. In this task, she approximates the chantwell, the broadcast journalist, or the (oral) writer. Interestingly enough, Santo, the narrator in the three linked Fire Eater stories in *A Brief Conversion and Other Stories*[26] is a journalist, albeit a print journalist.[27]

If the chantwell paradigm is not too overt a trope in *The Dragon Can't Dance* and *The Wine of Astonishment*, the same cannot be said for the film *Joebell and America*.[28] 'Joebell and America', the short story, opens with a third-person limited omniscient narrator relating the story of Joebell's frustrations in Trinidad and his decision to migrate to America where he hopes to realize his dreams of a life of pleasure:

> Joebell find that he seeing too much hell in Trinidad so he make up his mind to leave and go away. The place he find he should go is America, where everybody have a motor car and you could ski on snow and where it have seventy-five channels of colour television that never sign off and you could sit down and watch for days, all the boxing and wrestling and basketball, right there as it happening.[29]
>
> *A Brief Conversion*

Like Joebell, the narrator is a gambler and the language of narration approximates Joebell's language as well as the language of dialogue. As a participating third-person narrator, the narrator can only be privy to the contents of public events to which he is a witness. For most of the first part of the story, he operates within this narrative parameter. However, when he narrates the first meeting between Alicia and Joebell, he slips out of narrative focus and plausibility:

> The first time she see him in the snackette, she watch him and don't say nothing but, she think, Hey! Who he think he is? He come in the snackette with this foolish grin on his face and this strolling walk and this kinda commanding way about him and sit down at the table with his legs wide open, taking up a big space as if he spending a hundred dollars, and all he ask for is a coconut roll and juice.[30]

And later:

> But Alicia was thinking, Lord, just please let him get to America, they will see who is vagabond. Lord, just let him get through that immigration they will see happiness when he send for me.[31]

Since the snackette is a public space, it is possible to conjecture how the narrator could have gained access to the external details of the meeting. It would, however, have been impossible for him to discern Alicia's thoughts. This slip casts doubt on the narrative integrity of the story, and in the second part of the story, more questions about narrative agency, narrative plausibility, and narrative consistency are raised when the narration switches from third-person limited omniscience to a first-person perspective. On the surface, the narrative does not provide any justification for this seemingly arbitrary shift.

To appreciate the rationale behind the switch, however, it is important to recognize that the second part of the story, which is narrated by Joebell, is an account of Joebell's ordeal at the immigration in Puerto Rico. The third-person limited omniscient narrator, located in Cunaripo, could not have witnessed that event.

For him and the village to have become privy to it, they had to have been told by someone who was present at the scene. Joebell is the only one who fits that bill in the narrative. Once this point is recognized, the other parts of the narrative puzzle begin to fall in place: Joebell attempts to enter America through Puerto Rico on a false passport to fulfil his dreams but he is caught and deported. He returns to Cunaripo and tells his story to the villagers, among whom he must now settle and make a life for himself and Alicia, the girl friend he was going to send for once he was in America. On the basis of the story of his American misadventure and what the villagers already know about his dream to go away and his relationship with Alicia, the third-person narrator sets out to tell us the Joebell story. Presumably, in telling it, he borrows liberally from the collective memory of the community, including snippets of Alicia's account of the courtship between herself and Joebell, hence his access to Alicia's thoughts.

The switch from third- to first-person narrator illustrates the complex and organic relationship between the subjects of stories and their tellers. Both at the structural and thematic levels, the switch can be seen as a technique that allows Joebell to testify, as in a religious ceremony when the new convert testifies before the congregation, to both his experience and his resolution, or conversion, to return to find himself among his people. When the third-person narrator re-tells Joebell's story he implicitly provides the community with a cautionary tale, in the tradition of the chantwell/griot.

Though commonsensical, the conclusions about the chantwell paradigm in *The Dragon Can't Dance, The Wine of Astonishment,* and the short story 'Joebell and America' implicit in this paper would have remained speculative criticism if Lovelace had not written the film script for *Joebell and America* and been forced by the demands of the medium to reveal the identity of his primary narrative agent. *Joebell and America* opens with a sequence that answers all the questions about the narrative structure of the story and, by extension, confirms the speculations about the narrative strategies in *The Dragon Can't Dance* and *The Wine of Astonishment*:

> MIGHTY LICKS, the village calypsonian, and some other FELLARS are gathered outside the club singing extempo. They sing and

laugh about each other. As Joebell walks out, Mighty Licks sings a verse about Joebell.

MIGHTY LICKS

Is Joebell coming out the club again,

once again his face full of pain.

He still waiting to win out the wappie,

but up to now his pockets still empty.

Joebell boy you better go home

and leave the gambling alone.

They all laugh. Joebell responds with a clever verse.

JOEBELL

Licks, you better watch your mouth,

you really don't know what you talking about.

Very soon I will have the ace

when I get up and leave this place.

I will send you a postcard

because you will still be here singing bad calypso in Trinidad.

The introduction of Mighty Licks identifies the narrator as a chantwell/calypsonian/griot. He is used for most of the film to comment extemporaneously on events, especially as they impinge on Joebell or as Joebell impinges on them. Also, in order to indicate the organic relationship between the chantwell-narrator and the first-person narrator from whom the chantwell inherits most of the story, Joebell, the closet-chantwell, shares the narration with Mighty Licks, the champion-chantwell. With this outing/ unmasking of the narrator in the short story 'Joebell and America' and the fact that the primary narrator in Lovelace's 2005 novel-in-progress, tentatively titled 'It's Only a Movie', is a poet/ calypsonian, it is now possible to explicitly affirm the identity of Lovelace's unmarked narrators as variations of the chantwell. With this enthronement of the chantwell/calypsonian as one of his dominant narrators, Lovelace signals the calypsonian, both in his/ her style and content, as one of the prototypes for a native voice of authority.

Notes

1. Earl Lovelace, *The Dragon Can't Dance* (London: André Deutsch Limited, 1979).
2. Earl Lovelace, *While Gods Are Falling* (London: André Deutsch Limited, 1965).
3. Earl Lovelace, *The Schoolmaster* (Oxford: Heinemann Educational Publishers, 1968).
4. Gordon Rohlehr, *Calypso and Society in Pre-Independence Trinidad* (Trinidad: Gordon Rohlehr, 1990), 52.
5. Ibid., 51–52.
6. Ibid., 52.
7. Ibid.
8. Ibid., 52–54.
9. Philip M. Peek and Kwesi Yankah, eds., *African Folklore: An Encyclopedia* (New York London: Routledge, 2004), 162–64.
10. Chinua Achebe, *Anthills of the Savannah* (New York: Doubleday, 1987), 114.
11. Earl Lovelace, *Growing in the Dark (Selected Essays)*, ed. Funso Aiyejina (Trinidad: Lexicon Trinidad Limited, 2003), 169.
12. Lovelace, *The Dragon Can't Dance*, 10–13.
13. Lovelace, *Growing in the Dark*, 94.
14. Earl Lovelace, *The Wine of Astonishment* (Oxford: Heinemann Educational Publishers, 1982).
15. Lovelace, *The Wine of Astonishment*, 22–23.
16. Ibid., 25.
17. Ibid., 89.
18. Ibid., 104.
19. Ibid., 107.
20. Ibid., 128.
21. Ibid., 46.
22. Ibid., 83.
23. Ibid.
24. Ibid., 87.
25. Earl Lovelace, *Salt* (London: Faber and Faber, 1996). For more on this subject, see Funso Aiyejina, 'Novelypso: Indigenous Narrative Strategies in Earl Lovelace's Fiction', *Trinidad and Tobago Review* 22, nos.7–8 (2000): 15–17 and; Aiyejina, '*Salt*: A Complex Tapestry', *Trinidad and Tobago Review* 181, nos. 0–12 (1996): 13–16.
26. Earl Lovelace, *A Brief Conversion and Other Stories* (Oxford: Heinemann International, 1988).
27. It should be noted that, although outside of the focus of *The Wine of Astonishment*, the flow of influence between the calypso tradition and Eva as Mother of a Spiritual Baptist church is a two-way affair as can be seen in the influence of the rhythm of Spiritual Baptist/Orisa traditions on calypsonians in Trinidad like Super Blue, Sugar Aloes, Singing Sandra, David Rudder, and Ella Andall.
28. Asha Lovelace and Earl Lovelace, *Joebell and America* (film). Trinidad: CCN Six Point Production, 2005.
29. Lovelace, *A Brief Conversion*, 111.
30. Ibid., 114.
31. Ibid., 117.

TEN TO ONE IS MURDER:
GENDER, SEXUALITY AND THE BODY POLITIC

8

JAMETTE CARNIVAL AND AFRO-CARIBBEAN INFLUENCES IN THE WORK OF JEAN RHYS

Cynthia Davis

Most art critics would agree that since the Universal Exhibition of 1900 in Paris, African aesthetics have profoundly influenced twentieth-century sculpture and painting. Literary critics have paid less attention to ways in which West African culture and rhetorical patterns have shaped twentieth-century writing. A case in point is the Dominican writer, Jean Rhys (1890–1979) who has been located within the discursive spaces of formalism and feminism and, in the case of *Wide Sargasso Sea*,[1] postcolonialism. Aside from Caribbeanists who, as Kamau Brathwaite points out in 'A Post-Cautionary Tale',[2] bat Rhys back and forth as 'The Helen of Our Wars', critical response to Rhys's work usually privileges its European modernism and concern with form over its Caribbean cultural context. Even though Ford Madox Ford trumpets her Antillean origin in the introduction to her first book, *The Left Bank and Other Stories* (1927),[3] critics of Rhys's first four novels rarely mention her West Indian identity. Such an oversight is puzzling, considering that every text, European setting notwithstanding, includes such identifiable Afrocentric elements as parody, satire, masquerade, hybridity, heteroglossia, and the rhetorical technique of call-and-response. Critics who do acknowledge the culture of the Black Atlantic in all of Rhys's work include Kenneth Ramchand and Elaine Savory. Ramchand contextualizes her style, 'essentially image and rhythm', as part of the *Negritude* movement of the 1930s,[4] while Savory contends that Rhys's texts 'conduct important conversations between gender, national, racial and class positions'.[5] Janette Martin further asserts that Afrocentric spirituality provides all of Rhys's protagonists with an 'alternative epistemology',[6] 'to transcend or, more important, to transgress conventional modes of knowing and behaving'.[7] It is surprising that even after the publication of her specifically West Indian novel, *Wide Sargasso Sea* (1966), A. Alvarez hailed her as 'the best living *English* novelist', and Carole Angier, her British biographer, never visited Dominica as part of her research. Annette Gilson, however, maintains that Rhys's Afrocentric identity is always present in her European texts, albeit coded and manifested as presence-as-absence.[8]

Like Picasso and Modigliani, to whose art she alluded in her novels, Jean Rhys drew on African sources, mediated in her case through the culture of her Dominican homeland. Just as visual artists learned, from West African masks and sacred artifacts, to streamline and stylize form, so Rhys borrowed cultural and oral tropes from the Yoruba and other West African peoples. These cultural markers had crossed the Atlantic with the slave ships and evolved into the trickster tales, ghost stories, obeah spells, talismans, satirical calypso songs and carnival street performances of Dominica and the other Caribbean islands. In privileging Afro-Caribbean orality, heteroglossia, hybridity, and satire, Rhys stands as a foremother to Anglophone writers such as Olive Senior, Michelle Cliff, Rambai Espinet, Jamaica Kincaid, Pauline Melville, Velma Pollard, Erna Brodber, and Opal Palmer Adisa. Like the Martinican novelist Mayotte Capecia (Lucette Combette), Rhys writes against the racist travelogues of 'local colorists' like Lafcadio Hearn and subverts the stereotype of the *guiablesse* (female demon) in both West Indian and European sites.[9] Rhys's protagonists, like Capecia's, have been dismissed as apolitical and Eurocentric when in fact the reverse is true. Rhys's interrogation of power relations across racial, sexual and economic lines is subversive, and she approaches her subject in the indirect, elliptical style of Afrocentric social criticism.

This paper contextualizes Rhys within Afro-Dominican culture and argues that the texts set in Paris and London are deeply informed by the culture, specifically by the rhetorical device of call-and-response and by the persona of the female carnival street performer, or *jamette*. *Jamette* is Trinidadian Creole, from the French *diametre*, the name given to the working-class women who took part in carnival.[10] The term is used in a broader sense here to include the transgressive, parodic style of the Dominican female street performers of Rhys's childhood. I would argue that for Rhys, the *jamette* signifies an opposition to the legal and cultural 'limitations ... that seek to close women and to enclose [them] "safely"'.[11] Rhetorically, Rhys uses Afrocentric 'forms of verbal artistry such as calypso that require economy and highly developed verbal play [and] permit a depth of signification without many words'.[12] Rhys thus indirectly interrogates colonial and metropolitan power structures. In combining modernism and African aesthetics with the hybridity and heteroglossia of her own background, she shapes the satirical tone and parodic structure of her work.

It is not surprising that Jean Rhys was drawn to subversive Afrocentric orality. She was born on a predominately African island at the height of the British Empire; her father was a Welsh physician and her mother, a Lockhart, came from an old Creole family. Rhys, who began writing at an early age, was also musical; she played the piano and sang traditional West Indian melodies: folk songs like 'Brown Girl in the Ring' and 'Roseau Town'; French Creole ballads; and carnival songs like 'Charlie Lulu'.[13] Since there was constant musical exchange between Dominica and Trinidad, some of the tunes she learned as a child may well have been of Yoruba origin, brought to Trinidad by indentured Africans between 1841 and 1867.[14] Fluent in Dominica's French patois, she translated carnival songs for her disapproving English relatives, and soon grasped the heteroglossic implications of nation language. The British administrators in Dominica, as in Trinidad, 'nurtured a mistrust of the [Afro-]Franco-Catholic element ... [and] had settled on a policy of systematically anglicizing the island, both with respect to language and population'.[15] Rhys was aware of the politics of pronunciation and knew that accent denoted class: 'Now that I've spoken you can hear that I'm an ... English gentlewoman. I have my doubts about you. Speak up and I'll place you at once.'[16] Deprecated throughout her life for her West Indian accent, Rhys trained herself to speak in a whisper. However, her 'acute memory of West Indian speech' served her well as she composed the 'remarkable and convincing dialogue' in *Wide Sargasso Sea* and stories like 'Let Them Call It Jazz'.[17] In her seventies she recorded Afro-French lullabies and Houdini's (Edgar Leon Sinclair) 1926 calypso 'Woman Sweeter Than Man' in a flawless Dominican accent.[18]

In addition to her musical interests, Rhys was knowledgeable about Afrocentric folklore: witches, ghosts, shape-shifters, tricksters, soucriants, and zombies. She researched Voudou and left copious notes on Baron Samedi and other Haitian deities.[19] Rhys often mentioned obeah in her correspondence and claimed she could cast spells. She 'enjoyed alluding to herself as a witch, especially when she thought others so imaged her'; in fact, her neighbours in the remote Devon village of Cheriton Fitzpaine accused her of witchcraft more than once.[20] In later years, Rhys used trickster skills to avoid intrusive fans and importunate interviewers. When a reporter in possession of a batch of Rhys's book reviews appeared for an interview, Rhys appropriated the reviews before rushing her out, whispering '*Merde*, dearie, that's what they say for good luck.'²¹ Rhys's 'malicious grin' made the reporter think of 'voodoo ... of little dolls with pins ... (of) shades of Martinique'.²² Rhys was aware of the Afrocentric power of names: 'I have a thing about names ... they are very important indeed.'²³ She often changed hers, either because she hoped a new 'identity' would improve her luck, or for self-protection. In *Voyage*, Anna Morgan is teased about her West Indian heritage and retorts: '[m]y real name isn't Morgan and I'll never tell you my real name.... Everything that I tell you about myself is a lie.'²⁴ Dissimulation, witchcraft and shape-shifting appear frequently in Rhys's work: the black cat in 'Kikimora', either a familiar or a shape-shifting spirit, suddenly attacks a patronizing male guest.²⁵ Rhys's meek, passive protagonists are deeply angry women who fantasize about changing into animals: 'one day the fierce wolf that walks by my side will spring on you and rip your abominable guts out.'²⁶ Rhys's interest in shape-shifting and tricksters may have been inspired by the Dominicans who transformed themselves through the elaborate masks and costumes of the road march and sang carnival songs of *picong* (provocation) and *mepris* (scorn). Satire, as an approach to musical expression, had survived the Middle Passage and blended with Catholic ritual to create a uniquely Dominican cultural synthesis. Rhys was aware, however, that calypso songs and carnival performances were not simply entertainment, but were modes of resistance to an unjust and exploitative system.

The only eyewitness accounts of African celebrations in the Caribbean are filtered through a voyeuristic European gaze although, as Jean D'Costa and Barbara Lalla point out, 'even in . . . travelogues written by white visitors survive echoes of the voices of those who, having neither quill nor printing press, left the mark of their exile upon the minds of white observers'.²⁷ Jamaica, Trinidad, Dominica, Saint Lucia, and the Virgin Islands all developed unique approaches to holiday performance, and although the Jamaican Set Girls and the Trinidadian j*amettes* represent different cultural phenomena, they shared a common parodic and subversive response to social and economic repression. In 1687, Sloane described holiday dances or 'plays' in Jamaica that involved costumes, props, and 'great activity and strength of body in keeping time'.²⁸ In all of the islands, the role of women is well documented. Even before the advent of the *jamettes,* entrepreneurial women had hosted public parties and fetes. One woman in pre-emancipation Trinidad 'gave dances and made a great deal of money by them; she paid for everything — supper, liquor and music; and each negro paid half a dollar for admission'.[29] In the Virgin Islands, the Bamboula queen composed extemporaneous verses to which the other dancers sang a chorus in call-and-response style.[30] In Jamaica, during Christmas week, the Set Girls danced through the streets of Kingston. They wore elegant frocks trimmed with red or blue and sang satirical, topical songs.[31] Another witness of the Jamaican festivities reported that,

> the creole negro girls of the towns . . . dressed with much taste . . . Their gowns are of the finest muslin with pink or blue satin spencers . . . gold necklaces, ear-rings and other expensive trinkets shine to advantage on their jet black skins.[32]

The Queen at the head of the procession 'eclipse[s] all the rest in the splendor of her dress'.[33] Similarly, the Saint Lucian La Rose Society featured Queens 'with bright coloured head dresses, sparkling with jewelry (who) sang in cadences (with) dangerous gracefulness'.[34]

There was always a subversive undercurrent to these performances which sometimes masked slave uprisings. Between 1649 and 1833, one third of the 70 documented slave revolts in the Caribbean occurred at holiday time.[35] By the turn of the century, the harsh conditions of the urban poor had perforce altered the 'stateliness, subtle eroticism and decorum' of the early nineteenth-century street performances.[36] In fact, Rhys's eyewitness account of Dominican carnival women is remarkably similar to newspaper descriptions of Trinidadian *Jamette Carnival*.[37] By Rhys's time, the colonial press had become sufficiently discomfited by the subversive nature of these masked female performers to complain that,

> the obscenities, the bawdy language and gestures of the women in streets have been pushed to a degree of wantonness which . . . cannot be tolerated. The young girls will become the curse of the country if these yearly *saturnalia* are allowed to continue.[38]

Undeterred, the Dominican carnival women, in 'whiteface', wearing 'masks made of close meshed wire covering the whole face and tied at the back of the head — the handkerchief that went over the back of the head hid the strings and over the slits for the eyes mild blue eyes' and 'little red heart-shaped mouths',[39] continued to parody and lampoon powerful colonial interests.

In Rhys's Dominica in the early 1900s, political and economic power was vested in the British civil servants who administered the country, in the Catholic Church, and in the privileged proprietor-class, which included both whites and people of colour. The island had bounced between French and British control until 1782 when a decisive naval battle determined its status as a British possession. French patois remained the language of the folk and is still spoken by some older, rural Dominicans.[40] According to Lennox Honeychurch, the 'mulatto' or coloured elite of Dominica had challenged white hegemony more successfully than on any other Caribbean island.[41] People of colour, predominantly Catholic and of Afro-French descent, controlled the outspoken local press, as Rhys shows in stories 'Again the Antilles', 'Fishy Waters', and 'Pioneers, O Pioneers'. In the former story, Papa Dom, the editor of the fictional *Dominica Herald*, 'was against the Government, against the English, against the Island's being a Crown Colony'.[42] Rhys's father was satirized by the editor of the real *Dominica Dial* for his 'conviviality', his constant bridge playing, and the suspicion that he had parlayed his assignment to a remote medical district into a more lucrative one in the capital.[43] Although racial discrimination in Dominican politics had been illegal since 1831 — photographs of the House of Assembly in Rhys's time show a representative number of delegates of colour — tensions were evident between the Afro-French planters and the British administrators. Rhys interrogates Dominica's complex hierarchy of race and class in 'Pioneers, O Pioneers'. 'The black women were barefooted, wore gaily striped turbans and highwaisted dresses',[44] while Afro-French Madame Menzies maintained the dignity of her old-fashioned riding habit, and British Mr Ramage lived out an imperialist fantasy in his 'tropical kit, white suit, red cummerbund, solar topee'.[45] These different perspectives are linked through the consciousness of the young protagonist who rejects the reductive, hegemonic vision of colonial society.

Between the uneasy alliance of Afro-French and British interests and the black working class, there stretched a wide divide. Slavery had been abolished officially since 1834 but the former bondsmen and women were only marginally better off in the 1900s. A mercantilist economy discouraged local industry and tied the people to subsistence farming and domestic service. The poor possessed little mobility and had minimal recourse to the courts. Christophene, the obeah woman in *Wide Sargasso Sea,* is clearly based on Anne Truitt, the Rhys family's cook who was arrested and accused of practising obeah by Governor Hesketh Bell. Truitt's photograph is among Bell's papers at Cambridge University; the Governor seems to have photographed many of his female prisoners.[46] Truitt's low opinion of British justice has undoubtedly come down to us in the words of her fictional counterpart: 'No more slavery! She had to laugh! "These new ones have Letter of the Law. Same thing. They got magistrate. They got fine. They got jail house and chain gang".'[47] Through Christophene, Rhys interrogates a legal system that defines obeah and other aspects of African spirituality as evil and illegal.

In the absence of a just legal solution in Dominica, such as land reform, carnival and calypso provided a sanctioned outlet for resistance. Caribbean calypso, as Rohlehr points out, derives 'from an older West African tradition of social commentary, in which praise, blame or derision were conveyed in song'.[48] African music 'often served the purpose of social control ... leaders of society recognized the value of such satirical songs in which the ordinary person was given the privilege of unburdening his mind ... in a controlled context'.[49] Stylistically, the old Yoruba songs, 'whether sacred or secular, indicate a source of that satire-cum-boast tradition within the calypso'.[50] Rhys would have heard topical songs of 'praise, blame, picong, ridicule, improvisation; and the themes of women and love-intrigue',[51] all structured in call-and-response or litany form, 'which consisted of a couplet in recitative form and a chorus'.[52] Although both Rhys and her cousin Emily Lockhart wrote calypsos in nation language, including one by Lockhart about 'the gold Sargasso Sea' that provided the title of Rhys's novel, actual participation in carnival was limited to the black working class.[53] The proprietary class, people of colour and whites, watched from behind louvred windows as masked and costumed revellers composed extemporaneous verses and chorused responses to percussion and string bands. Rhys recalls that:

> In the afternoon, from four to six, the singing, dancing mobs thronged the streets. I used to hang out of an upstairs window and watch. ... Dancing, swaying people, dressed in every colour of the rainbow ... the women-masks were powdered and scented. You could see the powder like bloom on the dark skin of their necks and arms ... (the dancers) passed under the window, singing, headed by three musicians — a man with a concertina, another with a triangle, and a third with a "shak-shak" ... I used to think, "Imagine being able to do that — to dance along the street in the sun ... dressed in red or yellow, to concertina music; and to sing and shout your defiance ".[54]

While Dominicans may not have used the term *jamette* to describe carnival performers, Rhys would have been familiar with the word since it appeared in the Antillean newspapers to which her father subscribed, as well as in repressive legislation and in references to official documents such as R.G.C. Hamilton's 1881 report to the Secretary of State for the Colonies on Trinidad's Canboulay Riots.[55] Because some of the African dances that survived the Middle Passage were fertility-oriented, the carnival performances that Rhys observed included movements that were routinely banned by European colonizers who 'had brought to the New World, a horrendous history of anti-feminism',[56] of witch-hunts and misogyny. The language used by the colonial press to describe the moves of the transgressive *jamettes* anticipates that expressed by characters in Rhys's texts, who object to both black carnival dancers in Dominica and to solitary women of all races in European cities. In *Voyage,* an English aunt, watching the dancers, repeats angrily, 'It ought to be stopped ... it's not a decent and respectable way to go on.'[57] Through the trope of masking, Rhys specifically connects her protagonists with the *jamettes*. In *Good Morning Midnight,* Sasha's face is 'a tormented mask' that she can 'remove and hang on a nail'.[58] Wandering through Paris, she wonders whether she should place over her face 'a tall hat with a green feather, hang a veil over the lot, and walk about the dark streets merrily ... Singing defiantly "You don't like me, but I don't like you either"... Singing "one more river to cross, that's Jordan, Jordan".'[59] Sasha's defiance and her reference to an African-American spiritual reveal an Afrocentric epistemology. Writing in the persona of a *jamette*, Rhys rejects the hypocrisy and oppression of European belief systems:

> They had their feet well on your necks; and they paid you barely enough to live on and then called you "lazy devil"... for not doing more work; and imagined that you envied them, their pale faces and their pursed-up mouths, half-cruel, half-sanctimonious, and the stiffly-wooden gestures of their bodies. And, after all, they could only look on at you leaping in the sun and envy you.[60]

Rhys's Afrocentric belief system may be grounded in her own ambiguous ethnicity. 'Who's white?' the Rhysian father expostulates whenever the question of people's 'colored blood' on Dominica comes up, 'damn few!'.[61] While Rhys's father may have warned his family that the racial identity of *all* West Indians was suspect, he may also have encouraged his daughter to embrace her mixed heritage. Gilson writes that in the metropolis 'she was subject to disparagement reserved by the English for West Indian colonials whose racial identity was suspect and whose social position was questionable at best'.[62] In 1959, Francis Wyndham reported on the BBC that Rhys was 'Welsh and Scottish'. She immediately wrote: 'I am not a Scot at all. My father was Welsh ... my mother's family was Creole.... *As far as I know I am white* but I have no country really'[63] (emphasis added). Her great-grandfather Lockhart had married a 'pretty Cuban countess ...emphasis added with dark curls and an intelligent face', who never fully assimilated the language and mores of the British plantocracy. Lockhart was 'jealous and suspicious not only of other men but of her possible attempts to get in touch with Catholicism again'.[64] In 'Elsa' the narrator suspects that she is of mixed race: 'my grandfather and his beautiful Spanish wife. Spanish. I wonder'.[65] While one must be careful of conflating excessively, as Angier does, Rhys's fiction and her history, Aunt Hester's insinuations to Anna in *Voyage* that her mother is racially mixed and that her father was pressured into the marriage may be grounded in Rees Williams's family history. Rhys recalls that Aunt Clarice, the 'real' Hester, made similar remarks. Clarice claimed that her brother was 'continually brooding over his exile in a small Caribbean island...."Poor Willy," she would say meaningfully, "poor, poor Willy".'[66]

Although Rhys was considered white in Dominica, English people, including her biographer, routinely questioned her race. Adrian Allinson, a painter for whom Rhys once modelled and on whom she in turn based Marston in 'Till September, Petronella', criticized her 'drawling' West Indian voice and suggested that she was of mixed race.[67] Ford Madox Ford and his common-law wife Stella Bowen both claimed that Rhys was passing for white,[68] and described her as such in their books. Bowen justified her complicity in 'l'affaire Ford' by othering Rhys as 'savage' and 'cannibal', while asserting her own 'superior' Anglo-Saxon values.[69] The sinister Lola Porter — read 'Ella Lenglet', Rhys's name at the time — in Ford's turgid potboiler *When the Wicked Man* (1931)[70] is modelled on Rhys. Lola is a Creole from the West Indies and, like Rhys, is tall and thin. Lola has a 'soft, stealthy voice' and 'gipsy blood'.[71] She is 'a seductive blackamoor';[72] her breath 'pours in and out of her large nostrils'.[73] Lola frequents Harlem nightclubs, is an expert on 'Negro music', and tells 'fantastic and horrible details of obi and the voodoo practices of the coloured people of her childhood home'.[74] The scenes in which Lola alternates between kissing the protagonist's hands 'continuously, as if she had been a slave'[75] and threatening him with death by obeah,[76] are very similar to Rhys's description of Marya's behaviour toward Heidler (Ford) in *Quartet*.[77] A milder version of Rhys inspires another character in Ford's novel. Henrietta Faulkner Felise is an American, of Spanish descent. Henrietta is from the 'Deep South' — 'Missouri or Tennessee' as Ford puts it — and has 'a slightly dusky accent'.[78] Like Rhys, Henrietta has an unusual intonation and the protagonist 'experience(s) a singular revulsion ... at her voice'.[79] Henrietta is ostensibly white but Ford makes a Carib–cannibal association with her necklace of pink coral, her sharp little white teeth, her 'very full and pouted lips', high cheek bones, and 'extremely large-pupilled eyes'.[80] Like Rhys, both Lola and Henrietta are expert horsewomen and 'spent their childhood on horseback'.[81] Lola, dressed in riding clothes, inspires lurid dominatrix fantasies in the hapless protagonist. Although Rhys and Ford both said their novels, *Quartet* and *When the Wicked Man*, were not autobiographical, there are remarkable similarities in the racial othering of the Lola–Marya–Henrietta characters.

Rhys makes the women in her texts functionally white but codes them as nonwhite, and gives them her own experiences. Anna's classmates call her 'the Hottentot'[82] and her landlady objects to her 'drawly voice';[83] in 'Overture and Beginners Please,' the narrator's schoolmates refer to her as 'West Indies' and demand she translate the lyrics of 'coon songs'.[84] Marya in *Quartet* has a 'strange little Kalmuk face': broad-cheekboned, with 'wide nostrils' and 'thick lips'.[85] Julia's Brazilian mother in *After Leaving Mr. Mackenzie*[86] is, like Rhys's own mother, dark with high cheekbones and long black hair. The functionally white Heather in *Tigers are Better Looking*,[87] betrays her Caribbean origin when she pronounces her name 'Hedda'.[88] 'Her language/enunciation defines her as Other'; a would-be suitor sees her as 'disdainful, debonair and with a touch of the tarbrush too, or I'm much mistaken.... Why is it that she isn't white? — Now why?'[89] In 'The Blue Bird' the callous narrator notes 'a lovely creature' sitting alone in a café, 'her face framed by a silver turban' from which 'wisps of wooly hair' denote her race.[90] In 'Let Them Call it Jazz', Selina, a 'fair coloured woman' from the West Indies is provoked into assault and sent to Holloway Prison[91] just as Rhys was incarcerated for the same charge in 1949.

Through her writing Rhys reassembles the fragmented elements of her Afrocentric identity. She draws a parallel between the street performance of the transgressive *jamette* and the solitary urban woman, both of whom assert their right to move in public spaces. Heteroglossia and calypso infuse her texts: she grasps calypso's coda of resistance; the interplay of multiple voices; the condensed and telescoped imagery; the rhetorical devices of satire and call-and-response; and the themes of betrayal, exploitation, and oppression. Rhys understands calypso's technical structure and the strictly prescribed form belied by an apparent improvisational quality. In 1964, she sent a friend a calypso and implied that she had just dashed it off explaining, 'a real calypso is done on the spot ... words and music. The audience judges who's best'; yet her papers contain several carefully worked out drafts of the same tune.[92] She differentiates between the authentic voices of Emily Lockhart and respected calypsonians like Attila the Hun (Raymond Quevedo) and Houdini (Edgar Leon Sinclair) and the 'ersatz', commercialized music promoted by 'foreigners like Noel Coward and Katherine Dunham who always (get) it wrong'.[93] Like the calypso composer, she shapes her controversial material elliptically, creating dramatic tension through patterns of call and response.

According to Rohlehr, African call-and-response is an important element in the structure of calypso. 'The tendency of the Yoruba to repeat the first lines of their songs ... is still evident in the stanza structure of calypsos today.'[94] Proponents of calypso in the early twentieth century 'viewed the Call-and-Response calypso as being of Yoruba origin and encouraged singers ... to retain the form'.[95] Within this pattern, either the leader calls out a line and the group repeats it exactly, or the leader sings a couplet to which the group responds with a chorus, as demonstrated in Lord Caresser's (Rufus Callender) 1938 lyric about Trinidadians mining gold in Guyana:

Call:	I left America to go down Demerara
Response:	No surrender
Call:	On the Mazaruni River I was a gold digger
Response:	No surrender
Call:	When I am in the jungle the lions tremble.
Response:	No surrender
Call:	An old-time flunkser and a sweetie vendor
Call:	No surrender.[96]

Rhys uses call-and-response when she opposes the voice of a repressive, misogynistic society against the solitary urban women. Between the 1860s and World War I, Britain passed a number of laws related to the Contagious Diseases and Defence of the Realm Acts. Such legislation purported to control prostitution and venereal disease, but in fact discouraged the presence of single women in public; due to this sexualized stigma, 'respectable' women married and accepted confinement in the home. According to William Harris, Assistant Commissioner of Police in late nineteenth-century London, 'any woman who goes to places of public resort, and is known to go with different men, although not a common streetwalker *should be considered a prostitute*' (emphasis added).[97] This label was dispensed freely, as female promiscuity was assumed to be inherent: a London policeman in 1882 argued that 'in every large town without exception, where a woman has a chance of this course and runs no danger of serious loss or inconvenience ... she will embrace it'.[98] As Rhys knew from her own work experience, these laws ignored the fact that women barely earned subsistence wages in legitimate occupations. In 1911 women constituted less than 28 per cent of the labour force, and 66 per cent worked in manufacturing or personal service.[99] During World War I, when clerical jobs became available, Rhys was one of the women who earned one-third the salary paid to men in the same jobs.[100] Her earlier jobs, as a chorus girl and artist's model, were not only poorly paid but were considered forms of prostitution. When the Rhysian woman rejects these options and still insists on the right to be out of doors in cafes, streets, taxis, and restaurants, she threatens social stability and inspires an angry chorus from former lovers, landladies, employers, and strangers. Anna mentions that she met her lover 'at Southsea', and his friends chorus sly innuendo about loose women 'on the pier at Southsea'.[101] When she is abandoned, the pillars of society gloat over her plight. 'What about what's-her-name? She got on, didn't she? Get on or get out, they say ... everybody says "Get on" ... Everybody says the man's bound to get tired.'[102] In *Quartet,* Marya imagines both parts of the call-and-response: 'What's the matter with you? ... Why are you like this ... Pull yourself together! ... No self-control ... that's what's the matter with me.... No training.'[103] Marya provokes a hostile response simply by her unprotected state: 'As she walked she was certain that every woman she passed was mocking her gleefully and every man was mocking her contemptuously.'[104] In *Good Morning Midnight,* Sasha continually intercepts comments by 'them' on her sexualized solitude. Even inanimate objects join the ironic chorus, as when she returns to a Paris hotel where, as a much younger woman, she had lived with her lover: '"Quite like old times," the room says. "Yes? No?"'[105]

Not all call-and-response is oppositional. Sometimes Rhys creates call-and-response when minor characters repeat the protagonists' concerns and reflect their values. Rhys thus avoids the reified or voyeuristic stance of the omniscient narrator, and maintains the moral relativism of her modernist universe. Since exile, isolation and marginalization are major themes in Rhys's work, the 'respondents' in the European novels are often racially marginalized 'others', specifically Jews and Arabs. Miss DeSolla in *Quartet* is triply marginalized as a Jewish, female artist. Although she considers Marya 'pathetic', the pathos of DeSolla's situation as a struggling female painter, the butt of Anglo-Saxon humour, underscores Marya's vulnerability. In her bleak studio, DeSolla like Marya exhibits a 'hunger for the softness and warmth of life'.[106] Similarly, in *Good Morning Midnight,* Sasha's marginalized status and iconoclastic philosophy are echoed first by Serge, the Russian Jewish painter from whom she purchases a Soutine-like canvas, and later by Rene the gigolo, who was possibly an Arab. Serge, like Miss DeSolla, is poor but generous; he places an 'African' mask — that he has carved himself — over his face and dances to a Martinican Beguine in order to distract Sasha from sadness: 'Pourquoi etes-vous si triste?';[107] Serge's compassion, his ironic humour, his Afrocentric sensibility, and his authentic values respond to Sasha's 'call' for connection. Rene's lack of nationality links him to Sasha whose own citizenship is suspect: 'the patron tells me he wants to see my passport.... Nationality ... that's what has puzzled him'.[108] Sasha cannot identify Rene's accent; he describes himself as a *mauvais garcon,* a roughneck; he claims to have escaped from the Foreign Legion in North Africa. Although he echoes Sasha's desire for a relationship of authenticity and acceptance, their call-and-response does not result in communication or connection.

The abortive relationship between Sasha and Rene is prefigured at the beginning of the novel when she overhears someone singing 'Sombre Dimanche' (Gloomy Sunday), a popular song that establishes the year as 1937. Rhys achieves a variation on call-and-response when lines from popular songs comment on the action, much as calypsonians sample and reference one another's work. 'Important textual reference to songs is a Rhys hallmark', according to Savory.[109] Rhys both establishes the period and implicates the British upper classes in the impending First World War in 'Till September, Petronella' through references to 'La Reve Passe' and other songs associated with aristocratic English regiments.[110] Instead of describing Anna's exile from the Caribbean, Rhys contrasts a harsh, Cockney tune with West Indian folksongs that express her loneliness: 'Adieu, sweetheart, adieu'[111] and 'Connais-tu le pays ou fleurit l'oranger?' (Do you know the country where the orange trees flower?)[112] In *Good Morning Midnight,* Rhys comments on the hypocritical double standard of morality, when Sasha finds herself 'walking to the music of

L'Arlesienne'.[113] Daudet's naturalistic drama, for which Bizet composed the music, concerns an engagement broken up by the man's family because the young woman has 'a past', a situation applicable to all Rhys protagonists. Rhys knows Paris geography and has carefully worked out Sasha's route so when she hears Bizet's music, she is close to the Odeon Theatre where *L'Arlesienne* had its premier in 1872.[114]

In addition to adopting the calypsonian rhetorical pattern of call-and-response, Rhys explored the genre's thematic concern with exile and power relationships. Ford attributes to her Dominican background, her 'terrifying insight and a terrific — an almost lurid — passion for stating the case of the underdog'.[115] Like the calypsonian, Rhys chooses cryptic language and double-entendre because her texts challenge powerful interests. Both Rhys and C.L.R. James reference the 1933 calypso sung in duet by Attila the Hun and Roaring Lion, 'Doggie Doggie Look a Bone', to critique the economic exploitation of women and the commodification of sex.[116] Rhys uses it in the radio script of *Voyage in the Dark* and James associates it with the nurse in *Minty Alley*[117] who is both exploited by men and abusive toward her child. Economic exile also begets abuse of power; just as Callender sings about Trinidadians forced to migrate to the gold mines of Guyana, so Rhys writes stories and calypsos about West Indian women working in London. The patois words of *Tired Song* describe an exhausted woman; another tune, also in patois, notes the lack of trees in the urban landscape and deplores the spiritual aridity of Western culture: 'They don't hear no rivers running / They ain't got no ease'.[118] Both songs prefigure the protagonist of 'Let Them Call It Jazz' whose original calypso is commercialized and distorted on the radio.

Perhaps because her protagonists are so marginalized, Rhys's work has been described as morbid and depressing. Such critics miss her sly deflation of pomposity and her perfect comic timing. In fact, writes Elaine Savory: 'Rhys's humour can be understood better if viewed through the lens of Caribbean humour which is so often political, full of word-play, skeptical of institutions and power, and essentially survivalist.'[119] Her fragile women are resilient tricksters who mock and outsmart their oppressors. In 'Till September, Petronella', a man boasts about his amorous skills: 'I know what women like…. They like a bit of loving, that's what they like, isn't it? They like it dressed up sometimes — and sometimes not, it all depends. You have to know and I know. I just know.'[120] Petronella's ironic response — 'You've nothing more to learn, have you?'— goes over his head.[121] Like the Caribs in 'Temps Perdi', Rhys's women speak a different language from men.[122] In *After Leaving Mr. Mackenzie,* Rhys employs two Afrocentric tropes, the trickster and the zombie. Loe maintains that Rhys knew all about zombification, and that her 'allusions to zombies (are) an important narrative patterning'.[123] Julia, Mr Mackenzie's discarded lover, keeps appearing in the wet Paris streets. It is twilight, 'the hour between dog and wolf',[124] a time of shifting shapes and prowling spirits. Julia's face is pale with 'black specks in the corners of her eyes'[125] ... and deep, bluish circles under (them).[126] She walks 'slowly, aimlessly, her head down'.[127] Approaching the man as a zombie, Julia plays on his guilt; then swiftly she shifts shape and manipulates the startled Mackenzie into lending her a lot of money.[128] Like Anansy, the trickster spider of Jamaican folklore, Rhys's women must turn weakness to advantage in a predatory world. Given their marginalized status, they realize that 'cunning, rather than overt male/female confrontation is the preferred strategy' for getting what they want.[129]

The abuse of power, the exploitation of the weak, and 'disillusionment at the colonial, patriarchal lexicon of ideas that pass for universal truths' are central themes of Rhys's oeuvre.[130] The texts link two subversive and marginalized groups: the Afro-Caribbean *jamette* and her experience of misogyny, racialized motilities of the body, and legal restriction; and the single, urban woman of any race who encounters a similar hostility, sexualized stereotyping and legal deterrents to her mobility. In exposing relations of sexual commodification and economic oppression, Rhys challenges powerful social forces which, as she knew from her own experience, deal severely with those who destabilize the social order. As an artist wishing to interrogate controversial issues of gender, race, and class, Rhys calls upon her cultural heritage and utilizes Afrocentric rhetorical and stylistic strategies of parody, satire, and masquerade. Since 'linear European narrative cannot register plausibly her own experiences and those of her characters',[131] Rhys creates a multiplicity of voices and perspectives through heteroglossia and call-and-response. The Rhysian woman always rejects a 'single compartmentalizing vision in favor of one that opens up the realms of possibility'.[132] Rhys, through her exiled and marginalized characters, through the psychological fragmentation of their personalities, and through their deconstructed narratives and minimalist milieu, creates the quintessentially modernist text. Her protagonists, though temporally and geographically removed from carnival, are yet informed by an Afrocentric aesthetic of resistance, survival and celebration.

Notes

1. Jean Rhys, *Wide Sargasso Sea* (1966), in *Jean Rhys: The Complete Novels* (New York: Norton, 1985).
2. Kamau Brathwaite, 'A Post-Cautionary Tale of the Helen of Our Wars', *Wasafiri* 22 (1995): 64–81.
3. Jean Rhys, *The Left Bank and Other Stories*, Preface by Ford Madox Ford (London: Jonathan Cape, 1927).
4. Kenneth Ramchand, *The West Indian Novel and its Background* (London: Faber & Faber, 1970; reprinted Kingston: Ian Randle Publishers, 2004).
5. Ibid., 198.
6. Janette Martin, 'Jablesses, Soucriants, Loup-garous: Obeah as an Alternative Epistemology in the Writing of Jean Rhys and Jamaica Kincaid', *World Literature Written in English* 36, no.1 (1997): 5.
7. Ibid., 4.
8. Annette Gilson, 'Internalizing Mastery: Jean Rhys, Ford Madox Ford, and the Fiction of Autobiography', *Modern Fiction Studies* 50, no.3 (2004): 654; A. Alvarez, 'The Best Living English Novelist', *New York Times Book Review* 17 (March 1974): 6–7.
9. Sybil Jackson Carter, 'Mayotte or Not Mayotte', *CLA Journal XLVIII* 4 (2005): 446; Mayotte Capecia, *Je Suis Martiniquaise* (Paris: Editions Correa, 1948); Lafcadio Hearn, *Two Years in the French West Indies* (New York: Harper & Row, 1923).
10. Hollis 'Chalkdust' Liverpool, *From the Horse's Mouth: Stories of the History and Development of the Calypso* (Port of Spain, Trinidad: Juba Publications, 2003).
11. Mona Fayad, 'Unquiet Ghosts: The Struggle for Representation in Jean Rhys' *Wide Sargasso Sea*', *Modern Fiction Studies* 34, no.3 (1988): 451.
12. Elaine Savory, *Jean Rhys* (Cambridge: Cambridge University Press, 1998).
13. Jean Rhys Collection [Series I, Box 5, Folder 13] Department of Special Collections, McFarlin Library, The University of Tulsa.
14. Gordon Rohlehr, *Calypso and Society in Pre-Independence Trinidad* (Tunapuna, Trinidad: Gordon Roehler, 1990), 16.
15. Ibid., 51.

16. Jean Rhys, *Voyage in the Dark* (1934), in *Jean Rhys: The Complete Novels* (New York: Norton, 1985), 35.
17. Savory, *Jean Rhys*, 166.
18. Jean Rhys Collection [Series I, Box 2, Folder 3] Department of Special Collections, McFarlin Library, The University of Tulsa.
19. Jean Rhys Collection [Series I, Box 4, Folder 15] Department of Special Collections, McFarlin Library, The University of Tulsa.
20. Savory, *Jean Rhys*, 110; Jean Rhys, *The Letters of Jean Rhys*, ed. F. Wyndham and D. Melly (New York: Viking, 1984).
21. Donna Litherland, 'Jean Rhys. GOOD MORNING MIDNIGHT', Jean Rhys Collection [Series I, Box 6, Folder 13] Department of Special Collections, McFarlin Library, The University of Tulsa.
22. Ibid., 1.
23. Rhys, *Letters*, 170.
24. Ibid., 78.
25. Jean Rhys, *The Collected Short Stories* (New York: Norton, 1987).
26. Jean Rhys, *Good Morning, Midnight* (1939), in *Jean Rhys: The Complete Novels* (New York: Norton, 1985), 375.
27. Jean D'Costa and Barbara Lalla, eds., *Voices in Exile: Jamaican Texts of the 18th and 19th Centuries* (Tuscaloosa: University of Alabama Press, 1989), 8.
28. Edward Long, *The History of Jamaica* (1774; reprint, London: Frank Cass, 1970; reprint, Kingston: Ian Randle Publishers, 2003), 384.
29. Rohlehr, *Calypso and Society*, 13.
30. Ibid., 25.
31. Matthew 'Monk' Lewis, *Journal of a West Indian Proprietor Kept During a Residence in the Island of Jamaica 1815–1817* (London: Murray, 1834), 56.
32. James Stewart, *A View of the Past and Present State of the Island of Jamaica* (1823, reprint, New York: Negro Universities Press, 1969).
33. Ibid., 274.
34. Rohlehr, *Calypso and Society*, 33.
35. Robert Dirks, *The Black Saturnalia* (Gainesville: University of Florida Press, 1987).
36. Rohlehr, *Calypso and Society*, 33.
37. Hollis 'Chalkdust' Liverpool, *From the Horse's Mouth*, 3.
38. Rohlehr, *Calypso and Society*, 31.
39. Rhys, *Voyage in the Dark*, 113.
40. Lennox Honeychurch, Personal interview, February, 22, 2005.
41. Lennox Honeychurch, *The Dominica Story: A History of the Island* (Roseau: The Dominica Institute, 1984).
42. Rhys, *The Collected Short Stories*, 39.
43. Savory, *Jean Rhys*, 6.
44. Rhys, *The Collected Short Stories*, 275.
45. Ibid., 276.
46. Honeychurch, Personal interview, February, 22, 2005.
47. Rhys, *Wide Sargasso Sea*, 471.
48. Rohlehr, *Calypso and Society*, 1.
49. Ibid., 2.
50. Ibid., 17.
51. Ibid., 2.
52. Ibid., 2.
53. Jean Rhys Collection [Series II, Box 1, Folder 2], Department of Special Collections, McFarlin Library, The University of Tulsa.

54. Jean Rhys, 'Lost Island: A Childhood', Jean Rhys Collection [Series I, Box 1, Folder 14] Department of Special Collections, McFarlin Library, The University of Tulsa, p.10.
55. Liverpool, *From the Horse's Mouth*, 21.
56. Rohlehr, *Calypso and Society*, 4.
57. Rhys, *Voyage in the Dark*, 113.
58. Rhys, *Good Morning Midnight*, 370.
59. Ibid.
60. Rhys, 'Lost Island', 10.
61. Rhys, 'The Day They Burned the Books', in *The Collected Short Stories*, 156.
62. Gilson, 'Internalizing Mastery', 636.
63. Rhys, *Letters*, 172.
64. Jean Rhys, *Smile Please: An Unfinished Autobiography* (UK: ISIS Large Print Books, 1996), 26.
65. Jean Rhys, 'Elsa', Jean Rhys Collection [Black Exercise Book, Series I, Box 1, Folder 1a] Department of Special Collections, McFarlin Library, The University of Tulsa.
66. Rhys, *Smile Please*, 55.
67. Dorothy Miller Richardson Collection [Series II, Box 1, Folder 11] McFarlin Library, The University of Tulsa.
68. Carole Angier, *Jean Rhys* (Harmondsworth: Penguin, 1986).
69. Sue Thomas, 'Adulterous Liaisons: Jean Rhys, Stella Bowen and Feminist Reading', *Australian Humanities Review* 22 (2001): 4.
70. Ford Madox Ford, *When the Wicked Man* (London: Jonathan Cape, 1931).
71. Ibid., 157.
72. Ibid., 249.
73. Ibid., 183.
74. Ibid., 175.
75. Ibid., 162.
76. Ibid., 259.
77. Jean Rhys, *Quartet* (1928), in *Jean Rhys: The Complete Novels* (New York: Norton, 1985).
78. Ford, *When the Wicked Man*, 75.
79. Ibid., 78.
80. Ibid.
81. Ibid., 183.
82. Rhys, *Voyage in the Dark*, 7.
83. Ibid., 18.
84. Rhys, *The Collected Short Stories*, 316.
85. Rhys, *Quartet*, 199.
86. Jean Rhys, *After Leaving Mr. Mackenzie* (1931), in *Jean Rhys: The Complete Novels* (New York: Norton, 1985).
87. Jean Rhys, *Tigers are Better Looking* (London: André Deutsch, 1968; reprint, UK: Penguin, 1996).
88. Rhys, *The Collected Short Stories*, 181.
89. Veronica M. Gregg, *Jean Rhys' Historical Imagination: Reading and Writing the Creole* (Chapel Hill: University of North Carolina Press, 1995); Rhys, *The Collected Short Stories*, 181.
90. Rhys, *The Collected Short Stories*, 60.
91. Ibid., 158.
92. Rhys, *Letters*, 281; Jean Rhys Collection [Series I, Box 3, Folder 8] Department of Special Collections, McFarlin Library, The University of Tulsa.
93. Rhys, *Letters*, 108.

94. Rohlehr, *Calypso and Society*, 17.
95. Ibid., 18.
96. Ibid., 146.
97. Mary Anne Emery, *Jean Rhys at 'World's End'; Novels of Colonial and Sexual Exile* (Austin: University of Texas, 1990).
98. Ibid., 96–97.
99. Ibid., 92.
100. Ibid.
101. Rhys, *Voyage in the Dark*, 53.
102. Ibid., 46.
103. Rhys, *Quartet*, 190.
104. Ibid., 211.
105. Rhys, *Good Morning Midnight*, 347.
106. Rhys, *Quartet*, 122.
107. Rhys, *Good Morning Midnight*, 371.
108. Ibid., 350.
109. Savory, *Jean Rhys*, 168.
110. Rhys, *The Collected Short Stories*, 125.
111. Rhys, *Voyage in the Dark*, 19.
112. Ibid., 100.
113. Rhys, *Good Morning Midnight*, 396.
114. Ibid.
115. Rhys, *Left Bank*, 24.
116. Raymond 'Attila the Hun' Quevedo, *Atilla's Kaiso: A Short History of Trinidad Calypso* (St. Augustine, Trinidad: University of the West Indies, Deparment of Extra Mural Studies, 1983), 46–47.
117. C.L.R. James, *Minty Alley* (London: New Beacon Books, 1971).
118. Jean Rhys Collection [Series I, Box 3, Folder 9] McFarlin Library, The University of Tulsa.
119. Savory, *Jean Rhys*, 109.
120. Rhys, *The Collected Short Stories*, 141.
121. Ibid.
122. Ibid., 256.
123. Thomas Loe, 'Patterns of the Zombie in Jean Rhys' *Wide Sargasso Sea'*, World Literature Written in English 31, no.1 (1991): 35.
124. Rhys, *Leaving Mr. Mackenzie*, 343.
125. Ibid., 240.
126. Ibid., 343.
127. Ibid.
128. Ibid.
129. Carolyn Cooper, *Noises in the Blood* (London: MacMillan, 1993).
130. Thomas, 'Adulterous Liaisons', 100.
131. Ibid.
132. Fayad, 'Uniquiet Ghosts', 451.

9

'BIG FAT FISH': THE HYPERSEXUALIZATION OF THE FAT BLACK WOMAN'S BODY IN CALYPSO AND DANCEHALL

Andrea Shaw

The stage has traditionally been a space where people expect to be confronted with the spectacular, with acts that amuse and astonish. One of the primary components of the spectacular is that it crosses the boundaries of the normative. These border crossings occur as somewhat dichotomized possibilities. On one hand, a performer may cross the boundaries of the normative because she supersedes socially desirable criteria: for example, she may be extremely beautiful or her voice particularly outstanding. On the other hand, she may traverse those boundaries because she exceeds a socially undesirable standard, and within the context of the Western beauty arena, this could be because she is fat or black. The result has been that fat black women are welcomed into performative spaces because of the transgressive qualities of these spaces and because the site of the fat black woman's body is in itself a source of social disruption and she is a poignant embodiment of transgression.

Both dancehall and calypso are musical traditions associated with acts that generate astonishment. Aside from their politically and sexually charged lyrics, both traditions are contextualized within the unruly dance/performance rituals of carnival and the dancehall, which feature the extensive costuming of the female body in highly revealing attire. The fat black woman's body has come to play an instrumental role in the creation of spectacle in these two performative spaces.

Dancehall and calypso are historically associated with disruption and colonial resistance and both present a perpetual challenge to neocolonial cultural norms. Dancehall, one of reggae's offshoots, originated in Kingston's inner-city ghettos, and the music disrupts Jamaica's Eurocentric codes of propriety on multiple planes. Sound system 'clashes' are a regular and important feature of dancehall music and perhaps these events best help shape the most appropriate metaphor for defining one aspect of the relationship between dancehall and the Jamaican public. During a clash, groups of deejays affiliated with different sound systems try to outplay one another by selecting songs that best arouse the audience; additionally, the respective deejays compete based on their oratory skills. The conflictive context for these clashes mirrors dancehall's numerous other sites of contestation. For example, the promoters of outdoor street dances and neighbours in surrounding vicinities often clash over the noise from the sound system and issues of public disturbance. Additionally, the evolution of a 'vulgar' dancehall cultural aesthetic, as well as its subversive lyrical content consisting of lewd sexual references, clashes with middle-class bourgeoisie propriety.[1] Furthermore, dancehall lyrics are rendered exclusively in the island's local dialect or patois, contesting the privileged position of English as Jamaica's authentic discourse.

Trinidadian calypso has a similar legacy of contestation. In the early twentieth century the term calypso came into use in association with Trinidadian carnival music.[2] One of carnival's earliest expressions was the weekend slave dance, which often came under the suspicion of the ruling planter classes as a venue for coordinating rebellion.[3] Calypso's intimate association with carnival helped fuel its rebellious posture, and this musical tradition started to attract many of the same criticisms currently associated with dancehall. According to calypso scholar Gordon Rohlehr, articles in the *Port of Spain Gazette* from the late nineteenth century 'usually complained about the obscene and abusive songs, as well as the disrespect shown by lower-class masqueraders to the high and mighty in the society'.[4]

These complaints regarding carnival music often found themselves specifically located on the site of the female body, and an 1884 article in the *Port of Spain Gazette* situates the young women of Trinidad as the locus for the country's moral decay:

> In Port of Spain we have shown how the bands had been cowed down, but the obscenities, the bawdy language and gestures of the women in the street have been pushed to a degree of wantonness which cannot be surpassed, and which must not be tolerated. Obscenities are no longer veiled under the cloak of words of doubtful meaning, but lechery, in all its naked brutality was sung, spoken and represented by disgusting gestures in our public streets. The growing generation of young girls will become the curse of the country if these yearly saturnalia are allowed to continue.[5]

The 'jamettes' to whom the article refers were women associated with both carnival and calypso, and their astonishing gyrations simultaneously attracted the public's attention and its disgruntlement. Within a pan-Caribbean context, these jamettes are the performative ancestors of the Jamaican dancehall queens as are Jamaican set girls. During slavery as part of the Christmas season Jonkonnu festivities, set girls paraded through the streets of Jamaica festooned in elaborate clothing and competed with one another to see who was the best dressed.[6] These set girls as well as the jamettes have bequeathed their legacy of spectacular behaviour that specifically manifests as dancehall's outrageous fashion.

Dancehall 'divas' populate the literal dancehall, and their bodies are reflective sites for an emergent dancehall aesthetic.[7] Their notoriety within the dancehall setting expresses itself primarily on two planes: first with regards to their sexually explicit dance performances and second in terms of their elaborate fashion and accessories, which have perhaps become the most familiar visual expression of dancehall. However, unlike carnival, the dancehall operates in a contained space, and the public is not readily privy to the performances that take place within. As a result, the dancehall diva's ghetto-fabulous style, which is readily observable on the streets of Jamaica, has become one of the primary targets of middle- and upper-class disdain — along with dancehall lyrics disseminated on the radio stations. Just as over a century ago the jamette's 'disgusting gestures' were situated as a source of national decline, so is the female dancehall body situated as a representation of cultural degradation.[8] In a 1994 newspaper article, Jamaican columnist Morris Cargill comments on the flesh-exposing haute couture, no doubt dancehall inspired, that had by then taken hold on the local fashion scene: 'Males can become bored by over-exposure. Women's clothing, including bathing suits and including the crotch-cutters worn by beauty contestants, should titillate and promise, not hand out the prizes before they are won.'[9]

The tight and revealing nature of female dancehall fashion has not only led to national outrage but to attempts to police the Jamaican female body. In 1993 signs appeared at the Bustamante Children's Hospital in Kingston stipulating that dancehall fashion was not permitted in the waiting area of the emergency room.[10] Additionally, in preparation for the funeral of past Prime Minister Michael Manley, guidelines were issued in the newspaper encouraging women to dress 'appropriately'.[11] This 'encouragement' was particularly meaningful against the backdrop of another funeral gathering, that of Jim Brown, a popular don in the Kingston area.[12] One newspaper's fashion commentator conveyed her distaste for the mourners' apparel when she stated that 'No mini was too short, no tights too tight, no chiffon too sheer, no lace too see through'; moreover, she summed up the women's dress as a 'homage to bareness'.[13]

The fat black woman's body has come to play an instrumental role in the creation of spectacle in both the calypso and dancehall arenas. Fat bodies contribute to the disruptive spectacle of these two expressive forms, primarily because of the hypersexualizing of those bodies, which is immediately apparent in dancehall tradition. Dancehall has been the venue for the exposure of the fat black female body beyond the platform of the hefty higgler whose association with food and later the supply of scarce imported goods helped to firmly cross-pollinate the higgler's social function as both a literal supplier of goods and an icon of abundance. Gina Ulysse suggests that, 'Dancehall not only projected this full black female form into public arenas, but asserted both its desirability and sexuality'.[14]

Nowhere has this projection of the large sexualized black body been more apparent than with the unofficial crowning and sustained reign of Carlene the dancehall queen. Carlene came to power in the dancehall arena in the early 1990s via a series of fashion clashes in which she and her posse of women competed against professional models from a local agency.[15] Carlene and her crew were situated as part of the underprivileged Jamaican masses, although technically they did not necessarily fit into this category, while the bodies of the professional models were read as middle/upper-class commodities. The models performed fashion appropriations of female behaviour that fell within the boundaries of middle-class propriety, but Carlene and her group set out to astonish. Uninhibited by codes of female propriety, at one clash, barely clad in fishnet and lingerie, Carlene did a dance routine in which she imitated the experience of an orgasm.[16] This willingness to shock her audiences by engaging in sexually risqué behaviour has helped Carlene become a permanent fixture in Jamaican popular culture, and she has appeared on television in a variety of commercials and has been spokesperson for a brand of condoms.

However, Carlene's ascendancy to fame is complicated because not only is she full-figured, but she is of mixed-race and very light-skinned. Carlene's embrace by Jamaica's corporate world suggests that her 'brownness' has facilitated her corporate and social mobility by rendering her crude public displays more palatable since the site of enactment is a brown and not black body.[17] Nevertheless, Carlene's size has been instrumental in her success and I believe in sustaining her popularity with the black working class on whose approval she is ultimately dependent. I read her fat as an evocation of blackness that helps to resituate her near-white body as part of the extended body politic of Jamaica's masses.

In Trinidad, size has an equally compelling role in carnival–calypso iconography, and a number of female calypsonians are women of size. Calypso Rose, Singing Sandra, and Lady Iere are among several fat black women whose bodies reflect the subversive lyrics of their music and the disruptive potential of calypso in general. Soca has become to calypso what dancehall is to reggae, its most recent offshoot, and one of the very popular contemporary soca artists is Denise Belfon, a fat black woman famed for her energetic performances. According to Denise, 'People are always amazed at how a woman my size could move so I think a lot of woman respect me for that'.[18] This comment indicates how Denise's size contributes to the spectacular nature of her performances because audiences are amused by the assumingly incongruous juxtaposition of her large body and her energetic dancing capabilities. Interestingly, Denise names Aretha Franklin, Billie Holiday, and Mahalia Jackson as important artistic influences — all women whose full bodies helped create the spectacle of their performance and aided in their success.

Carlene and Denise's large bodies may also be read within the context of the carnivalesque. In Mikhail Bakhtin's text *Rabelais and his World*, he describes the carnivalesque as a mode of resistance to highbrow culture, and this resistance is accomplished via a redeployment of 'proper' upper-class rituals such as language and fashion.[19] The carnivalesque aspects of carnival and dancehall activities — the elaborate hair, makeup and costumes — comprise a sort of role-playing, a pretence at being part of the upper class. The fat black woman neatly fits into this inverted order because she is not beautiful according to Eurocentric aesthetics just as the carnival/dancehall participants are not wealthy. This is why the large female body is such a dominant image in these performative spaces; it encapsulates the inverted essence of the space.

Both soca and dancehall are musical traditions that have emerged from a social legacy of racism and oppression, and the rituals associated with each style of music address that oppressive heritage. Fat black women have contributed to the musical engagement of this shared diasporic experience of marginalization by providing bodily sites that counter the aesthetic values of the historically white hegemony. Additionally, these bodies gain popularity because they are more readily seen as an acceptable, and in some cases more desirable, form of embodiment. Furthermore, largeness has come to symbolize abundance and prosperity, especially important signifiers throughout the African Diaspora, which has undergone perpetual economic marginalization. The specifics of how large female bodies debase propriety varies across the disaporic creative genres, but the hypersexual connotations attendant on these large bodies seem to specifically inform the quality of their disruptive nature.

This disruptive potential is also evident among some of the earliest African-American female recording stars whose visual image, song lyrics, and performance reviews support the notion that both their bodies and performances, like Denise and Carlene's, mirror the transgressive qualities of the stage. Blues diva Ma Rainey was a full-bodied performer who crafted an extravagant stage persona that symbolically corresponded to her large body. Like the set girls and jamettes in the Caribbean, Ma Rainey and other black female blues singers such as Bessie Smith, Mamie Smith, June Richmond, Ida Cox, Ella Fitzgerald and Big Mama Thornton are also 'performative ancestors' to Carlene and Denise.

Dubbed 'Mother of the Blues' by Paramount, her record company, Ma Rainey was the first black woman blues singer to rise to fame, and during the five years that she worked for Paramount, she made over 90 recordings.[20] She was known for her outlandish dress and often performed in outfits extravagantly decorated with rhinestones and sequins.[21] She festooned herself with flashy headdresses and horsehair wigs and had a weakness for elaborate jewelry.[22] Additionally, Ma Rainey had her makeup applied to lighten her dark features, and this ended up heightening her outlandish appearance as the powder and rouge made her seem yellow in the glow of the stage lighting.[23]

Furthermore, her full figure was prominently featured in promotions for her show and on album covers, which suggests that her girth was an important aspect of the spectacle she created.[24] One advertisement that appeared in the *Chicago Defender* bore the headline, 'Dead Drunk Blues', and featured a cartoon drawing of Ma Rainey dancing and balancing her large body on top of a dining table where three black men are seated.[25] The men are dressed in formal suits and appear quite delighted with her performance as they sip from champagne glasses. The bucket of champagne is conspicuously placed in the forefront of the picture, situating the performance as an upper-class event, but even more importantly implying a demarcation between her and the patrons of her performance. The men's formal attire and financial access indicate middle- to upper-class values and propriety, while Ma Rainey's comical dance suggests that her performance provides a carnivalesque escape for the patrons from middle-class behavioural norms. Furthermore, her position on top of their dining table implies that observing her performance is an act of consumption, an act rife with sexual undertones.

Early in her career Ma Rainey recognized the potency of the spectacular, and beyond the production of her elaborate entertainment persona, her shows were staged to astonish. In a 1914 performance in New Orleans she sang a popular number, and at a certain point in the song the stage came apart and caved in.[26] A 1926 newspaper review further indicates Ma Rainey's penchant for unusual stage antics as well as her popularity. The writer states: 'Blues singers come and they go, but the way Ma draws them in she should be called the "mother of packin' 'em in" along with her title of being the mother of the "blues"'.[27] During the same performance that the reviewer is discussing, he describes her grand entrance to the stage: 'Ma Rainey is introduced. She is heard singing as only the mother of the "blues" can sing, but unseen until she steps from a big Paramount talking machine. Oh boy! What a flash Ma does make in her gorgeous gowns.'[28] In addition to stage gimmicks, the words of Ma Rainey's songs and the musical style in which they were performed helped sustain her outrageous performance persona.

Ma Rainey wrote several of her songs, and she was considered one of the blues performers most firmly anchored in the folk music tradition from which the blues had sprung.[29] Her loyalty to her African American musical heritage must have rendered her a somewhat more 'black' and hence genuine blues diva than her contemporaries such as Bessie Smith, whose style evolved away from its roots as her career progressed.[30] Ma Rainey's unwillingness to dilute her art form enhanced the racialized underscoring of her performance, and her black body performing historically black music must have imbued her with even more heightened levels of alterity and transgression. Her song lyrics also preserved her subversive persona. They covered a range of subjects, but the most popular theme was the passion and turmoil of intimate relationships.[31] Unlike most of the white female singers of her time, Ma Rainey sang of highly spirited women who were aware of their sexuality and aggressive in asserting their emotions.[32] In 'Explaining the Blues' Ma Rainey tells the story of an abandoned woman whose man has left her because of her involvement with another man.[33] As in several of her songs, the protagonist in 'Explaining the Blues' is quite a worldly woman who does not feel compelled to display any false modesty and who covertly indicates her comfort with the masculinized act of having concurrent intimate partners. In 'Titanic Man Blues' co-written by Ma Rainey, the protagonist goes a step further and actually abandons her man for another.[34] These direct sexual references and Ma Rainey's very frank engagement of the raw emotions attendant to romantic relationships aid in making her performances spectacular during an era when cultural norms discouraged female sexual agency.

In addition to Ma Rainey's overt engagement of sexuality in her songs, her off-stage life was also a source of sexual innuendo and transgression. Rumoured to be bisexual, as was Bessie Smith, Ma Rainey developed a reputation as sexually aggressive towards younger men as well as actively involved in lesbian encounters.[35] During one incident Ma Rainey was arrested in Chicago after the police were called because of the noise she and a group of young women were making.[36] When the police arrived, Ma Rainey and her party were all undressed; she then tried to escape through the back door, but she had picked up the wrong dress.[37] One of Ma Rainey's band members even implied that she and Bessie Smith were lovers because Ma Rainey was quite protective of Bessie while the two toured together.[38] Ma Rainey's life and her sexual exploits may not have been that unusual, but what is significant is the extent to which her sexual activities have become an element of her historical legacy, further symbolizing her as disobedient.

Ma Rainey's extravagant dress and her fat body both complemented each other as agents of transgression.[39] Furthermore, her dark skin, broad face and flat nose challenged normative criteria for feminine beauty, and she even became known as 'the ugliest woman in show business'.[40] The impact of Ma Rainey's fashion legacy on contemporary African-American entertainers is apparent, and like her, many modern rap artists sport numerous gold fillings and garnish their bodies with a plethora of jewelery.[41] This connection helps shed light on how transgression continues to be a crucial constituent of success in modern performative arenas. It also illuminates the criticisms levied against rap stars for their outlandish dress and extravagant jewelry — affronts to mainstream *haute couture* — as a means of reinforcing class and social hierarchies and simultaneously re-inscribing African Americans as well as their cultural spaces as deviant. These modern fashion choices of rap performers are surely informed by the same cultural tensions that affected Ma Rainey, which she manipulated for her professional success. This achievement was in part due to her recognition that the fat black woman's body was already an item of spectacle in American culture and that further embellishing that body to be more spectacular, efficiently reinforced America's assumptions of blackness as deviance as well as America's desire to witness the astonishing.

Rhythm and blues queen Aretha Franklin, named by Denise as a primary artistic influence, has continued Ma Rainey's legacy by placing in the foreground women's sexuality and romantic heartache in her music. Daughter of a religious minister, Franklin began her singing career in the church, and has released a number of gospel songs; however, she rose to fame in the 1960s with hits such as 'Respect', 'Natural Woman', and 'I Never Loved a Man', which earned her the title, 'Queen of Soul'.[42] For most of her illustrious career, Aretha's passion-filled songs about relationships have often been delivered via her ample body. At one concert Aretha teased the audience, remarking that she managed her weight via a mixture of 'Slim Fast and young men'.[43]

This is an intriguing comment given Ma Rainey's history and suggests that Aretha recognizes the potency of her large body and black skin as a source of sexual transgression. In fact, she is aware of the need to market herself as a sexual transgressor/ aggressor in order to attract and maintain her audience. This desire must surely be linked to Aretha's reputation for the tendency to overexpose herself, specifically her bust, through her revealing fashion choices. During the Clinton administration she performed in the Rose Garden, and for the event she wore an extremely low-cut dress, her large bosom forming high mounds above the dress's plunging neckline.[44] In an essay exploring black female sexuality, critic, bell hooks makes a similar observation as she comments on a PBS documentary featuring Aretha:

> throughout most of the documentary Aretha appears in what seems to be a household setting, a living room maybe, wearing a strapless evening dress, much too small for her breast size so her breasts appear like two balloons filled with water about to burst.[45]

On yet another occasion Aretha's bust became the subject of controversy as she prepared to make a television appearance. The directors of *The Tonight Show* asked that she change her dress because it exposed too much cleavage; she refused, citing the novelty of her appearance — a black woman with huge breasts — as the show's real issue.[46] In other words, Aretha implied that the directors of *The Tonight Show* were unaccustomed to the spectacular potential of black female sexuality. Assuming that Aretha has some say in the manner her image is staged, her choice of revealing outfits for very public appearances suggests that she is trying to embellish the astonishing nature of her already highly eroticized persona.

While Aretha's background in the church might seem in contradiction with her inclination to overplay her sexuality, her gospel legacy and this impulse to over-eroticize herself actually cooperate in the structuring of an astonishing image. Gospel is renowned for its highly emotive style and its facility for expressing a divine variety of passion. It is not unusual to see gospel singers, especially in the black church, dance, sway, and pivot across the stage in frenzied movements that have strong sexual inflections and closely resemble an orgasmic climax. Aretha and other large black women such as Mahalia Jackson and CeCe Winans evoke this sensuality during their performances — even though with Jackson and Winans there might be far fewer sexual references.

A major contributor to Aretha's success has been her ability to combine the divine and the erotic to create the spectacle of transformation through a musically framed sexual/spiritual encounter.

One performance where this amalgamation is particularly apparent is the 'Divas Live' concert during which Aretha performs with some other pop music royalty, including Mariah Carey and Celine Dion.[47] Susan Sarandon introduces Aretha and summarizes her accomplishments in very reverent tones.[48] Sarandon speaks of Aretha being 'anointed' queen of soul and describes her voice as a 'beacon' that represents everyone (*Divas Live*).[49] Before Aretha even appears on stage Sarandon invokes the divine by shrouding her in religious imagery and situating her singing talents as akin to a divine capacity for ministering. For the finale Aretha appears dressed in a floor-length, black dress with a very regal jacket, and the outfit resembles ministerial garb. She is wearing an elaborate necklace, and around her head she has a glittery black headdress similar to the ones Ma Rainey often wore. Although the other divas join in this final number, Aretha is the featured performer, and as she works her way to the chorus, she contorts her face and stiffens her body in a vivid overture to both the sensual and the divine. For portions of the chorus she raises her hand in the air, gospel style, as if she is witnessing about God's mercy while she sings about the glory of sexual ecstasy when the right man comes along. This entanglement of sexuality and divinity is quite aptly captured in one line of the song during which Aretha declares that her new found man rescued her soul (*Divas Live*). The concert ends with Aretha leading the divas in an unexpected, overtly religious finale that consists of them all repeating 'Jesus' in a variety of tonal inflections. This inarticulate repetition is actually quite appropriate as it suggests both the breathless and speechless aftermath of sexual intercourse as well as the incomprehensibility associated with the transformation that results from a divine religious experience.

In her study *The Holy Profane*, Teresa Reed explores the relationship between both black religious and black secular music, and her conclusions help explain why Aretha so effortlessly flowed between two songs that on the surface appear quite disparate.[50] Reed proposes that these religious and secular musical traditions often merge boundaries because of their African roots: 'In the West-African worldview, music is intrinsically spiritual, the sacred is intrinsically musical, and both music and the divine permeate every imaginable part of life.'[51] She further elaborates by referring to renowned African American musician Thomas Dorsey:

> Dorsey himself considered the connection between gospel and blues to be self-evident, as the two styles had a similar emotional effect upon its participants. To [Dorsey], both were equally valid vehicles of feeling, and the nature of the feeling — sacred or secular — was unimportant.[52]

Dorsey's perspective helps illuminate Aretha's performance and recognizes the intimate nexus between the emotions aroused by a saviour and those aroused by a lover, and mark somewhat of a spiritually infused hypersexualization.

Ma Rainey, Aretha, Carlene and Denise's performances are in fact feisty and 'vulgar' recastings of the hypersexualized large black female body and these performances function as a subconscious retaliation to historical events like the dehumanizing exhibit of the Hottentot Venus's fat caged body, which was displayed across Europe in the nineteenth century. Furthermore, these performances resist the pervasive objectification of the black female body in both Caribbean and North American cultures. Carlene performs with the recognition that her gyrations and scantily clad body offend the religiously underscored Western behavioural norms of Jamaican society. Additionally, the women, both fat and slender, who attend the dancehall and expose their bodies within that performative arena and on the streets of Jamaica at large, similarly engage in their fleshy displays as both a celebration of their sexuality as well as a subconscious class-inflected social affront. This retaliatory affront is propelled by both collective and individual subconscious responses to contemporary manifestations of economic as well as social marginalization, a marginalization that shares similar roots with the racialized oppression enacted against the Venus Hottentot.

Some may interpret Carlene and Denise's sexual agency as problematic and find it difficult to read their spectacular displays as empowering because of the supposedly deviant nature of their performances. However, this problem only arises if Carlene's dancing and Denise's sexually suggestive lyrics are read within the framework of Western, Judeo-Christian behavioural norms and gendered sexual regulation. Beyond the constraints of these or any other behavioural codes, there is no stable reading of this 'deviant' sexual agency; the choice to perform in these sexually unruly ways is iconoclastic and, I believe, a form of chosen sexual impropriety and resistance.

Notes

1. Carolyn Cooper, *Noises in the Blood: Orality, Gender, and the 'Vulgar' Body of Jamaican Popular Culture* (Durham: Duke University Press, 1995). I use the term 'vulgar' in keeping with Cooper's use of the term.
2. Errol Hill, 'On the Origin of the Term, Calypso', *Ethnomusicology* 11, no.3 (1967): 359–67. Hill suggests that the initial use of the term 'calypso' in reference to Trinidadian carnival songs was in the *Port of Spain Gazette* in 1900.
3. Gordon Rohlehr, *Calypso and Society in Pre-independence Trinidad* (Port of Spain: Gordon Rohlehr, 1990), 3.
4. Ibid., 47.
5. Ibid., 31.
6. Avia Ustanny, '200 Years of Christmas', *Jamaica Gleaner Online*, December 15, 2001 <http://www.jamaica-gleaner.com/gleaner/20011215/life/life2.html> (accessed November 29, 2005).
7. Norman C. Stolzoff, *Wake the Town and Tell the People: Dancehall Culture in Jamaica* (Durham: Duke University Press, 2000), xiii. I am indebted to Stolzoff for the term 'dancehall diva'.
8. Belinda Edmondson, 'Public Spectacles: Caribbean Women and the Politics of Public Performance', *Small Axe* 7, no.1 (2003): 1–16. See Edmondson's essay for a discussion of how female public performance in the Caribbean has been invested with nationalistic representational value.
9. Morris Cargill, *Gleaner*, 1994, p. 217.
10. Gina Ulysse, 'Uptown Ladies and Downtown Women: Female Representations of Class and Color in Jamaica', *Ariel* (1999): 165.
11. Ibid., 164–65.
12. A 'don' refers to inner city area leaders who often control their territory through a combination of illegal activities, including drug trafficking and blackmail.
13. Soas cited in Ulysse, 'Uptown Ladies', 164.
14. Ulysse, 'Uptown Ladies', 159.
15. Ibid., 161.
16. Ibid., 162.
17. Edmondson, 'Public Spectacles', 7.
18. 'Denise Belfon: Saucy Babe', Queenofsoca.com, June 14, 2004 <http://queenofsoca.com/ProfileDenise.html>
19. Mikhail Bakhtin, *Rabelais and his World*, trans. Helene Iswolsky (Cambridge: MIT Press, 1968).
20. Daphne Duval Harrison, *Black Pearls: Blues Queens of the 1920s* (New Brunswick: Rutgers University, 1988), 35. See Harrison for more details on

Ma Rainey's recording history; Donald Bogle, *Brown Sugar* (New York: Harmony Books, 1980), 21. Also see Bogle for information on Ma Rainey's career.
21. Bogle, 21.
22. Ibid., 18.
23. Sandra R. Lieb, *Mother of the Blues: A Study of Ma Rainey* (Amherst: The University of Massachusetts Press, 1981), 8.
24. Ibid., 10.
25. Ibid., 11.
26. Ibid., 7.
27. Bob Hayes, 'Ma Rainey's Review', *Chicago Defender*, February 13, 1926.
28. Ibid.
29. Lieb, *Mother of the Blues*, xiv.
30. Ibid.
31. Ibid., 82.
32. Ibid.
33. Ibid., 104.
34. Ibid., 110.
35. Ibid., 18.
36. Ibid., 17.
37. Ibid.
38. Ibid., 18.
39. Bogle, *Brown Sugar*, 16. Ma Rainey was rumoured to be bi-sexual, further enhancing the transgressive quality of her persona.
40. Bogle, *Brown Sugar*, 21.
41. Ibid., 18.
42. Aretha Franklin, 'Respect', *Respect*, Wea, 2002; Aretha Franklin, '(You Make me Feel Like a) Natural Woman', *Respect*, Wea, 2002; Aretha Franklin, 'I Never Loved a Man (The Way I Love You)', *Respect*, Wea, 2002.
43. Franklin cited in Stephen Holden, 'Playful Aretha Franklin Plumbs Roots of Soul', *New York Times*, November 5, 1994, late ed., 15.
44. Aretha Franklin and David Ritz, *Aretha: From These Roots* (New York: Villard Books, 1999).
45. bell hooks, *Black Looks: Race and Representation* (Cambridge MA: South End Press, 1992), 70.
46. 'The Original Do-Right Woman: The Queen of Soul talks about her life, her loves, her fear of flying and the time she and Sam Cooke "almost went there",' *Newsweek* 134, no.14 (October 4, 1999): 68.
47. *Divas Live*, dir. Michael A. Simon, perf. Mariah Carey, Gloria Estefan, Shania Twain, Aretha Franklin, Celine Dion, and Carole King, Epic Music Video, 1998.
48. *Divas Live*.
49. Sarandon specifically refers to Aretha's demands for 'respect' in the 1960s as a universal call on everyone's behalf; however, Sarandon's comment strikes me as a subconscious effort by the white/male power structure to dilute the black and female undertones of the song. This act of ostensibly embracing Aretha seems more an act of delivering her artistry from its racialized and gendered roots, hence making her otherness less specific to certain socio-historical occurrences.
50. Teresa Reed, *The Holy Profane* (Lexington: The University Press of Kentucky, 2003).
51. Ibid., 5.
52. Ibid., 11.

10

MEN IN THE YARD AND ON THE STREET: CRICKET AND CALYPSO IN CARIBBEAN LITERATURE

Claire Westall

If you told Man-man you were going to the cricket, he would write CRICK and then concentrate on the E's until he saw you again.

V.S. Naipaul, *Miguel Street*

Introduction

Based on a fabled Port of Spain resident whose Messianic tale is captured by The Mighty Wonder's calypso 'Follow Me Children', Man-man is the 'mad-man' of *Miguel Street* (1959)[1] whose descent into religious fantasy results in a mock (and failed) crucifixion and, thereafter, permanent incarceration. Man-man's identity, his very name, expresses the dialectic of 'Man' — capitalized and universal — a supposedly homogenous collective, and 'man' — uncapitalized and singular — a sometimes lonely and socially isolated being. In *The Crucifixion* (1987)[2] Ismith Khan also employs the story of the preacher's self crucifixion while Lovelace recreates the motif of Christlike sacrifice in Taffy and then Bolo, and even resurrects Man Man (no hyphen) as the martyred leader of a secret African society in the opening lines of *Salt* (1997).[3] In all these cases the heroic and/or mock heroic martyr is part of the ongoing and concurrent construction and interrogation of the self-sacrificing leader — the *man* whose 'man-ness' will lead the people to freedom, liberty and, crucially, Nationhood. In attempting to write CRICKET into the dust of Miguel Street, Man-man reaches CRICK before his inscription and his story stutter at the letter E; a letter that obviously evokes England and his surprisingly English accent. Man-man repeatedly carves Es into the landscape of Trinidad, into the poverty of Port of Spain, until Naipaul's young narrator returns from his out-of-sight cricket game. Only then can Man-man mark the final letter T. Much like Alford's repetition of As and his eventual arrival at C in Lovelace's *Salt*, Man-man's linguistic stutter is part of a wider concern with literacy and mimicry that reflects a coming into language, an obsession with the word and a faltering relationship with the old colonial master whose imposition of English and cricket coincide in his inscription. It is in the context of Man-man's story that this discussion proceeds as the seemingly mad, suspiciously astute double-man of *Miguel Street* embodies calypso, inscribes cricket into the landscape of his island with a stick — a miniature version of the phallic implements used by both stick fighters and cricketers — and eventually refuses to become the heroic saviour of his fellow men, and, Man.

In 'Music, Literature and West Indian Cricket Values',[4] Gordon Rohlehr establishes the aesthetic, cultural, political and economic intersections between cricket, calypso and the Caribbean literary imagination. Further, in 'I Lawa: Masculinity in Trinidad and Tobago Calypso',[5] Rohlehr examines the tradition of the warrior-hero of the stickfight, his evolution into the heroes of calypso and cricket (among others) and calypso's ability, ironic and humorous, to 'elevate and deflate the ideal of phallocentric masculinity'.[6] Building on these insights, this paper considers the place and purpose of cricket and calypso in Errol John's yard play *Moon on a Rainbow Shawl* (1958)[7] and V.S. Naipaul's collection of interwoven short stories *Miguel Street*. By reviewing the cricketing narratives provided by the men in the yard and on the street, this paper suggests how and to what consequence John and Naipaul reflect upon and interrogate the models of masculinity and heroism laid before them as young Caribbean men in postwar Trinidad.

Moon on a Rainbow Shawl and *Miguel Street* were both composed in London in 1955 and represent something of a literary re-crossing of the Atlantic as each author recalls and recreates the post-war Trinidad they left behind and fictionalizes, if not rationalizes, their own departure to England. Both pieces exhibit similarly cutting and unromanticized visions of poverty in Port of Spain and bear the marks of the 1930's barrack tradition of Alfred Mendes, C.L.R. James and others. In doing so, John and Naipaul rely heavily upon the sounds, styles and humour of calypso to localize, unify and animate their writing. Calypso also enables them to clear a cultural and psychic space for Caribbean identities, particularly working-class male identities, in between — though very much affected by — the competing economic and social influences of England and America during the transitional period before the federation, and thereafter, independence. Calypso is a dominant feature of *Moon*'s soundscape, it is the local sound and the sound of the *locale* inserted and asserted in between 'Land of Hope and Glory' and Frank Sinatra, and is personified onstage by Ketch, the calypsonian forced to run after the yankee dollar '.[8] Calypso is also the principle intertextual resource of *Miguel Street* as Naipaul uses at least 14 calypso songs from the 1930s and 1940s.[9]

More importantly, Naipaul and his characters operate almost entirely within the ironic idiom of calypso and, as in *Moon*, the picong, machismo and gender-battle of calypso remain omnipresent. Against Lamming's condemnation of 'castrated satire', Rohlehr argues that the employment of ironic and satirical strategies, as found in calypso, actually enables Naipaul to 'examine the past without sentimental self-indulgence'.[10] The same can be said of John. Moreover, Thieme's rightly suggests that Naipaul imaginatively returns from England through calypso to express, perhaps for the only time, a 'genuine concern for' and 'degree of sympathy' for 'the ordinary West Indian', specifically the black male.[11] In examining the past, and the men or examples of masculinity from their past, John and Naipaul employ calypso to probe the 'Big man' complex — the problem of how '[t]o be a man, among we men'.[12] They do this by presenting calypso and cricket as spaces in which men and male identities are at once established and undermined, performed and revealed as performance, remembered and exposed as false remembering.

In the yard and on the street, cricket exists as a boy's game and a manly topic of discussion that serves to distract from the reality of male boredom and, quite often, a physical sense of stasis or paralysis. For many Caribbean men, the sport appears to be a means of escape but it is portrayed by John and Naipaul as a Janus-faced illusion whose dreamlike promise of success and prosperity — obtained by an exceptional few — exists alongside defeat, exclusion, drinking and jail (for a wider majority) as experienced by Charlie and Hat. The works have, at their core, narratives of cricketing remembrance that illustrate the dialectic of cricket, its connection with calypso and the problems these fields of masculinity present for the leading male figures. In both texts, surrogate father–son relationships are created between the generationally separated male characters — Charlie and Ephraim in *Moon* and Hat and Naipaul's narrator in *Miguel Street* — which are clearly tied to their cricketing exchanges. In *Moon*, Charlie Adams shares the memory of his 'broken' career as a fast bowler with Ephraim. In *Miguel Street*, Naipaul's anonymous boy narrator tells of his first trip to the Oval with Hat, relays the details of his uncle's cricket-related wife beating and describes the earlier cited example of Man-man. In each case the act of memory functions to recall and re-member (to imaginatively put back together) the older men and their previous masculine performances but also serves to expose the instability of those past performances and the disjuncture between them and their present emasculation; a disjuncture which pushes the younger men, Eph and the narrator (read John and Naipaul), to flee to the Mother Country. In addition, these stories of cricket, and cricket's relationship to masculinity, are read through calypso and calypso in fact influences the very style of cricket on display. Like numerous other commentators, Richard Burton has pointed out that the 'street values' of calypso — reputation, aggression, bravado, et cetera — inform or mould the type of cricket played in the Caribbean whether on the beach, on the street or in the international arena. Mobilizing the works of Roger Abrahams and Peter Wilson, he believes that because of the two traditions found in West Indies cricket, those of Englishness and 'Caribbeanness', the game must be read through the dialectic of inside/respectability/yard/women and outside/reputation/street/man that structures carnival.[13] In this context, the following sections first address the men of John's yard and then move to consider those of Naipaul's street. While Burton's understanding of cricket, its two traditions and the values association with the yard and street is useful, this paper ultimately suggests that the battle to establish and maintain a coherent and stable masculine identity is one that takes place in both these sociocultural places/spaces because it is central to the pattern of gender relations that characterizes the picaroon society portrayed.

In the Yard

Moon on a Rainbow Shawl won the 1957 Observer play competition and went on to become a seminal piece of Caribbean theatre which, though dated, continues to be reproduced around the world. Although *Moon* was first published in 1958, John's revised 1962 version (published in 1963), set in the East Dry River District, home of the pan, emphasizes and expands the play's cricketing and calypso aspects and consequently is used herein.[14] The play's rainbow shawl is an obvious metaphor for the colours and 'texture' of Trinidad's racially mixed population which is physically presented onstage as a bedcover and security blanket upon which the light, promise and hope of the moon shines. The play depicts a small yard in which all of the characters feel trapped and dream of escaping to a bigger, fuller, happier life whether this is through cricket (Charlie), marriage (Rosa, Mavis) or departure (Sophia, Esther, Ephraim). The yard itself is a female, even feminine space dominated by Sophia Adams, matriarch, 'bully' and 'moral centre' of the play. Nevertheless, in this womb-like retreat from the street, it is the men, Charlie Adams and Ephraim, and their desperate actions that drive the piece forward. The play circles around Charlie's theft from Ole Mack's café and reaches its dramatic climax when Ephraim (Eph), the disillusioned young trolley bus driver, storms out of the yard to head for Liverpool, England, regardless of his girlfriend Rosa or their unborn baby. The struggles and relationship of Charlie and Eph is the key to the play's investigation of masculine identities and is principally negotiated through Charlie's cricketing story.

Charlie Adams is the 'ruined cricketer' Naipaul identifies as a recurring figure in 'Trinidad lore'.[15] Beckles notes that even his name evokes 'a regular, common kind of being — if not the first man in terms of biblical text'.[16] This first-everyman is the representative of all failed cricketers and, more specifically, the tradition of West Indies fast bowling. In his youth, Charlie attempts to 'grow to his full stature' through cricket; he is 'slim and handsome', real 'spit and polish', a man too good for Sophia.[17] He was, in fact, the young attractive male body Eph presents to the audience. However, on stage we see the once powerful sporting performer reduced to a rum-drinking thief who steals to provide for his daughter's education. 'Broken' by his cricketing past, Charlie's fall from masculine self-assertion, achieved through 'real quick' bowling, is written onto his 'big, bloated, brown skinned'[18] body which is soft, fat and effeminized by its similarity to his wife's 'plump'[19] figure. Eph reads Charlie and his body as a warning, as vision of his own future if he does not leave the island. Indeed, Charlie's body, especially in comparison to the sexual appeal of Eph, speaks of the older man's social, economic and, perhaps, sexual impotence.[20] Yet, Charlie is never violent or abusive — as men are ordinarily in *Miguel Street* — and his character is marked by his kindness and the single affection everyone has for him. When in the yard, his loosely worn mask of drunken happiness, that of a man of the street celebrating the heroes returning from war, quickly evaporates. In this feminine/homely space, he breaks down crying as he confesses his crime to Sophia. When she comforts him in her maternal fashion Charlie becomes a boy in her arms reliant upon his wife for any solution or help. He is a far cry from the man he re-members.

In the 1920s, Charlie had been a fast bowler of international promise until he protested against the unfair boarding conditions for coloured players while on an intercolonial tour of Jamaica. The 'stink' got into the papers, ending his career and his chance to escape the clutches of poverty by moving to an English league side. Remembering himself, approaching 30, 'strong as a bull — and at the height of his power of as bowler', he tells Eph:

> my big talent was with the ball. I used to trundle down to that wicket — an' send them down red hot! ... in my time, John, Old Constantine, Francis, them fellas was fast! Fast! Up in England them so help put the Indies on the map.... But for the West Indian tour to England that year — I didn't even get an invite to the trials.... In them days, boy — The Savannah Club crowd was running most everything.... They broke me.[21]

Speed, aggression and 'red hot' bowling were the qualities that used to anchor Charlie's sense of 'manliness' and his position in the world. He had a local 'reputation' and was considered a hero-in-waiting who would become one of the 'selected individuals [who] played representative roles which were charged with social significance'.[22] He stands as one of a long line of similar black fast bowlers. Initially employed by plantation owners for batting practice, they gradually entered the ideologically protected space of cricket — of Englishness, imperialism and white racial supremacy — in the nineteenth century as they were allowed to perform cricket's most physically demanding task; bowling.[23] Frank Birbalsingh summarizes the situation: '[b]y the last decade of the [nineteenth] century, the plantation origins of West Indian society had produced a situation in which the best batsmen were generally white and the best bowlers were black *and fast.*'[24] In his canonical *Beyond A Boundary* (1963), C.L.R James clearly relates the West Indies tradition of quick bowling to the region's complex colonial history and the consequences of that history.[25] Maurice

St. Pierre asserts that the frustrations caused by colonialism were sublimated into the socially accepted channel of cricket and made visible in fast bowling.[26] In literary terms, George Lamming captures the ferocity of the 'bloodthirsty fast bowler' with Crim (as in criminal), in *Season of Adventure* (1960), who uses speed as his 'weapon' against the racial and class distinctions in which he lives.[27] Through carnival and play, Burton claims that such bowling, where there is '[a]lways... the same emphasis on speed and aggression',[28] is intrinsically bound to the reputation-based values of the street and of calypso. In this context, fast bowling is a route to masculinity, to an understanding of one's self as the warrior-hero and such a sporting warrior could propel himself and his weapon — the ball — at those above and beyond his immediate social and economic reach. He could use his physical and mental strength to challenge and endanger the system that excluded him on the very field that was supposed to protect and reproduce imperial Englishness and white superiority.

Charlie Adams is based on Errol John's fast bowling father, George John, whom James describes as the 'knight-errant of fast bowling',[29] 'the fast bowlers' bowler',[30] 'not hostile but hostility itself'.[31] He 'incarnated the plebs of his time' and he and the white gentleman batsman George Challenor embodied their cricketing generation.[32] John's career was interrupted by the First World War but he toured England in 1924, aged at least 39, when his bowling and that of Learie Constantine and George Francis (the 'fellas' Charlie recalls) made them all heroes and helped the West Indies gain Test status in 1928, to 'put them on the map'. Also, in playing their part in a mixed racial and regional team, these men planted the seeds of what Beckles, in his book of the same name, calls 'A Nation Imagined'. It is this moment, this historic and collective entrance onto the world stage as potential sporting equals to England, still the colonial and cricketing Massa, from which Charlie is excluded in the second edition. As a cricketer, he is not only denied the chance 'to be measured against international standards'[33] but he is even refused the opportunity to prove himself worthy to compete, that is, he is denied the right to a 'trial'. Consequently, he haunts the yard, and Eph specifically, as a reminder of the racial and class injustices that structure Caribbean cricket and society generally preventing such black working-class men from making their way in the world.

However, as a fictional member of this 'generation of black men bowling fast [which] was more sure of itself',[34] it was Charlie's position of confidence that caused his downfall. When he acted outside of the field of play as a man confident or defiant enough to confront the realities of racial discrimination he became another tragic hero, another fallen figure at the feet of the Savannah crowd and their cricketing/colonial power. By not knowing his place he loses everything he hoped to become. On one hand, Charlie's story tells us that for the men of his generation fast, aggressive bowling was a physical and ideological weapon they could throw, or bowl, at the colonial power base represented by the (white) batsman. It was a means by which these men could build a sense of importance, a sense of achievement and masculinity. On the other hand, and especially before Frank Worrell's transformative arrival as captain of the West Indies in 1960, the black bowler was not only tortured by his physical duties but also by the obvious and life determining power of the cricketing/colonial authority under whom he bowled. Such a black bowler stood, like the calypsonian 'chasing the yankee dollar', in between agency and subjection, resistance and complicity, masculinity and emasculation. Thus, in *Moon* Charlie's bowling can be read as both his means of self expression and masculinity-in-action and the self-alienating labour white men (as batsmen and captains, et cetera) control.

While his previous life and self was tied to bowling, in the yard Charlie is reduced to a bat mender reliant on the patronage of the wealthy cricketing elite who expelled him. In fact, he is working when he tells Eph of his past and the bats onstage stand as physical references to the phallic power of the white batsman, hegemonic masculinity and the colonial order; all of which structure their lives and their exchange. Eph comforts Charlie with the knowledge that he was 'class' but he blames Trinidad, as a nation, for what happens to him. Eph, like Charlie and others before him, wants to make it 'big', to be a 'big man' and no 'small boy' but in his desire to achieve this size-based masculine sense of self he rejects what he knows and loves — his grandmother and Rosa — only to end up predicting his own future collapse, reminiscent of Charlie in Sophia's arms, by labelling himself a 'big boy'.[35] When Eph takes up the cricket bat to play some 'air shots' he reconnects with the game, with Charlie and the island whilst simultaneously seeking to move away from Charlie's position as black bowler and failed hero. His handling of the bat points to his attempt to grab, acquire and perform the phallic power he thinks he will be able to obtain in England even though England is the source of the colonial imagination that destroyed Charlie and, with a depressing irony, Liverpool — Eph's exact destination — was a key port for the slave trade. At the end of the play Young Murray arrives to collect these bats and reclaim these symbols of power. Charlie and Eph had discussed his talent and his father's wealth as they believed him to be a future international player. When Sophia returns from visiting Charlie in jail, Murray explains that he has arranged for Charlie to coach the 'juniors' at Queen's Royal College. This last painfully ironic blow could have provided Charlie with a road out of the yard and with such a job he could have re-established his sense of masculinity by being husband–father–provider. Yet, it would have resituated him in the position of black bowler, employed by the white colonial and cricketing elite and only able to perform *at* them if it is also *for* them. Instead, he resides in jail. It seems that the power of the bat has not yet become available to the men of the yard, though it is used and abused on the street.

On the Street

Miguel Street is a collection of 17 short stories told from the point of view of a nameless and seemingly fatherless boy narrator; all depict the residents of Naipaul's fictional Port of Spain street. Only one of the sketches, 'The Maternal Instinct', concentrates on a woman, Laura, and Naipaul uses her to humiliate her partner Nathaniel whom she beats in a reversal of the calypso message of 'Knock Dem Down'. The other sketches present the men of the area and the narrator's examination of them where his role models and examples of masculinity are found outside the domestic sphere on the street. The young narrator and his friends, Errol and Boyee, learn from and attempt to imitate Eddoes, Bogart and Hat, the street's dominant males, the men who present 'life lived ... on the pavement'.[36] The narrator tells of the performances of masculinity offered on the street but also explores the depths, problems and insecurities of these characters.

Although the narrator journeys through his adolescence with varying heroes or male icons, he enjoys a special bond with Hat — the street's 'smartman', a version of the hero of calypso. Hat is the man that boys and men aspire to be, who sets the street's standards of behaviour and the limits of laughter, who, more than anyone else, perceives 'the pain beneath the pose'.[37] In the penultimate story, simply entitled 'Hat', the narrator tells of his first encounter with Hat when Hat took him and 11 other children to the Oval for the last day of Trinidad versus Jamaica. This memory is placed alongside the narrator's outgrowing of Hat and the calypso culture of the street and Hat's fall from his previous, seemingly heroic, position. The last story is the narrator's own and tells of his parting with Hat and his departure to England.

Throughout *Miguel Street* cricket is played by the young boys and their games exhibit not only the makeshift nature of street cricket from which so much of West Indies cricket is said to derive, but as their ball regularly gets wet 'in the stinking gutter'[38] their game is quite literally tainted with the 'stink' of the poverty in which they live. The men of the street discuss, bet on and observe cricket. It is a part of the supposed 'leisure' of street life and a space in which they can invest their hopes, dreams and emotions whilst escaping the realities of their lives. The trip to the Oval provides the event in which Hat's personality, his persona, is most clearly revealed. He takes 12 of the street's children to the game not as a kindness but as a joke, as a trick. His mock-fatherhood grants him attention, importance and respect among the crowd of interested eyes as the children appear to attest to his manliness, to his fertility, to his phallic credentials. However, the validity of such an idea has already been undercut by the tale of Mr Morgan, the Pyrotechnist, whose ten children did not prevent his public emasculation at the hands of his wife. Whilst watching the game, the two sides of Hat's persona are revealed. On one hand, Hat shouts, gesticulates, places 'impossible bets'[39] and acts in accordance with the values of the street. His exuberance and excitement are very much part of the game's action and are examples of the close spectator–player relationship that characterizes West Indies cricket. At the same time, he conveys cricket's traditions of gentility and honour to the narrator by teaching him about the beauty of the game, the cricketer's names, the scoreboard and that a batsman can be said to have 'finished batting'[40] rather than just being 'out'. Here Hat embodies the two traditions of West Indies cricket that Burton categories as the white elite and its coloured imitators versus the black masses or the Anglo-Creole 'play up, play up, and play the game' versus the Afro-Creole 'play'. Burton's position seems to accurately reflect Hat's behaviour when he explains that:

> West Indian men, it seems to me, watch and play cricket with minds, hearts, values and expectations shaped by the street culture of boyhood, adolescence and early manhood. Concerned as they are with the enhancing of individual and group reputation, those values are potentially — though rarely in fact — at odds with the values of respectability, seriousness, moderation and obedience associated with the home, the church and the ethos of the dominant white and coloured elites.[41]

Burton's point is made when Gerry Gomez reaches 150 runs and Hat cries out, without a hint of irony, 'White people is God'.[42] Whilst Hat's support for Trinidad's captain is entirely understandable in the context of an intercolonial game he does not praise Gomez individually but white people collectively. His shout proclaims the complexity of his own identity, of his identification with and alienation from both his own people and the 'whites'. In this situation Gomez the 'white', Cambridge blue captain stands in for the traditions of England and Englishness that continue to dominate cricket and colonial hierarchies on and off the field: he is one of the 'Savannah crowd'. Hat's 'crazy bets' also set Gomez against George Headley of Jamaica, who, in 1948, became the first black man to lead the West Indies team on the field and whose presence therefore gestures forward to a black regional collectivity and leadership within and beyond cricket. As the first black, working-class batsman hero, Headley was a hero to the entire region. He was a great batsman, if not the greatest that the West Indies ever produced and James writes about him as such in *Beyond A Boundary*.[43] Headley carried the batting of the West Indies throughout the 1930s, and was largely responsible for the team's innings and, too often, the majority of their runs. Consequently, he earned the name 'Atlas'. He was also nicknamed the Black Bradman in reference to the most famous of Australian batsmen — Sir Donald Bradman. As such, Headley is the cricketing counterpart to Black Wordsworth, *Miguel Street*'s struggling poet and calypsonian who claims that he and his brother, the White Wordsworth, are two halves of a single poetic whole. In counterpoising Gomez and Headley, and, Headley and Wordsworth, Naipaul lays bare the two sides of Hat's identification with cricket and the pressure it exerts on his own sense of self. Hat's calypsonian persona of masculine bravado and self-assurance is unsustainable when faced with the supremacy of and his admiration for 'white people'. Hence, it is in the same penultimate sketch that we learn of how, through marriage, domestic violence and jail, Hat becomes another aged calypsonian whose mask shatters under its own weight causing Naipaul's narrator to distance himself from his last and most significant masculine hero. Like Eph in *Moon*, the narrator continues to feel affection and sympathy for the older, now fallen man but he, again like Eph, fears for his own future and leaves in search of a bigger life outside of the calypso-island.

The act of wife beating that sends Hat to jail is a repeated feature of *Miguel Street* and Naipaul's works more generally. Both John and Naipaul situate their concern with men and masculine identities within male–female relationships and both show the cricket bat as a phallic weapon used in domestic violence where wife beating is accepted as commonplace, performed in a kind of calypso comedy and is supposedly undercut by the emasculating tongues of the women. In *Moon*, Prince takes up one of the bats Charlie mends and makes as if to strike Mavis, his new fiancée. When she rebukes him declaring that they 'aren't married yet' he retreats to become 'the patsy' again.[44] In *Miguel Street*, Mr Bhakcu, 'The Mechanic' and narrator's uncle, beats his wife with a cricket bat and the narrator describes the situation:

> For a long time I think Bhakcu experimented with rods for beating his wife, and I wouldn't swear that it wasn't Hat who suggested a cricket bat. But whosoever suggested it, a second-hand cricket bat was bought from the Queen's Park Oval, and oiled, and used on Mrs. Bhakcu.
>
> Hat said, "Is the only thing she really could feel, I think."

> The strangest thing about this was that Mrs. Bhakcu kept the bat clean and well-oiled. Boyee tried many times to borrow the bat, but Mrs. Bhakcu never lent it.[45]
>
> [Bhacku] hated his wife, and he beat her regularly with the cricket bat. But she was beating him too, with her tongue, and I think Bhakcu was really the loser in these quarrels.[46]

Whilst the humour of the scene is undeniable it only adds to the seriousness with which one views these ritualistic acts. These examples point, quite obviously, to the emasculating effects of the colonial system, microcosmically contained within cricket, being re-directed into the physical domination of women. One can argue that the cricket bat is used to suppress, control and emasculate men of colour before they re-direct it against their womenfolk. In this sense, one should appreciate that when the traditional battle was between white batsman and black bowlers a coloured man taking up the bat is an attempt to offer some kind of anticolonial stroke, a move to seize power from the grip of the white (bats)man. This is why black batsmen like Headley, Sobers, Richards and Lara are crucial in offering a symbolic reversion of the traditional colonial order. However, Bhacku's situation disrupts this black–white dynamic and draws in Trinidad's wider racial picture. A probable descendent of indentured Indian labour, Bhakcu's seizure of the bat symbolizes his struggle against white hegemonic masculinity and its black opposition. His performance follows Reddock's explanation of Niels Sampath's depiction of:

> Indo-Caribbean masculinity as a difficult and sometimes confusing struggle against creolization, on the one hand seeking acceptance within this paradigm, but at the same time seeking to maintain Indian domestic patriarchal power. This is a struggle, following Wilson (1969), between the values of honour (Indian) and reputation (Creole).[47]

Still, even if the effeminized Prince and Indian Bhakcu are contesting hegemonic and black calypso-related masculinities, they reinforce the point that masculinities are typically united by their oppression, or attempted oppression, of women. Although Mrs

Bhakcu appears complicit in this oppression, the power of her tongue may recall the relatively strong position of Indian women during indentureship and male attempts to regain control over them post-indentureship. Importantly, in both instances the female tongue — standing in for the female voice and sexuality — defeats the men but does not improve their condition. This only happens when the men decide to do something else, in Bhacku's case to become a pundit. Mavis and Mrs Bhakcu are only able to 'emasculate' their partners by destroying the mask of masculinity they wear because the men are afraid of losing this mask but are constantly doing so; a feature that may actually cause the violence. I suggest that in the same way that the objectifying gaze of the women in *Moon* may be a displacement of the white male gaze, one suspects that the verbal attacks of the women are really the verbalization of the cricket bat's white hegemonic voice speaking back to the man of colour who uses it, and that the women are on the receiving end of both.

Conclusion

The examples of Charlie, Hat and Bhakcu are united by the Queen's Park Oval that is, as James puts it, the 'boss of the island's cricket relations'.[48] The Oval is the socio-political force that Charlie describes as 'pushing yer out of the stream — and on to the bank — So that yer rot in the sun'.[49] As a bastion of white power and prejudice, the Oval embodies the corrupting pressures white hegemonic masculinity places on the other male identities seen in *Moon* and *Miguel Street*, particularly those based on the street values of calypso and its popular expression within cricket. Eph and Naipaul's narrator blame Trinidad itself for the situation they see before them and bemoan that 'It ent much different'[50] for them than it was their elder counterparts and their point is supported by the two decades that pass between Charlie's cricketing career and the trip to the Oval. Consequently, these young men run away from Trinidad and the men they think they will become if they remain. Unfortunately, they are running toward the very epicentre of the colonial imagination which will not provide them with any easy solutions, as the *Windrush* generation discovered. In contrast, Charlie and Sophia believe that Trinidad is changing and that it has and will continue to improve for men like Charlie and Eph. In cricketing terms, black men have risen since Frank Worrell and a black man has led the West Indies cricket team from 1960 onwards. West Indies cricket has become a vehicle for the history and future of the Caribbean region. Over the course of the twentieth century it has increasingly become a means of the Caribbean expressing itself and its desires to the world. Yet, the continuing dominance of white hegemonic masculinity remains. Situated within the Oval and white cricket-playing nations like England and Australia its residual influence means that West Indies cricket still exists within a system of white, predominantly colonial, masculine and cricketing signification. For the men and nation of Trinidad, the historically situated performances of masculinity demonstrated by Charlie, Hat and Bhakcu, operating as they do within the traditions of cricket, calypso and calypso-cricket, seem to only entrench their identities within typical and accepted masculine domains of achievement via control and defeat over other men and gender identities. One suspects that they must engage with, learn from and ultimately unite with the very gender identities they seek to dominate or exclude. Finally, the disintegration of the heroes of calypso and cricket seen in *Moon* and *Miguel Street* seems to steer us away from an investment in the individual male as hero and towards a common collective based on something other than phallic power.

Notes

1. V.S. Naipaul, *Miguel Street* (London: André Deutsch, 1959).
2. Ismith Khan, *The Crucifixion* (London: Peepal Tree Press, 1987).
3. Earl Lovelace, *Salt: A Novel* (New York: George Braziller, 2004).
4. Gordon Rohlehr, 'Music, Literature and West Indian Cricket Values', in *An Area of Conquest: Popular Democracy and West Indies Cricket*, ed. Hilary McD. Beckles (Kingston: Ian Randle Publishers, 1994), 55–102.
5. Gordon Rohlehr, 'I Lawa: Masculinity in Trinidad and Tobago Calypso', *Interrogating Caribbean Masculinities: Theoretical and Empirical Analyses*, ed. Rhoda E. Reddock (Kingston: The University of the West Indies Press, 2004), 326–99.
6. Rhoda E. Reddock, ed. *Interrogating Caribbean Masculinities: Theoretical and Empirical Analyses* (Kingston: The University of the West Indies Press, 2004), 345.
7. Errol John, *Moon on a Rainbow Shawl: A Play in Three Acts*, 2nd Edition (London: Faber and Faber, 1963).
8. Ibid., 50.
9. See John Thieme, 'Calypso Allusions in Naipaul's *Miguel Street*', *Kunapipi* 3, no. 2 (1981): 18–33 for a full account of the calypsos alluded to by Naipaul and their individual uses. Like many of us, myself included, Thieme draws heavily upon the knowledge, writing and insight of Professor Rohlehr.
10. Gordon Rohlehr, 'The Ironic Approach: The Novels of V.S. Naipaul', in *The Islands in Between: Essays on West Indian Literature*, ed. Louis James (London: Oxford University Press, 1968): 121–39.
11. Thieme, 'Calypso Allusions', 19.
12. Naipaul, *Miguel Street*, 14.
13. This paper does not support Burton's argument that one can use these two positions to explain the crowd trouble and rioting during the MCC tours of 1953–55, 1960 and 1968. C.L.R. James's *Beyond A Boundary* (London: Stanley Paul & Co, 1963) offers a more insightful reading of that behaviour and those incidents.
14. The 1958 first edition employs the same examples of cricket and calypso and they are invested with the same symbolic significance. However, the 1963 version sharpens the attack made by John on the cricketing authorities and expands the discussion of cricket by and about Charlie whilst also increasing its calypso references. All citations are taken from the 1963 edition. There are some notable differences between the two versions, including John's decision to move the action from Woodbrook, the residential area in which he grew up, in the first edition to the East Dry River District in the second. Also, in the first edition Charlie is said to have missed the 1924 tour to England but this is moved forward to the 1928 tour in the second version. This discussion addresses the second case. Whilst the historical detail shifts, and these movements have been a notable part of my consideration of the play elsewhere, the arguments attached to Charlie's role and his exclusion from the international trials remains consistent.
15. V.S. Naipaul, *The Middle Passage: impressions of five societies – British, French and Dutch – in the West Indies and South America* (London: André Deutsch, 1962), 42.
16. Hilary McD. Beckles, *The Development of West Indies Cricket: Vol. 1 The Age of Nationalism* (Kingston: The University of the West Indies Press, 1998), 105.
17. Naipaul, *Middle Passage*, 41.
18. Ibid., 39.

19. Ibid., 23.
20. In both editions it is strongly suggested that Charlie is not the biological father of Esther.
21. Naipaul, *Middle Passage*, 61–62.
22. James, *Beyond a Boundary*, 66.
23. For a fuller discussion of the emergence of black bowlers see Hilary Beckles, *The Development of West Indies Cricket* Vol 1: 41–57.
24. Frank Birbalsingh, The Rise of West Indian Cricket: From Colony to Nation (Antigua: Hansib Publishing, 1996), 16.
25. James, *Beyond a Boundary*, 72–81.
26. Maurice St. Pierre, 'West Indian Cricket – Part 1: A socio-historical appraisal', in *Liberation Cricket: West Indies Cricket Culture*, eds. Hilary Beckles and Brian Stoddart (Manchester and New York: Manchester University Press, 1995), 107–24.
27. George Lamming, *Season of Adventure* (London: Michael Joseph, 1960); Gordon Rohlehr also makes this observation about Crim in 'Music, Literature and West Indian Cricket Values', 72. However, where Rohlehr suggests that the reference to cricket is 'a mere detail', I would posit that cricket is used by Lamming as a significant structural device at the start and end of the novel and one that deserves critical investigation.
28. Richard D.E. Burton, *Afro-Creole Power, Opposition and Play in the Caribbean*. (London and New York: Cornell University Press, 1997), 181.
29. James, *Beyond a Boundary*, 73.
30. Ibid., 81.
31. Ibid.
32. Ibid., 79.
33. Naipaul, *Middle Passage*, 42.
34. James, *Beyond a Boundary*, 79.
35. John, *Moon*, 54.
36. William Walsh, *V.S. Naipaul* (Edinburgh: Oliver & Boyd, 1973), 11.
37. Lillian Feder, *Naipaul's Truth: The Making of a Writer* (New York: Rowman & Littlefield, 2001), 165.
38. Naipaul, *Miguel Street*, 22.
39. Ibid., 156.
40. Ibid., 155.
41. Burton, 'Cricket, Carnival and Street Culture in the Caribbean', 98.
42. Ibid., 155.
43. See James's full and eloquent depiction of Headley in *Beyond A Boundary*, particularly, 139–48.
44. John, *Moon*, 55.
45. Naipaul, *Miguel Street*, 119.
46. Ibid., 123.
47. Reddock, *Interrogating Caribbean Masculinities*, xxii.
48. James, *Beyond a Boundary*, 49.
49. Ibid., 63.
50. Naipaul, *Moon*, 62.

WHEN ALL THE WORLD'S A STAGE: PERFORMING CULTURAL IDENTITY AT HOME AND ABROAD

11

WITH A TASSA BLENDING: CALYPSO AND CULTURAL IDENTITY IN INDO-CARIBBEAN FICTION

Paula Morgan

> It is only in the calypso that the Trinidadian touches reality.
> V.S. Naipaul, *The Middle Passage*[1]

Calypso occupies a privileged position in the Trinidadian cultural imagination. Given its enormous popularity within the island, regional and diasporic populations, calypso retains strong associations with home and with 'the Trini mentality'. Indeed calypso, along with Carnival, is often cited as possessing the power to convey the Trinidadian 'spirit' and worldview in the way that few other cultural practices can. Associated with lower-strata Afro-Trinidadian cultural identity, calypso is a hybrid form, the origin of which has been the subject of much contestation and debate.[2] The peculiar creation of the Afro-Caribbean urban folk, the calypso has been traditionally regarded as the lash of the small man who deploys picong and wit for boastful self-assertion and for sustained counter discourse with the hegemonic worldview, in the protected arena of the performance space. Drawing from the African tradition of the praise and blame song,[3] calypsonians have, by dint of struggle, created and maintained a relatively permissive platform for stinging, incisive humour, cutting criticism and for simultaneously airing and masking fear and antipathy through verbal power play and excess.

Over time, calypso has drawn from and fertilized myriad crossover music forms and has risen to prominence in the contemporary commoditization and globalization of local sound. In terms of its content and significance as a cultural practice, this shape-shifting nation-music occupies pivotal interface with literary and other textual discourses on gender, ethnicity and nation. Contextualizing a reading of the calypso in Indo-Trinidadian literature against a broader framework of gender and ethnic identity politics, this paper examines a range of symbolic associations, which attend the calypso as pointers to evolving gender constructions and as metaphors for cultural hybridity. It argues that the calypso with its cohesive links with Afro-Creole cultural assertion and identity also functions predominantly as an ambivalent trope for freedom and belonging for Indo-Trinidadian writers and protagonists.

Scholars have carefully documented the process by which a shared history of enforced labour through slavery and indentureship — with common legacies of anomie, institutionalized poverties, social and cultural dislocation, loss of ancestral heritages, and traumatic gender relations — has been transmuted into inter-ethnic hostility and rivalry.[4] The tenuous nature of the nation state in the resultant, fragile, island societies is reflected in the contestation over markers of rootedness and belonging. Citing calypso and Carnival as manifestation of both 'the theatres and metaphors through which Trinidad's social history is encoded and enacted', cultural critic, Gordon Rohlehr argues in 'Calypso Reinvents Itself':

> The Trinidad experience has involved an intense expenditure of energy in a process of continuous indigenization, enacted on ground stolen from the terribly reduced though not totally erased Amerindian presence, committed to create out of this teaming welter of ethnicities, a restless and according to V.S. Naipaul, "half-formed" society, sufficiently flexible to accommodate the paradox of homogeneity and difference, of one heart and yet multiple heartbeats; a jarring, jamming Carnivalesque collusion and clashing counter point of rhythms.[5]

Trinidadian discourses of cultural belonging have deployed tropes of hybridity and emblems of nationhood drawn from a range of icons. Seeking fluid and varied locations on a complex matrix of inclusions and exclusions, Indo-Trinidadians have for the most part rejected notions of an essentializing 'creole' social fabric to which their Indianness adds an 'exotic' flair. Nationalist discourses continue to revolve around questions such as: Should the steel pan, the percussion instrument created by the Afro-Trinidadian urban folk in the 1930s be emblematic of national creativity? At the time of writing (March 2005), the Trinidad and Tobago High Court was adjudicating a motion that questions the legality of the state's institution of the Trinity Cross, as the highest national award in a multi-religious society, given the symbol's associations with Christianity. The contestations continue from decade to decade and even generation to generation, with unsullied freshness and fervour.

Calypso is another such icon. With its attendant culture of competition and performance, it is a barometer of public opinion, a reflector of collective identity and a manifestation of the construction of individual and communal identity through performance. Its seasonal projection onto the national stage hinges on a strong, obtrusive, visual presence by performers who are identified by characteristic costumes that project lavish stage personas. What would a Shadow, Black Stalin, the soca artiste Ronnie Macintosh, or the chutney soca queen Drupatie Ramgoonai be without their trademark garments? In the performance, there is an increasing propensity to incorporate mime and playacting. Each of these elements adds to the texts to be decoded thus pushing the signification beyond the semiotic and verbal to incorporate the mimetic, dramatic and performative. This process becomes all the more contentious within the multi-ethnic environment. In 2003, Denise 'Saucy Wow' Belfon famed for her dizzying pelvic gyrations, crossed boundaries when she constructed the Indo-Trinidadian male as sexually desirable. Hitherto, the Indian male had been constructed in calypso, and arguably by virtue of selective representation and erasure in the mass media advertising industry, as weak, small bodied and feminized. Conservative elements within the Indo-Trinidadian community took issue with her other boundary crossing action — the use of a sari for her performance. They contended that she was thereby defiling the sacred garment.

In terms of its verbal dimension, the calypso is one facet of a diverse oral tradition, which has been used by all ethnic groups to express racial antipathy — a deep-rooted self-derision and contempt for the other through music and childhood rhyming songs. Indeed the intra-racial and inter-racial diatribes are an extension of the self-contempt and reductive laughter which Caribbean folk art forms, reflecting an historical legacy of ethnic denigration and disempowerment through naming, democratically employed within the ethnic group and toward other ethnicities. Rohlehr recalls the rhymes of his Guyanese childhood, through which children expressed the hostilities of their elders and of their societies in verses which groups of Indian and African children would hurl at each other.[6] He argues that these cancerous racial stereotypes are inculcated from childhood and hence are all the more insidious and resistant to erasure.

Reflecting this history of latent and manifest racial antipathy, calypso provides a most effective medium for race and gender stereotyping and for satirizing the other. Shalini Puri comments that the 'them and us' constructions, which continue to dominate Trinidad's discourses of cultural nationalism until today, posits notions of racially distinct ethnic parties who exist in racial antipathy and to a large extent in culturally specific spheres with a minimum of admixture. Puri contends:

> racialization of politics in post-colonial Trinidad, the persistence and active redeployment of colonial stereotypes, and the importance of stereotype in the popular national art form, calypso, result in a public discourse in which racial stereotypes are unusually prominent. What these stereotypes produce for contemporary dominant nationalist discourse is the fiction of a seamless and monolithic racial community with common interests, pitted against another seamless and monolithic racial community with common interests.[7]

Indo-Trinidadian cultural identity has been savagely satirized in calypso through mockery of mannerism, food, religious ceremonies and other cultural traditions. Conversely, there are the calypsos that offer rhapsodies about the sexual desirability and beauty of Indian women. Invariably this genre of calypso thinly disguises male–male competition with a primary focus on phallic boasting about the amazing capability of the Afro-Caribbean male for conquest within and across ethnic lines. Let the implicature of phallic inadequacy fall where it may.[8]

This tendency surfaces also in literary discourse. George Lamming, in his address to the Cultural Studies Conference in Trinidad, January 2004, 'Language and the Politics of Ethnicity', commented on literary representations of African–Indian relations:

> There are numerous examples in our literature of hostility between individuals which derive from these toxic sources of power that manipulate the original neutral difference between characters — the innocent malice for example of Masie directed at Philomen in

James's *Minty Alley;* the censoring of Pariag's inclusion and participation by the yard in Lovelace's *The Dragon Can't Dance.* The strategy of ensuring allegiance by dramatizing the menace of the Indian was most effectively used by the old colonial power and it has often been called into service by both African and Indian political leadership in the new independent countries. It has been a major obstacle to the realization of an *authentic, civic nationalism* that will embrace and recreolise all ethnic types in Caribbean society. (emphasis added)[9]

Through analysis of Indo-Trinidadian literary examples, I argue that the calypso in its broader discursive associations with ethnic dissociation and stereotyping, functions as a trope of hybridity and belonging which, nevertheless, is constructed differently depending on the gender of the writer.

The earliest mention of calypso in Indo-Caribbean fiction is in Seepersad Naipaul's *Gurudeva and other Tales* (1943?).[10] Seepersad Naipaul alludes to women, even those from conservative Indian homes, who took advantage of the American presence in Trinidad to enter into transactional sexual relations with the prosperous soldiers. The brief allusion is telling. While her parents are fretting about Daisy Seetohal's late nights and frequent absences, the latter laces her ablutions and denial of misbehaviour with snatches of the calypso 'Rum and Coca Cola', signifying that she is in fact 'working for the Yankee dollar'.[11]

A generation later, V.S. Naipaul refines his father's allusion to calypso to point to complex and diverse social movements in *Miguel Street* (1959).[12] Calypsos offer a running unifying commentary on its vignettes, which are also united through expanded character development from story to story, temporal progression and a shared narrator for whom keen observation of the complex social history of the Miguel Street residents is inextricable from his coming of age process. In the final segment, the youthful narrator equates walking into his future with walking into his own shadow: 'I left them all and walked briskly towards the aeroplane, not looking back, looking only at my shadow before me, a dancing dwarf on the tarmac.'[13] The novel is both a celebration of vivacity and coping strategies of a people doomed ultimately to fail, and a lament at an inevitable creeping loss, disillusionment, and the passing of a world of innocence. In V.S. Naipaul's *The Middle Passage* (1962) his whose perceiving eye and voice combines those of the journalist, the traveller/adventurer and social commentator. Naipaul ties the peculiar dynamic which characterizes Trinidad society to the calypso:

> The Land of the Calypso is not a copy-writer's phrase. It is one side of the truth, and it was this gaiety, so inexplicable to the tourist who sees the shacks of Shanty Town and corbeaux patrolling the modern highway, and inexplicable to me who had remembered it as the land of failures, which now, on my return, assaulted me.[14]

Published in 1959, nine years after Naipaul migrated to England, *Miguel Street* unfolds against the backdrop of World War II (1939–45) and the American military occupation of Trinidad. This period also coincided with increased urban–rural migration of Indians in Trinidad and the heightened pace and visibility of the acculturation process. This is the 1940s to 1950s during which Calypsonians vented their resentment at the intrusion of Indo-Trinidadians into the urban space. In this period Mighty Terror sang 'Grinding Masalla' (1947), 'Indian Women with Creole Names' and 'Indian Politicians' (1950), all of which thinly masked fear at intrusion and enhanced competition.[15]

Significantly though, this is not the focus of Naipaul's *Miguel Street* where calypsos provide an underlying philosophical frame for the narratives. The texts mentions no fewer than 'The More They Try to do me Bad' (1938) by Lord Caresser (Rufus Callender);[16] 'The Burning of the Treasury';[17] 'Cuff Dem Down' (n.d.) by The Mighty Sparrow (Slinger Francisco) which both The Roaring Lion (Hubert De Leon) and Lord Beginner (Egbert Moore) claimed to have invented;[18] 'Chinese Children Calling me Daddy' (1950) by The Mighty Terror;[19] 'Is Love Love Love Alone' (1937) by Lord Caresser;[20] 'All Day All Night Miss Mary Ann' (1954) by The Roaring Lion;[21] 'Working for the Yankee Dollar' (1943) by Lord Invader;[22] 'The Soldiers Came and Broke up my Life' (1944) by Lord Invader;[23] 'I Living with my Yankee Soldier' by Lord Invader;[24] 'Matilda' (1953) by King Radio and popularized by the famous American entertainer of Jamaican parentage — Harry Belafonte.[25]

Miguel Street deals with the issue of what it means to be a 'man among we men'. Its characters — some of whom are transient — grapple with turbulent gender and family relations. The calypso forms an ironic counterpoint to the feverish machinations of a small world in which individuals seek in vain for heroic stature, but are dogged by failure and frustration. The frustrated artiste exemplified in the Carpenter Popo does not work gainfully, preferring to strive to create the elusive 'thing without a name'.[26] The calypso becomes an ambivalent symbol of low culture creativity for the failed artist Black Wordsworth, who strives to write 'the greatest poem in the world' but sheepishly confesses that he makes his annual income by singing calypsos during the calypso season.[27] *Miguel Street* also represents frustrated careerists like the aspiring doctor turned Scavenger Cart driver in 'His Chosen Calling',[28] and the mechanical genius Mr Batchu who is more skilled at deconstruction than construction.[29] Moreover, in this world of men among men, an inordinate number meet misfortune and frustration in their pursuit of love.

Threaded throughout the narratives, the calypsos — the majority of which deal with the debacle of violent male–female relations — variously amplify and undercut the action. Although the narrator is proud to affirm that Miguel Street is a cut above the barrack yard environment, the eruptive violence in male–female relations does not reflect this differentiation. The scripts are varied but with a common thread. There is the failure of one party or the other to meet expectations; the escape of the aggrieved party from the disappointing relationship; and the attempt to win the loved one back with the help of violence, often eliciting the intervention of the law.

The calypso serves to analyse and magnify the domestic dramas. It lifts the petty events out of their specific confines and makes them representative experiences. When Popo beats his wife's lover, the incident becomes the basis for the road march 'Emelda'[30] which the popular all-female American vocalists The Andrews Sisters subsequently recorded for an American company.[31] The smallness of Miguel Street through which a stranger could drive and dismiss as a slum, is alleviated by the notoriety of the calypso which projects the community's mundane dramas onto the national and international stage and thereby amplifies its tragedies. In the process it lends significance and import to all. The narrator declares: 'It was a great thing for the street.'[32]

Naipaul also deploys reversals or spins on popular calypsos providing an alternative take on the popular lore. 'The Maternal Instinct' alludes to the infamous calypso-expounding wife beating which popularizes the assumption that 'women and them like a good dose of blows': 'Black up their eyes and bruise up their knee / And then they love you eternally.'[33] This ironically named narrative reverses the male beater/female beaten paradigm by presenting a female abuser. This woman, who is said to love her children, regularly deals them murderous verbal abuse. The lover Nathaniel, who is physically abused also, suffers from an ego-retrieving need to project the fabrication that he is the beater and not the beaten. Laura is reminiscent of the matador woman, that is, the woman who provides clothes, food and lodging for her 'sweet man' in exchange for his sexual favours and exclusive attention. Equipped with both physical and verbal ascendancy, she follows through on her beatings with a verbal emasculation suggestive of the African-American tradition of the dirty dozens — the male-dominated verbal power play that is a safer substitute for physical violence. In a public verbal game of one-upmanship, she emerges the victor by stripping him naked: 'Yes, Nathaniel, is you I talking to, you with your bottom like two stale bread in your pants.'[34] Yet the abusive matador woman is eventually stumped not by her own childbearing potential but by the prospect of the generational continuity of her impoverished lifestyle. She faces the likelihood that her daughter may follow her pattern of bearing eight children for seven men. In a bizarre double reversal, Laura's abuse of her pregnant daughter would have been indicative of love; her terrible silence seems a form of rejection of the girl who eventually resorts to suicide. Naipaul zeroes in here on a cultural tradition that habitually greets tragedy with laughter that becomes both a palliative and a substitute for more explosive and dangerous forms of expression.

A similar reversal is deployed in the short story 'Is Love Love Love Alone', which is named after Lord Caresser's calypso about Edward VIII who forsook the British throne to marry a commoner and divorcee. This statement on the ennobling power of love to transcend class barriers is the counterpoint to the story of a woman who leaves a sanitized, professional husband and luxurious lifestyle for a Miguel Street slum dwelling and an unkempt, drunken, abusive lover. The community disciplines the abuser with a severe beating, not because wife beating is unacceptable, but because his practices are sufficiently extreme to transgress even their boundaries. Arguably too, because the couple is unmarried, the violence does not securely remain under the category of 'husband and wife business' as may be the case in George's pink house.

In the 1940s–50s, lower strata gender relations in Trinidad were dealt a harsh blow with the intrusion of American soldiers during World War II. The chagrin was great among calypsonians who found that prosperous American soldiers had muscled in on their turf. This move which coincided with Indian rural–urban acculturation, crossed ethnic barriers so that Indian women became complicit in the sex as commodity exchange, which left their former partners out in the cold. Culturally conservative Indians and Afro-Creole calypsonians agreed on the destructive power of cultural assimilation. In 'Indian People with Creole Names' by Mighty Killer, the calypsonian decries a shift in naming conventions as evidence of an Indian takeover of naming, privilege, occupation and cultural identity. The stripping away of markers of cultural distinctiveness is seen as a threat which drives the calypsonian to seek to protect his name, status and wealth from impending 'trouble':

> Now what's wrong with these Indian people,
>
> as though their intention is for trouble?
>
> Long ago you meet an Indian boy by the road
>
> with his capra waiting to tote your load,
>
> but I notice there ain't no Indian again
>
> since the women and them taking Creole names.
>
> Long ago was Sumitra, Ramaleela, Ramaliwa
>
> But now is Jean and Dinah and Dorothy etc. etc. etc.[35]

More explicitly the calypso notes admixture in terms of hitherto taboo aggression, food and intimate relations:

> Long age you hadn't a chance
> To meet an Indian Girl in a dance
> But nowadays it is big confusion
> Big fighting in the road for their Yankee man
> And see them in the market they ain't making joke
> Pushing down nigger people to buy de poke.[36]

The naming to which Mighty Killer refers in 'Indian People with Creole Names' is indicative not simply of a shift in cultural identification but a muscling in on the transactional sex turf. The calypso cleverly links anglicized naming with prostitution when Killer attributes to the Indian working girls, the names of Sparrow's prostitutes (Jean and Dinah) whom the latter threatens with sexual revenge in the wake of the Yankees' departure. This dubious form of women's work attracts the censure of the licentious and libidinous calypsonian turned moralizer, the better to document the process of degeneration. As indicated by Rohlehr:

> The American presence undermined the traditional saga boy pose of the calypsonian who had presented the woman as an easily exploitable and expendable commodity. With American soldiers there to provide both mother and daughter with a "better price", the woman had become a sort of professional who no longer needed her parasitical saga boy.[37]

The Yankee soldier with his almighty dollar was instrumental in the unmasking of the Trinidadian male whose phallic boasting and control over a series of women disguised his fear of commitment. *Miguel Street* makes fictional allusions to this in 'Edward's Wife' in which the protagonist's pale, sickly woman leaves him for an American soldier. This is related even more directly to the issue of potency because Edward, the longing and the fearful, claims that he is constrained to marry the woman because she is pregnant with a baby that never materializes. His impotence is exposed when his wife leaves him and conceives by an American soldier lover. In this instance, life imitates the calypso, which amplifies, explains and rationalizes life. As it often is in reality, the narrator creates a seamless weave between the grim facts of characters that are grappling with crises, and the scripted fictionalized lives of characters of calypso. Hence Popo's actions make him the subject of a calypso which becomes the road march, while, in 'Until the Soldier Came,' Lord Invader sings the calypso first and subsequently Edward's wife mouths the calypsonian's scripted words. When he begs her to come back to him, she responds:

> "Invader, I change my mind
>
> I living with my Yankee soldier."
>
> This was exactly what happened to Edward.[38]

Despite the community's willingness to blame the wife and embrace the cuckolded husband, Edward — Hat's brother — takes himself and his shame away from Miguel Street.

In terms of the construction of a national community, the Miguel Street dweller lives side by side, for the most part, blissfully ignorant of markers of ethnic divisiveness. The construction of ethnicity surfaces here in relation to whiteness which in this grim scenario becomes ugly because of ugly actions:

> Hat said … "You see what a dirty thing a white skin does be sometimes." And in truth he had a nasty skin. It was yellow and pink and white with brown and black spots. The skin above his left eye had the raw pink look of scalded flesh.[39]

In the *Miguel Street* world, there is no contestation over national identity. Hat, subtly signalling his potency, is surrogate father to children of all ethnicities whom he proudly instructs in the intricacies of the national game — cricket. And calypso is the common repository into which all characters dip variously for reference points. Indeed, the calypso is also indicative of patriotism and the good life. Morgan the pyrotechnist turned arsonist sings: 'The more they try to do me bad / Is the better I live in Trinidad.'[40]

Calypso in *Miguel Street* becomes a unifying force in its promotion of patriotism and in its construction of the nation as a shared homeland. Its barbs and balms are applied in an egalitarian manner to all ethnicities and classes. As a marker of communal identity and affirmation, it functions as an indigenous boundary marker. Naipaul comments in *The Middle Passage*:

> It is only in the Calypso that the Trinidadian touches reality. The Calypso is a purely local form. No song composed outside Trinidad is a calypso. The Calypso deals with local incidents, local attitudes and it does so in a local language. The pure calypso, the best calypso, is incomprehensible to the outsider. Wit and verbal conceits are fundamental; without them no song, however good the music, however well sung, can be judged a calypso.[41]

In *The Middle Passage,* Naipaul insists on the indigenity of the calypso and its inability to travel as exemplary of its rootedness and its power to bind Trinidadians to locality, communal perspectives and worldviews. Yet, it is precisely as rooted, ethnic music that it travels so very well.

The tension between calypso as a culturally and geographically rooted form and its ability to reinvent itself on foreign terrain is explored in Selvon's short story collection *Ways of Sunlight*. In 'Basement Lullaby', the inability of the musicians to get the melody of the new calypso right, is associated with their growing alienation and dissociation within a hostile environment in which they live half lives, submerged in underground burrows. The alienation operates on several levels. They are divorced from the natural environment of both Trinidad and London. They seem to be suffering from lack of exposure to the energizing, life-giving sun. And access to the sun is a tall order with smog blocking out its feeble rays on the streets of London. The quality of their calypso performances is suffering because they are playing before non-discerning English audiences. The calypso symbolizes here a cultural rootedness and an inner well-being which they are losing hold of, and therefore, they find themselves producing discordant, jangling music.

In Samuel Selvon's 'Calypso in London', the art form is deployed as a contradictory marker of Trinidadian distinctiveness and the translocation of Anansi-style coping strategies within the metropolitan scenario. Trapped within the harsh wintry environment, bereft of employment and the support of extended community, Mangohead, the Vincentian, hones his skills as a hustler seeking to sell his lyrics to the composer Hotboy for quick money. The flash-in-the-pan creativity becomes an alternative to soul destroying, burdensome, manual work. Its financial reward is swiftly dissipated on basic necessities. More significantly, the story unveils the impulses that impact cultural production. This creation on foreign soil needs to be both distinctly Trinidadian and acutely relevant to the broader metropolitan framework, in this case the Suez Canal issue. The composition must satisfy opposing impulses — a parochial backward glance to Trinidad and its homegrown foci, rhythms and roots; and the outward oriented global appeal, which was always a facet of the traditional calypso, but becomes even more vital to its success in the new terrain. The Trinidadians as the 'authentic' owners of the cultural form are proprietary and defensive: Hotboy the composer berates Mangohead as a Vincentian who should leave Trinidad calypso alone; while Rahamut the 'legitimate' arbiter of the calypso's worth, berates his enthusiastic English assistant: 'Why you don't shut you mouth? What you English people know about calypso.'[42] Yet it is clear even to displaced Trinidadians the calypso must speak both to nationals abroad thirsty for connections to home and the growing circle of foreign consumers. To accomplish the second goal the calypso must move away from a thematic focus on the specificities of individuals' lived experience. The brief story is a telling commentary on how calypso travels and the impact of forces that shape cultural production on calypso as a commodity with increasing global appeal.

In Naipaul's and Selvon's fiction of the 1950s and 1960s, the calypso is reflective of shared experiences of poverty, social adversity, individual and communal disempowerment, and of adversarial gender relations. As Indo-Trinidadian writers who adopted calypso for their thematic and stylistic emphases, they resisted the propensity to use this nation song to signify ethnic dissociation. Instead the calypso as literary emblem was associated with belonging, rootedness, homecoming, and the formation of a common front in relation to external global events such as war, American army occupation and its paradoxical impact on the social conditions of Trinidadian life.

The construction of the Indian woman within this male-dominated lower-strata Afro-Caribbean art form became a pivotal element of inter-racial tension and contestation. The early literary expressions of Naipaul and Selvon did not follow this mould. Their location on the ever-shifting continuum of discourses in relation to nationalism in Trinidad saw muted possibilities for an emerging Creole cultural aesthetic. Even for a writer of Naipaul's persistent pessimism, denigration and self-exclusion, the calypso with its vigour, inventiveness and ebullience signalled a bewildering rootedness and potential in the face of all evidence to the contrary.

Selvon's perspectives in *Ways of Sunlight* were qualified in his 1979 Opening Address to the India in the Caribbean Conference, when he called for an end to ethnic antipathy and divisiveness. He is particularly critical of Caribbean islanders in the metropolis whose diseased sense of national belonging was susceptible to a shape-shifting fluidity which readily wrapped itself around political expediency: 'With no tradition, no national pride, no patriotism, lacking values but full of calypso and Carnival and what happening boy, it was as easy as kissing hand to deny their birthright.'[43] And in relation to the Caribbean island dweller he comments, 'in spite of the cultural growth in these islands since the last war, we are still being identified on a level which does not seem to rise above cricket, calypso, steelband and limbo'.[44] Issuing a call for unity, Selvon cites Black Stalin's 'Caribbean Unity' (more popularly known as 'The Caribbean Man') as a grassroots expression of the dream of Caribbean unity, which 'transcends the parochial and becomes regional rather than insular'.[45] The calypso's function as reflector and shaper of mass perspectives demonstrates the potential for significant ideological intervention. Ironically, such is the state of racial tension, that this very calypso generated intense and sustained public dialogue much of which was focused on its racist character in its supposed exclusive identification of the Afro-Caribbean as 'the' Caribbean man.[46]

The second part of this paper demonstrates that calypso and other predominantly Afro-Caribbean cultural forms play a divergent role for Indo-Trinidadian women writers. Indo-Trinidadian women, reflecting their secluded positions within the home, their traditional silencing, and later access to education, came to fictional expression later than both Indo-Trinidadian men and Afro-Trinidadian women. The post-independence period gave Indian women free primary education, access to jobs in public service and in the private sector. This was accompanied by intensified urban migration, and a shift to more nuclear type families. These women writers' fictional deployment of calypso and Carnival as emblematic of Afro-Creole society can be located variously on a continuum whose poles are attraction and revulsion.

Lashkmi Persaud, the first published Indo-Trinidadian female novelist (*Butterfly in the Wind*, 1990),[47] articulates in her second novel *Sastra* (1993)[48] the flip side of the negative ethnic stereotyping that emerges prominently in Afro-Caribbean fiction. The writer evokes a polarized position in her account of a single brutal murder of a moneylender and his family, which lacerates the entire Indian community who read it as racist in its motivation. The stereotypical 'them against us' binary is trotted out when the murder is related to the Indian's economic wealth and the criminal waste of Africans seeking money for criminal frivolities. Carnival functions as a shadowy symbol of criminal waste and licentiousness, the opiate of a people who hold their participation so dear that they are prepared to murder in order to steal the resources of the honest, enterprising and diligent. In the melee of voices, this is an extreme though not uncommon view.

Persaud, who is married to a prominent Guyanese and makes the topic of her third novel *For the Love of My Name* (2000)[49] the demonic insanity and extreme racial hatred of Guyanese political life, has had first hand insight into the race wars that have fuelled the Guyanese diaspora since the 1960s. Persaud reveals the sense of alienation, vulnerability and fear of defilement, which caused Indians to complain bitterly of exclusion, and yet remain constrained by their sense of distinctiveness and superiority to avoid assimilation. The emerging Creole nationalism, with Carnival as its pivotal cultural icon, becomes a troubled social framework for a besieged ethnic minority. This is not to imply that Persaud does not seek to negotiate through her fiction a space for a more liberatory female location within the traditional Hindu framework. Indeed, an overt embrace of the traditional location for women in the Brahminical Hindu framework is counterbalanced by an elaborate range of kinetic images — butterflies struggling to escape over imprisoning walls and girls being crushed under the icebergs of tradition and collapsing houses.[50]

The younger Indo-Caribbean women writers strike out for more transgressive representations of their position in relation to a broader, multi-ethnic social order. Calypso and Carnival are evoked as tropes of intentional hybridity signifying a different way to be Indian and female within a Trinidadian context. The difference between the portrayal Naipaul and Selvon explored earlier and that of the younger women Joy Mahabir, Rajandaye Ramkissoon-Chen and Ramabai Espinet is reflective of the nuances of Robert Young's differentiation between unconscious and intentional hybridity: the gap between 'unconscious processes of hybrid mixture or creolization and a conscious and politically motivated concern with the deliberate disruption of homogeneity'.[51] Participation and right of access to all of the cultural forms of all of the Caribbean peoples is the stance embraced by Ramabai Espinet the Trinidad-born Canadian writer and performance poet, who claims her right to perform her 'Indian Robber Talk' — her unique version of the boastful grandiloquence of the traditional African descended masquerade figure 'The Midnight Robber'.

The intentional hybridity finds fullest expression in Ramkissoon-Chen's 'When the Hindu Woman Sings Calypso'[52] which was inspired by Drupatee Ramgoonai, the Queen of Chutney Soca. The Chutney tradition which came to Trinidad with indentured Indians and survived in pockets in villages, represented resistance to a colonial hegemonic order which sought to nullify and demonize Hindu culture. Chutney derived from the non-Brahmanic caste and rural folk song and dance tradition associated with the Matikor ritual — that is, the exclusively female space in which women frankly instructed the bride-to-be on sexual matters through song, dance and ribald humour. Brinda Metha, in *Diasporic (Dis)locations*,[53] associates 'wining' with the birthing contractions of the body as it breaks free from itself and releases new life.[54] This female-dominated space, Kanhai suggests in *Matikor*,[55] served to affirm the sensuality of Hindu women but it may also have been the site of surreptitious female-to-female caresses under guise of preparing the bride for her most important traditional role. Until today, Chutney runs afoul of Brahminical notions of purity and seclusion as ideal behaviours for Hindu women. According to

Metha, 'the political dimensions of chutney are located in women's contestations of class distinctions.... The suggestive movements of chutney dancing are a public demonstration of women's efforts to defy normative codes of Hindu patriarchal morality.'[56]

By the time chutney reached the national stage in the 1980s, some of its elements had previously been appropriated by the calypso. Acknowledgement of the Indian presence in terms of lyrics as well as musical instruments was evident from about the 1970s onwards:

> This new style of music included the Indian instruments of the tassa, dholak & sitar. It also incorporated the more Calypso flavor of the steel pan and synthesizer and even the electric guitar. The lyrics were also mostly sung in West Indian creole with maybe the exception of only a few Hindi words. However, by far the most significant change in this new style was the fact that it was almost solidly dominated by Afro West Indians during its early days. Songs such as Baron's "Raja Rani", Mighty Trini's "Curry Tabanca", Sugar Aloe's "Roti & Dhalpourie" & Sparrow's "Marajin" dominated the Indian Soca scene from 1980–1987. (Saywack)[57]

The impact of this was to push chutney far more decisively and centrally onto the national stage. Many of these songs were about the sexual attractiveness of the Indian woman to the calypso persona. Given the systematic effort to construct this persona as a sexual predator bent on rake and scrape type inter-tribal penetrations or revenge through miscegenation, it is understandable that the conservative Indian elements in the society were not pleased with this appropriation of Indian cultural forms.[58]

Predictably the emergence of Hindu female chutney artists on the public stage occasioned a veritable outbreak of male censure and censorship. Ramkissoon-Chen pens a poetic intervention in the dialogue in 'When the Hindu Woman Sings Calypso', based on the career of Drupatee Ramgoonai, who emerged out of the rural village of Penal of South Trinidad via the Afro-Trinidadian male dominated calypso state, to enjoy international fame, at a period when few Indian men were willing to make their presence felt in this location. To appropriate this space was to violate numerous deeply intense taboos. Her intrusion can be contextualized by Rosanne Kanhai's statement on the traditional Bhowjee, the term applied to 'old fashioned' Indian ladies who had arranged marriages and who stayed 'at home to take care of the children and do housework':[59]

> Indeed the figure of the traditional Bhowjee, humming at the masala stone is familiar to the Indo-Caribbean landscape…. She hums under her breath because breaking into song is bolder than her life of repression and rigorous domesticity allows…. A hardworking woman is likely to be docile and virtuous, and Bhowjee's skill in grinding masala is proof of her chastity and morality; she symbolizes all that is wholesome and proper in the Indo-Caribbean community. Expressions of playfulness or waywardness are curbed, and creativity is channelled into household chores. The masala stone receives her complaints, reflections, longings, griefs, joys…. The massala stone sings. (Kanhai)[60]

The 'Bhowjee' in Drupatee Ramgoonai's initial composition 'Pepper, Pepper' brought into the public arena, the hardships endured by young East Indian women in the marriage relationship. It posed a simple strategy for taking revenge by putting excessive quantities of pepper in the husband's food.

Swift and strong censure was leveled against Drupatee Ramgoonai for her trangressive act: 'No Indian woman has any right to sing Calypso', and 'Indian women have been a disgrace to Hinduism' were cries from the fraternity.[61] Mahabir Maharaj writing in the Sandesh paper added:

> for an Indian girl to throw away her high upbringing and culture to mix with vulgar music, sex and alcohol in Carnival tents tells me that something is radically wrong with her psyche. Drupatee Ramgoonai has chosen to worship the gods of sex, wine and easy money.'[62]

Drupatiee's defiance of patriarchal dictates has been made more visible by her dramatic success.[63]

Rajandaye Ramkisoon-Chen's poem, 'When the Hindu Woman Sings Calypso', traces the journey of her protagonist from the rural peasant environment and the female-only matikor prenuptial ritual to the national calypso stage. The old restrictions and symbols of enclosure are reconstituted with radically divergent meaning. Progress in the form of electric light and glaring stage light replaces the gloaming, moonlight and lamplight. The poem unfolds:

> Strings of rhinestone now
> "*Purdah*" her forehead
> Hair frizzled to a "*Buss-up-shot*"
> The long tresses of
> A long tradition
> Seared in the electricity
> Of the mike's cord length.[64]

Within the broadened social framework, purdah — the tradition of sex segregation, which functioned traditionally to restrict women to the domestic space, has been radically reinterpreted. The only purdah enclosures that the persona entertains are the ones that enhance her glamour and sensuality. Her clothing reflects her selective incorporation of her Eastern ancestry. Significantly it is not the traditional Hindu female's sari, but trousers that reflect the wealth and opulence of the rich Mogul's garb. Her long hair, emblematic of traditional beauty and that most telling ethnic marker within the Caribbean framework, is 'frizzled' into a 'buss up shot' (a flour and butter roti whose flakes resemble a torn shirt). This uneasy metaphor signifies linguistic, culinary and phenotypical fusions that have been enthusiastically embraced by all members of Trinidadian society. Frizzling of the hair is suggestive of the admixture — a douglarization (read bastardization) — of hair quality and culture. Her disruptive and transfiguring location calls the world, even the natural world, to come and see. The sleeping 'fowl cocks' of the villages are replaced by the silenced night insects who stop their churrings to pay obeisance to the chutney artiste's resounding voice. Her act includes a signifier of the brotherhood of the boat or ocean crossing — the limbo, which has traditionally been emblematic of the burial and re-emergence of slaves from the survived middle passage to the arise to a new life in a new land:

> Her midriff's bare
> Looped white with pearls
> Her body sinuous
> With the dance of muscle
> She stoops as for a "limbo" number
> Head held backwards from the rod-fire
> Leaves of flame
> Play on her bodice.[65]

Ultimately the poem is about the power of border crossing and the potential and release that can be afforded by hybridity. Her music remains rooted in the oral tradition of the matikor, but it reinterprets traditional socially restrictive conditions.

Even moreso than Ramkissoon-Chen, Joy Mahabir evokes associations between Indian female sensuality and Afro Caribbean cultural expressions. In 'Fire and Steel', Mahabir explores potentiality and ambivalence in relation to pan as a symbol of spontaneous cultural fusion:

> Steel bursting into song
> Sticks clenched in sweating hands
> ...
> I remember only intense union
> freeing uplifting minutes of living
> and after I forget.[66]

The passionate sensuality offers momentarily the possibility of a near orgasmic union, but this is swiftly supplanted by a deliberate forgetting of the process and of the possibility. The protagonist is condemned subsequently to an amnesiac existence, conveyed as lacking, or existing in happenings I forget.[67] The transitory intense nature of the possibility begs the question how to sustain or crystallize the potential and the enrichment; how to cause the minute of heightened living to be sustained, to endure, to remain and not to be relegated to oblivion. Persistent images of bodily heat, of fever and passion are translated into energy that, in turn, fuels the beating of the pan and internal compulsion that produces sweating hands. In contrast to this transitional ecstatic moment is the absence and lack that endures. The persona sets up a tension between the brevity of the remembering which is entrenched by frequent repetitions: 'I remember only one night ... one moment ... intense union.'[68] This is counterbalanced by the persistence of the forgetting. Yet the narrative inscription of the experience disputes the dominance of the forgetting and privileges the fire and the steel and it is this, which the reader remembers. This formulation recalls Lamming's poignant statement of the power of such remembering as the tongue probes the space left by an extraction and intensifies the memory of loss all the more.[69] Highly sexualized orgasmic pulsation becomes the barely veiled metaphor for creative awakening and cultural hybridity. Why is the persona of 'Fire and Steel' constrained to forget the orgasmic moment? Amnesia is indicated because the potentiality of the ecstatic moment to give way to a lifetime of communal dissociation and disconnectedness. Not to forget may be to court disaster.

Ramabai Espinet's novel *The Swinging Bridge*[70] makes the connection between the matrilineal ancestor the indentee Gainder, the entertainer of the Hindu feast, and her progeny who seek cultural and sexual autonomy in the contemporary framework of Trinidadian cultural nationalism. The Trinidadian born Indian family migrate to Canada only to discover a peculiar inability to cut their navel strings, which remain buried in the former family lands in Manahambre Road, Princess Town. Spatial rootedness, ethnic identity and sexual citizenship are the issues confronted by Mona the protagonist as she explores a dark hinterland of female cultural and sexual oppression, and the grim outcome of desire judged inappropriate on the basis of ethnicity and gender. The eldest son, who unknown to the majority of the close knit family is dying of AIDS in a discrete Toronto hospice, is insistent that his sister, who has been unable to thrive in Canada, should return to Trinidad to repurchase the family land. A submerged theme in the narrative is the dark, unbridled sexuality which is paraded in the Carnival festivities, but which intrude in veiled forms throughout the narrative. Mona and her father sneak off like secret sharers every J'Ouvert morning to gaze at the raw passions, which are powerful enough to drive men to gyrate against lampposts in a flouted hunger for release. It surfaces initially in the new arrivants, the indentee Gainder, whose upwardly mobile Presbyterian husband cuts her off from the role of the village entertainer; whose insistence on her right to sing and dance in public signals her availability to men, who perhaps sings the vulgar snatches of songs to invite them in, or who sings the sacred bajans to ward them off. In the shadowy interstices of the narratives we are never certain which truly obtains. The legacy passes down to generations of women who experiment in art and / or in sex with the potentiality of making hybrid connection in this land of their migration.

Rich potentiality and violent oppression assault generations of women and men who gravitate towards hybridity. This is the fate of Grandmother Lill whose fierce love for the offspring of the Creole overseer culminates when her father beats her lover's burgeoning seed out of her nubile body. Alienation settles deep in Mona's spirit after she dares to love a black man, Bree, for which wantonness her father constrains her to cross the gravely yard on her knees. Indeed undercutting assumptions of the value of intentional aesthetic hybridity is the haggling over the possession of Indian women's fertility as the repositories of ethnic distinctiveness. The threat is so menacing that to marry a Creole is to invite sure alienation and to risk insanity. 'It good for she! Who tell she to marry Creole?'[71] Potentiality and oppression are the fate of the closeted homosexual, whose intent of re-establishing the family's rootedness in Trinidad is matched by his intention to carry his secret sexual practice with him to his imminent grave. Underlying the scenario is the magnetic appeal and equally compelling fear of the consequence of unbridled sensuality, the passions and spiritual energies that are figured in the narrative most prominently by Carnival.

In conclusion, 'With a Tassa Blending' argues that calypso with carnival as its encompassing ritual context originated in Afro-Caribbean resistance and cultural affirmation in the face of Eurocentric denigration and repression. Despite the fact that it has been a creative vehicle of African towards Indian diatribe and racial stereotyping, it emerges in Indo-Caribbean literary expression as emblematic of the possibility of raising a common voice against Eurocentric hegemonic discourses and asserting shared cultural belonging and national pride. It is not at all surprising that the explosive, spiritual energies of calypso and carnival should fuse with the eruptive, reproductive energies of the low caste matikor folk ritual to usher chutney and chutney soca unto the national stage. The musical and literary allusions and blendings reveal both the impulse towards intragroup competitions and communalism, and the inevitably of its fusions, all of which proceed simultaneously in the Trinidadian project of feverish hybridization which Rohlehr describes as in 'Calypso Reinvents Itself' as 'a jarring, jamming Carnivalesque collusion and clashing counter point of rhythms'.[72] These rich energized fusions now coexist comfortably on a public stage.

Indo-Trinidadian women writers like Ramkissoon-Chen and her real life model Drupatee Ramgoonai, have moved beyond the confines of a deliberate forgetting and an oblique testimony of erased ecstasy. For Indo-Trinidadian writers, calypso has always signalled belonging to the multi-ethnic social order. For the earlier male writers, it signifies an unintentional hybridity. For the younger female writers, it signifies an intentional trope and a liberationist aesthetic associated with sensuality and sexual autonomy. Notwithstanding legal contestation among conservative Indian elements in the society in respect to national symbols and emblems, today's Bhowjee has laid claim to a densely textured, inclusive narrative of intentional hybridity and 'she sings and "*winds*"/ To calypso and "*pan*"/ With a "*tassa*" blending'.[73]

Notes

1. V.S. Naipaul, *The Middle Passage: Impressions of Five Societies — British, French and Dutch in the West Indies* (1962; reprint, Harmondsworth: Penguin, 1969).
2. The origins of calypso have variously been traced to the West African praise blame songs which utilized litany or call-and-response forms. See Gordon Rohlehr, *Calypso and Society in Pre-independence Trinidad* (Port of Spain: Lexicon Publishing, 1990); J.D. Elder, 'Evolution of the Traditional Calypso of Trinidad and Tobago: A Socio-Historical Analysis of Song Change' (PhD dissertation, University of Pennsylvania, 1996); and Errol Hill, *The Trinidad Carnival: Mandate for a National Theatre* (Austin, TX and London: University of Texas Press, 1992).
3. Rohlehr indicates:

> African music often served the purpose of social control, and the roots of the political calypso in Trinidad probably lie in the African custom of permitting criticism of one's leaders at specific times, in particular contexts, and through the media of song and story. The leaders of society recognized the value of such satirical songs in which the ordinary person was given the privilege of unburdening his mind while the impact of his protest was neutralized by the controlled context in which criticism was possible. (Rohlehr, *Calypso and Society*, 2)

4. See Brinsley Samaroo, 'Two Abolitions: African Slavery and East Indian Indentureship', in *India in the Caribbean*, eds. Dabydeen and Samaroo, 43–60 (London: Hansib Publishing, 1987); and Kusha Haraksingh, 'Control and Resistance among Indian Workers: A Study of Labour on the Sugar Plantations of Trinidad 1875–1917', in *India in the Caribbean*, 61–80.
5. Rohlehr, 'Calypso Reinvents Itself', in *The Scuffling of Islands* (Port of Spain: Lexicon Publishing, 2004), 374.
6. The Indo-Guyanese children would tease:

> Black man salla pound massalla
>
> Who is yuh daddy
>
> Coolie is yuh daddy.

The Afro-Guyanese children would tease:

> Coolie water rice
>
> pork and spice
>
> get some cow dung
>
> to make it nice

And both groups would intone variously:

> Nigger / Coolie is a nation
>
> very botheration
>
> Go to police station

Reflecting the stereotype of Indian husbands as jealous vengeful wife-beaters, the Afro-Guyanese children interpreted the message of the tassa drums which heralded the Hindu wedding procession thus:

> Bum bum bum
>
> Ra taa taa taa
>
> Lil lil gyal me going to marry to yuh
>
> And if yuh take another man
>
> Ah going to cut off yuh neck.

Gordon Rohlehr, unpublished interview, February 2005, University of the West Indies, St. Augustine.

7. Shalini Puri, 'Race, Rape, and Representation: Indo-Caribbean Women and Cultural Nationalism', in *Matikor: The Politics of Identity for Indo-Caribbean*

8. *Women*, ed. Rosanne Kanhai (St. Augustine: University of the West Indies School of Continuing Studies, 1999), 240.
9. Klass, in his study of an Indian village that he names Amity, notes the assumption of overwhelming sensuality of the young Indian girl which needed to be strictly policed to avoid the disgrace of pregnancy out of marriage and, even more so, vulnerability to the excessive phallic prowess which was the boast of Afro-Caribbean populations as represented through the calypsonian.
9. George Lamming, 'Language and the Politics of Ethnicity', (unpublished address delivered at the Cultural Studies Conference, Cross Culturalism and the Caribbean Canon, the University of the West Indies, Trinidad, January 13–17, 2004).
10. V.S. Naipaul dates the first publication of *Gurudeva and Other Indian Tales* (reprint, London: André Deutsch, 1976) as 1943, in his Foreword to the André Duetsch edition in 1976. No date is recorded in the original publication.
11. The original lyrics to 'Rum and Coca Cola' were composed and sung by Lord Invader (Rupert Grant) in Trinidad in 1943. This calypso was subsequently recorded by The Andrews Sisters with Vic Schoen and His Orchestra, October 18, 1944. Credits for the words and music were given to Morey Amsterdam (words), and Jeri Sullavan (music) and Paul Baron (music). The dispute over ownership was settled in court in Invader's favour.
12. V.S. Naipaul, *Miguel Street* (1959; reprint, London: Heinemann Caribbean Writers Series, 1974).
13. Ibid., 222.
14. Naipaul, *Middle Passage*, 58.
15. These are not the earliest calypsos focusing on the Indian presence. Rohlehr notes:

> Consciousness of the East Indian presence would begin to emerge in the twenties, and by the thirties calypsos such as Executioner's "My Indian Girl Love", Lion's "Bhago Pholouri", and "Ara Da Da", Tiger's "Gi Rita Ram Gi" and King Iere's "Madras Wedding" would be sung. (*Calypso and Society*, 40–41).

No recording information is available for the calypsos 'Grinding Masalla' (1947), 'Indian Women with Creole Names' (1950) and 'Indian Politicians' (1950).
16. Naipaul, *Miguel Street*, 82.
17. Ibid., 91.
18. Ibid., 111.
19. Ibid., 127.
20. Ibid., 136.
21. Ibid., 166.
22. Ibid., 185.
23. Ibid., 196.
24. Ibid., 197.
25. Ibid., 210.
26. See chapter, 'The Thing Without a Name', Ibid., 17–25.
27. Ibid., 63.
28. Ibid., 36–43.
29. See chapter, 'The Mechanical Genius', Ibid., 147–54.

30. I have not been able to trace a calypso on this topic named 'Emelda'. John Thieme in *The Web of Tradition: Uses of Allusions in V.S. Naipaul's Fictions* indicates the same and surmises that it may be an invention on Naipaul's part (Thieme 205). This calypso is not to be confused with Young Killer's 'Emelda's Nightmare' (1959) which is about Emelda's night long attack on the persona's 'little finger' and his inability to find a police man to rescue him.
31. The Andrews Sisters were an extremely popular all-female trio who maintained their impact on the entertainment industry for about 30 years. According to their official website, they sold over 90 million records, recorded approximately 700 songs and earned nine gold records. Their energy, virtuosity and harmony helped to brighten a dark period in American history. The Andrews Sister popularized the calypso 'Rum and Coca Cola'. <http://www.cmgww.com/music/andrews/about/bio3.htm> (accessed December 2005).
32. Naipaul, *Miguel Street*, 22.
33. Ibid., 111.
34. Ibid., 113.
35. Mighty Killer [Cephas Alexander], 'Indian People with Creole Names'.
36. Ibid.
37. Rohlehr, *Calypso and Society*, 365.
38. Naipaul, *Miguel Street*, 197.
39. Ibid., 137.
40. Ibid., 82.
41. Naipaul, *Middle Passage*, 75–76.
42. Sam Selvon, 'Calypso in London', *Ways of Sunlight* (1957; reprint, London: Macgibbon & Kee, 1961), 129.
43. Selvon, '"Three Into One Can't Go—East Indian, Trinidadian, West Indian", Opening Address to East Indians in the Caribbean Conference, University of the West Indies, Trinidad, 1979', in *India in the Caribbean*, eds. David Dabydeen and Brinsley Samaroo (London: Hansib Publishing, 1987), 18.
44. Ibid., 19–20.
45. Ibid., 22.
46. For a detailed study of the media debates surrounding 'The Caribbean Man', see Ramesh Deosaran, 'The "Caribbean" Man: A Study of the Psychology of Perception and the Media', in *India in the Caribbean*, eds. Dabydeen and Samaroo, 81–118.
47. Lashkmi Persaud, *Butterfly in the Wind* (Leeds: Peepal Tree Press, 1990).
48. Lashkmi Persaud, *Sastra* (Leeds: Peepal Tree Press, 1993).
49. Lashkmi Persaud, *For the Love of My Name* (Leeds: Peepal Tree Press, 2000).
50. For a fuller discussion of this text see: Paula Morgan 'East / West Indian / Woman / Other: At the Crossroads of Gender and Ethnicity', *Ma Comere Journal of Association of Caribbean Women Writers and Scholars* 3 (2000): 109–22.
51. Robert Young, 'Hybridity in Post Colonial Studies', in *Post-Colonial Studies: The Key Concepts*, ed. Ashcroft Griffith and Tiffin (London: Routledge, 1998), 120.
52. Rajandaye Ramkissoon-Chen, 'When the Indian Woman Sings Calypso', in *Creation Fire: A Cafra Anthology of Caribbean Women's Poetry*, ed. Ramabai Espinet (Toronto: Sister Vision, 1990), 50.
53. Brinda Metha, *Diasporic (Dis) Locations: Indo-Caribbean Women Writers Negotiate the Kala Pani* (Kingston: The University of the West Indies Press, 2004).
54. Ibid., 98.

55. Rosanne Kanhai, *The Politics of Identity for Indo-Caribbean Women* (St. Augustine, Trinidad: University of the West Indies School of Continuing Studies Press, 1999).
56. Metha, *Diasporic (Dis) Locations*, 98.
57. Rajendra Saywack, 'From Caroni Gyal to Calcutta Woman — A History of East Indian Chutney Music in the Caribbean' (Black and Puerto Rican Studies Department. Thomas Hunter College, December 1999) <http://www.saxakali.com/caribbean/Hemchandra1.htm> (accessed March 2005).
58. For obvious reasons the thought of Afro-Trinidadian male and East Indian female sexual relations was disturbing for most East Indians. Saywack notes that Sparrow's 'Marajin', where he describes his love interest for a Pandit's (Hindu Priest) wife, was banned in Guyana for several years, after a huge outcry from the Hindu community in that country. Puri mentions the outrage that greeted the nani songs. This term which means grandmother on the mother's side is in Trinidad also a vulgar name for vagina. It therefore lends itself to the double entendre so well, so that it became the subject of the popular Crazy's 'Nani Wine', Scrunter's 'Nanny' and Becket's 'Nanny Revival'. The uproar was great when Drupatee Ragoonai sang the chutney soca song 'Lick Down Me Nani', thereby disrupting the 'idealization of a desexualized Indian grandmother' (Puri, 'Race, Rape, and Representation', 257–62).
59. Kanhai, *Matikor*, 3.
60. Ibid., 209–10.
61. Drupatee Ramgoonai quoted in Zeno Obi Constance, *Tassa, Chutney and Soca: The East Indian Contribution to the Calypso* (San Fernando, Trinidad: Jordan's Printing Service, 1991), 51.
62. Ibid.
63. Drupatee made history as not only the first female chutney soca artist to hit the national stage, but the first Indo-Trinidadian to successfully crossover into the soca charts and to have a number one hit.
64. Ramkissoon-Chen, 'When the Indian Woman Sings Calypso', 50.
65. Ibid., 51.
66. Joy Mahabir, 'Fire and Steel', in *Creation Fire*, ed. Ramabai Espinet, 45.
67. The full text of 'Fire and Steel' reads:

> I remember only
>
> One night
>
> Nights of fever and beating
>
> Brought us to his place
>
> Voices, stilled passion
>
> Movement in anticipation
>
> I remember only
>
> One moment:
>
> Steel bursting into sound
>
> Sticks clenched in sweating hands
>
> Now lacking, existing,
>
> In happenings I forget.

> I remember only:
>
> Intense union
>
> Freeing, uplifting
>
> Minutes of living
>
> And after, I forget
>
> *Creation Fire*, 45.

68. Mahabir, 'Fire and Steel', 45.
69. George Lamming, *In the Castle of My Skin* (Trinidad and Jamaica: Longman, 1970), 279.
70. Ramabai Espinet, *The Swinging Bridge* (Toronto: Harmony Flamingo, 2004).
71. Ibid., 260.
72. Rohlehr, 'Calypso Reinvemts Itself', 374.
73. Ramkissoon-Chen, 'When the Indian Woman Sings Calypso', 51.

12

BOP GIRL GOES CALYPSO: CONTAINING RACE AND YOUTH CULTURE IN COLD WAR AMERICA

Michael S. Eldridge

In early July 1957, United Artists rushed into wide release its latest contribution to the burgeoning 'teen-pic' genre. The film's improbable plot revolves around a dour psychology grad student (played by a 38-year-old Bobby Troup) whose empirical data on mass hysteria show incontrovertibly that rock and roll is about to be supplanted by calypso — much to the dismay of his bald, bespectacled, rock-loving thesis adviser. The professor's club-owner chum, Barney — a crass, cigar-chomping lunkhead who has bet his business's future on rock and roll — belligerently dismisses young Bob's findings. But Professor Winthrop, who ruefully understands that 'you can't argue with science', contrives to save his sceptical friend from ruin by persuading the club's main attraction, perky ingénue Jo Thomas (Judy Tyler, who would co-star that same year with Elvis Presley in *Jailhouse Rock*), to study under his own star pupil behind her boss's back. When Barney belatedly learns of Jo's clandestine flirtation, he sees red — until he watches her raise the roof at a rival venue with a vaguely tropical tune exhorting calypso to 'roll' and 'rock' in order to 'raise [its] flock'. Then, with all the zealotry of the fresh convert, he re-christens his own nightspot 'Club Trinidad', strings palm fronds and fishnets on the walls and ceiling, bedecks himself and his staff in tattered shirts and straw hats, and takes to addressing his patrons as 'Gatos' ('That's calypso for "Cats",' he explains). Vindicating Bob's thesis, the youthful club-goers at the former 'Club Down Beat' are duly hysterical over Jo's new act. Record executives materialize out of thin air, falling over each other to sign her, and everyone, we are given to understand, lives happily ever after.

The fairytale ending actually would not have seemed so implausible when filming began a couple of months earlier. The Calypso Craze was then at its zenith, and brash predictions of rock's imminent demise filled the air. But the reason it later seemed preposterous — and the reason for the studio's nervous haste in hustling the movie, strangely titled *Bop Girl Goes Calypso*,[1] to market — was that it turned out to be a very late entry in the calypso derby. Following on the heels of two earlier contenders, Allied Artists' *Calypso Joe*[2] (with Ellington alumnus Herb Jeffries in the title role, opposite a then unknown Angie Dickinson) and Columbia's *Calypso Heat Wave*[3] (featuring aspiring song-and-dance man Joel Grey and lounge singer Maya Angelou), the United

Artists' picture hit the screens in a much different climate, as the fad was fizzling, and the film's 'Rock versus Calypso' premise was largely moot. Calypso, it was generally agreed, had lost.

Never mind that United Artists had hedged its bets on the outcome of the contest all along: advertising the picture as a battle of 'Rock 'n' Roll vs. Calypso!' committed the studio to neither one combatant nor the other. Indeed, the film's promotional packet encouraged theatre owners to sell 'tropical' tchotchkes in their lobbies while hosting neighbourhood 'Rock-'n'-Roll Nights', and to stage 'Rock vs. Calypso' competitions by recruiting placard-carrying teenagers, soliciting 'campaign' coverage from hometown radio DJs, and holding mock elections officiated by local personalities and music writers. But in the rubble of the calypso craze crash, *Bop Girl*'s promoters scrambled to play down its Caribbean content even further. Exhorting 'hepsters' of all stripes to 'beat those bongos and let those trumpets wail', they generously pledged that 'rock-'n'-roll addicts ... calypsomaniacs, and just the plain jazz lover will all find something to cheer about'. Though some posters, lobby cards and newspaper ads still billed the film as the 'Greatest Calypso Carnival' — 'A fiesta with a bongo beat about a curvy calypso cutie who taught a square prof all the angles!', others dubbed it the 'Greatest *Rock 'n' Roll* Carnival', and still others (less ambiguously, if more provocatively) the 'Greatest Rock 'n' Roll *Riot* Ever' (emphasis added). In some cities, moreover, the film's title was mysteriously truncated to *Bop Girl*. Finally, while a handful of ads and posters retained an image of Judy Tyler in an outlandish 'creole damsel' get-up with frilly cuffs and collar, the majority showed her busting off the page as a tight-skirted, open-shirted rocker striking an insolent juvenile delinquent pose.[4]

What makes this marketing muddle of lasting interest, however, is not so much its schizophrenia as the candour — perhaps the cynicism — with which it unveils the broken-down mechanism of the calypso fad's promotion, which had been slapdash and jury-rigged all along. *Bop Girl*'s own thematic viewpoint is similarly haphazard. Even as the film cheerfully alleges that calypso carries the day, it makes a much more convincing case for the *real-life* winner of the rock-versus-calypso sweepstakes. A crucial exchange midway through the picture between Bob and a still-skeptical Jo, for instance, apologizes for rock and roll at some length. Explaining that the hysteria over rock is a 'symptomatic reaction' of 'American youth' to their many 'problems, fears, and hopes', Bob feelingly philosophizes about how rock songs make one feel 'emotionally ... safe, by anchoring you to Mother Earth even as you soar like a balloon'. Sadly, he explains, the mooring that rock provides cannot last, because 'we're in a very restless world, always demanding something new'. But luckily, calypso has not only 'tremendous excitement potential', but 'roots ... [that] go very deep in the ground', and lyrics which (in his bizarre estimation) 'are the plaintive lament of the wearied worker ... the escape valve that makes it possible to go on living'. 'Like our [sic] very own spirituals!' marvels Jo. Making room for a '*calypso* spiritual' on the American cultural scene, she and Bob agree, is the one remaining challenge. Yet even Tyler's pivotal tune complains that calypso 'Don't move my feet' because it's 'Too soft and sweet'. If it ever hopes to attract a young audience, she scolds, it will have to 'Get with the beat' — the Rock 'n' Roll beat. ('Oo-ba, shoo-ba / Rock, Calypso! / Oo-ba, shoo-ba / Roll, Calypso!' she chirps, with her backup band, Lord Flea and His Calypsonians, gamely seconding the motion.)

 Her sound proposal is undercut by the fact that in the world of the film, calypso *does not* become more like rock; nor, contrary to what the narrative ostensibly proposes, does rock become more like calypso. Rather, both come to sound more like Les Baxter, and the fact that the film's logic leads to such a tawdry musical compromise — what one wag calls 'a cultural hybrid native to no place outside the San Fernando Valley' — betrays the even-handed timidity of its message.[5] What this underscores again is that the supposed battle between rock and calypso — which the press had played up from the earliest days of the Calypso Craze — had been bogus from the outset, a pseudo-contest which the music industry had gladly countenanced if not staged outright. It stood to profit from the outcome either way.

 At the same time, however, the film's wishy-washy proposition that the dispute might be resolved by having it both ways cannily reflects not just Mr and Mrs America's Atomic-Age anxiety over the potential explosiveness of rock and roll, but their fundamental ambivalence about substituting calypso as the object of their daughter's musical affections. On its face, that is, the story — even the title — of the film is a tidy encapsulation of the wishful fantasy that the American teen (personified as a spunky, fresh-faced, yet dangerously sexual 'girl') might renounce her unhealthy fascination with that degenerate Negro music and 'Go' for the altogether more wholesome calypso.[6] But what, in the context of such fantastic racial and sexual psychothematics, could it have meant to 'Go Calypso'? For calypso was surely an unlikely candidate for the salvation of American girlhood from the imminent peril of rock and roll.

The underlying logic of the pipe dream was incoherent on at least two counts. That calypso was *also* an historically black cultural form had long been conveniently overlooked in the US, explained away with the tacit understanding that the refined manners and quaint accents of its indigenous practitioners rendered them a different *sort* of black — black with an asterisk, as it were. (One reason that 'boatloads of returning tourists' from the West Indies had come home to America 'the most ardent calypso disciples', opined one contemporary magazine, was that '[y]ou're no sooner off the boat than you're regaled with a personalized calypso tone-poem rendered in Oxford accents'.[7] West Indian blacks, moreover, were not currently demanding to 'integrate' with the American body social then, or so it seemed. While Lord Flea and his calypsonians — in reality a souped-up mento band 'discovered' and promoted in the US by a Miami hotelier — might add a tinge of authentic tropical colour, not to mention a gust of sensual tropical 'heat', to the cool pallor of *Bop Girl*'s collegiate clubland, structurally speaking the film's true calypso champion — and the title character's designated love interest — is the woodenly dispassionate Bobby Troup. Calypso's blackness is thereby provisionally erased, or at least tightly enclosed, within a blonde, crew cut wrapper. Flea and company signify in a different register, evoking a happy-faced, tropical version of plantation-apartheid in which dark-skinned people still exist primarily to serve and entertain white people. At home or abroad, West Indian blacks were thus exoticized, held symbolically at a tourist's distance, confined to the stage or the other side of the serving tray. Flea and his 'calypsonians' conform to the type: as grinning, head-waggling, straw-hat caricatures, they are props for Bop Girl to regard and perhaps mimic, but never touch, figuratively or otherwise. In fact, the one time Tyler so much as shares the stage with Lord Flea, is when she is pointedly refusing to 'dig' calypso:

'I gotta bring down and knock Calypso / 'Cause you don't rock, Calypso.' In the face of her censure, he and the band are reduced to barely articulate, bongo-playing 'savages' complaisantly parroting the 'Oo-ba, Shoo-ba' chorus. To the extent that calypso ever 'get[s] with' rock and roll's 'beat', then, it does so within the starched confines of white-bread romance.

More awkward was the fact that if rock and roll was held by anxious parents to be inherently salacious, calypso could hardly be thought less so, least of all in its typically American incarnations, which by the mid 1950s made a great show of being spicy and risqué. Even journalist Robert Metz, who seems to have originated the orthodox line that calypso was doing 'what a multitude of mothers and a corps of cops could never do: drown out rock 'n' roll music', deadpanned that '[w]hether [calypso's ascendance] will be good or bad for the morals of teenagers ... is a question open to debate'.[8] One pulp monthly, *Real: The Exciting Magazine for Men*, was even blunter. The joke was on the 'blue-noses,' it smirked: 'If they were rattled by some naughty rock tunes, they will become positively obstreperous' once they really listen to calypso. Its 'animalistic' beat is 'throbbing' across the country, *Real* leered, while its lyrics (on 'Ekberg's bosom [and] Elvis' pelvis') 'swim free-style from one line of sex to another'.[9]

The observation was specious, if only partly so. It is true, of course, that an important strain in calypso tradition (about which most Americans were in any event thoroughly ignorant) made creative use of double entendre and innuendo, usually in the service of boilerplate boasts of romantic prowess or jabs at the moral hypocrisy and sexual indiscretions of the rich and powerful. Indeed, the Trinidadian middle classes had for decades waged a quixotic campaign to launder calypso and other carnival practices of such embarrassing tendencies, and calypsonians had repeatedly mounted spirited defenses of the redeeming social merits of their art.[10] Yet to acknowledge this racy subgenre hardly implies that calypso *per se*, as many Americans seemed to think, was 'all about' sex. When it took matters sexual as its subject, Trinidadian calypso was often suggestive, sometimes ribald, but rarely crude. Yet the same could hardly be said for much of what passed for calypso in mid-1950s America — which was determinedly, exaggeratedly, vulgar, even as it wore this vulgarity as a badge of authenticity. *Real*'s pulp sensationalism was an extreme case, but among

American journalists it was nevertheless an article of faith that in its pristine, 'unexpurgated' state, calypso was variously 'sassy', 'shady', 'naughty', 'risqué', 'earthy', 'bawdy.' Genuine calypsos, every hack knowingly reported, were 'strictly suitable for stag parties'— 'so spicy they ha[d] to be laundered for American audiences'.[11] It is hardly surprising, then, that for many American fans, calypso's alleged lubricity was the very basis of its appeal. Even the sober *New York Herald-Tribune* stated matter-of-factly that 'the not-too-well-hidden meaning is basic to calypso's success'.[12] The Duke of Iron (Cecil Anderson), a Trinidadian émigré who sang calypso in Harlem and Manhattan throughout the 1940s, had recently staged a comeback on the strength of such sophomoric single-entendres as '[She Had] Lovely Parakeets', 'She Has Freckles On Her, But', 'I Left Her Behind for You', and his signature tune, the notorious 'Big Bamboo'.[13] To the *Herald-Tribune*'s interviewer, he simply shrugged: Americans demand songs about sex, so what's a poor calypsonian to do?

How, then, could suburban parents in a panic over rock and roll's threat to their children's moral hygiene — and, by implication, its menace of contagion of the social order with the germs of restiveness increasingly associated with black people — possibly see calypso as a preferable alternative to the demon rock and roll? They could do so, above all, by personifying it in Harry Belafonte.

This was hardly a stretch. Though Belafonte was a native New Yorker, his infatuation with calypso was rooted in long spells of his childhood spent in Jamaica, where he was exposed to a wide variety of Caribbean music — including Trinidad's carnival music, whose practitioners regularly circulated throughout the West Indies, both in person and on disc. After refashioning himself as a folk singer in 1951 — the makeover followed a critically encouraging but personally unfulfilling debut as a jazz-pop crooner — Belafonte had begun incorporating Caribbean material into his repertoire, quickly turning two old 78s by King Radio, 'Man Smart, Woman Smarter' and 'Matilda', into reliable show-stoppers.[14] In 1954, his puckish performance of 'Hold Him Joe', a traditional (and somewhat risqué) West Indian tune also known as 'My Donkey Want Water', in the Broadway revue *John Murray Anderson's Almanac*, garnered rave reviews. By this point, Belafonte's star was rising fast: his nightclub act, which easily sold out the largest rooms in the bigger cities, was drawing fanatical audiences and sensational notices in the trade papers, and he was beginning to land promising roles in high-profile Hollywood films. Finally, when a segment he headlined for NBC-TV's *Colgate Comedy Hour* ('Holiday in Trinidad', conceived as a kind of musical tour of the West Indies) in October 1955 won him still more national acclaim, he lobbied RCA to let him put out an entire album's worth of West Indian songs. The result, *Calypso!* was recorded that same autumn but diffidently issued by RCA only in May 1956.

Belafonte's legions of fans sent the album to number one on the charts by September (it would become the first LP ever to sell a million copies in its first year), but the befuddled label neglected to release a single until late October, after a hitherto obscure folk trio called The Tarriers began climbing the charts and appearing on *Your Hit Parade* with an adaptation of 'The Banana Boat Song' they had learned from folksinger Bob Gibson, who had in turn picked it up while working on cruise boats off the coast of Florida.[15] RCA then rush-released Belafonte's *own* 'Banana Boat Song (Day-O)', which his frequent collaborator Irving Burgie had lifted from other Jamaican folk sources.[16] Belafonte's version quickly eclipsed The Tarriers', though both were covered instantly by everyone from Steve Lawrence to Sarah Vaughan. By the time *Billboard* announced 'Hot Trend: Trinidado Tunes' in hyperventilating headlines on the cover of its December 26th issue, the calypso craze was well underway.

For all the sound and fury associated with it, however, the calypso wagon was always firmly hitched to Belafonte's star. And despite Belafonte's famous reluctance to accept the title of 'Calypso King' conferred on him by an eager press — he decried the craze loudly and repeatedly — the hundreds who tried, and mainly failed, to hit big with calypso were largely riding the king's coat-tails. Every newspaper and magazine article about the craze devoted an obligatory paragraph or two to speculation on its causes, with explanations ranging from the sociological (the postwar rise in Caribbean tourism) to the mystical (calypso's 'irresistible' beat). Most, however, eventually settled on what one fan magazine dubbed 'the Belafonte-Did-It-Theory': without Belafonte, this hypothesis went, calypso would have been nothing.[17] Lead singer Tony Williams of the Platters, quizzed by *Melody Maker* as he toured the UK for his own analysis of the latest rage back home, put the matter succinctly: 'if you don't dig [calypso] in the States, then you're square', he allowed. Yet he quickly cautioned against making too much of that fact, as 'all that craze is due to Belafonte'. And in any case, he demurred, calypso 'won't go as far as rock-'n'-roll'.[18]

For the vast majority of Americans, then, the calypso craze was really what *Look* magazine dubbed a 'Belafonte Boom': in the popular mind, the exciting singer and the exotic song were virtually synonymous. That Belafonte's followers were overwhelmingly white no doubt speaks to the racial politics of the entertainment business in general, but in particular it shows how easily whites could embrace Belafonte as the exceptional black man: well-spoken, intelligent, charismatic, and, well … *sexy*. While his nightclub act was all class, his open-shirted, tight-trousered costume deliberately emphasized his trim, muscular physique. At this point in his career, moreover, Belafonte was not only a top-drawing nightclub entertainer and a chart-topping recording artist, he was beginning to look like the first *bona fide* black screen idol, as well. Women, white and black, teenaged and middle-aged, regularly mobbed him backstage, captivated by what one fan magazine called 'his "Valentino-like" spell'.[19] His sultry, light-skinned good looks, together with the lilting accent he affected for his West Indian repertoire, imbued him with a marketable 'exotic' racial ambiguity, and Belafonte himself admits that he was someone of whom a liberal-minded white father might comfortably, if disingenuously say, 'that's the kind of Negro I'd like my daughter to date.' If the overriding aim of the all-American dad were to contain his daughter's fascination for the Big Bad Black Man, then, it would seem to make perfect sense to channel her errant attraction towards the genial Belafonte.[20]

Of course, this 'Negro' whom many whites saw as non-threatening was actually a political radical whose leftist sympathies and support of the Civil Rights movement became more open as the repressive climate of the Cold War eased. But the ironies surrounding Belafonte in this context are multiple. For starters, the man who exuded (and cultivated) an undeniable sex appeal was himself on a mission to clean up calypso's slack image. As he saw it, American calypso's vulgar penchant for titillating double entendres pandered to the worst racist clichés about black folks in general and lascivious island 'natives' in particular. To counteract such demeaning representations, Belafonte now says that he aimed to project a more dignified and sophisticated image of West Indians and West Indian culture.[21] But in some sense Belafonte's earnestness missed the point. That is, it overlooked the likelihood that the scurrilousness at which he took such umbrage was itself being propounded ironically: in performance, songs like 'The Big Bamboo' and 'Don't Touch Me Tomato' were insufferably cute and corny, their hokey sexuality brimming with ostentatious camp.[22]

Such irony can cut both ways, of course. If all those blue calypsos were only ironically — and therefore safely — outrageous, it was in part precisely *because* of what Belafonte had alleged: that they were openly trading on shopworn stereotypes about 'natives' of all sorts, whose sexuality — as the West has perennially delighted in discovering, from Vespucci to Gaugin to 'South Pacific' — is at once thrillingly uninhibited[23] and disarmingly innocent. *Real: The Exciting Magazine for Men* put the paradoxical chestnut just that baldly: calypso was unquestionably all about sex, yet at the same time it was 'childishly naïve',[24] infused with 'a kind of perverse purity': 'no matter how shady the implication ... seems to be', *Real* insisted, calypso 'retains an underlying native innocence that the staid statesider can't quite comprehend'.[25] The standard calypso costume — the garish colours, the exaggerated tatters, the outlandish straw hats, et cetera — overplayed the point, fairly screaming carefree poverty and cornball rusticity. Even many of calypso's more serious explicators wound up shilling it as a sort of siren song with the power to transport repressed Northerners to more easygoing mental climes. Geoffrey Holder, the phenomenal young Trinidadian dancer-choreographer who had risen to fame after bringing his own troupe to the United States on a shoestring (he eventually danced in *Aida* at the Met and acted in *Waiting for Godot* on Broadway, though his breakthrough came in Harold Arlen's exoticist *House of Flowers*), sympathetically explained to the *Herald-Tribune* that '[i]n a tense city like New York where people are busy making money, they seize upon calypso as a way to make them lose their inhibitions'.[26] And dance instructor Robert Luis concluded the purple-prosed introduction to his booklet *Authentic Calypso: The Song, the Music, the Dance* even more amenably:

> To the native of the Indies calypso means unbridled happiness, a release from life's tensions and frustrations ... rum and drums ... dance and romance. To his North American counterpart, the tense, overworked businessman of our bustling metropoleis [sic], calypso can also offer a wonderful fount of relaxation. (N.p. [5], ellipses in original.)

The travel industry had long drawn from the same well of clichés about tropical paradises filled with lithe black bodies, touristic truisms that served as comforting reconfirmations of familiar stereotypes. There was nothing inherently unsettling, then, about the idea of morally unrestrained 'natives' so grateful for our financial attentions that they might freely grant certain other favours in return. Contained within such colonialist paradigms of knowledge — not to mention symbolically sidelined to an offshore environment where the racial and sexual strictures of Cold War America were understood to be more or less suspended — calypso was thus effectively neutered, and any potential disturbance it might pose to middle-class America's moral equanimity was checked in advance.[27] This begins to explain how calypso, for all its vaunted licentiousness, could be envisioned as a more acceptable (black) suitor for the wayward affections of white American girlhood. The 'camp' factor ensured that calypso's sex appeal — like Belafonte's, in a way — was largely notional. Like the standard-issue straw-hat-and-tattered-trouser costume of the American calypso performer, it was *schtick*, albeit a schtick which quietly maintained the old colonialist myth of native simplicity while loudly protesting that any soupçon of suggestiveness in the infantilized *indigène* was merely a put-on. Under such guise, any over-the-top sleaziness could be excused as apparently off-colour but ultimately all in fun. To lure teens away from hot rods, rock and roll, general disaffection and delinquency, then, calypso had to seem naughty enough to be appealingly transgressive — but the naughtiness had to be scripted, managed, and *contained.*

The teens, to their credit, were not falling for it. As a strategy of containment, the calypso switch was perhaps too cheerfully transparent. And anyway, if the teens weren't quite buying calypso, then neither, exactly, were the adults who peddled it. In fact, the patent phoniness of the fad was another theme that was sounded early and widely: the distinction between authentic and synthetic, ersatz and genuine, 'the bonafide Calypsonian and the commercial singer of calypso songs who merely pretends to legitimacy' (*Calypso* fanzine 25) [28] — this was a commonplace in Craze reportage. So when Belafonte inveighed against the record industry's shameless opportunism, irritated that what was being fobbed off on a credulous public as calypso was not in fact calypso (and incensed, moreover, that calypso's true folk roots were being obscured and perverted in the bargain), he was not really saying anything that dozens of others had not remarked upon before. Robert Metz, for instance, taking *Variety*'s sardonic cue about 'the Brill B[uilding] set' churning out calypsos 'by the steel drumful' ('Calypso Here I Come'),[29] likewise disparaged Tin Pan Alley's slapdash cynicism: 'professional tunesmiths have thrown away their handbooks on rock 'n' roll,' he reported, 'and have begun grinding out "calypso" songs which have little if any relation to the real thing.'

There was a general awareness, too, of the hokum factor behind the Craze's prevailing aesthetic: no story was complete without a throwaway line about the scads of nightclubs nationwide that (like *Bop Girl*'s Club Trinidad) were hastily flinging up 'a batch of fishnet cork floats' and relaunching themselves as calypso lounges (*Trinidad Time*).[30] That this stock theme-décor was conceived as pure theatre is borne out by a description in Harlem's *New York Amsterdam News* of the Ekim Calypso Dock, newly opened in the back room of a venerable Irish bar near Columbia University. '[D]esigned and created by Danny Wright, a former off-Broadway producer', the club was 'an actual reproduction [!] of a Caribbean pier, as culled from the travels of its creator: fish nets, rum barrels, ropes and costumed waiters, will add to the atmosphere' ('New Calypso Room Opens').[31] Meanwhile, *Variety* noted 'the rapidity with which a lot of Harlemese have hidden their origins, accented the wrong syllables and are now passing themselves off as being from the islands' ('Could Calypso').[32] When *Time* finally weighed in on 'Calypsomania' a month later, it led off by dryly observing the brisk sales of ready-made 'Calypso Kits (including bongo drums, a gourd and a pair of maracas)' at New York's 'august music-house', G. Schirmer — the entry-level kit listed at $24.50.

In fact, to hear Robert Dana tell it in the New York *World-Telegram and Sun*'s weekend magazine, it was an open secret that American calypso was deliberately, slickly inauthentic, and that many if not most of the top performers favoured 'highly commercial adaptations' that were 'streamlined to fit the untutored American taste'.[33] In view of this, The Fabulous McClevertys, a successful calypso act from the Virgin Islands, struck Dana as having found the perfect middle ground: they 'make no unnecessary concessions to commercialism but compromise only in making lyrics intelligible'. Moreover, '[t]hey retain the authentic rhythms but expurgate lyrics and watch their diction' — exactly the qualities that critics were applauding in the reluctant King of Calypso, Harry Belafonte. At this relatively early stage of the craze, in fact, while many observers prized Belafonte precisely — though misguidedly, as he was at great pains to point out — for his supposed 'authenticity', others were of the opinion that imitation calypso was actually *preferable* to whatever the real thing might be.

A comparison of two notices in the January 2nd issue of *Variety* is telling. The same (anonymous) reviewer found the material performed at Montreal's 'El Morocco' by King Caribe and his Steel Bandits ('all legit personalities from Trinidad,' he asserted — though unbeknownst to him, they had only lately, and expediently, taken up calypso) lively and colourful, but too 'specialized': it 'would perhaps be more effective in these climes to work in a few of the more familiar West Indies chants'. By contrast, the effete frippery of Lord Lance (a white Englishman whose gimmickry included a monocle and top hat) actually 'boosts overall values because [he stays] with the more obvious items' — that is, the pseudo-calypso standards that North American audiences had come to expect — rather than 'the more obscure calypso routines that a native group might inject' ('New Acts'). That this frank preference for *faux* was justified by appealing to a need for latitudinal adjustment is striking, especially considering the rather distorted geographical lens through which Americans habitually viewed the Caribbean. It amounts to an unabashed contention that Americans' dopey ideas about the West Indies should govern the performance aesthetic of what they took to be West Indian music — there were shades of this sentiment even in Belafonte's well-intentioned ambitions to dramatize and 'interpret' West Indian folk music for American ears. The Versatones, alumni of Harold Arlen's *House of Flowers* and protégés of Belafonte, put the claim more bluntly: authentic calypso, they declared, was beat-heavy but melodically dull and monotonous; Americans, to their credit, 'try to make it more musically interesting'.[34]

Perhaps the most influential proponent of this line of thinking, however, was Manny Warner, talent scout, (self-) promoter, and founder of Monogram Records, which somewhat grandiosely claimed to have the 'largest [and] latest [calypso] catalogue in the world'. While lamenting the dearth of 'authentic talent' in the US — and he meant to get right on top of that problem — Warner insisted nevertheless that

> [f]or the general public ... some Calypso songs must be tailor-made. Authentic Calypso, being the folk medium it is, deals with local problems and is delivered in the patois of the Islands. Much of its meaning is lost when presented to a mass American audience.

To answer 'the need for songs which retain the native flavor, but are more suited to the requirements of an American audience, then, Warner simply decided to write his own stuff ('Behind the Scenes'). Thus was born 'Big Bamboo', 'Parakeets', and a flood of other off-colour tunes, which undoubtedly figured among the 'more obvious items' that *Variety* had in mind. Jean Ferdulli, who had opened Chicago's pioneering calypso nightclub The Blue Angel in 1953 largely at Warner's instigation, was just as brazen if a bit more incoherent: 'Calypso,' he told *Ebony*, 'must be treated with respect' — which, for him, meant precisely that '[it] must be embellished and glamorized. It must be packaged correctly,' he clarified. 'If it is not treated with respect,' he concluded, more presciently than he realized, 'I believe it will die' ('Fad').

In short, if most American fans preferred calypso processed, glamourized, and embellished — 'Calypso, American Style', one fanzine called it — and if, in the end, this was 'not really calypso' ... well, then, as *Time* magazine breezily concluded, 'no one seem[ed] to care'.[35] At least, not anyone who much mattered. 'Already complaints are being heard,' *Time* fretted, 'that U.S. calypso ... is corrupting a fine old tradition, just as old-time jazz lovers thought big-band, arranged jazz was a sad decline from the old, improvised New Orleans roughhouse.' But the tone of *Time*'s report also implied an awareness that nostalgia would be an ineffectual response to the taste of the American consumer. And the analogy it employed suggested that in any event, such wistful sentiments were largely confined to reverent paternalists who (like LeRoi Jones's 'Dixieland revivalists') arrogantly imagined they knew what 'ancient colored men' should sound like, now and forever.[36]

That assessment was not so far from the mark, actually — though in calypso's case, the self-styled purists were actually romantic types more concerned with preserving certain imaginary qualities possessed by dusky tropical maidens. In the summer of 1955, the eminent jazz critic Leonard Feather led the way as he haughtily recounted his own recent visits to Jamaica and The Bahamas, pronouncing himself disappointed in the profusion of 'bastardized' calypso he found there, clearly the product of American tourists' predilections. Trinidad itself, he speculated ignorantly, might still be relatively unspoiled, and he hoped to get there one day. In the meantime, at least, Belafonte was giving us the real hot item back home.

The idea that American brutes had deflowered West Indian virgins, pressuring them to surrender what *Real* magazine referred to as their 'native musical innocence ... [by] consciously catering to what they believe Americans will like',[37] was not new: novelist, composer and amateur orientalist Paul Bowles had founded this school of criticism in response to the passing calypso fad of late-1930's New York, and many calypsonians also maintained (with more than a little chauvinist pique) that American GIs had ravished Trinidad and its culture during World War II, usually with the compliance of what they figured as a two-timing local jezebel. This was not quite what Feather, Sasso, and Co. had in mind, as their version of the gripe ascribed all agency to the big, brawny Americans, without considering whether their Trinidadian partners might have had some role in engineering, or indeed profiting from, the long, complicated affair. In any event, their brand of paternalism characterized a whole cottage industry of self-appointed experts and purists full of sniffy indignation over the dreck that now passed for calypso.[38] Some, especially early in the decade, were holdouts from the New York-based Folk Song movement of the 1930s and 1940s which under the banner of a kind of popular-front internationalism had earnestly championed calypso as the unvarnished expression of one of the world's folk cultures. Though the dwindling disciples of this vision — artists, activists, intellectuals and college students — were ever more marginalized as 'arty' and elitist, or simply persecuted as un-American in the early 1950s, for all such true believers 'the folk' were *ipso facto* authentic, and the slightest taint of commercialism was anathema. An October 1950 *New York Times* review of a performance by Massie Patterson's Carib Singers, one of several ethnographically-oriented folk troupes in New York that catered to liberal white audiences, gives a glimpse into the widening schism between two competing aesthetics: what Miss Patterson's singers and dancers provided, said the *Times* approvingly, was 'authentic' folksong from the islands, 'not a night-club Trinidad'.

Other devotees had actually come by their enthusiasm for calypso via commercial means, a sin for which they sought to atone by cultivating the supercilious authority and fanatical attention to detail characteristic of the jazz buff and the record collector. Unlike the tasteless, gullible masses, they knew what the 'real thing' was, and they sought it out intensely. Though these afficionados rarely spoke for themselves, they were alluded to in the press as the nameless 'purists' who 'will no doubt tell you that ... true calypso ... like ... Dixieland jazz ... should be extemporized',[39] the connoisseurs whose collective opinion formed the basis of the authentic/synthetic split that structured so much of the reporting on the calypso craze. Belafonte — who, *Variety* once said gratefully, had taken folk singing out of the 'arty' confines of Greenwich Village — was often conscripted to serve as spokesman for this camp. According to the sidebar of a *Newsweek* story whose overriding purpose was to decide the degree to which the current craze (which 'embrace[d] all manner of rhythmic Caribbean aberrations') could 'claim some legitimate kinship with the true calypso,' Belafonte wanted 'no identification with 'this so-called calypso'.... No matter how big this craze gets [he declared], I will never sing one of those phony numbers merely to sell a lot of records' ('Calypso Craze').[40] Surveying the 'burgeoning battle between the calypso purists and the make-a-quick-buck copyists', Robert Sasso of *Real* found that Belafonte's hot (if half-accurate) denunciations even suited the pulp magazine's punchy prose style:

> Authentic calypso is a very special song form. ... Synthetic calypsos are just gimmicky tunes that lack the throbbing 2/4 or 4/4 beat.

This current mania for some of the musical nonsense conveniently labeled calypso is due in large measure to Tin Pan Alley. They feel that rock 'n' roll has just about lost steam — and they are starting to push calypso and the poor imitations for all they are worth. I want no part of the hysteria or to be associated with any cult form whatsoever.[41]

When Belafonte could not be trotted out to make this point, however, actual Trinidadians — or Trinidadian expatriates, or even singers commonly mistaken for Trinidadians — would do. *Down Beat* set the precedent in mid 1956 with a feature on the Mighty Panther, a well-regarded veteran of the Young Brigade Tent who was then making his American debut at Chicago's Blue Angel. The story dutifully followed Panther's lead in distinguishing between dues-paying tent calypsonians and all the 'commercial singers of Calypso only pretending to legitimacy' (by which he principally meant Belafonte) who were showing up on US marquees (L. Brown).[42] That Panther had laboured to '[make] Americans keenly aware of the difference between the true calypso and the ersatz', however, did not prevent him from claiming authorship of the notoriously phony 'Big Bamboo', which he recorded, along with several other famous pseudo-calypsos, for an album promoted by his American label as 'A Party Record for Adults to Enjoy'.[43] Some months later, Robert Metz called upon another *bona fide* calypsonian, Gorilla, who likewise explained that the ability to compose extemporaneously was the main distinction between 'pure' calypsonians and calypso *singers*, who merely memorized other people's tunes. (In Gorilla's opinion, Belafonte was strictly speaking of neither one nor the other.) This axiom was lazily echoed by scores of journalists, who dropped it into potted histories in which calypso was romanticized as having descended from the secret language of slaves forbidden to speak but permitted to sing. Only on rare occasions, as in Jesse DeVore's profile of the Mighty Dictator, 'one of the few authentic calypsonians in the United States', in the *New York Amsterdam News*, was the difference elaborated upon more precisely.

For *Real* magazine, meanwhile, it was the US-based Duke of Iron, whose calypso résumé dated back to 1940, who assumed the role of grizzled veteran authorized to draw such a distinction.

> The current crop of ersatz calypso chanters, [he scoffed] were 'parasitic parrots. They memorize the melody and lyrics to a handful of songs and spend their time singing them repeatedly. They have no imagination. No fervor. Nothing. ... A true calypsonian is an artist, a creator, a man of deep sensitivity. He creates his lyrics from what is at hand. ... Calypso in its truest form is a topical kind of music'[44]

How the Duke squared this principled stand with the fact that he himself had had no experience as a calypsonian before emigrating to America, wrote almost none of his own material, and had lately revived his flagging career by flogging a handful of off-colour tunes he had recorded for Manny Warner's Monogram Records, is not known.[45] Even *The New Yorker* descended from its Olympian heights, in the company of its 'eloquent friend' Joseph Willoughby, gentlemanly elder statesman of the West Indian community in Harlem, who had served the preceding autumn as the magazine's native informant on the quaint customs of West Indian carnival ('Mardi Gras').[46] As the composer of several popular calypsos himself (he co-authored Louis Jordan's 1946 hit 'Run Joe', which had been dusted off for the current craze), Willoughby was in a hard place: he stood to profit personally from the current fad, and was understandably loath to invite a 'conspicuous and regrettable diminution of the possible financial rewards.' Yet he obligingly regretted the sensational character of the more commercially oriented calypsos, fearing 'that the cause of calypso [was] not being well served artistically,' and he spent the bulk of the piece holding forth on the characteristics of the more genteel and erudite brand of calypso that he personally preferred ('Life and Love').

In the end, though, all of this semi-informed and sometimes self-contradictory quibbling — this ventriloquizing of Trinidadians in order to bolster one's otherwise dubious authority (clearly the word of a Geoffrey Holder, 'a man who first heard [calypso] from his mother,' could not be gainsaid) — was not about the distinction between ersatz and authentic per se. The cheesy material that Lord Kitchener — whose credibility was hardly in question (he was perhaps the most revered calypsonian in Trinidad of the past half-century) — was then performing for audiences in Britain rendered those categories problematic, at the very least. The paramount thing was the mere act of *making* the distinction. Declaring one's quasi-ethnographic knowledge of 'the real thing', asserting one's power to discriminate between the genuine and the phony, clucking your tongue over slick American louts perverting pristine folk traditions — this was finally a way of establishing and defending imperial claims of knowing. The smirking insinuation that 'we know what the real thing is, and it's much too earthy for clean-living Americans' — at root another effort at racial and sexual containment, albeit a more titillating and seemingly transgressive one — was an earlier variation on the theme. But the implied argument, nearly Conradian in nature, behind the sniggers went something like this: Yes, we're foisting this cute hokum on the American public, though we all know what lurks underneath its campy veneer. Namely, the lure of the *real* calypso: its full-strength, 'animalistic', island sexuality, to which American nightclub calypso continually refers, if only as the shadow refers to the substance. For decency's sake, the truth of calypso has got to stay suppressed — but it is still there, hidden (luckily, luckily).

Depending upon the character it ascribed to the authentically exotic (virgin or whore, noble savage or savage she-devil) then, the discerning pose was rooted in an off-the-shelf ethnography or the sophomoric self-regard of an adolescent empire. In either case, it reflected a uniquely American brand of callow internationalism, the geopolitical and cultural outlook of a nation eager to claim a worldly sophistication at just the moment it was claiming ownership of the world — and remaking it in its image.[47]

Elaine Tyler May argues that the relative security of the suburban domestic idyll was always felt by those who lived it to be precarious and fragile, under a tacit but ever-present threat from all sorts of shadowy outsiders as well as from more immediate rumblings of social disintegration. It is crucial to keep in mind, then, that as Americans went crazy for calypso, the *birthplace* of calypso like much of the rest of the Third World, was clamouring for independence from its colonial masters. Often with relative order and civility, though sometimes with considerable rancor and bloodshed, black people the world over were seizing control of their destinies, and it must have been plain to anyone who cared to look that, as James Baldwin had put it in 1955, 'the world [was] white no longer.'

Obliviously depicting 'natives' as simple, languorous and oversexed — more concerned with dancing, drinking rum and fooling around than with fomenting revolution — could have a certain sedative effect; repeating those ragged stereotypes, one might delude oneself into thinking that there was no trouble in paradise.

The trouble brewing at home, however, where the Civil Rights movement was coalescing and race relations were growing tenser all the time, would have been harder to ignore. The Montgomery bus boycott dragged on through all of 1956, for instance, and various challenges to court-mandated school integration, including that of Arkansas Governor Orval Faubus, played out in the spring and summer of 1957.[48] But an even more salient context for the calypso craze was the gruesome murder of Emmett Till, the black teen from Chicago killed by racist thugs in Mississippi in August 1955 for the crime of dallying (as they saw it) with a white woman. Indeed, despite — or perhaps because of — what Patricia Williams calls our nation's 'complexly libidinous history', segregationists' most reliable bugbear was the perennial spectre of miscegenation. That the full integration of blacks into the American body politic would entail the mixing of flesh and the amalgamation of the gene pool was for them no flight of fancy but a dead certainty. Keeping the Negro in his place unquestionably meant keeping him *out* of white women's pants.[49]

While right-thinking Northern whites ordinarily did not voice such cracked thoughts so freely, that is not to say that they perceived African-American aspirations as any less threatening to their newly prosperous way of life — or even that their own libidinous logic was any less twisted. Rock and roll, which after all came straight into the bedrooms of the sons and daughters of suburbia via the record-player and the radio, might well be regarded as the stealthiest agent of a thoroughgoing corruption of the social order; and by such paranoid reckoning, it would have made a certain amount of sense to prescribe calypso as preventive medicine. Unlike rock, calypso was not *seriously* threatening to contribute to the sexual delinquency of white American girlhood. Yet, the more Hollywood elucidated the calypso craze's racial and sexual unconscious, the more incoherent its logic appeared. *Bop Girl*'s ending, for instance, would seem to represent a fatal compromise of the original plan for calypso to oust rock, since the 'Calypso Rock' that its heroine ultimately embraces is a conscious hybrid, and hybrids are inevitably the product of cross-breeding. Granted, the film offers no suggestion that calypso-rock's conception has taken place any way other than immaculately — which is to say, symbolically. But according to the heroine's climactic anthem, helping calypso to increase and multiply in a non-indigenous North American environment would have to involve some rocking and rolling somewhere along the line. Such an outcome hardly constitutes a successful sublimation of America's inter-racial anxieties. Even so, at the end of the day Hollywood was satisfied with seeing calypso — or a facsimile of it — merely *tame* rather than displace rock and roll. Rock, so *Bop Girl* would have it, could paradoxically be domesticated by taking up with a 'foreign', more rustic, yet somehow less 'savage' version of itself.

But whether calypso's proponents fondly hoped that it could help banish the twin threats of black sexual and political upheaval from American consciousness altogether or simply box them into a more manageable package, in the end it failed to do either. As one nay-saying record store owner told The *Miami Herald*: 'the kids just [were]n't going for it.' To be sure, there may have been credulous kids who were briefly taken in by the Calypso Craze, just as they were gulled by a dozen other manufactured fads. But Eisenhower-era teens related to rock and roll more profoundly than they did to, say, Davy Crockett caps. And as long as everyone else treated calypso ironically (or mock-ironically), it was impossible for teenagers to see it as truly subversive — or consequently, as attractive — as rock. By the end of 1957, rock and roll was not only more popular than ever, but more closely associated in the minds of its white teenage fans with black political causes. And youth culture, now openly identifying with the outsider status and restrained rebellion of American blacks, was, in the words of Andrew Ross, ever more firmly centred around 'interracial affiliations[,] fantasies of sexual mobility',[50] and a general 'willingness to cut across class-coded and color-coded musical tastes'.[51] In retrospect, then, Bop Girl's brief affair with Calypso amounted to an experiment gone awry. The upshot was that although calypso was now in some sense permanently entrenched in the gene pool of American pop culture, the gene had been altered in such a way as to be effectively neutered, stripped of any power to affect that culture meaningfully.[52]

Joe Klein, writing of the Folk Revival of the late 1950s and early 1960s, contends that 'the patina of integrity and authenticity covering white collegiate folk music ... offered record companies an exit from ... the racial and sexual fears that had generated mainstream disapproval of rock and roll'.[53] If Klein is right, then the calypso craze was in its own botched way a warm-up exercise for this negrophobic 'exit strategy'. And even though the dry run failed, one could still argue that the diffuse but pervasive tendency towards containment that characterized the 1950s ultimately succeeded even while backfiring. Even if rock and roll had not been thwarted by calypso, that is, calypso *itself* was lastingly relegated to the province of the quaint, the corny, and (above all) the un-hip. At best, calypso was Rat Pack cool *avant la lettre*: savvy, supercilious, and slightly louche, the cool of 30- and 40-year-olds behaving like teenagers. Despite its indigenous history of incisive social critique, and despite the increasingly open political radicalism of its American avatar Belafonte, calypso's embroilment in the failed effort to 'contain' rock and roll helped discredit it as a music of squares and social reactionaries, thereby cementing its lasting reputation in the US as kitsch.

Now, it is possible that some stealth strain of Caribbean culture has still had the last laugh here: Bo Diddley famously (perhaps unwittingly) based his eponymous beat — one of the founding rhythms of rock and roll — upon the *clave*, and before you know it, the Buena Vista Social Club has colonized suburban CD players and the 'Reggaeton Virus' has infected North American dancehalls. Indeed, Ned Sublette has convincingly demonstrated how Cuban music and Caribbean traditions have 'insinuated themselves into every breakthrough moment in American music',[54] and Mimi Sheller has argued that while the North's 'consumption' of the Caribbean—its 'landscapes, plants, food, bodies, and cultures'[55] — has been central to the narrative of Western modernity, nevertheless where America is concerned, 'the Caribbean is already within, and to consume it is really to regurgitate what is already there'.[56] America may *think* it knows what it is ingesting when it heaps up the Caribbean on its plate — white sand beaches, spliff-smoking rastas, hurricanes, boat people, and 'Hot Hot Hot'— when history shows that a much subtler and more complicated sort of Caribbean was a key ingredient of the American recipe all along. And it is an ingredient that remains undigested, or so we might like to believe. No matter how 'much the Caribbean is ... eaten [by America],' Sheller muses, 'it is never eaten up'; no matter how thorough America's success in containing it, it 'can never be simply consumed, swallowed ... and discarded'.[57] This, no doubt, is what Harry Belafonte meant, in part, when he paternalistically prophesied in May of 1957 that 'calypso [would] survive all of us ... no matter what's done to it now'.[58] But whenever some ironic hipster or drunken baseball fan performs a casual act of modern-day minstrelsy by breaking into a jokey chorus of 'Day-O,' why, then, it can be difficult to maintain that in America, calypso has not been chewed up and spat out, its only 'undigested' remainder a dimpled wad left on top of the nation's bedpost. Still, there is always a degree of self-conscious sheepishness to this minstrelsy, not unlike the campiness that characterized the calypso craze in general — and this ought to remind us of what Eric Lott pointed out a decade ago. All such acts of racial impersonation involve a peculiar kind of mimicry: they express both a deep-seated loathing and a twisted longing, equal parts ridicule and desire, for their object. White America 'went calypso' precisely in order to *avoid* black America — and failed. Perhaps this strand of unresolved longing and loathing, for African-Americans *and* for their fantasy stand-ins, the West Indians, is what remains, undigested, of calypso in America.

Notes

> Research for this article was carried out under a generous grant from the National Endowment for the Humanities during 2001–2002.

1. *Bop Girl Goes Calypso* [a/k/a *Bop Girl*]. Pressbook. United Artists, 1957.
2. Calypso Joe. Allied Artists, 1957
3. *Calypso Heat Wave.* Dir. Fred Sears. Perf. Johnny Desmond and Merry Anders. Columbia, 1957.
4. Michael Barson and Steven Heller's *Teenage Confidential: An Illustrated History of the American Teen* (San Francisco: Chronicle Books, 1998), provides a concise and accessible pictorial survey of the sensationalist iconography of the wild teenage delinquent. The *Bop Girl* poster is of a piece with the artwork of hundreds of other pulp novels, magazines, comic books, movie posters and advertisements of the day directed primarily at teens.
5. Judy Tyler's 'calypso' numbers were penned by Les Baxter, the godfather of Exotica — an ersatz-tropical idiom of the 1950s that mixed 'Afro-Cuban rhythms, unusual instrumentations, [and] environmental sounds' with 'lush romantic themes from Hollywood movies [and] evocative titles like "Jaguar

God'" ('What Is'). For a brief biography and discography of Baxter, see 'Les Baxter', *Hyp Records/Vinyl Safari*, ed. Tony Wilds, 1998, September 9, 2003 <http://www.hipwax.com/music/exot_lb.html>; and 'Les Baxter', *The Space Age Pop Music Page*, September 10, 2003 http://www.spaceagepop.com/baxter.htm; (Wilds's 'Exotica' page <http://www.hipwax.com/music/exotica.html> is also excellent.) A more thorough overview of Baxter's work can be found at 'The Exotic World of Les Baxter', *Club Velvet*, ed. Dean Vaccaro, September 10, 2003 <http://www.tamboo.com/baxter/index.html>. The piece that makes a calypso convert of Barney is strongly tinged with *son* and *mento*, while Jo's costumed showstopper at the newly metamorphosed 'Club Trinidad' is more mambo than calypso.

6. How 'Bop' figures into this shorthand is a bit more complicated: it evidently stood for a loosely forged metonymic chain of black musical forms that all somehow threatened to unravel the moral fiber of the nation. As LeRoi Jones (Amiri Baraka), *Blues People: The Negro Experience in White America and the Music that Developed From It* (New York: Morrow, 1963), 187–88 points out in discussing the social implications of bebop's eccentric style, 'the white musicians and other young whites who [in the 1940s] associated themselves with this Negro music identified the Negro with ... separation [and] nonconformity'; bebopper (and later, beatnik) jokes generally 'referred to *white nonconformists* ... and not to Negroes' (190). Oddly, the pseudo-calypso of the mid 1950s took on certain beatnik trappings — notably bongo drums — and its afficionados were not infrequently lampooned as finger-snapping, beret-wearing hipsters. Like *Bop Girl*'s Barney, ads for calypso clubs often employed hep-cat lingo (Maxim's Calypso Den in New York invited patrons to come hear the 'Cool Cats from the Caribbee'), and one self-consciously swinging magazine characterized the entire phenomenon as one centred around 'Those wild Trinidaddies': 'What started many years ago as a parochial passion in certain chi-chi cliques is now throbbing and reverberating in virtually every hamlet from here to Squaresville.' Arthur J. Sasso, 'They're Going Crazy for Calypso!', *Real: The Exciting Magazine for Men* 10, no. 2, June 1957, 80.

7. Sasso, 'They're Going Crazy for Calypso!', 80.

8. It was actually Boston's celebrated 'jazz priest' Norman O'Connor who had first made the prediction, relayed excitedly by *Variety*, that calypso would soon write rock's epitaph ('Warning'). But Metz's seminal article for the International News Service was syndicated — and pilfered — repeatedly. The formulation just cited, from the Chicago-based African-American picture magazine *Hue* ('Will Calypso Craze Doom Rock 'N' Roll') was further stylized in *Ebony* ('The Fad from Trinidad'); 'The calypsomania also did what the police and PTA couldn't do. It nudged rock 'n' roll off the front pages.' Metz's original read: 'Calypso ... may accomplish what platoons of parents, sociologists and police have failed to do. It may push rock 'n' roll from the top spot in popular music.'

9. Sasso, 'They're Going Crazy for Calypso!', 80; In addition, marvels one wolfish club-owner quoted in the article, calypso's beat seems to have a 'narcotic effect' on many 'females'.

10. The most eloquent, perhaps, came from Atilla the Hun (Raymond Quevedo), who in 'The Banning of Records' (1938) protested:

> To say these songs are sacrilegious, obscene or profane
> Is nothing but a lie and a burning shame

> If kaiso is indecent then I must insist
> That so is Shakespeare's "Venus and Adonis"
> Boccaccio's tales and Voltaire's *Candide*
> *The Martyrdom of Man* by Winwood Reade
> But o'er these authors they make no fuss
> But want to take advantage of us.

11. The two final quotes are from Sasso and 'The Fad from Trinidad: Sassy, syncopated calypso is hottest craze in entertainment world', *Ebony*, June 1957, 48–52, respectively. The litany of adjectives was plucked randomly from Dana, 'The Fad', Sasso, 'Will Calypso', and 'Calypsomania', but similar descriptors were repeated ad nauseum elsewhere. (One of the second-tier promoters of calypso in New York, R. Jason Phillips, billed one of his early shows at the Calypso Room on East 59th Street as the 'Mad Fad from Trinidad' with 'the slightly sinful lyrics and tricky rhythms'. The show's headliners were Lance Haven, 'The Bad Lad from Trinidad', and Lady Calypso, 'The "Tomata" from Jamaica'. (See advertisement in the New York *Sunday Mirror*, February 24, 1957, 57.)
12. Lucy Kavaler, 'Where go calypso? We've given Manhattan back to the (West) Indians. When will it be ours again?', *New York Herald-Tribune*, May 26, 1957; 'Today's Living', 4.
13. The first stanza and chorus should be sufficient to convey the song's character:

> I asked my lady what could I do
> to make her happy and to keep her true.
> She said, "My friend, one thing I need from you
> is a little tiny piece of the big bamboo."
> She wanted big bamboo four feet long,
> big bamboo so full and strong.
> Big bamboo stands up straight and tall;
> Only big bamboo pleases one and all.

14. These calypsos were also among the first tunes Belafonte recorded after signing with RCA in 1953.
15. Some of the preceding factual information comes from Arnold Shaw's *Belafonte: An Unauthorized Biography* (Philadelphia: Chilton, 1960) and Colin Escott's essay, 'Harry Belafonte: Island in the Sun', *Harry Belafonte: Island in the Sun* ([book accompanying CD boxed set of the same name] Hambergen, Germany: Bear Family Records, 2002. 1–37), accompanying a boxed-set survey of Belafonte's early career on Bear Family Records; some comes from interviews with Belafonte himself. For material on The Tarriers and Bob Gibson, I am indebted to entries by Ronnie D. Lankford, Jr. and Richie Unterberger, respectively, in the online version of the *All-Music Guide* <www.allmusic.com>. It is perhaps of passing interest that the original, mixed-race line-up of The Tarriers, unsung heralds of the Folk Revival, included a young Alan Arkin.
16. A Brooklyn native of Barbadian parents, Burgie was a university-trained musician who had flirted with the leftist Folk Song movement in the late 1940s. He had been performing calypsos for several years as 'Lord Burgess' when he was tapped first to assist with the *Colgate Comedy Hour* segment (where 'Day-O' debuted) and then the *Calypso!* album. (He also recorded two albums of his own in 1954 and 1955, 'Lord Burgess: Caribbean Folk

Singer' for Paragon and 'Lord Burgess' Calypso Serenaders: Folk Songs of Haiti, Jamaica and Trinidad', on the Stinson label.) Though many of his tunes were merely 'inspired' by Caribbean material, Burgie's practice of appropriating and/or embellishing West Indian folk melodies and copyrighting them as his own was neither rare nor unprecedented. Belafonte eventually recorded 36 of his tunes.

17. Leonard Green, 'Calypso sweeps the nation...', *Calypso* 1 (1957): 21. While it took months for many promoters to stop believing their own hype, everyone ultimately came to realize the full implications of the theory: economically speaking, apart from Belafonte, calypso really *was* nothing — something the big record company A&R men had suspected all along — and moreover, Belafonte was the only performer with 'legs'. The fanzine article's author, a theatrical agent whose firm boasted 'a larger stable of calypso entertainers than any other' (Green 17), must eventually have appreciated this fact more ruefully than many. For a survey of calypso's rise and fall on the *Billboard* charts, see Ray Funk, 'The Calypso Recording Craze of 1957', in *Harry Belafonte: Island in the Sun* [book accompanying CD boxed set of the same name], ed. Colin Escott (Hambergen, Germany: Bear Family Records, 2002), 92–94.

18. Tony Williams quoted in Tony Brown, 'Will Calypso Knock the Rock?: The Stars Answer your Question', *Melody Maker*, March 16, 1957, 3.

19. 'The Girls Are Wild About Harry', *Harry Belafonte: His Complete Life Story*, ed. Hy Steirman (New York: Hillman Publications, 1957), 45.

20. White southerners, maniacally sensitive even to make-believe miscegenation, brooked no such fine distinctions. Blanching at the whiff of romantic attraction between characters played by Belafonte and Joan Fontaine in *Island in the Sun* (adapted from Alec Waugh's bestselling novel and released after months of advance publicity in June 1957), they demanded that their scenes together be censored from screenings in Southern cinemas. That Belafonte, divorced from his first (black) wife, Marguerite, actually called the white liberal bluff by then marrying a white woman could only have confirmed the worst fears of Southern racists.

21. Belafonte was not a prude, yet leaving aside the truth that a kind of grotesque caricature was in fact being routinely passed off as 'calypso' — sometimes with the collusion of West Indian and/or West Indian–American performers, his stance is still open to charges of presumptuousness and condescension. (It would be one thing if his point were that West Indians' image had been commandeered and exploited by others, and he, who had exceptional access to the media, were setting about to correct things on their behalf. But if his point were that West Indians were perfectly capable of deciding how to portray themselves and were simply, in his opinion, doing a bad job of it, that would be something else again.) Statements Belafonte made in 1957 and repeated in subsequent interviews often seem to point a scolding finger at Trinidadian calypsonians themselves. But in conversation with me (April 12, 2002), he clarified that his condemnation was really targeted at the sorts of calypso-burlesques that were spread ad nauseum by 'Hotel Calypso' singers and other lesser stars in the calypso firmament.

22. From another point of view, though, he was spot on — since, after all, this type of irony habitually cuts both ways. As the deconstructive adage has it: the man who says one thing while meaning another still says that first thing. Besides, there's every possibility that calypso's insinuating kitsch was an instance of 'stealth' irony — something that feigns not to mean what it says when it actually *does*.

23. An ad for an appearance by singer-dancer Josephine Premice ('and her company of Afro-Cuban [sic] Calypsonians') at the Dunes, Las Vegas, featured a bust of Premice with sensuous lips and downcast eyes framed by her own sinuously beckoning fingers, and promised that the show would be 'Wild! Savage! Electric! Pagan! Primitive! Passionate!' (Advertisement, *Las Vegas Sun*, January 7, 1957) 3.
24. *Real: The Exciting Magazine for Men*, 81.
25. Sasso, 'They're Going Crazy for Calypso!', 80.
26. Kavaler, 'Where go Calypso?', 4.
27. Even if suburbanites' affinity for calypso constituted a pallid rejection, however feeble or subconscious, of stultifying middle-class domesticity — some may have understood that calypso was associated in some distant way with 'bacchanal' — any hint of insurgence it might have entailed was so thoroughly policed as to be rendered impotent. In our own day, the locus of 'safe abandon' has moved northward to the margins of the Caribbean, as *The New Yorker*'s Rebecca Mead explained in a brilliant analysis of the rituals of Spring Break, especially as they are ritually enacted for the hugely popular 'Girls Gone Wild' exploitation videos: 'The popularity of [such] hokey simulacra', wherein gleefully uninhibited co-eds 'spontaneously' bare their breasts for the camera, demonstrates on the part of participants and spectators alike a 'conscious enjoyment' of a pre-scripted moment of mock-daring that is 'both visually persuasive and unmistakably inauthentic ... at once convincing and implausible'. Its editing into such tediously repetitive (and tame) pornography yields an 'atmosphere of exemption ... [that's] surprisingly orderly'.
28. 'Mighty Panther and "The Big Bamboo"', *Calypso* 1 (1957): 25.
29. 'Calypso Here I Come — Maybe: Can Kids Dance to Caribe Beat?', *Variety*, January 23, 1957, 41+.
30. '"Trinidad Time" Up In N.Y.; Hub's 1st.', *Variety*, February 6, 1957, 58.
31. 'New Calypso Room Opens', *New York Amsterdam News*, February 9, 1957, 12.
32. 'Could Calypso Go Into Collapso By Too Rapid Rise in Salaries?', *Variety*, February 6, 1957, 58; Lucy Kavaler struck a similar note in the *New York Herald-Tribune* several months later ('Many a night club owner is hurriedly putting up palm leaves, stepping up his rum order, and importing talent from one of the islands, be it Trinidad, Staten, or Manhattan'), as did *Ebony* magazine ('Owners of plush supper clubs are sprinkling sawdust on the floor, hanging fishnets on the ceilings and re-opening as calypso clubs. American singers, striving for that fresh-from-the-islands effect, are wiggling like Elvis and broadening their A's').
33. Robert W. Dana, 'The Big City Is Stomping to Calypso!: The Primitive Rhythm Was Slow to Catch On, But Now It Has the Night Clubs in a Tizzy', [New York] *World-Telegram and Sun Saturday Magazine*, March 2, 1957, 10–11. Of course (as I argued above) the 'taste' being kow-towed to had just as much to do with orientalist assumptions as deficient understanding.
34. The Versatones quoted in Dana, Ibid., 10.
35. 'Calypsomania', *Time*, March 25, 1957, 50.
36. Jones, *Blues People*, 203.
37. Sasso, 'They're Going Crazy for Calypso!', 81.
38. It is hard not to read their opprobrium as yet another prohibition against racial and cultural mixing — masquerading as, of all things, a self-directed sanction against cultural imperialism.

39. Mary Ellin and Marvin Bennett, 'Trend: Up from Trinidad', 'On Our List: A monthly report on what the intelligent American may want to read, see, hear, and talk about', *Good Housekeeping*, May 1957, 8.
40. Easy for him to say; he was *already* selling a lot of records. An alternate citation prefaced this adamant declaration with a further refusal: '[I]f phony synthetic cliché calypso material floods the market, they're not going to get me to sing it or pose with one of those straw hats' (Ralph J. Gleason, 'The Music's Got to Have Truth Or Belafonte Won't Sing', *San Francisco Chronicle*, June 23, 1957: 'This World', 10+.) Having posed in just such a ridiculous, straw-hatted getup in John Murray Anderson's *Almanac*, of course, he had already paid his dues in that regard.
41. Sasso, 'They're Going Crazy for Calypso!', 80.
42. Les Brown, 'The Mighty Panther Tells Roots, Meanings of Calypso', *Down Beat*, May 30, 1956, 42.
43. Given calypso's 'blue' reputation, it may come as no surprise to learn that some consumers placed it, in the continuum of recorded music, alongside the stag records that were also in vogue at the time, or the raunchy comedy albums of Redd Foxx, or even the gently naughty albums by comediennes Ruth Wallis (of 'Boobs' fame) and Rusty Warren. In fact, Wallis capitalized on the calypso craze by composing an entire album's worth of 'Saucy Calypsos'.
44. Duke of Iron quoted in Sasso, 'They're Going Crazy for Calypso!', 80–81.
45. My catty side is perhaps too unkind. The Duke was a genuinely talented (and tireless) performer and a longtime fixture in New York, a favourite of both white and black audiences. Though fan magazines like *Calypso Album* went to some lengths to fabricate a pedigree for him as an 'authentic' tent champion in Trinidad, this line from the same magazine's puff-piece profile is probably a more accurate assessment of his credentials: 'His act is characterized by an authenticity few Calypso singers presently in vogue can achieve. The Duke imitates the exact style of the Trinidad singers who perform during carnival time in Port-of-Spain' ('Duke of Iron'). By this point in his career, however, he took pleasure in posing as the dean of calypsonians in America, and his claim generally went unquestioned. In February 1957, in distinguishing 'natives' (or 'islanders') from 'non-natives', *Variety* unhesitatingly placed the Duke in the former category — along with Lord Burgess (Irving Burgie, from Brooklyn), Lord Flea (a Jamaican), and Johnny Barracuda (a student at Columbia who emigrated from Jamaica as a child, but who was often billed — as in the 'Calypso Mambo Panorama' sponsored by 'The Jewish Men of Queens' — as having come 'Direct from Trinidad') ('Non-Trinidadians'). A month later, *Time* also counted the Duke — and Lord Flea — under the elastic category 'authentic' ('Calypsomania'). By May, the *New York Times* could be a bit more exacting in its taxonomy, thanks largely to a piece it had run a few weeks earlier by Trinidadian dancer and showman Geoffrey Holder, then headlining a monumental 'Calypso Festival' at Loew's Metropolitan in Brooklyn, exhaustively dissecting for the *Times*'s discerning readers the difference between 'true Calypso' and 'Manhattan Calypso'. Clearly echoing Holder, John S. Wilson divided his review of recent calypso records into 'Calypsonians' (not to be mistaken for mere 'Calypso singers') and 'slicked-up Calypso'. In the former slot he put Trinidadians Lord Beginner, Lord Melody, and Small Island Pride, along with 'older practitioners' such as Wilmoth Houdini (another Trinidadian expatriate who had at least

competed, but never quite 'made it', in Port of Spain), and ... the Duke of Iron.

46. 'Mardi Gras', 'The Talk of the Town', *The New Yorker*, September 1956, 35–36.

47. Thanks to Hope Munro Smith, who voiced this idea at the Joint Annual Meeting of the Society of American Music and the Center for Black Music Research in Port of Spain, May 2001.

48. The year 1957 also saw the establishment of the US Civil Rights Commission and the passage of the first Civil Rights Act — relatively toothless compromise measures intended, no doubt, to contain any more radical or violent aspirations on the part of African Americans. (For a compelling account of the behind-the-scenes machinations that scuttled any more effective civil rights legislation in 1957, see Robert Caro's *Master of the Senate: The Years of Lyndon Johnson, Volume 3* (New York: Knopf, 2002).)

49. I have already mentioned Southern hysteria over the hint of inter-racial romance between Harry Belafonte and Joan Fontaine in Darryl F. Zanuck's *Island in the Sun*, a steamy melodrama that generated notoriety in the press even as it was under production in Trinidad in late 1956. But it is fair to say that Zanuck's confused parable of US racial tension, clumsily displaced into the Caribbean (with Belafonte again embodying American and West Indian blacks at once), is itself fairly shot through with anxiety over miscegenation. Belafonte plays David Boyeur, a charismatic labour organizer and populist agitator on the fictional island of Santa Marta ('our homegrown revolutionary', the grandfatherly colonial governor lightheartedly dubs him) who ominously instructs a visiting American journalist that the island's most pressing concern is 'the colour problem'. ('What we want is equality,' he vows grimly.) The correspondent's take on this tip, oddly, is to 'out' the mixed-race ancestry of the fading planter-aristocracy's most prominent family — much to the consternation of its marriageable teenage daughter, who is secretly pregnant by the governor's dashing son (himself passing through Santa Marta on his way to Oxford after a Middle Eastern stint in the colonial service). By contrast, the family's resentful, ne'er-do-well son, who is standing against Boyeur for a seat in the island's legislature, briefly tries to make political hay out of his newfound pedigree by eagerly pleading to a surly and skeptical crowd, 'I am one of you!' The governor's young (white) aide-de-camp, meanwhile, has openly, if chastely, taken up with Margaret Seton, a self-possessed West Indian shop clerk (played by sultry Ohioan, Dorothy Dandridge) who has grown tired of a lengthy but unproductive flirtation with Boyeur. Of all the film's mixed-race couples, then, separatists should have found the least to object to in Belafonte and Fontaine, as theirs — the only pair composed of a black man and white woman — is also the only one to abort before it ever lifts off. In a disjointed climactic dialogue in which the would-be lovers testily trade racial suspicions, recriminations, and regrets, Belafonte ultimately spurns Fontaine's advances: 'My people wouldn't understand,' he concludes. 'They'd think I'd betrayed them.' Segregationists could breathe easy: black men would *voluntarily* keep to their own kind.

50. Andrew Ross, *No Respect: Intellectuals and Popular Culture* (New York: Routledge, 1989), 64.

51. Ibid., 77.

52. In view of the fact that rock and roll was so often denounced as 'degenerate' music, a final aside on *Bop Girl*'s romantic subplot may be of interest. In order for the union of Bob-the-calypso-herald and Jo-the-erstwhile-rocker

to be completed, Bob must dump his domineering fiancée, a eugenics enthusiast with a single-mindedly clinical ambition to bear her crew-cut boyfriend's baby. That the *new* couple implicitly eschews the ideology of race purity (according to the reading I advanced earlier, Bob rather laughably stands in for the domesticated Negro) presumably signifies their broad-mindedness.

53. Gene Santoro, 'Folk's Missing Link', *The Nation*, April 22, 2002, 34.
54. Alex Ross, 'Rock 101', *The New Yorker*, July 14 & 21, 2003, 91.
55. Ibid., 22.
56. Ibid., 178.
57. Ibid., 175.
58. Kavaler, 'Where go Calypso?', 21.

13

(NOT) KNOWING THE DIFFERENCE: CALYPSO OVERSEAS AND THE SOUND OF BELONGING IN SELECTED NARRATIVES OF MIGRATION

Jennifer Rahim

Culture is an embodied phenomenon. This implies that one's cultural location is not fixed to any one geographical space. Cultures, in other words, are not inherently provincial by nature. They move and evolve with the bodies that create and live them. The Caribbean civilization understands the logic of travelling cultures given that the dual forces of rootedness and itinerancy shape its diasporic ethos. Travel is how we 'do' culture. Indeed, the Caribbean's literary tradition is marked by a preoccupation with identity constructs that display allegiances to particular island locations and nationalisms, on the one hand, and transnational sensibilities that are regional and metropolitan on the other. This paper is interested in the function of the calypso as a sign of cultural identity and belonging in selected narratives that focus on the experiences of West Indian immigrants to the metropolitan centres of England and the United States. It discusses Selvon's *The Lonely Londoners*[1] and his short stories 'Calypso in London' and 'Basement Lullaby' from the collection *Ways of Sunlight*,[2] Paule Marshall's *Brown Girl, Brownstones*,[3] and Lawrence Scott's *Aelred's Sin*.[4]

No circumstance tests the relevance of a local or regional cultural form better than that of migration. Such has been the case of the calypso. The aesthetic and thematic use made of the art form in these West Indian narratives of migration is evidence of the persistent ability of its expressive modes to supply meaning, signify identity, shape consciousness, and create community. The issue of belonging is never without its intense politics of recognition, made so by the timeless difficulty of dealing with difference, primarily because difference is also what it means to be human. In this regard, the common thread that unites these texts is the calypso's function as an axis of instability around which the shifting status of cultural identity, communal and individual identification rotates. In all cases, issues of belonging, cultural 'authenticity', and reinvention are contingent upon a series of variables that include nationality, race, ethnicity, class, gender, and sexuality. These inherently restless signifiers make the terrain of identity and identification rough going given culture's radically uncontainable nature. Further, the texts are all shaped by a transnational ethic. As such, they reveal a socio-psychic cartography marked by the often-turbulent crosscurrents of relations with homes left behind and new spaces of dwelling.

Calypso and the Emigrant Community

Popular cultural forms, like music, can be powerful tools for externalizing a community's collective consciousness, communicating its sensibilities and consolidating its codes of belonging. The representational authority of popular culture, though never complete, is partly facilitated by its associative link with elements that signify the 'traditional', the 'indigenous' and the 'people'. In the case of immigration, the value of cultural markers associated with originating homelands may indeed increase to serve the need to remain connected and to maintain a distinct identity from the host country. This is partly the logic that facilitates what Paul Gilroy notes as the emergence of Jamaican reggae as a unifying catalyst for Caribbean immigrants to London. He argues that reggae 'ceased, in Britain, to signify an exclusively ethnic, Jamaican style and derived a different kind of cultural legitimacy both from a new global status and from its expression of what might be termed a pan-Caribbean culture'.[5] A similar case can be made for the Trinidadian calypso, which would have predated reggae in this capacity. For the characters depicted in Selvon's *The Lonely Londoners* and relevant short stories collected in *Ways of Sunlight*, calypso music operates as an important indicator of identity and as a means of bridging the gap with home. The narrator of *The Lonely Londoners* reveals that inquiries about the 'latest calypso number'[6] are among the first questions that more seasoned emigrants put to new arrivals at Waterloo station.

Indeed, Selvon's narratives supply moving and humorous accounts of West Indians attempting to insert themselves in an unwelcoming British environment. The music is depicted as offering a means to more aggressively assert a collective, regional identity across ethnicities and nationalisms as a front against British discriminatory practices. Homesick and socially displaced West Indians in metropolitan London turn to calypso music for a much-needed sense of community. Cultural anchoring and connectivity become increasingly necessary as they confront the traumatic reality that their race and island origins take on greater or differently politicized meanings, which keep them on the margins of the British social order. Selvon depicts calypso fetes as sites where islanders, disadvantaged by race, origin, and economic deprivation find strength in community and affirm their resilience in spite of the exclusionary status quo. The parties are not only occasions for cultural celebration; they are contexts for engineering strategies for survival and for performing subversive counter-cultural behaviour. The latter is evident, for instance, in the habit of the Barbadian Five of 'jocking waist' during the playing of the British national anthem, 'God Save the Queen' (*Londoners*).[7]

Furthermore, the art form is a vital source of income for emigrants who seem to be forever dodging the prospect of starvation and homelessness. These include characters like Mangohead and Hotboy from 'Calypso in London', Bar 20 and Fred from 'Basement Lullaby'. For those with the talent, whatever the measure, to produce the music and songs, London provides opportunities for globalization of the music, and for the possible escape from poverty and anonymity. These narratives, in particular, give useful insights into the precarious lifestyles and creative processes of struggling practitioners. In fact, the informal contexts for artistic consultation and creation, such as those provided by Rahamut's tailor shop in 'Calypso in London', corroborate, to a certain degree, Gordon Rohlehr's note with regard to the camaraderie forged by calypso artistes in metropolitan centres, where they establish the practice of meeting to exchange ideas.[8] The intensified sense of community that engenders closely knit relations among Caribbean peoples in 'exile', prompts Rohlehr to suggest the possibility of understanding this particular cultural phenomenon from the perspective of an 'unacknowledged, Caribbean federation'.[9]

What happens when cultural expression is deployed as transgression in contexts of discrimination and marginalization? What happens when traditional or 'native' cultural practices are evoked as signifiers of 'authenticity' in places distant from home? What is the role of cultural expression in conditioning modes of belonging? Questions like these focus attention on the ambivalences and paradoxes inherent in cultural performance, an arena of activity where identification practices are defined by the interplay between processes of recognition and disavowal, resistance and transformation. On this shifting terrain, it is imperative, as Stuart Hall suggests, to remember that identities are 'subject to radical historization, and are constantly in the process of change and transformation',[10] which means that culture, where identities are lodged and defines, is always about relations of power, on the one hand, and temporality of expression, on the other. As such, cultural hegemonies are constantly affected by the very margins they create. Additionally, these marginal sites are troubled by their own internal 'wars' of belonging. Insider–outsider designations are in this way simultaneously contingent on affiliations to hegemonic codes from both locations. This is certainly the problem of the emigrants in the narratives under consideration as they seek acceptance in the British metropolis and, at the same time, struggle to maintain their West Indian identities.

The presence of Selvon's West Indians in London, for instance, operates as an important critique of British authority and civility, which have been erected as *the* measure of 'high' humanity and culture. Therefore, the Barbadian Five claims that Londoners are 'too quiet'.[11] He then proceeds to condemn the unforgivable 'slackness' of city authorities for not having more street fetes as when the Lord Mayor drove through London, with 'steel band beating', and 'jumping up as if it is a West Indian carnival'.[12] Whether or not the choice of the calypso to accompany the parade of British state authority is read as nothing more than the deployment of minority culture to gain political points, its appearance doubles with the emigrants' use of the music as an anti-establishment tool. The stubborn politics of unequal difference may remain in tact; however, this duality signals the subtle disintegration of the rigid cultural divide established between Britain and its 'Others', a disruption already encoded in the book's title.

Certainly, the emigrants are generally persistent in devising strategies that undermine the cultural hegemony of the unwelcoming, 'mother' country. These include the boys' strategic romancing of British girls, their boisterousness behavior and blatant refusal to behave like 'proper gentlemen', English style, at Harris's parties. (*Londoners*) [13] In addition, there is Tanty's gyrating, dance-floor performance to the calypso number, 'Fan Me Saga Boy Fan Me', in defiance of English ladylikeness. These counter-establishment performances signal the transgressive presence of West Indians bent on claiming the centre on their own terms. In this regard, the calypso fete functions as a theatre of crossroads, where complex cultural performances oriented towards several interdependent ends are played out. In Fanonian terms, the fete is a virtual 'zone of occult instability' (*The Wretched of the Earth*),[14] that is, the ground where the new conditions of the present open a dialogue with the expressive forms of the customary past and, in so doing, the process of reconstruction and redefinition is initiated.

The emigrants' excitable performances to the rhythm of calypso also hint at a certain degree of anxiety around the preservation of their West Indian identity in the host country, especially in the face of open prejudice and the ever-widening gulf that separates them from their originating homelands. The counterpoint of Moses' narrative distance, his tempering refrain, 'Take it easy' (*Londoners*),[15] his pensive aloofness, and his scepticism about the enactments of West Indian identification point to the arbitrary and temporal nature of cultural signification as it relates to either notions of 'authenticity', or to insider status. As the text's introspective consciousness and authorial mouthpiece, Moses' perspective unmasks the excessiveness and potentially counter-productive behavioural modes of the 'boys', which reveal a deeper experience of displacement. Anxiety about social integration and belonging is sometimes characterized by a contradictory oscillation between forces of recognition and disavowal in relation to both Britishness and West Indianness. The character of Harris is of particular interest in this regard.

Harris is the Jamaican-born, Trinidad-raised businessman whose assimilation of Britishness doubles as a product of his fear of rejection and as a survivalist strategy. He is associated with the daffodil, that infamous metaphor of English, cultural indoctrination, which Moses catches him purchasing as a gift for an influential lady-friend (*Londoners*).[16] The association sets him up as a representative of the schizophrenic subjectivity or uncomfortable hybridity sometimes symptomatic of postcolonial identities. His insecurity is evident in his repeated caution to the 'boys' that they should act like 'proper gentlemen' and not turn the fete into a 'brawl'.[17] However, to read Harris's assimilation of English dress, deportment and language as a one-sided accommodation is to minimize the complexity of his yet to be attained cultural confidence in his new identity-space that is both West Indian and British.

Harris's core mission is to make his way, as best he can, in his adopted home, which means he has to contrive methods to infiltrate the rigidly guarded status quo. Mimicry and the organization of tourist-friendly versions of the West Indian fete are his primary means of negotiating his social and economic insertion. Harris, therefore, simultaneously functions as a kind of Naipaulian mimic-man and as an ambassador for the very West Indian culture that is the source of his insecurity. Interestingly, Moses describes him as being attracted to 'English customs and thing', and liking to 'play ladeda'.[18] The word 'play' suggests the interdependence of his apparent crisis of identity and his deliberate performance of 'Englishness' as an expedient social mask to keep his white customers happy. The use-value nature of this self-construction is made all the more evident when the mask is inadvertently stripped, such as during his occasional linguistic slips into the Creole when he is in the company of other West Indians.

Seen from this perspective of the gap between hegemonic cultural assimilation and the indelible mark of his West Indian difference, the personality of Harris approaches the subversive mimicry of the 'white masked Black man' described in Homi Bhabha's reading of Fanon's *Black Skin, White Masks* (*Location*).[19] It is an image that speaks to the political agency available to the marginalized when the social constructions of race, ethnicity and nationality are manipulated to their advantage. Harris's pretence at being a 'proper gentleman' is a compensatory tactic to 'penetrate' London's exclusionary status quo, and is therefore not unlike Five's strategy of 'closehauling' the English girl to the upbeat rhythm of a calypso number as though it were a 'sentimental fox'.[20] Although they are apparent opposites, the men are not very different. Their excessive identity performances, on either side of a tenuous West Indian/British binary, reveal them to be conflicted threshold-characters in search of a comfortable social fit.

The often times uncomfortable effects of initial cultural change are the subtext of Selvon's 'Basement Lullaby', which is a painfully humorous story about two Trinidadian club musicians living in a dilapidated basement in London. During a strained, early-morning conversation, the insomniac Bar 20 accuses Fred of not getting the 'melody right' to a new calypso ('Basement Lullaby'),[21] an error he apparently repeats. Fred, however, retaliates for being kept awake by pointing out to Bar 20 that his 'drums not keeping up with the rest of the band these nights'.[22] From one perspective, the musicians' struggle to keep the calypso rhythm is a result of the physical and mental exhaustion of managing a lifestyle that is offbeat in a number of ways. They are exhausted by the unnatural hours they keep. They literally live a death-in-life existence below the ground where their very sense of the real is distorted and blurred, like the unhealthy, London smog that veils vision. Further, their basement apartment is described in almost hellish, Dantesque terms consonant with their underclass status in London. Bar 20's nostalgia for Trinidad and Fred's willed amnesia, along with his fugitive avoidance of domestic responsibility, establish them as 'exiles' in every sense of the word.

Yet, their failure to get the calypso-beat right is perhaps the influence of a 'foreign' environment that demands a different rhythm, adjustments to the tempo to suit the audience, just as the calypsos composed for the London market, according to the Trinidadian composer, Hotboy, have to transcend local/island concerns to address more international, 'topical subject[s]' ('Calypso in London').[23] 'Basement Lullaby' provides insights into the processes of change that impact on form and content, as well as on cultural sensibility, in the fledgling stages of calypso's globalization. Notions of the calypso's rhythmic 'authenticity', therefore, mediates between the musicians' alterations in its performance, whether mistakes or not, and the ignorance of 'English people' who enjoy the music, although they don't 'know the difference'.[24] The symbolic reversal of rhythmic associations suggested in the story's ironic title, 'Basement Lullaby,' one that is literally performed in Fred's vengeful piano rendition of a song to deny Bar 20 sleep, interplays with the slippage between the right and wrong beat, the known and the emergent in the enunciation of cultural performance and identification. Like the unstable 'play' of signification/enunciation of Derridean 'differance', this instability signals culture's temporality and openness to the changing conditions of historical time and place.

Homi Bhabha argues that in the case of subordinate peoples and cultures, like emigrants in dominant hegemonies, the 'issue of cultural difference emerges at points of social crises', either from a 'position of marginality or in an attempt at gaining the centre' (*The Location of Culture*).[25] He concludes that appeals to the 'authority of customary' and 'traditional practices' are in fact 'anchoring moments' that are revalued as a form of anteriority ... whose causality is effective because it returns to displace the present, to make it disjunctive'.[26] This necessary relocation of past or native cultural practices in the present is a means of ensuring historical continuity, and of erecting a political front against the marginalization of difference. However, it is possible to read this disjuncture of the totalizing logic of the dominant culture by the incommensurability of the marginal as having the dual effect of producing resistant forms of communal coherence that at the same time disrupt their own terms of representation or enunciation in light of the new conditions of the present. Therefore, when calypso and its associative behavioural patterns are evoked in the ritualized performances of West Indian cultural 'authenticity', those very 'anchoring moments' are destabilized as old, and emerging identities vie for space. The challenge of Selvon's characters, for instance, is to negotiate their way to a place of comfort with the 'newness' they are becoming, even as they appeal to 'customary' identity markers out of necessity for survival in conditions of threat, to become institutionalized as 'authentic' signs of West Indianness.

In Paule Marshall's *Brown Girl, Brownstones*, the ambivalent relationship between cultural belonging and change induced by immigration is also a powerful theme. The novel deals with the experience of first-generation Barbadians in New York City and focuses on the conflicts of integration and survival experienced by the Boyce family. In Marshall's narrative, the calypso operates as a surveillance tool, deployed by the American-Barbadian community to punish nonconformists and the rebellious. In the novel's key scene, that is, the wedding reception of Gatha Steed's daughter, the renegade Deighton Boyce is ostracized by the community for his rebellious stance on its materialistic identity-code. Significantly, it is during the band's playing of the 1943 calypso, 'Small island go back where you come from', by the Trinidadian Invader, that Deighton enters the dance hall. According to Paula Morgan, the song was originally composed to criticize the large-scale migrations of West Indians to wartime Trinidad.[27] However, Marshall's redeployment of the song transcends its original intention to generate several trajectories of overlapping meanings. For instance, the wedding guests affirm their Barbadian–West Indian identity and form a community frontline against North American politics of exclusion. The performance, however, is split along competing lines of differentiation consonant with the recognition of a generic West Indian identity, and its simultaneous disavowal in order to assert a distinctive, Barbadian nationality, now reconstructed in the capitalist terms of a transnational, Barbadian-American self-understanding.

Deighton's appearance on the dance floor demonstrates his insider–outsider status. An antagonistic terrain of inter-group discrimination is unveiled, with the calypso used as a weapon of exclusion. Following the lead of his wife Silla, the dancers form a virtual wall that blocks Deighton out of their circle. Sexuality and nationality intersect as his rejection is charted via his unfulfilled desire for Silla's body during her dance with Seon Brathwaite. Silla deliberately denies him access to its pleasure when she refuses to beckon him from the margins of the dance floor, and so claim him on behalf of the community. Instead, her laughter, which is stimulated by her seeing him and then disavowing his presence, coincides with the chorus of Lord Invader's 'Small Island' (1943):[28] 'Small island, go back where you come from'.[29] Deighton's unforgivable crime is that he is and is not a 'real-real Bajan Man'.[30] Further, in addition to being considered a delinquent in his Barbadian-American community, his womanizing, easy-going nature, and lack of productivity sets him up as a 'kind of Trinidadian', an identity that is reinforced by the fact that he is taunted and expelled during the singing of a Trinidadian calypso.

Interestingly, in this instance, Trinidadian identity emerges as the fetishized Other of Barbadian identity. The notion of a regional, West Indian identity is evidently fractured along territorial lines, where differentiation is based on popular stereotypes. For instance, when dancing begins at the reception, Bajan identity is distinguished from a truancy that is manifestly Trinidadian. So that on observing the dancers take to the floor, Florrie Trotman comments, 'Wha'lah, look at them. Their guts full now and they getting on worse than Trinidadians.'[31] The association of Trinidadians with bad behaviour or laissez-faire temperaments also appears in Selvon's narratives, and when performed by non-Trinidadians like the Barbadian Five, there is possibly a 'Trini' connection. Five grew up in Trinidad, the place where one apparently learns how to 'misbehave' in a number of ways. Similarly, in Selvon's 'Calypso in London', the composer Hotboy, a name that incidentally reinforces an associated licentiousness with the practitioners of the art form, is an opportunistic loafer who lives by mysterious means. Having no fixed employment, he spends most of his time loitering at Rahamut's tailor-shop, which serves as an improvised music studio when the need arises. Clearly, there is some kind of consensus about Trinidadians and slackness, a stereotype that concurs with Rohlehr's commentary on the origins of Atilla's 1944 calypso, 'Reply to Englishman'. The calypso was composed as a response to a letter written to the *Guardian* newspaper in which the writer whose penname was Englishman, accused Trinidad of 'having the greatest percentage of slackers in the Empire'.[32]

At the same time, however, this very capacity for enjoyment and spontaneity doubles as counter-hegemonic resistance in environments that marginalize West Indian emigrants and attempt to undermine their joy of life, making them, like Silla, insensitive, mechanized pawns in the capitalist race for survival. At the wedding, therefore, the older Brathwaite dismisses Silla's objection to dancing by recalling her youthful days in Barbados when, on Saturday nights, he would see her 'wucking up' herself to the Bajan Brumlee Band until, on one occasion, he witnessed her collapse from pure exhaustion on the grass.[33] Silla's physical energy, sexual vibrancy, and affinity with the earth are in direct contrast to her robotic, sexually frigid and joyless life in New York. For the emigrants, the island exists in memory as a pastoral paradise lost, whose past can only be reproduced in the ritualized performances of associated, often stereotypical, cultural practices. Brathwaite's rationale for having a good time is therefore as follows: 'we's in death. So le'we drink our little rum and have our little spree till it come.'[34] His philosophy captures both the temporality of human existence and the death-like, exilic condition that immigration represents. These conditions intensify the need to reclaim, in whatever measure, the culture of home. This accounts for his repeated use of the possessive pronoun 'our' with reference to 'rum' and 'spree', icons of a romanticized version of West Indian belonging, encoded in one of Lord Invader's calypsos to which they dance, 'Don't Stop the Carnival' (1939):[35] 'All the West Indian love their carnival / Lord, don stop the carnival.'[36]

A national Barbadian and transnational Barbadian–American binary is constructed with the former representing backwardness, poverty and failure. The latter serves almost cannibalistically to nourish the myth of immigration as a narrative of progress to be consumed in at least two ways. On the one hand, the myth functions as a placebo for emigrants in the throes of hardship and disillusionment in their new homelands. On the other, it offers inspiration to those left behind, who fuel its regeneration by buying into its promises. One can therefore understand, though not easily forgive, Silla's decisive act of rejection following Deighton's retreat into spiritualism and non-profit service. She reports his illegal status to the immigration authorities, which results in his deportation to Barbados. Her betrayal is consonant with her construction of the island as trapped in a state of stasis, or absence, evident in her reaction to Selina's consideration of the family's possible return to Barbados. Silla angrily asks her daughter, 'Live where! Barbados is a place to live too?'[37]

Deighton is irredeemably the small-islander, that is, Barbadian and not the transcendent Barbadian-American because he is the one who fails the community in the battle for survival in North America. He is therefore dishonorably discharged to his native homeland. His death by possible suicide before he actually reaches Barbados symbolizes his absolute displacement. He belongs nowhere since the island is largely his imaginary homeland, a paradise of dreams. The complexly combined national, regional and metropolitan features that circumscribe concepts of transnationality expose the tense relations that regulate identification. The nation and expressions of nationalism, however imagined or politicized, remain key players in the construction of transnational identities. As such, the theorizing of the Caribbean trans-nation should guard against its constitution in ways that either romantically privilege, perhaps inadvertently, the promises afforded by the prefix 'trans', or that suppress the presence and influence of the 'national' in the reinvention of identities in the new spaces of dwelling. This is so because, like its embattled root nationalism, the construction of the nation beyond fixed boundaries is a modality that is equally troubled and challenged by its own problems of differentiation and consolidation.

The Calypso and Sexual Citizenship

If it is accepted that the calypso, like reggae, has functioned with a certain degree of success as a barometer of social consciousness, an expression of collective identity, and a vehicle for anti-establishment critique, then the art form very much resembles a version of Glissant's notion of a 'natural poetics', which he argues expresses a community's 'shared attitude', facilitating the most 'daring or the most artificial of experiences'.[38] In other words, a social group's 'natural poetics' is potentially revolutionary or anti-establishment, even as it is also a stabilizing or consolidating representation of the everyday existence of the social body. The problem, of course, with any collective cultural paradigm is its tendency to enforce a reductive, homologous logic that usually compresses and blurs a series of variables that include race, ethnicity, age, class, and sexuality in the interest of promoting a notion of the whole. Similarly, with respect to a national or regional music, the unspoken presumption is its unproblematic symbiotic tie with a collective identity. In other words, a popular expressive mode like the calypso can, voluntarily or not, emerge as a signifier for a particular brand of cultural nationalism. This accounts for the production and dissemination of associations like calypso is to Trinidadian and reggae is to Jamaican.

The arena of sexuality, however, is one of the spaces where the antinomies inherent in any essentialist cultural paradigm, which may include a national or regional culture, will reveal the accommodative limits of its frame, or will 'disturb' what Bhabha calls 'its anointed horizons of territory and tradition' ('Culture's In-Between').[39] In all the texts under consideration, for instance, the calypso, as it relates to transnational identities, surfaces as a regulator of social fit in the tumultuous terrain of sexuality. Unlike Glissant's 'natural poetics', the music works to reinforce, rather than challenge the exclusionary politics of the status quo on the issue of sexual citizenship. The general rule seems to be that the music functions as a crusader against the legitimacy of nonheterosexual identities, operating as a disciplinary panoptic eye (Foucault, III. Discipline 3)[40] that sanctions 'right' sexual pairing and 'appropriate' reproductions of gender behavioural modes.

Like its Jamaican relative dancehall, calypso serves as a disseminator of anti-gay propaganda, feeding off the most derogatory stereotypes of homosexual identities. Timothy Chin's 'Bullers and Battymen: Contesting Homophobia in Black Popular Culture and Contemporary Caribbean Literature', for instance, raises the issue of Jamaican dancehall as a regulatory medium for a prescriptive heterosexuality. He particularly references the controversy surrounding the 'deeply rooted homophobia' evident in Buju Banton's song, 'Boom Bye Bye'.[41] Moreover, Chin identifies an intellectual strain that displays an aggressive territorial protectionism of 'indigenous' culture, one that is willing to skirt the issue of homophobia in the Caribbean in an effort to valorize its cultural productions. He therefore calls for a 'cultural politics that can critique as well as affirm — a politics that recognizes, in other words, the heterogeneous and contradictory . . . nature of all cultural forms'.[42]

In relation to the calypso's role as moral adjudicator of sexuality and sexual practice, Rohlehr's findings in his essay, 'The Construction of Masculinity in the Trinidad & Tobago Calypso', are particularly pertinent. Rohlehr admits the corpus of songs that target homosexuality is relatively small; however, he notes that the 'homotextuality of calypso' reveals, among other things, 'a possible connection between rigid constructions of masculinity, male fear of effeminization and homophobia',[43] with a significant number of popular performers including General Grant, Buju Banton and Shabba Ranks, who have 'called for the murder of homosexual males'.[44] Homosexuality, Rohlehr argues, is selected as 'one of the worse signs of masculinity gone off-track',[45] and points to an inherent double standard that infects the moral surveillance of sexuality as 'antigay paranoia has on occasion masked itself as moral righteousness, with calypsonians assuming the patriarchal roles of prophets, warners and spokesmen for the same "straight" society that they more normally un-mask and demolish with their reductive laughter'.[46]

In both Selvon's *The Lonely Londoners* and Marshall's *Brown Girl, Brownstones*, the dance floor of the calypso fete is a microcosmic social stage where heterosexuality or heterosexual performances to the music of calypso signify 'West Indianness'. Marshall's text tentatively approaches a questioning of a presumed or prescribed relationship between 'compulsory heterosexuality' and West

Indian trans/national identity in the calypso-dance between the pre-adolescent friends, Selina Boyce and Beryl Challenor. This occurs prior to the community's ostracism of Selina's father, Deighton, to the music of Invader's calypso, 'Small Island, Go Back Where You Really Come From'. After a tense exchange between the friends about the implications of dancing together, Selina's defiantly reacts to Beryl's caution that they were 'kinda of old for that' as follows: 'I don't give one damn, d'ya hear? Not one damn in hell about anything'.[47] The exchange signals the girls' awareness of the inappropriateness of the act given that their ages apparently place them in the zone of accommodation for such behaviour.

Despite the unspoken heterosexual code they know they will transgress by dancing together, the young friends still take to the dance-floor in the full presence of the community, and after a brief period of awkwardness, find their 'rhythm'.[48] However, with the appearance of Selina's father, the subliminal force of social norms triggers her anxious command to Beryl, 'My father's here. Lemme go,'[49] as the metatext of their inappropriate paring, momentarily transgressed, is reintroduced. Selina's desire to be free of Beryl oscillates between her desire to go to her father and substitute for her mother's refusal to partner him, and the fear of his disapproval. Neither materializes as Deighton signals to her 'to remain where she was',[50] a command that is an obvious contradiction of the tacit gender compatibility codes at work in the larger group. Father and daughter, are therefore ideologically positioned outside the consensual frame of the community's gender and sexuality behavioural modes at that seminal 'moment' of communal anchoring.

The adolescents, however, do not reap the rejection of the community as does Deighton for his failure to be a 'real', Bajan man. Their age apparently places them in a safety zone of indeterminacy, an intermediary position where meanings about a possible different orientation are as yet unclear, or not fully formed, given that this knowledge mediates between the girls' shared awareness of the inappropriateness of their pairing and the community's latent rejection of it. Suspicion is therefore suspended in the unknown territory of the girls being simultaneously still young enough and too old to dance together, that is, the play between knowing and not knowing the difference. Nevertheless, the heterosexual destination of Marshall's bildungsroman safely lodges Selina's adolescent sexual confusion as a symptom of maturation. This is all well and good, except that the plot's sub-textual engagement with sexual ambiguity interrupts any comfortable foreclosure regardless of an authorial design that seeks to 'right' the girls' dance and displaces, if not corrects, its appearance as a legitimate identity text within the West Indian literary canon and the wider trans/national cultural field.

Ambivalences around making a place for sexual difference within Caribbean literary and social culture are also evident even in Selvon's *The Lonely Londoners*. Ian Smith's insightful essay in 'Critics in the Dark', for instance, makes a convincing argument for the presence of a repressed homoerotic subtext in the novel. According to Smith, the homoerotic evoked and then disavowed by 'meta-narrative effects', through which writer and text are realigned to a literary canon that has 'no place' for nonheterosexual subjectivities in its discourse[51] and, by extension, as members of its national and diasporic citizenry. Selvon's text ends as follows: 'It was a summer night: laughter fell softly: it was the sort of night that if you wasn't making love to a woman you feel you was the only person in the world like that.'[52] Smith argues the 'homoerotic *double-entendre* of the closing lines' implies the difference of an unspoken *other* type of sexual union, which disrupts the heterosexual stability that the book's 'writerly consciousness,' filtered through Moses, seeks to regain at the end.[53] This corrective drive is propelled by the very 'ballads' or texts of life the narrative tells. Tales such as Cap's strange encounter with the transvestite and its subsequent regulation by hasty marriage reveal knowledge of the homoerotic, even if this is managed as sub-textual knowledge.

But even before the closing lines of *The Lonely Londoners*, Moses' largely non-participatory status at Harris's fete provides an obvious contrast to the womanizing, hyper-masculinity that figures as the West Indian, male prototype. If the fete is the space where ritualized gender performances are consolidated, Moses' posture of standing in a corner, telling Galahad 'ballads' while the fete is in full swing, is odd enough to draw the notice, if not suspicion, of Five who asks him why he is not dancing.[54] The question, of course, is weighted because it is also an unvoiced query about his not being seen dancing with a woman. Offering his age as an excuse further undermines Moses' defensive counter that he had danced 'one or two' sets: 'But you know the old man always taking things easy.'[55] His rationale, however, inadvertently associates youth with able, heterosexual partnering and relative old-age with resigned celibacy or its alternative, but not enunciated text of male partnering, albeit platonic, suggested by his standing in a corner with Galahad on the margins of the calypso fete.[56] That 'ballad', however, is merely sublimated, half-told within a script sanctioned by the normalcy of male camaraderie and Moses' bachelor status, lest it fractures the narrative's already self-conscious effort to keep its homosociality 'straight'.

Narratives of migration, whether real or fictive, that feature escape as an option from small-island homophobia have gained increasing visibility in the Caribbean literary canon and discourses on sexual identity over the last decade or so. On the whole, the known beneficiaries of these 'exits' include third generation writers like Dionne Brand, Patricia Powell, Shani Mootoo and Michelle Cliff. It seems that a combination of factors such as geographical distance, spatial largeness, and the ideological liberalism of Northern metropolises allow for greater sexual and creative freedom. Evelyn O'Callaghan, for instance, notes that immigration has allowed Jamaican writers like Powell and Cliff the space to act as ventriloquists for male homosexuality, coming as they do from an island where its 'virulent homophobia ... is almost exclusively directed in its most violent form at gay men' ('Homosexuality and Textual/Sexual Alternatives').[57]

However, is immigration the resolution to small-island discrimination against sexual difference? Shani Mootoo's lesbian lovers, Lavinia and Sarah, from *Cereus Blooms at Night* (1996),[58] for instance, disappear into the uncertain sunset of the 'Shivering Northern Wetlands',[59] to realize a love the island perhaps could not contain, albeit at the expense of Sarah's daughters. After a botched escape plan the children are left behind to suffer the consequences of living with an alcoholic, incestuous father. While there is ample evidence to establish a connection between immigration and creative freedom to 'write' homosexuality into the literary and social landscape of the Caribbean and its extended diaspora, there is a need to historicize and interrogate the myths that paint the 'North' as a haven of sexual freedom and acceptance, one that may well demystify the binary of 'foreign' liberalism as opposed to 'small island' homophobia. The already noted Janus-faced construction of immigration as narratives of socioeconomic 'progress' that at the same time conceal experiences of social exclusion and hardship may also mark the stories of immigration as escapes from small-island homophobia. Additionally, transnational reinventions of sexual identity undoubtedly continue to exist in a strained relationship with the very national and regional hegemonies emigrants may seek to escape, but to which they literally or imaginatively return.

In this context, it is interesting that calypso music surfaces at the end of Lawrence Scott's *Aelred's Sin*. The novel intricately reconstructs the life of Jean Marc de la Borde, a white Creole who, sometime in the 1960s, travels from his Caribbean island, Les Deux Isles, to become a Benedictine monk in an English monastery. The decision comes on the heels of an adolescent, same-sex relationship that ends tragically in public victimization and the 'accidental' death of his partner, Ted. After a brief experience of monastic life, Jean Marc/Aelred leaves to be with his lover, and ex-monk Edward. Both men later die of AIDS in the 1980s. The novel's epilogue, among other things, reveals the layered 'ironies' of Jean Marc's 'coming out' excursion with Edward, and their mutual friend, Joe in 1968, a period of radical sexual liberalism in Europe and North America. Several incidents converge in a critical scene when the men are walking along the seafront at Barmouth. The conflicting trajectories of Jean Marc's white, Caribbean identity, which include his Catholicism, homosexual orientation, and emigrant status, are consolidated in that symbolic borderline space, with the sea forming the bridge connecting Jean Marc's adopted English home to his Caribbean home, Les Deux Isles.

At the centre of these incidents is Jean Marc's discovery of a 'black guy playing a steel tenor pan' at the funfair.[60] The moment of recognition and connection is so powerful he exclaims: 'Calypso, man! Hear that calypso music!'[61] Reconnection with his island past via its music is actually preceded by a series of interconnected heterosexual metatexts that reinforce his condition of multiple 'exile'. Important in this regard is Joe's earlier sighting of the word QUEER written on the seawall. The discriminatory sign intersects with Jean Marc's disillusioned remark that the world outside the monastery is 'not much different',[62] in terms of its negating surveillance of homosexuality.

The inherent irony of the three men singing in unison The Drifters' song of carefree, even illicit love, 'Under the broadwalk'[63] is thereby reinforced as it excludes the men from the romantic conventions inscribed in its text. While the theme of concealment is normalized as a metaphor for heterosexual adventure, the scenario directly opposes the misadventure of the trios' defiance of the closet, as private and public space remain demarcated as illegitimate territories for their 'different' desire.

Further, several intersecting colonial and postcolonial histories that feature homosexual desire, both sadistically forced and consensual are uncovered in a palimpsest-like manner when Edward suggests, possibly in jest, that the pan player's name must be 'Jordan', Jean Marc's invented name for the slave-boy in the portrait of the eighteenth-century owner of Ashton Hall, the site of the Benedictine monastery he leaves. In the text's central mirroring scene, the narrator writes:

> Aelred stared and wondered. Then he saw his own face reflected in the glass of the portrait. His face was superimposed upon that of the boy whose face shone from beneath, so that the black face seemed to be his own.[64]

Jean Marc's/Aelred's identity therefore dovetails with the African slave in the portrait, with Mungo, the runaway slave whose story he learns from his childhood nanny Toinette, and with his adolescent mixed-race lover, Ted, whose shoes he literally wears as a junior monk. He particularly comes to recognize Jordan as his sexual and racial other, whose history reflects his own experiences of sexual violation by his homophobic schoolmates and the racialized construction of his body by his fellow English monks, one of whom seduces him in the chapel.

Significantly, the player's nationality remains unknown at the end of the 'encounter'. In spite of Edward's prompting, Jean Marc is unable to overcome his 'shyness' to ask the man where he is from. How does one read this timidity? The preference for anonymity rather than open conversation with a man possibly from his island, or one like his own, is undoubtedly entangled in John Marc's larger personal and collective history of displacement and rejection because of his ancestral connection with the white plantocracy and sexual orientation. First, Jean Marc is aware that the black panman represents a culture and race he has been taught to fear, echoing Kenneth Ramchand's designation of the phrase 'terrified consciousness' to describe the insecurity of the white, Creole elite in the context of burgeoning black postcolonial populations and cultures.[65] Second, in his case this terror takes on an additional dimension at the level of the exclusionary politics surrounding his sexual orientation, which he knows can prompt violent homophobic disapproval in his homeland. Scripts of sadistic sexual abuse by colonial masters, consensual same-sex love and homophobic violence therefore crisscross, corrupt, and interrupt each other as Lawrence attempts to undo narratives of homosexual negation in order to create a redemptive construct of Jean Marc's life. Ultimately, his recognition of the music of home doubles as a misrecognition of belonging to the island that cannot accommodate him, a religion that condemns him, and a 'mother country' that identifies him as 'QUEER'. Neither 'coming out' into the secular world, nor leaving his homophobic homeland, offers a space for real acceptance as his life is consistently policed by the same heterosexist codes, histories and laws that collude to outlaw and negate him.

While self-acceptance and reciprocated same-sex love seem to be the most treasured gifts of Jean Marc's rebellion against the moral codes of his faith and the legal surveillance of civic society, the disease AIDS brings an almost retributive closure to a life that loses, by the errors of its reactionary choices, that which it sought so hard to welcome and save. What Jean Marc finds irreconcilable as a Catholic monk is the moral grille that discriminates between his homosexual identity and his homosexual practice. For him, the recommendations of spiritual friendship in the tradition of his patron, St. Aelred, and the vow of celibacy central to his religious vocation and tradition represent an intolerable compromise and hypocrisy. His rebellion against the teachings of his faith consolidates his rejection of a host of religious, psychological and civic epistemologies that result in demonizing, pathologizing, and criminalizing his sexual orientation. What he misguidedly seeks to redeem from a history of denigration is the equal 'right' of homoerotic pleasure. However, what he also tragically discovers, as an active homosexual, are the deadly consequences of the practice.

The roots of *Aelred's Sin* certainly run too deep for oversimplification. Bolder experiments with 'homotexuality' in current Caribbean literature undoubtedly disturb the clearly demarcated boundaries around the 'anointed territory' of sexuality in their attempts to claim space for nonheterosexual identities on the terrain of human experience and knowledge. At the same time, however, they put on the table serious ethical and moral debates, often skirted by cultural theory and critical practice that are perhaps ill-equipped to address them. These issues must be the business of every human being and society: the acceptance of the complex nature of sexuality, the call to responsibility in relation to sexual practice, and the discovery of the particular sacrifices that 'desire' demands, whatever the name of its identity. The challenge remains to bravely engage the justice issues that attend claims for inclusion without compromising the very thing that legitimizes such claims, that is, the dignity of the human person.

Conclusion

The inherently fluid nature of culture and cultural identities does not change the fact that they are also territorially based and traditionalist in their behaviour and allegiances. These sample references to the calypso in the Caribbean's literary imagination point to its function as an agent of recognition, even 'authenticity' in relation to nationalist and transnationalist identity-frames, and to the changing constructions of these identities with time and travel. They also raise questions about the role of cultural artifacts or forms in the construction of discriminatory boundaries that circumscribe belonging, given their propensity to operate as signifiers of sameness that not only occlude differences, but also govern the dance-floor by exclusory means or unequal terms. West Indian belonging, indeed any identity space, is troubled by consensual and differentiation forces at the individual and collective levels. These constantly demand the re-negotiation of the terms that circumscribe insider–outsider positions. Further, the simultaneously changing and fixed dynamics of identification imply that the criteria for belonging or acceptance must also be left open to reformulations based on the differences that will always require a serious questioning of the implications of remaking codes and attitudes about belonging in order to better humanize the trans/nation dance.

Notes

1. Samuel Selvon, *The Lonely Londoners* (1956; reprint, London: Longman, 1979).
2. Samuel Selvon, *Ways of Sunlight* (1957; reprint, Essex: Longman, 1979).
3. Paule Marshall, *Brown Girl, Brownstones* (1959; reprint, New York: First Feminist Press, 1981).
4. Lawrence Scott, *Aelred's Sin* (London: Allison & Busby, 1998).
5. Paul Gilroy, *The Black Atlantic: Modernity and Double Consciousness* (Cambridge, MA: Harvard University Press, 1993), 82.
6. Selvon, *Londoners*, 10.
7. Ibid., 106.
8. Gordon Rohlehr, 'Calypso and Caribbean Identity', in *Bucknell Review: Caribbean Cultural Identities*, ed. Glyne Griffith (London: Bucknell University Press, 2001), 56.
9. Ibid.
10. Stuart Hall, 'Introduction: Who Needs "Identity"?', in *Questions of Cultural Identity*, eds. Stuart Hall and Paul du Gay (London: Sage Publications, 1996), 4.
11. Selvon, *Londoners*, 95.
12. Ibid., 94–95.
13. Selvon, *Londoners*, 96.
14. Frantz Fanon, *The Wretched of the Earth* (1961; reprint, London: Penguin Books 1990), 183.
15. Selvon, *Londoners*, 20.
16. Ibid., 95.
17. Ibid., 96.
18. Ibid., 95.
19. Homi Bhabha, *The Location of Culture* (London: Routledge, 1994), 121; Frantz Fanon, *Black Skin White Masks*, trans. Charles Lam Markmann (1952; reprint, New York: Grove Press, 1967).
20. Selvon, *Londoners*, 101.
21. Selvon, 'Basement Lullaby', in *Ways of Sunlight*, 176.
22. Ibid., 179.
23. Selvon, 'Calypso in London', *Ways of Sunlight*, 128.
24. Selvon, 'Basement Lullaby', 176.
25. Bhabha, *The Location of Culture*, 177.
26. Ibid.
27. Paula Eleanor Morgan, 'A Cross-cultural Study of the Black Female-authored Novel of Development' (PhD dissertation, University of the West Indies, St. Augustine, 1993), 141.
28. Lord Invader (Rupert Grant), 'Small Island', also 'Small Island, Go Back Where You Really Come From', in *Calypso and Society in Pre-Independence Trinidad*, Gordon Rohlehr (Tunapuna, Trinidad: Gordon Rohlehr, 1990).
29. Marshall, *Brown Girl*, 150.
30. Ibid., 173.
31. Ibid., 144.

32. Gordon Rohlehr, *Calypso and Society in Pre-Independence Trinidad* (Tunapuna, Trinidad: Gordon Rohlehr, 1990), 351.
33. Marshall, *Brown Girl*, 144.
34. Ibid., 145.
35. Lord Invader (Rupert Grant), 'Don't Stop the Carnival', in *Calypso After Midnight*. Rounder 11661–1841, 199.
36. Marshall, *Brown Girl*, 147.
37. Ibid., 43.
38. Édouard Glissant, *Caribbean Discourse: Selected Essays*, trans. with Introduction by Michael Dash (Charlottesville: University Press of Virginia, 1989), 120.
39. Homi K. Bhabha, 'Culture's In-between', in *Questions of Cultural Identity*, eds. Stuart Hall and Paul du Gay (London: Sage Publications, 1996), 54.
40. Michel Foucault, *Discipline and Punish: The Birth of the Prison*, trans. Alan Sheridan (New York: Vintage, 1995), 3.
41. Timothy Chin, '"Bullers" and "Battymen": Contesting Homophobia in Black Popular Culture and Contemporary Caribbean Literature', *Callaloo* 20, no.1 (1997): 128–29; Buju Banton, 'Boom Bye Bye', *Early Years (90-95)*. CD VP Records 2100, 2001.
42. Ibid., 128.
43. Gordon Rohlehr, 'The Construction of Masculinity in the Trinidad and Tobago Calypso', in *A Scuffling of Islands: Essays on Calypso* (Trinidad: Lexicon, 2004), 264–65.
44. Ibid., 272.
45. Ibid.
46. Ibid.
47. Marshall, *Brown Girl*, 146.
48. Ibid.
49. Ibid., 149.
50. Ibid.
51. Ian Smith, 'Critics in the Dark', *Journal of West Indian Literature* 8 no. 2 (1999): 2–9.
52. Selvon, *Londoners*, 126.
53. Smith, 3.
54. Selvon, *Londoners*, 105.
55. Ibid.
56. Ibid., 103.
57. Evelyn O'Callaghan, '"Compulsory Heterosexuality" and Textual/Sexual Alternatives in Selected Texts by West Indian Women Writers', in *Caribbean Portraits: Essays on Gender Ideologies and Identities*, ed. Christine Barrow (Kingston: Ian Randle Publishers, 1998), 309–10.
58. Shani Mootoo, *Cereus Blooms at Night* (Vancouver: Press Gang Publishers, 1996).
59. Ibid., 29.
60. Scott, *Aelred's Sin*, 441.
61. Ibid.
62. Ibid., 440–41.
63. Ben E. King and the Drifters, 'Under the Broadwalk', *Hits Collection*. 1XCD, 1997.
64. Scott, *Aelred's Sin*, 78–79.
65. Kenneth Ramchand, *The West Indian Novel and Its Background* (1970; reprint, London: Heinemann, 1983), 223–24.

14

'EVERYBODY DO THE DANCE': THE POLITICS OF UNIFORMITY IN DANCEHALL AND CALYPSO

Kezia Page

There is dancing in the calypso. Dance! If the words mourn the death of a neighbour, the music insists that you dance; if it tells the troubles of a brother, the music says dance. Dance to the hurt! Dance! If you catching hell, dance, and the government don't care, dance! Your woman take your money and run away with another man, dance. Dance! Dance! Dance!

Earl Lovelace, *The Dragon Can't Dance*[1]

I cannot be the only Jamaican that is sick of this "Dance Craze." What is happening to dancehall is what I hate most about soca. Don't get me wrong I can deal wid di one an two "SWINGING ENGINE" or any wining song for that matter. But the "put u rag in the air and jump" — "do the iwer, butterfly, shadow, wave" ... these are the songs that simply perpetuate a HERD MENTALITY. A mentality that has spilled over into dancehall

Anika Smith, 'Dancehall overhype ... or more like over the hype'.[2]

The Earl Lovelace and Anika Smith epigraphs interpolate two different moments in Caribbean history, though both are critically concerned with how dance functions in specific sub-contexts: one as a form of resistance in 1960s Trinidad and the other as a critique of hyper-similarity and banality four decades later in Calypso and Dancehall traditions of the last decade of the twentieth century and the first five years of the twenty first. In the prologue to Lovelace's *The Dragon Can't Dance*, dance is a means to subvert myriad problems, losses, and challenges. Besides resistance — on Calvary Hill where people gather to 'lime', the trinity of 'Idleness, Laziness, and Waste' does not reign, dance offers mobilization, action to the inactive masses, and more than just action — art. Dance. Dance! In statement and exclamation dance is intimately connected with music and lyric. The narrator's call to movement is resonant with a history Gordon Rohlehr traces in *Calypso and Society in Pre-Independence Trinidad*;[3] a movement which underscores that this call to dance was heard on the slave ship under command of the Captain's whip where, 'Africans were forced to dance for exercise',[4] and then in resistance and reclamation from the mouths of slaves in the New World:

> Slave dances were viewed by the planters with a mixture of suspicion and tolerance. On the one hand they provided gatherings of black people with private space and the power of assembly, and had been known to lead to rebellious uprisings throughout the Antilles. On the other hand, they provided therapy for the enslaved trapped in the tedious ménage of plantation labour.[5]

Anika Smith might be surprised to note that as West African dance forms evolved into West Indian dances, the therapy–resistance duo continued, and that dances such as the Calinda, the Jhouba, the Bel Air, and the Quadrille involved specific movements to specific rhythms, some more formalized than others, though Rohlehr points out in his discussion of the Calinda that, '[b]lack people retained, as ever, their own sound, sounds, style and distinctive aesthetic: atonality and kinesis, discord and ecstatic utterance under the power of the spirit.'[6] Rohlehr's description here suggests that while the Calinda was a *community* dance performed to specific music, the codes were understood without instruction, or didactic choreographing. Perhaps it is the latter that troubles Smith about this present dance moment, a moment that is similar yet for her disturbingly different from older forms of communal dancing even those beyond the Caribbean context to other dispensations of black culture. It is the instruction, 'everybody do the dance', the rapid rate of these instructions, move after move, and what for Anika Smith is most objectionable — the dances themselves, the 'Scooby Doo', the 'flowers a bloom', the 'summer bounce', the 'chakka chakka', dances that not only limit creativity and individuality, but shepherd the masses into dance after silly dance.

Rohlehr's 'Calypso and Identity' is empathetic to Smith's concerns. In this article he traces the development of Calypso and suggests that the music has evolved under a form and function rule: the call-and-response, the war song, work songs, and celebration. Among Rohlehr's criticisms of contemporary 'celebration calypsos', is that they become mere 'action songs': 'there is also the question of involving the listeners, the people who are celebrating, in the music, so that you create lyrics which give them something to do. There are many action songs in which the singer is telling the listeners, the party goers, what they should do.'[7] Rohlehr attributes this trend to the influence of Jamaican practices popularized, for example, by Byron Lee.[8]

With this background in mind, my paper considers the following questions: How do we make sense of the shift from dance organized as rebellion, and the contemporary moment both Smith and Rohlehr are concerned with, dance so organized and instructed that it generates uniformity–anti-rebellion — a herd mentality? How does this moment raise questions about artistes' desire to provide access to both Calypso and Dancehall by making them appear less political, less localized, and as music more concerned with reaching a global audience through dance? This paper focuses on the calypso 'Stranger'[9] by Shadow and Elephant Man's dancehall song 'Signal de Plane'[10] as evidence of the performative moment Smith is critical of. I want to suggest with careful analysis of the songs and important contextual evidence, that both songs and perhaps the moment they are apart of are more and do more than what Smith reduces them to in her critique. How do the songs 'Stranger' and 'Signal de Plane' capture an ethos that is at once concerned with making space for the outsider and marginalizing that same outsider? Is there in these dances another kind of dual moment — therapy–entertainment and resistance? Might these dances, in their invitation to uniformity, be a way of charting identity by using patriotic calls to assembly in a contemporary moment when identity is most easily defined around sameness?

Shadow's 'Stranger', the winning 2001 road-march song, is the narrative of how he, Shadow, a kind Trinidadian man, teaches a white Australian woman how to dance and how to enjoy Carnival:

> I'm a stranger said a pretty gal
>
> I came down here for the Carnival
>
> So this music, have me in a trance
>
> Want to play mas' teach me how to dance
>
> Buy a little rag and put it in your pocket

> Buy a little flag that's the way you do it
>
> Find yourself a band and find a good position
>
> When the music blast, you'll find out how to play mas'
>
> When they say rag, pull yu rag (repeat)
>
> When they say flag, pull you flag (repeat) an' wave it
>
> Do you ting — jump up jump up, wine up wine up (repeat)
>
> When they say wine roll you waist (repeat)
>
> Jump up jump up, wine up wine up.

In the first verse and the chorus the gist of the song is clear and so are the politics. It is the stranger who finds herself in Trinidad and who approaches Shadow for dance lessons. As part of this dance class, Shadow instructs the visitor on what to purchase — a flag and a rag, and then alerts her when to use the essential paraphernalia. Shadow's 'Stranger' is ironically not for strangers, but is a first place mobilizer for insiders who already know what to do when he shouts 'rag' and 'flag', and find in his narrative a kind of power and pleasure, as revellers dance along with the fictional stranger — only better. It is useful to note here that Shadow's 'Stranger' is quite similar to Kitchener's 'Miss Tourist', the 1968 road-march winner, save of course the lyrical genius of Lord Kitchener, and the fact that by stanza three 'Miss Tourist' unlike the stranger, looks as though she were born in Trinidad, and by stanza four she 'breaks away'.[11]

Kitchener and Shadow's narratives of white tourist women in Trinidad at carnival time desiring to be taught how to experience and enjoy carnival together provide an important context for the follow-along lyrics of Shadow's 'Stranger'. Both songs use carnival, more specifically dance in 'Stranger,' to talk about tourism and sex. Implicit in the tourists' search for a good time is a sexual experience with a local man. Indeed, both Kitchener and Shadow's songs imply that the developing friendships and the exotic dance classes do not all happen in public. Consistent also in both 'Miss Tourist' and 'Stranger', its 2001 road-march winning reincarnation, is a power shift between tourist and local. While these women might have expected to take advantage of friendly and easy access into Caribbean entertainment, they are in fact the ones who are exploited as they are made into spectacle, and perhaps worse. Their stories inspire Calypso lyrics that poke fun at tourists while simultaneously moving natives to dance beyond any stranger's learned reach. How might we use the purposefulness of Shadow's instructions in 'Stranger', that is, the way the song grants access to outsiders and facilitates a kind of choreographed unity for insiders, as a way to understand the shift from the unspoken intuited codes of community dance, to the overt speaking of these codes? Are some of these codes in effect non-transferable?

The song's call and response quality, 'when I say rag, show your rag', et cetera, though undoubtedly a call to solidarity, operates on two levels because of the inclusion of the stranger. These levels might be more clearly understood in the call, 'when I say wine, roll yu waist', where the call might be expected to yield thousands of black people performing at various skill levels the sexualized waist rolling that continues to be spectacle on Black Entertainment Television (BET) and MTV networks. However, with the presence of the first-timer 'stranger', that spectacle is reversed because waist rolling is not always as simple as it sounds. Here then is a song, apparently intent on including a white Australian visitor that might have as its result exclusion. While 'Stranger' seems to extend solidarity beyond national lines by including the white Australian woman in the revelry, encouraging her to join a band, it is possible to read this invitation as poking fun, as insiders are aware that these skills are not simply transferred by the instruction, 'roll yu waist'. In effect, Shadow, by making a spectacle of the outsider strengthens the bonds of the insider community, for here, knowing the dance is the way one indicates her or his place in the community. In addition, the idea of community is reinforced as the community knowing how, responds to the calls together. At the same time 'Stranger' does not simply reinforce community by speaking in the community lingo but also reinforces the community by drawing borders through what might be termed a choreographic map.

Shadow's 'Stranger' is part of a road-march tradition arguably begun in 1991 with Super Blue's road-march winner 'Get Something an' Wave'.[12] This call to solidarity, under the particular label of patriotism, is fuelled by the failed Abu Bakr uprising of the old year, and uses performative sameness to respond to political difference and discord. 'Get something an' wave', suggests that there is spiritual power in getting together, evidenced by mother Muriel who is ringing the Baptist bell and waving the flag. Paul Gilroy's discussion on sameness and hypersimilarity in *Against Race* is particularly compelling here as we consider the effect and meaning of Super Blue's song.[13] The call to solidarity and unity around spiritually based nationalist terms, the employment of a figure such as Matriarch Muriel, whose Baptist hands now wave the flag in an effort to engender national pride and conversely to reject anti-national sentiment, and the fact that this would be encouraged and disseminated by rallying the masses to 'get something an' wave' might be exactly what Gilroy takes to task:

> When we think about the tense relationship between sameness and difference analytically, the interplay of consciousness, territory, and place becomes a major theme. It affords insights into the core of conflicts over how democratic social and political life should be organized at the start of the twenty-first century. We should try to remember that the threshold between those two antagonistic conditions can be moved and that identity-making has a history even though its historical character is often systematically concealed. Focusing on identity helps us to ask in what sense the recognition of sameness and differentiation is a premise for modern political culture.[14]

Gilroy's discussion here is relevant to both the political and the popular: Super Blue's response to a national crisis is to encourage solidarity through the instructions to sameness, for by encouraging sameness difference is immediately identified, and such is the case with the white Australian stranger who even with a good position in a band, with flag and rag in hand, seems destined to standout.

Gilroy's discourse on hypersimilarity as it impacts the 'great resonance' of the term, identity, is both confirmed and complicated by a figure such as Mother Muriel whose response to the nation-upsetting, radical position of Abu Bakr and his followers is specific to her religious-cultural experience. A discussion of why this unlikely Afro-Trinidadian figure and the artifacts of her African-based Protestant faith with providential force are able to mobilize Trinidadians to get something an' wave and free the country from the grip of curfews might be connected to Gilroy's position here:

> Links can be established between political, cultural, psychological, and psychoanalytic concerns. We need to consider, for example, how the emotional and affective bonds that form the specific basis of raciological and ethnic sameness are composed, and how they become patterned social activities with elaborate cultural features. How are they able to induce conspicuous acts of altruism, violence, and courage? How do they motivate people toward social interconnection in which individuality is renounced or dissolved into the larger whole represented by a nation, a people, a "race," or even an ethnic group?[15]

One might argue that if mother Muriel inspires Trinidadians to 'get something an' wave', it is not because she is a figure with whom all Trinidadians can identify, nor because her bell and prophecies signify the political pull of the Spiritual Baptists in Trinidad, but instead it might be that if this old Baptist woman wants to jump up in Carnival it is clear that the political upheaval in Trinidad and the curfews in response have upset the patience of the very saints.

Conversely, Super Blue's employment of Mother Muriel might highlight for us the 'affective bonds' that compose sameness in the Afro-Trinidadian context. What is it about Muriel that would win a Road March title or 'motivate people to social interconnection'? There are at least two important factors that I wish to outline:

(1) Muriel calls on a tradition of subversion that inspired the very roots of Carnival. Not only does she subvert the efforts of the coup makers by encouraging patriotic sameness by waving flags, she simultaneously subverts the authority of the

government and the police by shouting with Super Blue 'no curfew'. Here Muriel joins or leads the national critique of government that is arguably a Caribbean 'pastime', often drawing ordinary Trinidadians together as nationals.

(2) In addition to these somehow small, nation-unifying rebellions, Mother Muriel's very presence in Carnival as a spiritual Baptist or religious woman unsettles (European based) notions that the spirit and the flesh are separate. To the 'ting a ling' of Mother Muriel's bell, Super Blue reclaims Carnival as seamlessly political, spiritual, and *pleasurable*. The weight of this 1991 call to sameness, though interestingly constructed around subversion interpolates a moment that is ripe for national compliance.

Still there is more to be made of this moment that understands sameness in dance, and sameness with a dance-teacher-to-boot, than as simply limiting access to distinct localized communities and identities and instead as a method of also allowing access to individuals outside of Caribbean and Caribbean Diaspora communities. Calypso and Dancehall artistes have contended that 'action songs' present another way to effectively take their wares to the global market, and that this means might appear less confrontational, less exclusionary — particularly with reference to homophobia — and therefore more suitable for international consumption.

The implications of seeming to include the stranger are numerous. Indeed, the narrative of Shadow's welcome and invitation to learn the codes of playing mas' is the very moment that demonstrates Shadow's — Calypso and dancehall artistes — global consciousness and market savvy. His willingness to at least gesture toward extending the community of revellers is appropriately configured around consumption, in this case the Australian is told what to purchase, 'buy a rag', and 'buy a flag', secure or purchase a place in a band; anything it seems, even access to the community can be had at a price. In fact, Shadow's posturing as the kind native, and more specifically the available and friendly native culture guide, is facilitated by the ease with which instructions can be given to become part of the community and by extension how narrowly this community seems to be defined. On the surface, Caribbean music is fun and accessible, and Caribbean artists are friendly to tourist-strangers. Songs such as 'Stranger' with dance instructions included are certainly more exportable, more global in their reach.

Many of these same questions raised in the Calypso tradition intersect with questions about hypersimilarity in dancehall music. Elephant Man's 'Signal de Plane' is one of the first in this new wave of dancehall songs to have contributed to the 'everybody do the dance', follow-the-instruction ethos. Elie's 'dancehall nice again' vibe like Shadow's 'Stranger' is couched in patriotic terms: 'dancing a Jamaica middle name'. Then, to solidify the bonds of what he terms the 'dancehall fraternity', he instructs — John, Bogle, Keeva, Stacy — his audience, on the codes of how to be good citizens: 'Visa fi go a Englan a strain / immigration a call out yu name / nuh mek yu fren get buss/signal de plane.' The call to 'signal de plane', that is, to do the dance is simultaneously a call to caution when there is danger ahead. The dance move actually mimics hand movements of ground crew agents or taxi agents — with added waist movement of course — as they guide airplanes in and out of parking spaces. This rhythmic warning certainly offers resistance to draconian US–UK anti-other immigration policies as well as includes dancers outside of the specific community (who can follow along and do the dance but do not know what they are doing), in the gesture of resistance.

Like Shadow, Elephant Man plays with the layers of insider–outsider as he creates resistance and access in the same lyrical brew. Unlike Shadow however, Elephant Man's resistance may not be about exclusion but inclusion; as he mobilizes both insiders and outsiders to 'do the dance', outsiders are included in the symbolic signalling against immigration laws. While the outsider in 'Stranger' is quite clearly the white tourist and perhaps tacitly those who are on the outskirts of Carnival culture, in 'Signal de Plane' insiders and outsiders are not always easily defined. At the centre is the dancehall fraternity, the ostensible party community who along with Elephant Man beckons to the rest of Jamaica to claim their national birthright — 'dancing a Jamaica middle name' — and use dance as a national unifying element. The 'dancehall nice again' vibe intended for those in the dancehalls and those outside is a call to stop the fighting and 'the segregation whey a gwaan'. Still, it is understood that despite Elephant Man's desire to dance unity into national policy, fractious behaviour in the dancehalls continues, and some Jamaicans will not participate in dance as anti-immigration plane signalling, or in dancing even for dancing sake. Jamaican culture maintains a strong puritanical strand in keeping with a protestant ethic that for many has meant a religious subculture that frowns on dance and most certainly the kind of dancing found in dancehalls. In addition, for many, their particular protestant subculture has been their entryway to middle-class society. The insiders — Jamaicans, might not have both feet inside as Elephant Man generalizes inside. In fact, Elie's call to dance/unity upsets an imbricated sociocultural history that maintains to the present. The outsider category might include Jamaicans who choose not to participate in this kind of dance as resistance and as unification, and it might include the numbers of non-Jamaicans in dancehalls all over the world who follow the 'energy god'[16] move after move but do not understand what he is saying and the symbolic resistance this move making implies.

Ultimately, 'Signal de Plane' does what 'Stranger' does: it makes insiders and outsiders of people around dance. Both Elephant Man and Shadow seem invested in solidifying identity around culture and nation, choreographing borders in Shadow's case by adding currency to the art form by introducing a foreign body that needs to be instructed on the codes of participation, and thus creating an insider community by virtue of the stranger. The white Australian's presence also adds to the complexity of the carnivalesque as the stranger becomes the spectacle and not the locals. Similarly, Elephant Man uses dance to inspire national pride and unity, and to engender in those willing to dance and enjoy themselves the symbolic and covert powers of community dancing. Elephant Man seems to be saying to those of the community audience that Jamaican dancing is a powerful thing with relevance beyond the dancehalls. In the same way that Shadow encourages Trinidad and Tobago unity in the face of an encroaching tourist participation in Carnival, Elephant Man proposes dance as a way to reclaim the violence-ridden dancehalls and by extension to stay national troubles with unified coordinated movement, while at the same time layering the meaning of the song with ironic symbolisms and the politics of borders.

These trends around inclusion and exclusion are consistent in the Calypso and Dancehall of the early 1990s, and are certainly popularized again in music of the first five years of the twenty-first century, specifically in songs focused thematically around dance and dance instruction. It is noteworthy that Colin Lucas's 'Dolla Wine'[17] released in 1991, a song whose popularity has been maintained in the Caribbean though primarily as easy dance instruction for tourists, raises similar questions as it relates to market access facilitated through access to dance moves. The 'she' in Lucas's song who calls him 'Mr. Trini' and wants to learn how he moves his body is the implied outsider or stranger. The 'big money wine' when compared to the other low currency gyrations, mimics the 'wining' of more accomplished dancers and is decidedly sexualized and consumer oriented. Though the international success of Lucas's instructions is evidently related to the simplicity of his instructions, the big money 'wine' when converted to local currency is clearly too simple to be worth as much to locals.

Lucas's hit seems to have influenced the next few years of Calypso and Dancehall and it reveals a dialectic between both music forms with politics that should move beyond who spoke first. Buju Banton's 'Bogle'[18] and Beenie Man's 'World Dance'[19] released in 1992 and 1994 respectively, both describe popular dances that are a little more complicated than the 'Dolla Wine', inspired by the dexterous Bogle of the Black Roses Crew.[20] Though both Buju and Beenie suggest these dances are for everyone (in Jamaica), people from uptown and downtown, both men and women with various skill levels, the songs by no means garnered the kind of international attention as 'Dolla Wine', as is the case with Burning Flames' 'Swing Engine'[21] and Colin Lucas's 'Iwer/Butterfly/Shadow/Wave'[22] both released in 1995. There seems to be in this early version of the dance instruction trend a relationship between the complexity of the dance move(s) and the market itself. In more recent dance songs the question of inclusion and exclusion is not only drawn along national lines, though patriotism is certainly part of the creation of dance communities.

Richie Feelings' Dancehall successes 'Dancin' Class Part 2'[23] and his collaboration with Tony Matterhorn in 'All About Dancing',[24] both released in 2004, are songs primarily about finding and performing dance even in the banality and triteness of everyday life. In 'Dancing Class Part 2' he begins with the mad walk dance — 'Bellevue', then moves to the 'Cut off yu head'. The dance class includes the 'call down the rain' and the 'umbrella'. The song ends, presumably after creating a dance community, with a call to everyone in the dancehall who does not 'bow', that is, take part in oral sex to do the final move the 'Zagga zow'. The community created by using specific local references and choreographing them into dances, is solidified with the call to the adherence of a sexual standard that is considered morally right. The implication is that everyone in the dance is in agreement with this standard and that dancers who do not comply cannot be included as members of the insider community. Destra Garcia and Machel Montano's 2003 'Carnival'[25] constructs a community of revellers as people infected with a kind of madness and dance frenzy around Carnival. This community will 'take a jump', start to wave and wine, inspiring a version of the oneness Destra and Machel see as Carnival in Trinidad and Tobago. The lyrics of 'Carnival' say little more than this and besides the presumption of heterosexuality from the description of the interaction between bodies, insiders of this community must know how to dance and enjoy dancing.

While 'Stranger' and 'Signal de Plane' certainly perpetuate what Anika Smith calls a 'herd mentality', using their repetitive 'action song' gimmicks to create communities around the dangerous hypersimilar that Gilroy is critical of, these songs are but the edge of the question as far as 'follow-fashion' lyrics go. Still we see in this mid ground trends in Calypso and Dancehall that cannot simply be dismissed:

(1)   There is a willingness to consider questions of exclusion and inclusion as these artistes create, protect, and define community, sometimes 'renouncing individuality in favour of community', or supporting the troublingly narrow spirit that, as Gilroy argues, such calls to uniformity engender. Indeed, when songs such as 'Get Some Thing and Wave', 'Stranger', and 'Signal de Plane' are analysed they share a common concern with nation building. These 'action songs' together offer choreography as an alternative means of nation building and resonate with, contradict, and exert

tensions against the more established modes that take place in the political arena. One might consider then that if these shifting movements in dance, though perhaps conceived with comparable motives, have the same effect as monuments, uniforms, and laws.

(2) While these songs encourage sameness, this sameness is often organized around resistance. For example, waving flags simultaneously against anti-government radicals and government imposed curfews, upsetting power dynamics associated with race and re-establishing authority around traditional knowledge, subverting the power of immigration laws and speaking against community violence, all complicate notions of sameness by encouraging subversion.

(3) Along with sameness and subversion, many of these songs are clearly concerned with marketing music for consumers of Caribbean culture. The follow-along lyrics, with dance instructions included, on one hand seem to extend the dance community and thus the consumer community in an ingeniously welcoming gesture; they on first read are shamelessly tourist oriented at the risk of compromising lyrics and art in these creative communities. However, while the above is true, these same lyrics by making fun of outsiders and making unsuspecting insiders of people along just for the dance are clearly more than just welcoming.

(4) Finally these songs are parody. They make fun of specific experiences and the everydayness of the world by mimicking anything and making a dance of everything; making fun of the music form itself, and making fun of themselves and those who dance along. Parody then functions as the recourse of the disadvantaged, choreographing out of hurt and hell an art in coordination that can be taken to market abroad and that makes the top of the charts at home. Dance to the hurt? Dance if you catching hell? Dance if the government don't care? Dance? Dance?

Notes

1. Earl Lovelace, *The Dragon Can't Dance* (New York: Persea, 1998).
2. Anika Smith, 'Dancehall Overhype ... more like OVER the Hype' (unpublished review, 2004).

3. Gordon Rohlehr, *Calypso and Society in Pre-Independence Trinidad* (Port of Spain: Gordon Rohlehr, 1990).
4. Ibid., 2.
5. Ibid., 3.
6. Ibid., 12.
7. Gordon Rohlehr, 'Calypso and Caribbean Identity', in *Caribbean Cultural Identities,* ed. Glyne Griffin, *Bucknell Review* XLIV, no. 2 (2001): 69.
8. Rohlehr argues that Byron Lee and the Dragonaires, a Jamaican band, began this trend: 'I can remember as early as the 1960s in Jamaica that Lee's band created songs telling people to "put your hand in the air" and "put your foot and jump up higher, higher, higher," and so on.' (Calypso and Caribbean Identity', 69) Both Rohler's statement about the Jamaican influence on these Calypso 'action songs' and Anika Smith's 20 recent commentary on the 'herd mentality' Trinidad and Tobago calypsos have inspired in dancehall music, make for useful parallel critiques, perhaps proving nothing but the cross-fertilization in Caribbean music forms.
9. Shadow, 'Stranger', *Just for You.* CD Crossroads Records CRCD008, 2001.
10. Elephant Man, 'Signal de Plane', *Good to Go.* Atlantic, 2003.
11. Lord Kitchner, 'Miss Tourist', *Classic Kitchener: Volume Two.* Ice 941002. Ice 919002,1994; The first and last verses of Kitchener's 'Miss Tourist' as well as the chorus offer a noteworthy parallel to the Shadow's lyrics in 'Stranger':

> A tourist dame I met her the night she came / well she curiously asking about my country/she said I hear about bacchanal and the Trinidad Carnival / So I want to jump in the fun, and I want you to show me how it is done / I said to her. (Chorus) Come in town j'ouvert morning, find yourself in a band / Watch the way the natives moving, have a time with a man/Sing along with the tunes they playing, and now and again you shouting / Play mas bacchanal, Miss Tourist, that is Carnival. (Last verse) She turn and say now I feel to break away / she said come on man and grabbed in front the band/Mama when we reached Independence Square / She kicked and she raised she dress in the air/ Bawling bacchanal, bacchanal, I am the queen of the Carnival / I said baby.

12. Super Blue (Boy Blue), 'Get Something an' Wave', *10th Anniversary.* LP Charlies BCR 3538, 1991.
13. Paul Gilroy, *Against Race: Imagining Political Culture beyond the Color Line* (Cambridge: Harvard University Press, 2000); I include here the words to the second verse and chorus of Super Blue's 'Get Something an' Wave' so that we understand the contextual importance of Mother Muriel and her mourning ground as they connect to that political moment in Trinidad.

> Prime Minister, Abu Bakr / no curfew, no curfew / Baptist woman, get a vision / no curfew, no curfew / while she was on the mourning ground / she saw a monkey and two pigeon / true my son she sey we will rise/ if police lock me up in a band / a wining to the station / Trinidad and Tobago I'm hearing ... Cho. Break away! Carnival is plenty action / Break away! 91' is wheels in action / Break away! I want to see some

bottoms rolling / Break away! I want to see my culture rising / Break away! I want to be free/ Get something an wave, get something an wave.

14. Gilroy, *Against Race*, 100,
15. Ibid., 101.
16. In Elephant Man's previous album 'Log On', he refers to himself as the energy god. It seems that this moniker has caught on.
17. Colin Lucas, 'Dolla Wine', *Caribbean Carnival Soca Party Vol. 4*. CD. Coral Sounds CSS018, 1996.
18. Buju Banton, 'Bogle', *Best of the Early Years: 1990–1995*. VP Records, 2001.
19. Beenie Man, 'World Dance', *Best of Beenie Man: Collectors Edition*. VP Records, 2000.
20. Bogle or Gerald Levy was a popular dancehall personality and the leader of the Black Roses Crew in Kingston, Jamaica. Bogle made his fame as a leading dancehall choreographer and an international dancer.
21. Burning Flames, 'Swing Engine', *Carnival Mega Mix: The Ulimate Party Mix*. CRS Music C-CD-0035, 1996.
22. Colin Lucas, 'Do the "Iwer/Butterfly/Shadow/Wave"', *One Foot Man*. LP Coral Sounds CSS012, 1995.
23. Richie Feelings, 'Dancing Class Part 2', *Ragga, Ragga, Ragga 2004!* Greensleeves, 2004.
24. Tony Matterhorn and Richie Feelings, 'All About Dancing 2', *Ragga, Ragga, Ragga 2004!* Greensleeves, 2004.
25. Destra (Destra Garcia), 'Carnival' (with Machel Montano), *Red, White, Black*. 2003. Socacds 2003-03; Machel Montano, 'Carnival', *The Circus*. CD. JWJW258, 2003.

BIBLIOGRAPHY

DISCOGRAPHY

Listing by Artist and Composition Titles

Banton, Buju (Mark Myrie)
'Boom Bye Bye'. *Early Years (90–95)*. CD VP Records 2100, 2001.
'Bogle'. *Best of the Early Years: 1990–1995*. VP Records, 2001.

Becket
'Nanny Revival'. *Fresh*. CD Cocoa Records ABC-F-00110, 1993.

Beenie Man (Moses Davis)
'World Dance'. *Best of Beenie Man: Collectors Edition*. VP Records, 2000.

Blakie, Lord
'De Doctor Eh Dey'. *Sparrow Lost/De Doctor Eh Dey*. 7" Telco TW – 3240, 1964.

Burning Flames
'Swing Engine'. *Carnival Mega Mix: The Ultimate Party Mix*. CRS Music C-CD-0035, 1996.

Chalkdust, The Mighty
'Brain Drain'. *Brain Drain/Devaluation*. 7" RA NSP 193, 1968.
'Two Sides of the Shilling'. *Answer to Black Power/Two Sides of the Shilling*. 7" Tropico T7-1109, 1970.
'Goat Mouth'. *Goat Mouth/Immigration Problems*. 7" Strakers S-0061, 1972.
'Who Next'. *Who Next/We're Ten Years Old*. 7" Strakers S0067, 1972.
'Somebody Mad'. *Somebody Mad/PNM Loves Me*. 7" Strakers S-104, 1973.
'Clear Your Name'. *Stay Up*. LP Strakers GS 7789, 1974.
'Let the Jackass Sing'. *Stay Up*. LP Strakers GS 7789, 1974.
'Eric Loves Me'. *Origins*. LP Strakers GS 2220, 1979.

Crazy

'Nani Wine'. *Nani Wine*. LP Trinity Records TR 001, 1989.

Cro Cro (Weston Rawlins)
'Face Reality'. *Face Reality 2004*. CD Abstracts Entertainment, 2004.

Cypher, The Mighty
'Last Election'. *Top 10 Calypsoes from the Original Young Brigade 1967* (aka *Calypso 1967 Top Ten*). Various Artists. LP National N.L.P. 8099, Hilary SP 3004, 1967.

DeFosto
'Reflections of Our Late Prime Minister'. *Reflections of Our Late Prime Minister*. EP TODH TODH 006, 1981.

Delamo
'Apocalypse'. *Apocalypse/Musical Rasta/Doreen Party*. 12" Semp SDI 24, 1981.

Destra (Destra Garcia)
'Carnival' (with Machel Montano). *Red, White, Black*. 2003. Socacds 2003-03.

Duke, The Mighty
'Find a Fellar'. No album information [c. 1970].

Elephant Man
'Signal de Plane'. *Good to Go*. Atlantic, 2003.

Feelings, Richie
'Dancing Class Part 2'. *Ragga, Ragga, Ragga 2004!* Greensleeves, 2004.

Franklin, Aretha
'Respect', *Respect*, Wea, 2002.
'(You Make me Feel Like a) Natural Woman', *Respect*, Wea, 2002.
'I Never Loved a Man (The Way I Love You)', *Respect*, Wea, 2002.

Grant, Eddy
'Neighbour Neighbour'. 12" Ensign, 1981.

Invader, Lord (Rupert Grant)

'Don't Stop the Carnival'. *Calypso After Midnight*. Rounder 11661-1841, 199.

King, Ben E., and the Drifters
'Under the Broadwalk'. *Hits Collection*. 1XCD, 1997.

Kitchener, Lord
'Miss Tourist'. *Play Ma's With Kitch*. Tropico TSI-2004, 1968.
'Sock it to me Kitch'. *Sock It To Me Kitch*. LP Tropico TSI-2018, 1970.
'Twenty to One'. *Tourist in Trinidad*. LP Trinidad TRCS – 0004, 1974.
'Miss Tourist'. *Classic Kitchener: Volume Two*. Ice 941002. Ice 919002,1994.

Lucas, Colin
'Do the "Iwer/Butterfly/Shadow/Wave"'. *One Foot Man*. LP Coral Sounds CSS012, 1995.
'Dolla Wine'. *Caribbean Carnival Soca Party Vol. 4*. CD. Coral Sounds CSS018, 1996.

Luta
'Pack Yuh Bags'. *Double Silver*. Double CD Dimensions DPR003C, 1999.

Maestro
'Dread Man'. *Savage/Dread Man*. 12" Charlies PKL 150, Kalinda PKL-15, 1976.
'To Sir With Love'. *Mr. Trinidadian/To Sir With Love/Poor Man*. 12" Hildrina H 1007, 1981.

Matterhorn, Tony (and Richie Feelings)
'All About Dancing 2'. *Ragga, Ragga, Ragga 2004!* Greensleeves, 2004.

Melody, Lord (Fitzroy Alexander)
'Mamma Look a Booboo'. *Mamma Look a Booboo / Missin' Chicken*. 78; 7" Monogram M950, 1955.
'Corbeau Flying High'. *The Devil/The Beast/Caroline/Corbeau Flying High*. 7" EP Cook CC 5811, 1958.

'Doctor Make Your Love'. *Again!! Lord Melody Sings Calypso.* LP Cook 914, 1959.

Montano, Machel
'Carnival'. *The Circus.* CD. JWJW258, 2003.

Panther, Mighty
'Songs of Dynamite'. 12" LP. Chicago: Drum Boy Records DBLM-1000, n.d. [1956].

Ramgoonai, Drupatee
'Pepper, Pepper'. *Pepper.* EP Kash Productions SP 2001, 1989.
'The Car Lick Down Me Nani'. *Down in Sando.* CD Multitone Records DMVI 1335, 1995.

Relator
'Deaf Panman'. *Deaf Panman/The Bomb.* 7" Pan Records P 3150, 1974.
'Take a Rest'. *The Real Master.* EP Makosssa MD 9060, 1980.

Rose, Calypso
'I thank Thee'. *Her Majesty.* LP Charlies CR 444, 1978.
'Balance Wheel'. *Mass in California.* LP Strakers GS 2234, 1982

Rudder, David
'Calypso Music'. *Calypso Music 10th Anniversary Album.* LP with bonus 7" Lypsoland CR06/CR07, 1987.
'Madness'. *Calypso Music 10th Anniversary.* LP Lypsoland CR06/CR/07, 1987.
'Panama'. *Haiti.* LP Lypsoland CR 008, 1988.
David Rudder 1990. Port of Spain, Lypsoland, 1990, 33S! rpm LP Record, CR013.
'Hoosay'. *Rough and Ready.* LP Lypsoland CR06/CR07, 1991.
'Another Day in Paradise'. *No Restriction.* Triple CD Lypsoland CR 027, 1997.

Scrunter
'Crapaud Revolution'. *Crapaud Revolution/Sheila Run Away.* 12" KN-003, 1981.
'Nanny'. *Nanny / John Dick.* 12" 2Guys SCR-002, 1986.

Shadow
'From Then to Now'. *National 25th Anniversary of Independence Calypso Competition*. Various Artists. LP Stag H18701, 1987.
'Stranger'. *Just for You*. CD Crossroads Records CRCD008, 2001.

Shorty
'The Art of Making Love'. *The Art of Making Love*. Shorty S-003, Caravan CX-160, Sakanda SAK-737, 1973.
'P.M. Sex Probe'. *The Love Man, Carnival '74 Hits*. LP Shorty SLP 1000, 1974.
'Oh Trinidad'. *Sweet Music*. LP Shorty SLP-1003, 1976.

Sparrow, The Mighty (Slinger Francisco)
'No Doctor No'. *No Doctor No*. 78 Pirates Records V 100, 1957.
'Sailing Boat Experience'. No album information [c. 1957].
'PAYE'. *Calypso Carnival 1958*. LP Balisier HDF 1005, Cook 920, 1958.
'Reply to Melody'. *Calypso Carnival 1958*. LP Balisier HDF 1005 Cook 920, 1958
'William The Conqueror'. William The Conqueror/Sailor Man/Yankees Back Again/Third Eye on the Finger. 7" EP Balisier EXJA 101, 1958.
'You Can't Get Away From the Tax [You Must Pay Tax]'. *This is Sparrow*. LP Balisier HDF 1008, 1959.
'Leave the Damn Doctor'. *Lulu/Leave the Damn Doctor*. 7" RCA 7-9030, 1960.
'Federation'. *This is Sparrow Again*. 7" EP Kalypso XXEP4, 1961.
'Present Government'. *Sparrow the Conqueror*. RCA LPB-2035, 1961.
'Mr. Rake and Scrape'. *Veronica/Mr. Rake and Scrape*. 7" RCA 7-2041, 1961.
'Wear Your Balisier'. *Wear Your Balisier/Panama Woman*. 7" RCA 7-2067, 1961.
'Dey Washin Dey Mouth'. *120 Calypsoes to Remember*. Port of Spain, 1963.
One Hundred and Twenty Calypsoes to Remember. Port of Spain: National Recording Co., 1963.
'The Slave'. *Kruschev and Kennedy/The Slave*. 7" Jump Up JU-507, 1963.
'The Village Ram'. *Bull Pistle Gang/The Village Ram*. 7" Jump Up JU-523, 1963.

'The Outcast'. *The Outcast.* LP National NLP 4199, 1964.
'Get to Hell Out'. *Congo Man,* LP National NLP 5050, Melodisc NLP 17 155, Hilary SP 3006, 1965.
'Congo Man'. *Congo Man/Patsy.* 7" National NSP 052, 1965.
'Get to Hell Outta Here'. *Get Outa Here.* Matrix NLP 5050 ½ c. pre carnival, 1965.
'Mas'. *Mas'/Birds Fly High.* 7" RCA 7-2172, 1965.
'Honesty'. *Going Home Tonight/Honesty.* 7" National NSP 078, 1966.
'Cockfight'. *More Sparrow More.* RaRa 2020, Island Series CCS 2020, 1969.
'Sa Sa Yea'. *More Sparrow More.* RaRa 2020, Island Series CCS 2020,1969.
'Jean and Dinah'. *Sparrow in London.* LP RA RA 2127, 1970
'Toronto Mass'. *Hotter Than Ever.* Matrix RA 3112, 1972.
'The Witch Doctor'. *Sparrow V/S The Rest.* Matrix DSR SP, 1976.
'Du Du Yemi'. *Sparrow N.Y.C. Blackout.* Matrix CR139, 1977.
'Idi Amin'. *Idi Amin/Du Du Yemi (Black Beauty).* Charlies 1906, 1978.
'Gu Nu Gu'. *London Bridge.* Matrix JAF-001, 1979.
'Love African Style'. *London Bridge.* Matrix JAF-001, 1979.
'Isolate South Africa'. *Sweeter Than Ever.* Matrix JAF 1005, 1982.
'Marajhin'. *Sweeter Than Ever.* LP with 12" Charlie's JAF 1005, 1982.
'Sam P'. *King of the World.* LP Bs BSR-SP-002, 1984.
'Invade South Africa'. *A Touch of Class.* Matrix BSR SP 041, 1985.
'I Owe No Apology'. *We Could Make It Easy If We Try.* Matrix BLS 1011, 1991.

Squibby
'Streaker'. *The Chook/Streaker.* 7" Strakers GS 188, 1975.

Stalin, Black (Leroy Calliste)
'Caribbean Unity'. *Play One/Caribbean Unity.* 7" Wizards MCR-147, 1979.
'Break Down Party'. *Just for Openers/This is it.* Double LP Makossa MD9054/55, 1980.
'Move'. *The Bright Side.* LP Strakers GS 2337, 1991.

Striker, King
'Don't Blame the PNM'. *Don't Blame the PNM/No Jobs Suit Striker.* 7" Cook CC5807, 1958.

Super Blue (Boy Blue)
'Get Something an' Wave'. *10th Anniversary.* LP Charlies BCR 3538, 1991.

Valentino
'No Revolution'. *No Revolution/Birth Control.* 7" Antillana 968, 1971.
'Barking Dogs'. *Barking Dogs/Be Aware.* 7" Strakers S-107, 1973.

Movies

Bop Girl Goes Calypso [a/k/a *Bop Girl*]. Pressbook. United Artists, 1957.
Calypso Heat Wave. Dir. Fred Sears. Perf. Johnny Desmond and Merry Anders. Columbia, 1957.
Joebell and America (film). Asha Lovelace and Earl Lovelace. Trinidad: CCN Six Point Production, 2005.

Newspapers

Chicago Daily Defender
'Calypso Fad Returns Home'. May 21, 1957, 17.
'Calypso Hits Hollywood With Bang: Allied Artist's [*sic*] First Is Called Greatest So Far'. May 11, 1957, 29.

Jamaica Daily Gleaner
Londoner (sic). 'West Indian Table Talk'. October 15, 1957.

Jamaica Sunday Gleaner
Mills, Claude. 'Lord Creator has a Passion for Ballads'. April 12, 1998.

Los Angeles Times
Schallert, Edwin. 'Calypso Craze Inspires Tide of New Films'. April 14, 1957, V1.

Miami Herald
Kennedy, William. 'Calypso Rhythms Are Here to Stay'. April 21, 1957, 3B.

Metz, Robert. '"Calypso Is A Thing I'm Telling You": New music craze edging rock 'n' roll'. [Allentown, Penn.] *Sunday Call-Chronicle*, February 3, 1957, 6. Abbr. and rpt. as 'Will Calypso Give Heave-Ho to Rock 'n' Roll?: GI Oil Drums in West Indies Help Spark New Dance Craze'. March 3, 1957, 12B.

Nation
Santoro, Gene. 'Folk's Missing Link'. April 22, 2002, 32–37.

New York Amsterdam News
DeVore, Jesse. '"Mighty Dictator"— A True Calypsonian'. April 27, 1957, 12.
'Loew's Musical Rhythm Battle'. *What's Cookin' in New York,* April 1957, 10–11. Abbr. and rpt. as 'Rock 'N Roll Vs. Calypso At Loew's'. March 30, 1957, 11.
'New Calypso Room Opens'. February 9, 1957, 12.
'Pearl Primus Brings Calypso Show Uptown'. May 25, 1957, 16.
Walker, Jesse H. 'Theatricals'. May 4, 1957, 14.

New York Herald-Tribune
Kavaler, Lucy. 'Where go calypso? We've given Manhattan back to the (West) Indians. When will it be ours again?' May 26, 1957. 'Today's Living', 4.

New York Post
Thirer, Irene. 'Calypso Takes Over Stage Of Loew's Met for 10 Days'. April 21, 1957, 15.

New York Sunday Mirror
Strassberg, Phil. 'Calypso Out, Tina In, at Le Cupidon'. June 23, 1957, 55.

New York Times
Holden, Stephen. 'Playful Aretha Franklin Plumbs Roots of Soul'. November 5, 1994, late ed., 15.
Scott, A.O. Review of Down With Love. (Nat'l Ed.) May 9, 2003, B1.
Wilson, John S. 'Belafonte and Others in Calypso Variety'. May 5, 1957, X15.

New York Times Magazine
Holder, Geoffrey. 'That Fad From Trinidad'. April 21, 1957, 14.

Trinidad Express
Best, Lloyd. December 13, 2002.
Black Brother. Letter to Editor. Wednesday, February 22, 1978.
Cato, Reuben. 'Oh Sparrow, You Have Shocked Me'. January 16, 1978.
Karamoko, Modibo. Letter to Editor. Wednesday, February 15, 1978.
Sampson, Valda. 'De Vice in Dey Own Head'. Letter to the Editor. December 20, 1984, 9.

Trinidad Guardian
Alleyne-Forte, Learie. 'Open letter to Sparrow on That Idi Amin Calypso'. January 21, 1978.
Freethinker. Letter to the Editor. February 16, 1965.
Milne, L. 'I Am Ashamed'. Letter to the editor. February 18, 1965.
Robinson, Arthur. 'The New Frontier and the New Africa'. Friday, January 17, 1964 (one of a series of articles running weekly in the *Trinidad Guardian,* January/February 1964.
Sealey, Clifford. 'Ah Mr. Censor'. Letter to the Editor. Thursday, February 23, 1965.
Sparrow, The Mighty. Interview by Wayne Brown. October 2, 1966.
Derek Walcott. 'Efficient Birdie Minus the Feather-ruffling'. Review of the Original Young Brigade. January 6, 1965.

Trinidad Sunday Express
Alexander, Vernon. 'The Noble Congo Man'. February 5, 1989.
Baksh, Vaneisa, 'The King and I'. October 6, 1991.
Jacob, Debbie. 'Sparrow's Own All-time Favourite'. February 10, 1991.
Trinidad Sunday Guardian
Anonymous. '"Chalkie was disrespectful" say women'. March 11, 1973, 1.

Trinidad Weekly Guardian
'Seditious Publications Act Passed'. March 27, 1920, 11.

Books, Journals, Magazines

Abrahams, Roger D. 'Traditions of Eloquence in Afro-American Communities'. *Journal of Inter-American Studies and World Affairs* 3, no. 4 (October 1970): 507–27.

———. 'The Shaping of Folklore Traditions in the British West Indies'. *Journal of Inter-American Studies and World Affairs* 9 (1967): 456–80.

Achebe, Chinua. *Anthills of the Savannah*. New York: Doubleday, 1987.

Anonymous. 'God help our gracious king'. *Tapia* (May 23, 1971): p.8.

Aiyejina, Funso. '*Salt*: A Complex Tapestry'. *Trinidad and Tobago Review* 181, nos. 0–12 (1996): 13–16.

———. 'Novelypso: Indigenous Narrative Strategies in Earl Lovelace's Fiction', *Trinidad and Tobago Review* 22, no. 7–8 (2000): 15–17.

Alvarez, A. 'The Best Living English Novelist'. *New York Times Book Review* (March 17, 1974): 6–7.

Angier, Carole. *Jean Rhys*. Harmondsworth: Penguin, 1986.

Anthony, Michael. *Parade of the Carnivals of Trinidad 1839–1989*. Port of Spain: Circle Press, 1989.

Atilla the Hun (Raymond Quevedo). 'The Banning of Records' (1938).

Bakhtin, Mikhail. *Rabelais and His World*. Trans. Helene Iswolsky. Cambridge: MIT Press, 1968.

Barson, Michael and Steven Heller. *Teenage Confidential: An Illustrated History of the American Teen*. San Francisco: Chronicle Books, 1998.

Beckles, Hilary McD. *The Development of West Indies Cricket: Vol. 1 The Age of Nationalism*. Mona, Kingston: The University of the West Indies Press, 1998.

———. *A Nation Imagined: First West Indies Test Team, The 1928 Tour*. Kingston: Ian Randle Publishers, 2003.

'Behind the Scenes King of Calypso'. *Calypso Album*, ed. Arthur Unger, 61. New York: Modern Music Publications, 1957.

Belafonte, Harry. Interview with Michael S. Eldridge December 18, 2001.

Belfon, Denise. 'Denise Belfon: Saucy Babe', Queenofsoca.com, June 14, 2004 <http://queenofsoca.com/ProfileDenise.html>

Bennett, Louise. 'Back to Africa'. In *Jamaica Labrish*. Kingston: Sangster's Book Stores, 1996.

Bhabha, Homi K. *The Location of Culture*. London: Routledge, 1994.

———. 'Culture's In-between'. *Questions of Cultural Identity*, eds. Stuart Hall and Paul du Gay, 53–60. London: Sage Publications, 1996.

Bogle, Donald. *Brown Sugar.* New York: Harmony Books, 1980.

Bowles, Paul. 'Calypso — Music of the Antilles'. *Modern Music* 17, no. 5 (April–May 1940): 154–59.

Boyce-Davies, Carole. 'The Africa Theme in Trinidad Calypso'. *Caribbean Quarterly* 31, no.2 (June 1985): 67–86.

Birbalsingh, Frank. *The Rise of West Indian Cricket: From Colony to Nation*. Antigua: Hansib Publishing, 1996.

Brathwaite, Kamau. 'A Post-Cautionary Tale of the Helen of Our Wars'. *Wasafiri* 22 (1995): 64–81.

Brown, Les. 'The Mighty Panther Tells Roots, Meanings of Calypso'. *Down Beat* (May 30, 1956): 42.

Brown, Tony. 'Will Calypso Knock the Rock?: The stars answer your question'. *Melody Maker* (March 16, 1957): 3.

Burton, Richard D.E. 'Cricket, Carnival and Street Culture in the Caribbean'. In *Liberation Cricket: West Indies Cricket Culture*, ed. Hilary Beckles and Brian Stoddart, 89–106. Manchester and New York: Manchester University Press, 1995.

———. *Afro-Creole Power, Opposition and Play in the Caribbean*. London and New York: Cornell University Press, 1997.

'Calypso, American Style'. *Calypso Album*, ed. Arthur Unger, 50–53. New York: Modern Music Publications, 1957.

'Calypso Can't Displace R&R as Teenage Box-Office Draw'. [Unsourced newspaper story, datelined (erroneously?) 'New York, Apr. 20 [1957]'.] *First Pressings: The History of Rhythm & Blues*, vol. 7 (1957), comp. and ed. Galen Gart. Milford, NH: Big Nickel, 1993.

'The Calypso Craze'. *Newsweek* 49, no. 8. (February 25, 1957): 72.

'Calypso Here I Come—Maybe: Can Kids Dance to Caribe Beat?' *Variety* (January 23, 1957): 41.

'Calypso Is Stone Cold Dead'. *Variety* (May 22, 1957): 41.

'Calypsomania'. *Time* (March 25, 1957): 55–56.

'The Caribbean, Ho! U.S. Tourists in Record Rush to the Indies'. *Life* 42, no. 6 (February 11, 1957): 24–33.

Capecia, Mayotte. *Je Suis Martiniquaise*. Paris: Editions Correa, 1948.

Carter, Sybil Jackson. 'Mayotte or Not Mayotte'. *CLA Journal XLVIII* 4 (2005): 440–51.

Castagne, Pat and Lu. *Trinidad's Sensational Calypso Dance*. Port of Spain: Guardian Commercial Printery, 1957. Abbr. and rpt. as 'Trinidad's Sensational Calypso Dance Instructions'. In *Leeds Calypso is like so: Authentic Calypso Songs with Words and Music including Ukulele Diagrams and Guitar Chords, plus dance instructions with Diagrams*, 41–48. New York: Leeds Music Corp, 1957.

Castagne, Patrick S. 'This Is Calypso'. *Music Journal* (January 1958): 32–33.

Chin, Timothy. '"Bullers" and "Battymen": Contesting Homophobia in Black Popular Culture and Contemporary Caribbean Literature'. *Callaloo* 20, no.1 (1997): 127–41.

Coester, Markus. '"Ghana is the Name We Wish to Proclaim" – Two Popular Caribbean Voices and the Independence of Ghana'. *Ntama Journal of African Music and Popular Culture*. <http://ntama.uni-mainz.de/content/view/92/29/>

Cohn, Norman. *Europe's Inner Demons*. 1975. Reprint, St. Albans: Paladin, 1976.

Conrad, Joseph. *Heart of Darkness*, ed. Robert Kimbrough. 1899. Reprint, New York: Norton, 1963.

Constance, Zeno Obi. *Tassa, Chutney and Soca: The East Indian Contribution to the Calypso*. San Fernando, Trinidad: Jordan's Printing Service, 1991.

Cooper, Carolyn. *Noises in the Blood: Orality, Gender, and the 'Vulgar' Body of Jamaican Popular Culture*. Durham: Duke University Press, 1995.

'Could Calypso Go Into Collapso By Too Rapid Rise in Salaries?' *Variety* (February 6, 1957): 58.

Cowley, John. *Carnival, Canboulay and Calypso: Traditions in the Making*. Cambridge: Cambridge University Press, 1996.

Cudjoe, Selwyn. 'Eric E. Williams and the Politics of Language'. In *Eric Williams Speaks: Essays on Colonialism and Independence*, ed. Selwyn Cudjoe, 35–110. Wellesley, MA: Calaloux, 1993.

Dabydeen, David and Brinsley Samaroo. *India in the Caribbean*. London: Hansib Publishing, 1987.

Dana, Robert W. 'The Big City Is Stomping to Calypso!: The Primitive Rhythm Was Slow to Catch On, But Now It Has the Night Clubs in a Tizzy'. [New York] *World-Telegram and Sun Saturday Magazine* (March 2, 1957): 10–12.

D'Costa, Jean, and Barbara Lalla, eds. *Voices in Exile: Jamaican Texts of the 18th and 19th Centuries.* Tuscaloosa: University of Alabama Press, 1989.

Davidson, Basil. *The African Genius.* Oxford: James Curry, 1969.

Davis, Cynthia. 'Calypso and Carnival Influences in the Works of Jean Rhys'. Calypso and Caribbean Literature Panel. Calypso and the Caribbean Literary Imagination. University of Miami, Coral Gables, Florida. March 19, 2005.

de Four, Linda. *Gimme Room to Sing: Calypsoes of the Mighty Sparrow 1958–1993: A Discography.* Port of Spain: Linda de Four, 1993.

Deosaran, Ramesh 'The "Caribbean" Man: A Study of the Psychology of Perception and the Media'. In *India in the Caribbean,* eds. Dabydeen and Samaroo, 81–118. London: Hansib Publishing, 1987.

Dirks, Robert. *The Black Saturnalia.* Gainesville: University of Florida Press, 1987.

Dorsinville, Max. *Le Pays Natal: Essais sur les littératures du Tiers-Monde et du Québec.* Dakar: Nouvelles Editions Africaines, 1983.

'Duke of Iron'. In *Calypso Album,* ed. Arthur Unger, 54–55. New York: Modern Music Publications, 1957.

Edmondson, Belinda. 'Public Spectacles: Caribbean Women and the Politics of Public Performance'. *Small Axe* 1 (2003): 1–16.

Elder, J.D. 'Evolution of the Traditional Calypso of Trinidad and Tobago: A Socio-Historical Analysis of Song Change'. Dissertation, University of Pennsylvania, 1996.

Ellin, Mary and Marvin Bennett. 'Trend: Up from Trinidad'. 'On Our List: A monthly report on what the intelligent American may want to read, see, hear, and talk about'. *Good Housekeeping* (May 1957): 8.

Elliot, Ann. 'Real, Real Calypso: How It Is Sung and Danced in Trinidad'. *Dance* (July 1957): 30–33 and (August 1957): 36–37.

Emery, Mary Anne. *Jean Rhys at 'World's End'; Novels of Colonial and Sexual Exile.* Austin: University of Texas, 1990.

Escott, Colin. 'Harry Belafonte: Island in the Sun'. In *Harry Belafonte: Island in the Sun* [book accompanying CD boxed set of the same name], 1–37. Hambergen, Germany: Bear Family Records, 2002.

Espinet, Ramabai. *Creation Fire: A Cafra Anthology of Caribbean Women's Poetry.* Toronto: Sister Vision, 1990.

———. *The Swinging Bridge.* Toronto: Harmony Flamingo, 2004.

'The Fad from Trinidad: Sassy, syncopated calypso is hottest craze in entertainment world'. *Ebony* (June 1957): 48–52.

Fanon, Frantz. *Black Skin White Masks.* Trans. Charles Lam Markmann. 1952. Reprint, New York: Grove Press, 1967.

———. *The Wretched of the Earth.* 1961. Reprint, London: Penguin Books, 1990.

Fayad, Mona. 'Unquiet Ghosts: The Struggle for Representation in Jean Rhys' *Wide Sargasso Sea*'. *Modern Fiction Studies* 34, no. 3 (1988): 437–52.

Feather, Leonard. 'Feather's Nest'. *Down Beat* (July 13, 1955): 4.

Feder, Lillian. *Naipaul's Truth: The Making of a Writer.* New York: Rowman & Littlefield, 2001.

Ford, Madox Ford. *When the Wicked Man.* London: Jonathan Cape, 1931.

Fortune, Leasa Farrar. 'Hollywood's Haiti: The Genesis of "Voodoo Movies"'. Abstract of paper presented at Conference of the Centre for Black Music Research, Port of Spain, Trinidad, 2001.

Foucault, Michel. *Discipline and Punish: The Birth of the Prison.* Trans. Alan Sheridan. New York: Vintage, 1995.

Franklin, Aretha, and David Ritz. *Aretha: From These Roots.* New York: Villard Books, 1999.

Funk, Ray. 'The Calypso Recording Craze of 1957'. In *Harry Belafonte: Island in the Sun* [book accompanying CD boxed set of the same name], ed. Colin Escott, 92–94. Hambergen, Germany: Bear Family Records, 2002.

Funk, Ray and Donald R. Hill. '"Will Calypso Doom Rock 'n' Roll"?: The Calypso Craze of 1957'. In *Harry Belafonte: Island in the Sun,* ed. Colin Escott. Hambergen, Germany: Bear Family Records, 2002.

Gibbons, Rawle. *No Surrender: A Biography of the Growling Tiger.* Tunapuna, Trinidad: Canboulay, 1994.

Gilroy, Paul. *The Black Atlantic: Modernity and Double Consciousness.* Cambridge, MA: Harvard University Press, 1993.
Gilroy, Paul. *Against Race: Imagining Political Culture Beyond the Color Line.* Cambridge: Harvard University Press, 2000.
Gilson, Annette. 'Internalizing Mastery: Jean Rhys, Ford Madox Ford, and the Fiction of Autobiography'. *Modern Fiction Studies* 50, no. 3 (2004): 632–56.
Girard, René, *Violence and the Sacred.* Trans. Patrick Gregory. Baltimore: Johns Hopkins Press, 1977.
'The Girls Are Wild About Harry'. In *Harry Belafonte: His Complete Life Story,* ed. Hy Steirman, 44–50. New York: Hillman Publications, 1957.
Gleason, Ralph J. 'The Music's Got to Have Truth Or Belafonte Won't Sing'. *San Francisco Chronicle,* June 23, 1957. 'This World', 10.
Glissant, Èdouard. *Caribbean Discourse: Selected Essays.* Trans. with Introduction by Michael Dash. Charlottesville: University Press of Virginia, 1989.
Green, Leonard. 'Calypso sweeps the nation'. *Calypso* 1 (1957): 16–24.
Gregg, Veronica M. *Jean Rhys' Historical Imagination: Reading and Writing the Creole.* Chapel Hill: University of North Carolina Press, 1995.
Hall, Stuart. 'Introduction: Who Needs "Identity"?' In *Questions of Cultural Identity,* eds. Stuart Hall and Paul du Gay, 1–17. London: Sage Publications, 1996.
Haraksingh, Kusha. 'Control and Resistance among Indian Workers: A Study of Labour on the Sugar Plantations of Trinidad 1875–1917'. In *India in the Caribbean,* eds. Dadydeen and Samaroo, 61–80. London: Hansib Publishing, 1987.
Harrison, Daphne Duval. *Black Pearls: Blues Queens of the 1920s.* New Brunswick: Rutgers University, 1988.
Hayes, Bob. 'Ma Rainey's Review'. *Chicago Defender,* February 13, 1926.
Hearn, Lafcadio. *Two Years in the French West Indies.* New York: Harper & Row, 1923.
Hill, Errol. 'On the Origin of the Term, Calypso'. *Ethnomusicology* 11, no. 3 (1967): 359–67.
———. *The Trinidad Carnival: Mandate for a National Theatre.* Austin and London: University of Texas Press, 1992

Hinds, Donald. *Journey to an Illusion: The West Indian in Britain.* 1966. Reprint, London: Bogle L'Ouverture, 2001.
hooks, bell. *Black Looks: Race and Representation.* Cambridge MA: South End Press, 1992, 70.
Honeychurch, Lennox. *The Dominica Story: A History of the Island.* Roseau: The Dominica Institute, 1984.
———. Personal interview. February 22, 2005.
Invader, Lord (Rupert Grant). 'Small Island', also 'Small Island, Go Back Where You Really Come From'. In *Calypso and Society: In Pre-Independence Trinidad*, Gordon Rohlehr, 313, 351. Tunapuna, Trinidad: Rupert Grant, 1990.
James, C.L.R. *Beyond A Boundary.* London: Stanley Paul & Co, 1963.
———. *Minty Alley.* London: New Beacon Books, 1971.
———. *Party Politics in the West Indies*, ed. R. Walters, 151–72. 1962. Reprint, San Juan, Trinidad: Inprint, 1984.
John, Errol. *Moon on a Rainbow Shawl: A Play in Three Acts.* 2nd Edition. London: Faber, 1963.
Jones, Leroi (Amiri Baraka). *Blues People: The Negro Experience in White America and the Music that Developed From It.* New York: Morrow, 1963.
Joseph, E.L. *History of Trinidad.* London: H.J. Mills, 1838. Reprint, London: Frank Cass & Co Ltd, 1970.
Joyce, James. *Ulysses.* 1922. Reprint, London: The Bodley Head, 1960.
Kanhai, Rosanne. *Matikor: The Politics of Identity for Indo-Caribbean Women.* St. Augustine: University of the West Indies School of Continuing Studies Press, 1999.
Lamming, George. *In the Castle of My Skin.* Trinidad and Jamaica: Longman, 1970.
———. 'Language and the Politics of Ethnicity'. Unpublished address delivered at the Cultural Studies Conference, Cross Culturalism and the Caribbean Canon, The University of the West Indies, Trinidad. January 13–17, 2004.
Lankford, Ronnie D., Jr. 'The Tarriers'. *All-Music Guide.* 2005. September 16, 2005. <http://www.allmusic.com>.
Lewis, Matthew 'Monk'. *Journal of a West Indian Proprietor Kept During a Residence in the Island of Jamaica 1815–1817.* London: Murray, 1834.
Lieb, Sandra R. *Mother of the Blues: A Study of Ma Rainey.* Amherst: The University of Massachusetts Press, 1981.

'Life and Love'. 'Talk of the Town'. *The New Yorker* (April 13, 1957): 34–35.

Litherland, Donna. 'Jean Rhys. GOOD MORNING MIDNIGHT'. Jean Rhys Collection [Series I, Box 6, Folder 13] Department of Special Collections, McFarlin Library, The University of Tulsa.

Liverpool, Hollis 'Chalkdust'. In *Kaiso and Society*. St. Thomas: Virgin Islands Commission on Youth, 1986.

———. *From the Horse's Mouth: Stories of the History and Development of the Calypso*. Port of Spain, Trinidad: Juba Publications, 2003.

Loe, Thomas. 'Patterns of the Zombie in Jean Rhys' *Wide Sargasso Sea*'. *World Literature Written in English* 31, no.1 (1991): 34–42.

Long, Edward. *The History of Jamaica*. 1774. Reprint, London: Frank Cass, 1970; reprint, Kingston: Ian Randle Publishers, 2003.

Lott, Eric. *Love and Theft: Blackface Minstrelsy and the American Working Class*. New York: Oxford University Press, 1993.

Lovelace, Earl. *While Gods Are Falling*. London: André Deutsch, 1965.

———. *The Schoolmaster*. Oxford: Heinemann Educational Publishers, 1968.

———. *The Dragon Can't Dance*. London: André Deutsch, 1979. Reprint, New York: Persea, 1998.

———. *The Wine of Astonishment*. Oxford: Heinemann Educational Publishers, 1982.

———. *A Brief Conversion and Other Stories*. Oxford: Heinemann International, 1988.

———. *Salt*. London: Faber & Faber, 1996.

———. *Growing in the Dark (Selected Essays)*, ed. Funso Aiyejina. Trinidad: Lexicon, 2003.

———. 'Working Obeah'. In *Growing in the Dark: (Selected Essays)*, ed. Funso Aiyejina, 216–26. Trinidad: Lexicon, 2003.

Luis, Robert. *Authentic Calypso: The Song, the Music, the Dance*. New York: Aloha Printing Company/Latin American Press, 1957.

Mahabir, Errol. 'Errol Mahabir'. Special Issue: *Capitalism and Slavery Fifty Years Later*. Eric Williams and the Post-Colonial Caribbean. Hosted by the Department of History, University of the West Indies, St. Augustine 1996. *Caribbean Issues* 8, no.1: 159–162.

Mahabir, Joy. 'Fire and Steel'. In *Creation Fire: A Cafra Anthology of Caribbean Women's Poetry*, ed. Ramabai Espinet, 45. Toronto: Sister Vision, 1990.

'Mardi Gras'. 'The Talk of the Town'. *The New Yorker* (September 1956): 35–36.

Marshall, Paule. *Brown Girl, Brownstones*. 1959. Reprint, New York: First Feminist Press, 1981.

Martin, Janette. 'Jablesses, Soucriants, Loup-garous: Obeah as an Alternative Epistemology in the Writing of Jean Rhys and Jamaica Kincaid'. *World Literature Written in English* 36, no.1 (1997): 3–29.

Mathews, Dom Basil. *Crisis of the West Indian Family*. Port of Spain: University of the West Indies, Extra Mural Department, 1952.

May, Elaine Tyler. *Homeward Bound: American Families in the Cold War Era*. Revised and updated ed. 1988; New York: Basic Books, 1999.

Mead, Rebecca. 'Endless Spring'. *The New Yorker* (April 1, 2002): 50–55.

Mehta, Brinda. *Diasporic (Dis) Locations: Indo-Caribbean Women Writers Negotiate the Kala Pani*. Mona, Kingston: The University of the West Indies Press, 2004.

Melody, Lord. Interview by Gordon Rohlehr. November 24, 1987. Library, University of the West Indies, St. Augustine, Trinidad.

Metz, Robert. 'Crazy For Calypso'. In *Harry Belafonte: His Complete Life Story*, ed. Hy Steirman, 37. New York: Hillman Periodicals, 1957. [Abbr. and rpt. version of 'Will Calypso Give Heave-Ho to Rock 'n' Roll?: GI Oil Drums in West Indies Help Spark New Dance Craze'. *Miami Herald*, March 3, 1957, 12B.]

'Mighty Panther and "The Big Bamboo".' *Calypso* 1 (1957): 25.

Morgan, Paula, Eleanor. 'A Cross-cultural Study of the Black Female-authored Novel of Development'. Dissertation, the University of the West Indies, St. Augustine, 1993.

Morgan, Paula. 'East / West Indian / Woman / Other: At the Crossroads of Gender and Ethnicity'. *Ma Comere Journal of Association of Caribbean Women Writers and Scholars* 3 (2000): 109–122.

Murray, Arthur. 'Arthur Murray Tells How to Dance the Calypso'. In *Calypso Album*, ed. Arthur Unger, 10–15. New York: Modern Music Publications, 1957.
Nadel, Alan. *Containment Culture: American Narratives, Postmodernism, and the Atomic Age*. Durham, North Carolina: Duke University Press, 1995.
Naipaul, Seepersad. *Gurudeva and Other Indian Tales*. n.d. Reprint, London: André Deutsch, 1976.
Naipaul, V.S. *The Middle Passage: Impressions of Five Societies – British, French and Dutch – in the West Indies and South America*. London: André Deutsch, 1962. Reprint, Harmondsworth: Penguin, 1969.
———. *Miguel Street*. London: André Deutsch, 1959. Reprint, London: Heinemann Caribbean Writers Series, 1974.
———. Foreword. In *Gurudeva and Other Indian Tales* by Seepersad Naipaul. London: André Deutsch, 1976.
'Natural Death or Murder?' *Variety* (June 12, 1957): 61.
'New Acts'. Reviews of King Caribe and His Steel Bandits and Lord Lance Trio. *Variety*, January 2, 1957, 55.
'Non-Trinidadians' Calypso Clicks'. *Variety* (February 27, 1957): 1.
O'Callaghan, Evelyn. '"Compulsory Heterosexuality" and Textual/Sexual Alternatives in Selected Texts by West Indian Women Writers'. In *Caribbean Portraits: Essays on Gender Ideologies and Identities*, ed. Christine Barrow, 294–319. Kingston: Ian Randle Publishers, 1998.
Oxaal, Ivar. *Black Intellectuals Come to Power: The Rise of Creole Nationalism in Trinidad and Tobago*. Cambridge, MA: Schenkman, 1968.
Paddington, Bruce. 'Caribbean Cinema: Cultural Articulations, Historical Formation and Film Practices'. PhD thesis, University of the West Indies, St. Augustine, Trinidad and Tobago, 2004.
Peek, Philip M., and Kwesi Yankah, eds. *African Folklore: An Encyclopedia*. New York London: Routledge, 2004.
Persaud, Lakshmi. *Butterfly in the Wind*. Leeds: Peepal Tree Press, 1990.
———. *Sastra*. Leeds: Peepal Tree Press, 1993.
———. *For the Love of My Name*. Leeds: Peepal Tree Press, 2000.
Philip, M. NourbeSe. 'Dis Place – The Space Between'. In *Genealogy of Resistance*. Toronto: Mercury Press, 1997.

———. *Coups and Calypsos: A Play.* Ontario: The Mercury Press, 1996.

———. 'The Absence of Writing or How I Almost Became a Spy'. In *She Tries Her Tongue: Her Silence Softly Breaks*, 10–25. Charlottetown, PEE: Ragweed Press, 1988.

Pouchet Paquet, Sandra. 'Documents of West Indian History: Telling A West Indian Story'. *Callaloo* 20, no. 4 (1997): 764–76.

Puri, Shalini. 'Race, Rape, and Representation: Indo-Caribbean Women and Cultural Nationalism'. In *Matikor: The Politics of Identity for Indo-Caribbean Women*, ed. Rosanne Kanhai, 238–82. St. Augustine: University of the West Indies School of Continuing Studies Press, 1999.

Quevedo, Raymond 'Atilla the Hun'. In *Atilla's Kaiso: A Short History of Trinidad Calypso*. St. Augustine, Trinidad and Tobago: University of the West Indies, Extra Mural Department, 1983.

Ramchand, Kenneth. *The West Indian Novel and its Background.* London: Faber & Faber, 1970. Reprint, Kingston: Ian Randle Publishers, 2004.

Ramkissoon-Chen, Rajandaye. 'When the Indian Woman Sings Calypso'. In *Creation Fire: A Cafra Anthology of Caribbean Women's Poetry*, ed. Ramabai Espinet, 50. Toronto: Sister Vision, 1990.

Reddock, Rhoda E., ed. *Interrogating Caribbean Masculinities: Theoretical and Empirical Analyses.* Mona, Kingston: The University of the West Indies Press, 2004.

Reed, Teresa. *The Holy Profane.* Lexington: The University Press of Kentucky, 2003.

Regis, Louis. *The Political Calypso: True Opposition in Trinidad and Tobago.* Barbados: The University of the West Indies Press; Gainesville: University of Florida, 1999.

Rhys, Jean. *After Leaving Mr. Mackenzie.* 1931. In *Jean Rhys: The Complete Novels.* New York: Norton, 1985.

———. 'Elsa'. Jean Rhys Collection [Black Exercise Book, Series I, Box 1, Folder 1] Department of Special Collections, McFarlin Library, The University of Tulsa.

———. *Good Morning, Midnight.* 1939. In *Jean Rhys: The Complete Novels.* New York: Norton, 1985.

———. 'Lost Island: A Childhood'. Jean Rhys Collection [Series I, Box 1, Folder 14] Department of Special Collections, McFarlin Library, The University of Tulsa.

———. *The Collected Short Stories.* New York: Norton, 1987.

———. *The Left Bank and Other Stories.* Preface by Ford Madox Ford. London: Jonathan Cape, 1927.

———. *The Letters of Jean Rhys,* ed. F. Wyndham and D. Melly. New York: Viking, 1984.

———. *Quartet.* 1928. In *Jean Rhys: The Complete Novels.* New York: Norton, 1985.

———. *Voyage in the Dark.* 1934. In *Jean Rhys: The Complete Novels.* New York: Norton, 1985.

———. *Wide Sargasso Sea.* 1966. In *Jean Rhys: The Complete Novels.* New York: Norton, 1985.

Roach, Eric. 'Hard Drought'. *The Flowering Rock: Collected Poems 1938–1974.* Leeds: Peepal Tree Press, 1992.

Rohlehr, Gordon. 'The Ironic Approach: The Novels of V.S.Naipaul'. In *The Islands in Between: Essays on West Indian Literature,* ed. Louis James, 121–39. London: Oxford University Press, 1968.

Rohlehr, Gordon. 'Calypso and Political Criticism after 1965'. *From Atilla to the Seventies* #20. Port of Spain: Government Broadcasting Unit, Sunday June 10, 1973.

———. *Calypso and Society in Pre-Independence Trinidad.* Port of Spain: Gordon Rohlehr, 1990.

———. 'Music, Literature and West Indian Cricket Values'. In *An Area of Conquest: Popular Democracy and West Indies Cricket,* ed. Hilary McD. Beckles, 55–102. Kingston: Ian Randle Publishers, 1994.

———. 'Calypso and Caribbean Identity'. In *Bucknell Review XLIV,* no. 2 (2001). *Caribbean Cultural Identities,* ed. Glyne Griffith, 55–72. London: Bucknell University Press, 2001.

———. 'Calypso Reinvents Itself'. In *The Scuffling of Islands,* 374–449. Port of Spain: Lexicon, 2004.

———. *A Scattering of Islands: Essays on Calypso.* Port of Spain: Lexicon, 2004.

———. *The Scuffling of Islands: Essays on Calypso.* Port of Spain: Lexicon, 2004.

———. 'I Lawa: Masculinity in Trinidad and Tobago Calypso'. In *Interrogating Caribbean Masculinities: Theoretical and Empirical*

Analyses, ed. Rhoda E. Reddock, 326–99. Mona, Kingston: The University of the West Indies Press, 2004.

———. 'The Construction of Masculinity in the Trinidad & Tobago Calypso'. *A Scuffling of Islands: Essays on Calypso*, 198–280. Trinidad: Lexicon, 2004.

Ross, Alex. 'Rock 101'. *The New Yorker* (July 14 & 21): 2003, 87–93.

Ross, Andrew. *No Respect: Intellectuals and Popular Culture*. New York: Routledge, 1989.

Rudnicki, Robert W. *Percyscapes: The Fugue State in Twentieth-Century Southern Fiction*. Baton Rouge: Louisiana State University Press, 1999.

Samaroo, Brinsley. 'Two Abolitions: African Slavery and East Indian Indentureship'. In *India in the Caribbean*, eds. Dabydeen and Samaroo, 43–60. London: Hansib Publishing Ltd, 1987.

Sasso, Arthur J. 'They're Going Crazy for Calypso!' *Real: The Exciting Magazine for Men* 10, no. 2 (June 1957): 23.

Savory, Elaine. *Jean Rhys*. Cambridge: Cambridge University Press, 1998.

Saywack, Rajendra. 'From Caroni Gyal to Calcutta Woman — A History of East Indian Chutney Music In The Caribbean'. Black & Puerto Rican Studies Department, Thomas Hunter College, December 1999. <http://www.saxakali.com/caribbean/Hemchandra1.htm> Accessed March 2005.

Scott, Lawrence. *Aelred's Sin*. London: Allison & Busby, 1998.

Selvon, Sam. 'Calypso in London'. In *Ways of Sunlight*, 125–31. 1956. Reprint, London: Macgibbon & Kee. 1961.

———. 'Basement Lullaby'. In *Ways of Sunlight*, 175–80. 1957. Reprint, London: Macgibbon & Kee. 1961.

———. *The Lonely Londoners*. 1956. Reprint, London: Longman, 1979.

———. *Ways of Sunlight*. 1957. Reprint, Essex: Longman, 1979.

———. '"Three Into One Can't Go—East Indian, Trinidadian, West Indian". Opening Address to East Indians in the Caribbean Conference, University of the West Indies, Trinidad, 1979'. In *India in the Caribbean*, eds. Dabydeen and Samaroo, 13–24. London: Hansib Publishing Ltd, 1987.

Shaw, Arnold. *Harry Belafonte: An Unauthorized Biography*. Philadelphia: Chilton, 1960.

Sheller, Mimi. *Consuming the Caribbean: From Arawaks to Zombies.* London: Routledge, 2003.
Smith, Anika. 'Dancehall Overhype...more like OVER the Hype'. Unpublished review, 2004.
Stewart, James. *A View of the Past and Present State of the Island of Jamaica.* 1823.
Reprint, New York: Negro Universities Press, 1969.
Stolzoff, Norman C. *Wake the Town and Tell the People: Dancehall Culture in Jamaica.*
Durham: Duke University Press, 2000.
St. Pierre, Maurice. 'West Indian Cricket – Part 1: a socio-historical appraisal'. In *Liberation Cricket: West Indies Cricket Culture*, eds. Hilary Beckles and Brian Stoddart, 107–24. Manchester & New York: Manchester University Press, 1995.
The Official Web Site of The Andrews Sisters. <http://www.cmgww.com/music/andrews/about/bio3.htm> Accessed December 2005.
Thieme, John. 'Calypso Allusions in Naipaul's *Miguel Street*'. *Kunapipi* 3, no.2 (1981): 18–33.
Thomas, Sue. 'Adulterous Liaisons: Jean Rhys, Stella Bowen and Feminist Reading'.
Australian Humanities Review 22 (2001): 1–9.
Thorne, Harcourt. 'Calypso and Calypsonians'. *The Crisis,* October 1957, 479–82.
'Tornado From Trinidad'. *Time* (May 6, 1957): 43–44.
'"Trinidad Time" Up In N.Y.; Hub's 1st'. *Variety* (February 6, 1957): 58.
Ulysse, Gina. 'Uptown Ladies and Downtown Women: Female Representations of Class and Color in Jamaica'. *Ariel* (1999): 147–72.

———. 'Uptown Ladies and Downtown Women: Informal Commercial Importing and the Social/Symbolic Politics of Identities in Jamaica'. Dissertation, University of Michigan, 1999.
Unterberger, Richie. 'Bob Gibson'. *All-Music Guide.* 2005. September 16, 2005. <http://www.allmusic.com>.
Ustanny, Avia. '200 Years of Christmas'. *Jamaica Gleaner Online.* December 15, 2001.
<http://www.jamaica gleaner.com/gleaner/20011215/life/life2.html> (accessed November 29, 2005).

Walcott, Derek. 'Crusoe's Journal'. *The Castaway and Other Poems*. London: Jonathan Cape 1965.

———. 'The Spoiler's Return'. *The Fortunate Traveller*, 53–50. London: Faber & Faber, 1980.

———. 'A Far Cry from Africa'. *Derek Walcott: Collected Poems 1948–1984*. New York: Farrar, Straus & Giroux, 1986.

Waldron, D'Lynne. 'Tribal War in Luluabourg, Belgian Congo'. 1960. <http://www.dlynnwaldron.com/Luluabourg.html>

Walsh, William. *V.S. Naipaul*. Edinburgh: Oliver & Boyd, 1973.

'Warning: Calypso Next New Beat; R.I.P. for R'n'R?' *Variety* (December 12, 1957): 1.

'What Is Exotica?: Some Definitions'. *The Space Age Pop Music Page*. 2002. April 1, 2002. <http://www.spaceagepop.com/whatis.htm>

'Will Calypso Craze Doom Rock 'N' Roll'. *Hue*, April 1957, 22–25.

Williams, Eric. W. *Inward Hunger: The Education of a Prime Minister*. London: André Deutsch, 1969.

———. *History of the People of Trinidad*. New York: Praeger, 1984.

Young, Robert. 'Hybridity in Post Colonial Studies'. In *Post-Colonial Studies: The Key Concepts*, ed. Ashcroft Griffith and Tiffin, 118–21. London: Routledge, 1998.

CONTRIBUTORS

List of Contributors

Funso Aiyejina is a lecturer in English in the Department of Liberal Arts, University of the West Indies, St. Augustine, Trinidad and Tobago, where he teaches African and Caribbean literatures and Creative Writing. Aiyejina is a prize-winning writer of fiction and poetry, a dramatist, and a scholar. He is the author of *A Letter to Lynda and Other Poems* (Nigerian Authors Prize, 1989), *The Legend of the Rockhills & Other Stories* (Best First Book, Commonwealth Writers Prize, Africa, 2000), *I, The Supreme & Other Poems*, and a one-act play, *The Character Who Walked Out on His Author*. He is the editor of *Earl Lovelace: Growing in the Dark (Selected Essays)*, and *Self-Portraits: Interviews with Ten West Indian Writers and Two Critics*.

Cynthia Davis is associate professor of English at Barry University in Miami, where she teaches African-American and Caribbean literature. She co-authored with Verner Mitchell, *Where the Wild Grape Grows: Selected Writings, 1930–1950*, a critical biography of African-American writer Dorothy West, and has published essays in both fields.

Ray Funk is a judge in Fairbanks, Alaska, and a leading researcher and collector of popular music materials. He is the host of a roots programme on public radio in Fairbanks (KUAC-FM), the producer and liner notes writer for numerous CDs of historic calypso and gospel music, and was a major lender of materials to the Smithsonian for its *Wade in the Water* gospel exhibition. He has been involved in calypso research for over a decade. He was co-curator of *Calypso: A World Music* (2004) and is writing a book on the 1950's 'Calypso Craze'.

Michael S. Eldridge teaches literature and culture at Humboldt State University in Arcata, California. His work has appeared in *Callaloo, Transition,* and *World Literature Today*, and he is working on a book about calypso, race and American culture.

Hollis 'Chalkdust' Liverpool is a seven-time winner of the coveted Calypso Monarch title of Trinidad and Tobago's legendary Carnival. A former Director of Culture in Trinidad and Tobago, he has a PhD in history and ethnomusicology from the University of Michigan and currently teaches at the University of the Virgin Islands in St. Thomas. He is the author of several books on calypso, among them *Culture and Education: Carnival in Trinidad and Tobago; Kaiso and Society; Rituals of Power and Rebellion: The Carnival Tradition in Trinidad & Tobago, 1763–1962*; and *From the Horse's Mouth: Stories of the Development of Calypso*. Chalkdust has also recorded more than 300 songs and is the eight-time winner of St. Thomas' (UVI) King of the World contest.

Earl Lovelace is a premier novelist of the contemporary Caribbean from Trinidad and Tobago. His novels include: *While Gods are Falling* (1965), *The Schoolmaster* (1968), *The Wine of Astonishment* (1982), *The Dragon Can't Dance* (1979), and *Salt* (Best Book, Commonwealth Writers Prize, 1997). He has published a collection of short stories *A Brief Conversation and Other Stories* (1988) and a collection of plays *Jestina's Calypso and Other Plays* (1984). He is also a cultural critic whose writing was a regular feature of the *Express* in Trinidad for many years. Some of his essays and lectures have been collected and edited for publication by Funso Aiyejina in *Growing in the Dark* (2003). While Lovelace is settled in Trinidad, he travels extensively and has taught at universities in the USA and the Caribbean.

Paula Morgan is a lecturer in the Faculty of Humanities and Education and an associate of the Centre for Gender and Development Studies, the University of the West Indies, St. Augustine. Her primary area of research, teaching and publication is women's literature of the Caribbean and the African Diaspora. She has edited a collection of essays with Funso Aiyejina entitled *Caribbean Literature in a Global Context* and co-authored a book with Valerie Youssef entitled *Writing Rage: Violence in Caribbean Discourse*. Her scholarship has also appeared in the *Journal of West Indian Literature, Journal of Popular Culture* and *MaComère: Journal of Caribbean Women Writers and Scholars*.

Kezia Page is an assistant professor of English at Colgate University where she teaches Caribbean literature and Ethnic American literature. Her research interests include Caribbean literature and culture and Diaspora literature. Her work has appeared in *Small Axe, Journal of West Indian Literature* and *Callaloo*. She is currently completing a manuscript entitled *Kingston 21: Diaspora Migrancy and Caribbean Literature*.

Marlene NourbeSe Philip is a poet, essayist, novelist and short story writer from Trinidad and Tobago who lives in Toronto. She is also a lawyer who practised law for seven years in Toronto before giving up the practice of law to devote more time to writing. Although primarily a poet, NourbeSe Philip also writes both fiction and non-fiction. She has published three books of poetry, *Thorns* (1980), *Salmon Courage* (1983) and *She Tries Her Tongue; Her Silence Softly Breaks* (1988), and has been the recipient of Canada Council awards, numerous Ontario Arts Council grants and a Toronto Arts Council award in 1989. NourbeSe Philip has published two novels: *Harriet's Daughter* (1988) and *Looking For Livingstone: An Odyssey of Silence* (1991). In 1994, her short story, 'Stop Frame' was awarded the Lawrence Foundation Award by *Prairie Schooner*. She has also published three collections of essays, *Frontiers: Essays and Writings on Racism and Culture* (1992), *Showing Grit: Showboating North of the 44th Parallel* (1993), and *Genealogy of Resistance and Other Essays* (1997), and a chapbook *Caribana: African Roots and Continuities— Race, Space and the Poetics of Moving* (1996). M. NourbeSe Philip's first play *Coups and Calypsos* (1996) was produced in both London and Toronto during 1999. In addition, a stage adaptation of *Harriet's Daughter* was work-shopped in both 2000 and 2001 using a script written by the author.

Sandra Pouchet Paquet is professor of English at the University of Miami where she teaches Caribbean literature and African American literature. She is the author of *The Novels of George Lamming, Caribbean Autobiography: Cultural Identity and Self-Representation* and numerous articles on Caribbean literature and culture. At the University of Miami, she is currently director of Caribbean Literary Studies and editor of *Anthurium: A Caribbean Studies Journal*

Jennifer Rahim is a lecturer in literature in the Department of Liberal Arts at the University of the West Indies, St. Augustine, Trinidad and Tobago. She has published essays on Caribbean literature, and is also a poet and writer of short fiction. She is the author of two volumes of poetry, *Mothers Are Not the Only Linguists* (1992) and *Between the Fence and the Forest* (2002). Her forthcoming collections include *Approaching Sabbaths: Poems* (Peepal Tree Press, 2007).

Louis Regis is a lecturer in the Department of Liberal Arts, University of the West Indies, Trinidad and Tobago. He is the author of *Political Calypso: True Opposition in Trinidad and Tobago, 1962–1987; Maestro: The True Master,* and *Black Stalin: The Caribbean Man.* He has published several articles on Caribbean literature as well.

Gordon Rohlehr is professor of West Indian Literature at the University of the West Indies, St. Augustine. He has lectured throughout the Caribbean, the US, Canada and the UK. Since 1968 he has published over 100 essays on Caribbean literature, calypso and popular culture. Among his several books are *Calypso and Society in Pre-Independence Trinidad* (Port of Spain, 1990); *My Strangled City and Other Essays* (Longman Trinidad, 1992); (co-editor) *Voiceprint: An Anthology of Oral and Related Poetry from the Caribbean* (Longman, 1989); and *A Scuffling of Islands: Essays on Calypso* (San Juan, Trinidad: Lexion, 2004)..

Patricia Saunders is an assistant professor of English at the University of Miami where she teaches Caribbean literature and popular culture, African Diaspora literature and postcolonial studies. Her scholarship has appeared in the *Bucknell Review, Small Axe* and the *Journal of West Indian Literature* and she is currently completing a manuscript entitled *Alien/Nation and Rapatri(n)ation: Caribbean Literature and the Task of Translating Identity.* She is also the assistant editor of *Anthurium: A Caribbean Studies Journal.*

Andrea Shaw is interim writing program coordinator and visiting assistant professor in the Division of Humanities, College of Arts and Sciences, Nova Southeastern University. She specializes in Caribbean and Diaspora Studies and her book, *The Fat Black Woman's Unruly Political Body* (Lexington Books, 2006). She is also a creative writer and is completing work on an MFA in creative writing from Florida International University. Her creative and scholarly work have been published in a range of journals, including *World Literature Today*, *MaComére*, *The Caribbean Writer*, *Gulfstreaming*, *Anthurium: A Caribbean Studies Journal*, *Feminist Media Studies*, *Social Semiotics* and *FEMSPEC*.

Stephen Stuempfle is chief curator at the Historical Museum of Southern Florida in Miami. He is the author of *The Steelband Movement: The Forging of a National Art in Trinidad and Tobago* (University of Pennsylvania Press and University of the West Indies Press, 1995). He has curated several exhibitions on Caribbean history and culture, including (with Ray Funk) *Calypso: A World Music* (2004).

Claire Westall is a doctoral student at the University of Warwick, England, where she also teaches Literature in the Modern World. Her thesis examines the place and significance of cricket in English and Caribbean literatures and is funded by the English Arts and Humanities Research Council.

www.ingramcontent.com/pod-product-compliance
Lightning Source LLC
Chambersburg PA
CBHW060938230426
43665CB00015B/1983